Communication
Research
Methods

John Waite Bowers
THE UNIVERSITY OF IOWA
& John A. Courtright
CLEVELAND STATE UNIVERSITY

Scott, Foresman and Company · · · · · · · · Glenview, Illinois
Dallas, Tex. · · · · Oakland, N.J. · · · · Palo Alto, Cal. · · · · Tucker, Ga. · · · · London

We dedicate this book to the future, especially that of John Steven Bowers, Jeanne Terese Bowers, Julie Michelle Bowers, Merissa Joy Courtright, and Abby Frances Courtright.

Library of Congress Cataloging in Publication Data

Bowers, John Waite.
   Communication research methods.

  Bibliography: p.
  Includes index.
   1. Communication—Methodology. 2. Communication—
Research. I. Courtright, John A. II. Title.
P91.B7 1984   001.51′072   83-11682
ISBN 0-673-15468-8

Preface

Communication Research Methods is an introductory text for upper-division undergraduate and beginning graduate courses in research methods. It incorporates both conceptual and statistical approaches to communication research and theory, describing with ample exemplary material the best of the contemporary research approaches to communication as a social science. Throughout, the book maintains a clear focus on applications. It should serve as a single text for courses where the norm has been to use two texts—one conceptual and one statistical.

Communication Research Methods, although it explicitly considers only social science research methods, is sympathetic to other approaches. It widens the scope of "social scientific" research, and treats covering law, rules, and systems (pragmatic) models as contemporary thrusts of that research. It also attends to the "qualitative" and "quantitative" distinction (or pseudo-distinction) in contemporary research.

The statistical approach of *Communication Research Methods* is the General Linear Model. This model serves as the source of other statistics, including Analysis of Variance, which is shown to be a special case of the Linear Model. Most importantly, the text demonstrates the links among statistical models and perceptions of research problems and methods.

Practical aids to the student include Chapter 7 (on finding a researchable idea), Appendix A (an index of variables used in the most prominent communication research during a three-year period), and Chapter 15 (on ethics, writing, and reacting to criticism).

Strict adherence to the sequence of the book is not mandatory, nor is it necessarily the wisest way to organize a research methods course. We favor an approach that combines instruction *about* research methods with experience *in* research. This gives students both cognitive and experiential modes of learning research methods.

We will not presume to prescribe the organization of any instructor's course, but we have found workable a sequence beginning with instruction in the philosophy and "rules" of science (Chapters 1 and 2), followed by immersion in a survey study (especially Chapter 3, but also Chapters 6, 7, and 15). In the remainder of the course, we ask students, usually in small groups, to generate an observational study (Chapter 4) and a rating study (Chapter 5), almost always using semantic differential technique. These studies profit from an a priori survey of Appendix A. We use the statistical material (Chapters 8 through 14) serially, but we emphasize sections germane to the studies occurring in the class from week to week. Other plans for the course doubtless would work equally well.

We acknowledge with gratitude the contributions of our reviewers: Judee K. Burgoon, Michigan State University; Joseph N. Cappella, University of Wisconsin—Madison; Gwendolyn Mettetal, Purdue University; and Carol Wilder-Mott, San Francisco State University. Their judgment and sound advice helped shape the final product.

We are grateful to the Literary Executor of the late Sir Ronald A. Fisher, F.R.S. to Dr. Frank Yates, F.R.S. and to Longman Group Ltd. London, for permission to reprint Tables III, V, and VII from their book *Statistical Tables for Biological, Agricultural and Medical Research*. (6th edition, 1974)

At Scott, Foresman, we were guided and assisted by Michael Anderson, Barbara Muller, and Susan Strunk. We are grateful for Scott, Foresman's commitment to the communication discipline.

J. Ann Selzer and Don Arenz skillfully and cheerfully compiled, named variables for, indexed, and typed Appendix A. Samuel L. Becker, Bruce E. Gronbeck, and Deborah Rutt contributed materials to Chapter 7. We hereby acknowledge our debt to them.

Carol Schrage, Rosemary Zimmerman, and Lisa Suter of the Department of Communication and Theatre Arts, University of Iowa, greatly eased the execution and completion of the work.

Illene Courtright and Nancy Harper commented substantively on the chapters as they developed and also helped in countless other ways.

Like many academic writers, we owe our greatest debt to our students, who have been the victims of our pilot studies with various manuscript versions. We thank them for the "true" variance they have contributed, both to the development of this book and to our own development.

John Waite Bowers
John A. Courtright

Contents

ix

Communication Research Methods

Social Science as a Mental, Behavioral, and Social Process

Communication scientists engage themselves in the quest for relationships among variables. They hope to explain how and why people produce messages and what consequences those messages might be expected to effect. In this chapter, we will introduce specifically (but also, paradoxically, abstractly) science as a process. To do so, we present two parables.

The Parable of the Boiling Water

After the Fall but before history, three cavepersons clothed in llamaskins were sitting in a circle. (For convenience, we will call them Marie, Calvin, and Isaac.) Thunderstorms had occurred the night before, and Marie suggested that they use some recently acquired technology to build a fire. Calvin and Isaac agreed, so they built the fire, and warmth returned to their circle.

By happenstance, a saucer-shaped rock that the thundershowers had filled with water rested partly in the fire. After a few minutes of conversation, Isaac, always alert to his surroundings, noticed that the water in the rock had begun to bubble. He watched the water carefully until its bubbling became violent. He called the phenomenon to the attention of Marie and Calvin.

Marie crept toward the fire, looked questioningly at Calvin and Isaac, and gingerly touched the water with her index finger. She withdrew immediately, shrieked in pain, and retreated hastily to the mouth of her cave. Her companions observed her activity but, noticing no ill effects to themselves, remained in their places, eventually inducing Marie to return. A dialogue ensued:

Marie: Stay away from that water. The fire god had a baby. The baby is in that water. The baby god bit my finger almost like the fire god does when you get too close to it. He might bite you too.

Calvin: Marie, you always take things too personally. We know that the fire god is a man, and we know that men don't have babies.

1

Marie: The fire god had a baby. I felt the bite.

Calvin: Babies don't bite. They don't have any teeth.

Marie (nonplused by this logic): If the fire god's baby didn't bite me, why does my finger hurt?

Calvin: Marie, you must learn to look at things from a broader perspective. Now think. The purpose of water is to disappear. Water is always going somewhere. Even when it stands perfectly still, it disappears. The water in this rock has been here too long. It must disappear. That's what it's *for*. That bubbling just helps it disappear faster. Look, you can see that much of it is gone already. It didn't hurt you because of any baby god that dislikes you. It hurt you because you interfered with its purpose. It would hurt anybody who did that. Things always hurt people when people get in the way of their goals. I agree that we should stay away from that water. But not because of any baby god.

Marie: I still think the fire god somehow had a baby or put one in that water. Or maybe the fire god is in the water himself.

Calvin: What makes you think so?

Marie: It bit me.

Marie and Calvin, if left to themselves, might have continued their conversation throughout the day and into the night. But during their discussion, Isaac had been closely observing the fire, the rock, and the water. At the lull in the conversation, Isaac picked up a branch and asked Marie and Calvin to help him move the now less-than-full rock away from the fire. They complied, and the water stopped bubbling. ("The baby god wants to stay close to its parent," said Marie.) Isaac then asked the others to help him move the rock back to the fire. When they did, the water soon resumed its bubbling.

Under Isaac's direction, the trio found another dish-shaped rock, filled it with water, and placed it near the fire. In a few minutes, they noticed the same violence in the water. "I think," said Isaac, "that when water in a rock is placed near this fire, it bubbles and disappears even more rapidly than usual. I wonder if it will do the same thing near another fire."

By this time, Marie and Calvin, having participated in Isaac's research, were interested. They cooperated to build another fire some distance from the first. Repeating the entire procedure from their first study, they noted the same phenomenon in the water. They had now used four rocks and two fires, always with the same result.

"That takes care of your argument against me, Calvin," said Marie. "The fire god is a man, but the rock god is a woman. The rock god had the baby. She has one each time she gets near the fire god. The fire god is the father. The babies are boys, so they want to stay close to their father. That's why the babies leave the water when we move their mother away from their father."

Isaac had not yet completed his research. "Unless I'm mistaken," he said, "water will bubble violently when we place it near a fire regardless of the vessel that contains it." He, Marie, and Calvin searched for and found some other natural vessels suitable for holding water—a bone, a piece of petrified wood. Though the time between placement near the fire and bubbling varied slightly, the new vessels did not otherwise affect the results.

"An interesting discovery," said Marie. "Gods of all hollow vessels are female."

"It proved my point," said Calvin. "Water, when placed near fire, wants to disappear more quickly. Bubbling helps it do that."

"Water, when placed in a hollow vessel near fire, bubbles violently and disappears quickly," said Isaac. "Also, when touched, it may bring about pain, but I'll delay that conclusion until I've done some more studies."

The Parable of the Fluctuating Thermometer

Several millennia after the discovery of boiling, four persons (we'll call them Gordon, Bernard, Charlotte, and Joan), indigenous to what is now the United States, met during a continental convention held in what is now Lawrence, Kansas. Gordon lived near what is now Iowa City, Iowa; Bernard and Charlotte, a brother and sister, lived near what is now Denver, Colorado; and Joan lived near what is now Death Valley, California.

After the council, they happened to find themselves seated around the same campfire, and they soon discovered that they had an epistemology in common. All had assimilated the skeptical and empirical tendencies displayed by Isaac, and most of the conversation related incidents in which they had debunked the witch doctors (epistemological descendants of Marie) in their respective tribes.

Eventually, they began discussing their other accomplishments. Gordon (anticipating Fahrenheit) mentioned that he recently had discovered a way to measure heat with mercury in a hollow tube and that he had been able to manufacture and identically calibrate two such instruments. He related a few of the experiments he had carried out with the instruments, noting that he had established to his satisfaction the validity of the statement: "Water, when heated to 212 degrees, boils."

During the discussion, Charlotte had changed her position in the circle so that she was now seated next to Gordon. She expressed great admiration for Gordon's accomplishments with his new instrument and indicated that she would like to see it work. Her brother Bernard, however, indicated his strong skepticism and implied that Gordon's talk was intended principally to impress Charlotte. Joan held her peace for the most part, though Charlotte noticed that she nodded occasionally when Bernard pursued his attacks on Gordon's slightly immodest exposition.

As is the way with scientists, Gordon invited Bernard to dispel his own skepticism by the only method acceptable under the rules of science—observation. Bernard accepted the invitation, and Gordon agreed to send his spare thermometer to Denver via the next messenger from Iowa City. Charlotte assured Bernard that she would check, and, if necessary, repeat Bernard's studies. The four drank a final toast to skepticism and empiricism, then dispersed to their homes in Iowa, Colorado, and California.

During the several succeeding months, awaiting the arrival of the thermometer, Bernard occasionally expressed to Charlotte his disbelief in the existence of such an instrument. But finally the messenger from Iowa City arrived with a cylindrical parcel for the brother and sister.

With no delay, Gordon found the notes on procedure that he had taken at the conference. With Charlotte's help, he built a fire and began to conduct his research. The mercury approached 203 degrees as the water began to boil, and it failed to rise above 203 degrees at full boiling. At Charlotte's insistence, they repeated the experiment with the same result.

Tom-toms sounded the message from Denver across parts of Kansas, Nebraska, and Iowa: "Sorry, Gordon. Your statement about temperature of boiling wrong. Congrats to me for correction. Water boils when heated to 203 degrees. Sincerely, Bernard."

Needless to say, Gordon did not accept Bernard's correction (and its attendant publicity) without resistance. His own research, which had been proceeding smoothly, depended on the law that water boils when it is heated to 212 degrees. As a scientist, however, Gordon knew that emotion must give way to observation. If Bernard had observed repeatedly that water boils at 203 degrees and if Charlotte had checked Bernard's observations as she had agreed to do, then Gordon recognized that he must search for hypotheses that, if verified, would explain the difference between his results and Bernard's.

First, he asked one of his colleagues in Iowa City to repeat his own experiments. The colleague did and found that water consistently boiled at a temperature very near 212 degrees. Still, Gordon was not satisfied that a real difference existed between his results and Bernard's. He thought that the apparent difference might be accounted for by a fault in one of the measuring instruments.

The next messenger from Iowa City to Denver carried Gordon's thermometer and a message instructing Bernard to send back the other thermometer. The message also reiterated for Bernard the exact procedures to be followed in the boiling experiments and reported the results of Gordon's most recent studies, all of which reinforced the 212 degree criterion.

Within a year, the exchange of thermometers was effected and the experiments were replicated. Again, the tom-toms sounded, and both Gordon and Bernard knew that the relationship between their respective findings continued to conflict. Both were now convinced that the conflict was not the fault of inconsistent calibration of the thermometers. The intensity of the emotional tone in their messages began to increase in a negative direction as their frustration became more severe.

Charlotte, who held both men in high esteem, became concerned with the deteriorating relationship. Also, as a scientist, she knew that invective never would solve the empirical question: At what temperature does water boil?

On the one hand, Charlotte had witnessed Bernard's experiments, and in her own checks of those experiments she had repeatedly seen water boil at 203 degrees. On the other hand, Gordon's reports of his studies were perfectly credible to her. She was convinced that he was a conscientious scientist. Even if he were not conscientious, Charlotte doubted that he would falsify results when others could so easily detect the deceit through direct observation. She was strongly motivated to seek an explanation compatible with both sets of findings, an explanation that would account for the anomalous results and transcend the conflict.

Charlotte confined herself for a month, during which she pondered the difference between Gordon's studies and Bernard's. She discarded, on the basis of her own informal observations, the idea that fires were hotter in Iowa City than in Denver. More reluctantly, she discarded the untestable idea that Denver water is always cooler than Iowa City water, other conditions being equal.

On the thirtieth day of her confinement, Charlotte managed to express an idea that had been gestating in her mind. Once more the tom-toms sounded between Denver and Iowa City: "Gordon: Could it be that the temperature at which water boils decreases with westerly movement? As always, Charlotte."

Gordon immediately accepted the generalization and published it among his friends as "Charlotte's Theory."

Bernard was less sanguine than Gordon about the theory. Knowing his sister and having various suspicions about Gordon, Bernard perceived that her attempt to transcend the conflicting results and Gordon's quick acceptance of her theory might be explained by personal rather than scientific considerations. Bernard insisted, and Charlotte agreed, that the theory must be tested.

Bernard remembered Joan's sympathetic participation in the original discussion, and he indicated to Charlotte the opinion that the Californian could be enlisted to cooperate in the test. He observed that Denver was about as far west of Iowa City as Death Valley was west of Denver. If Charlotte's theory was valid, Bernard deduced, the boiling temperature for water in Death Valley should be about as much below Denver's boiling temperature as Denver's boiling temperature was below Iowa City's. The calculation put the hypothetical boiling temperature for water in Death Valley at or about 194 degrees.

Bernard immediately dispatched a messenger to Joan, sending the thermometer, procedural instructions, the history of the controversy, and a closing statement expressing the hope that he and she might meet to discuss the results. Joan received the message, noted the possible personal implications to be inferred from the closing statement, and began her experiments.

In a few days, the tom-toms carried a message from Death Valley to Denver, thence to Iowa City: "Bernard and all: Charlotte's theory worse than bad. Water here boils at almost 213 degrees in repeated experiments—perceptibly above Iowa City's boiling temperature, and far above Denver's. I have found answer. Meet me at peace convention next year for details. Fondly, Joan."

Bernard saw in Joan's message the beginning of a friendly rivalry. Secretly pleased by the failure of Charlotte's theory, which Gordon had endorsed, he thought that he would be in the catbird's seat if he could propose a resolution to the conflicting results that would be superior to Joan's (whatever it was).

With the return of the thermometer, Bernard went to work. He began to travel east and west as widely as he could, repeating the experiment at the end of each day's trek, and he sent Gordon a message asking him to do the same. Both researchers kept careful records of their locations and the boiling points for all trials. Between them, they traveled the breadth of the continent, taking measurements at daily intervals. They arranged to arrive at the peace convention a day early, when they would discuss their findings.

Still responding to Charlotte's theory when they met, they devised a chart showing boiling temperatures as a function of longitudinal position on the continent. (See Figure 1.1, p. 6.)

When the four met around their campfire, Bernard and Gordon proudly produced their charts. Bernard made the presentation:

> When Gordon and I heard Joan's report from Death Valley, we perceived immediately that Charlotte's theory needed adjustment. For that reason, we thought that gathering more data would be desirable. Because boiling temperature is obviously in some way a function of geographic location, we decided to travel across the continent, performing the boiling experiment at regular intervals. Charting our data geographically, we saw that they fit an irregular curve that we hereby publish. We think that this curve amounts to a theory from which we can predict the boiling temperature of water at any point on a latitudinal path across the central part of the continent.

Joan and Charlotte applauded, and the coauthors received congratulations with becoming modesty.

FIGURE 1.1. Boiling Temperature as a Function of Longitudinal Location.

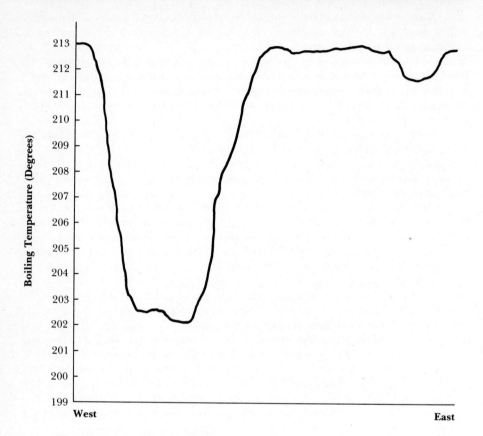

Then Joan asked for attention:

To my colleagues, I can do nothing but express my admiration for their ingenuity and my envy for their industry. Their scientific contribution certainly will prove to be significant.

However, I would like to propose an alternative to their theory. When I received the instructions and the account of the conflicting findings, together with Charlotte's theory, I fully expected that my little experiment would simply substantiate the theory of another. My surprise was great when the experiment not only failed to substantiate the theory but even contradicted it. I therefore searched for explanations other than geographical location. Maps are useful, but for the most part they describe rather than explain.

You all know that I lay no claim to genius. Only the most obvious possibilities occurred to me. In effect, I asked the following question: Will variations in environment that may change my physical feelings also change the temperature at which water boils? I therefore tried the experiment in the sun, in the shade, in the wigwam, even on a raft in the water. These manipulations did not significantly affect the boiling temperature.

As you know, Death Valley is located near a high mountain. The mountain is always in my vision. When climbing the mountain, I have noticed difficulty in breathing, even more difficulty than the physical exertion by itself would explain. As I gazed at the mountain, I wondered whether water would boil at the same temperature on top of it as in my valley.

I therefore decided to investigate. Taking a friend with me, I climbed the mountain. Whenever we could find a convenient place, we repeated the experiment, I observing and she checking my observations. My hypothesis was that boiling temperature and the distance we climbed would be related.

Imagine my delight when I discovered that as we climbed higher our experiments yielded regularly varying results. Soon we began to predict specific boiling temperatures at the various heights we reached. Our predictions were most accurate.

As a result of this research, I feel justified in expressing the following generalization, which, I think, is superior as a theory in some ways even to that of Bernard and Gordon: The temperature at which water boils is an inverse function of altitude. It decreases at the rate of about one degree every 500 feet.

My colleagues should not take this theory or this speech as a belittlement of their accomplishments. Their data can be most valuable in checking the validity of my theory. All we need to do is recalculate a little, predicting their results from my theory by using altitude rather than east-west axis as the predictor variable. No better test for the theory could be devised. Again, I congratulate them.

Joan took her seat next to Bernard to the accompaniment of sustained applause. An inspection of Gordon and Bernard's data did indeed confirm the theory.

The Justification for Social Science

In the two parables, which we will analyze later in this section, the subject of study is physical behavior—how the behavior of matter varies under varying environmental conditions. Communication—symbolic behavior—is material only in a trivial sense. Nobody would claim that "communication" consists in any important way of the sounds people produce when they talk or the squiggles people produce when they write or the electronic processes people employ when they broadcast or the photographic images people develop when they make a film. Communication is social behavior, probably unique to human beings. Some people think that human behavior is not a suitable subject for scientific study. In the minds of these critics, human behavior is not explainable and/or predictable in the same sense that physical phenomena are explainable and predictable. We will consider five such positions. Adolf Grünbaum (1952) has analyzed four of them:

1. Human behavior is not amenable to causal description and therefore not predictable, since each individual is unique and not exactly like anyone else.
2. Even if there is a causal order in the phenomena of human behavior, it is so complex as to elude discovery permanently.
3. In the physical sciences, a present fact is always determined by past facts, but in human behavior present behavior is oriented toward future goals and thus "determined" by these future goals.

4. If human behavior were part of the causal order of events and thereby in principle predictable, it would be futile to attempt to make a choice between good and evil, meaningless to hold people responsible for their deeds, unjust to inflict punishment, and naive to take seriously such remorse or guilt as is professed for past misdeeds. In short, the argument is that to assume the principle of causality in human behavior is incompatible with the known fact that people respond meaningfully to moral imperatives.

If social scientists are to feel secure in their attempts to explain and predict communication, they must frame replies to these propositions. And, in fact, they have done so.

The first proposition, the argument from uniqueness, is the easiest to answer. The critics are right when they say that each individual is unique. They might even go further and say that each individual *behavior* is unique. But each pot of boiling water and each air pump and each falling body is also unique. Every being and every event is unique, at least in space or in time. Social science tries to establish systematic relationships among the characteristics and activities of individuals, not among the individuals themselves. In Isaac's studies, the heating and the boiling, not the particular fire, the particular water, and the particular rock, were related by his generalization.

Your own commonsense observation belies the proposition that uniqueness of beings prohibits the formulation of general laws, even about communication, in a statistical (much more about that in subsequent chapters), if not in a particular, sense. You probably would subscribe to the generalization, "Infants, when awake and moderately hungry, cry." This generalization does not deny the uniqueness of particular infants; it simply relates an antecedent state of those unique individuals, hunger, to a consequent behavior, crying. You also might subscribe to the more powerful generalization: "A behavior, including a communicative behavior, is more likely to be repeated in a similar situation if it is positively reinforced." As an adult human being, you regularly have been affected by (and have affected others by) the relationships asserted in this generalization regardless of whether you have previously read or expressed it. (In a slightly more general form, it is called the "law of effect.") The uniqueness of individuals, *including the unique events and combinations of events that are positively reinforcing to them*, do not reduce (although they complicate somewhat) the explanatory and predictive power of the generalization.

The second argument, the argument from complexity, is phrased well by Bill Bumpers, the protagonist in Peter De Vries's novel, *I Hear America Swinging* (1976, p. 7). Bumpers is attempting to defend his proposed doctoral dissertation, a sociological study of the causes of divorce in eastern Iowa. The dissertation arrives at no conclusions, and, as things turn out, his defense is unsuccessful. In response to an examiner's objection to the dissertation's failure to arrive at conclusions, Bumpers says:

> . . . it can't be done, except with a cigarbox of meaningless digits. . . . That to think it can be scholastically achieved is to harbor a delusion, and to act on it to pursue a will-o'-the-wisp. . . . That these investigations are foredoomed, the result a mare's nest, the stuff we call human nature being finally incalculable as it is, utterly elusive to our poor attempts at mathematical statistical measurement.

Scientists can answer the argument from complexity by noting that the critics are right when they say that human behavior is complex. But all natural phenomena are complex; if they were not, science would be redundant, and each person could make all the predictions scientists make without benefit of research. Society would have no need for the self-correcting process (which we will explain later) provided by science. We think it likely that human behavior is not appreciably more complex than is the behavior of the rest of the universe. But (1) people have been trying to study human behavior from a scientific epistemology for a relatively short time, and (2) the process of treating human behavior as material for science is inhibited somewhat by the scientists' own direct involvement in the very behavior they are trying to explain. Participants in an event are not, generally, the best analysts of the event. The fact may be unfortunate, but it remains that if human behavior is to be explained, human beings will have to do the explaining (at least until the earth is colonized by extraterrestrials).

The third proposition, the argument from human purposiveness, gives the critics a stronger position, but not an impregnable one. Science attempts to explain causally, the argument goes, so that the present is a function of the past, the future a function of the past and present. For human behavior, the critics assert, such prediction is not possible, because human behavior is directed toward goals; goals, by definition, find their attainment only in the future. Therefore, the "cause" of behavior is something that has not yet occurred. This is the argument from teleology. You may recognize that Calvin expressed it in a primitive form when he asserted that the purpose of water is to disappear.

Answering this argument requires that you analyze, to some extent, the nature of your own behavior as a human being. At first introspective glance, you may be inclined to agree with the critics. Your present activities seem to be influenced by past, present, *and future* events. Chances are, you are reading this book *because* (in the past) your instructor assigned it. But you are also reading this book *in order to* (in the future) participate in a class discussion or do well on an examination or become a communication theorist. In causal reasoning, the future cannot cause the present, so causal reasoning is inappropriate for explanations of human behavior.

But pursue the thought a step or two further. Actually, your behavior is *not* a function of future events. It is a function of your *expectations* or *perceptions* of future events. These *expectations* (though not the events that are their subjects) exist in your *present*, not your future. In fact, the future outcomes you presently expect may well not occur at all (the class may disband, the teacher may cancel the test, you may die), so they can in no meaningful sense be called "events" at all.

One of the approaches to communication research and theory, the "rules" approach (to be discussed more fully later in this chapter), takes explicit account of people's present expectations (or rule systems) in its attempts to account for communicative behavior. While this approach is objectionable to some scientists because of its orientation to the future, our judgment is that the objection is not warranted. Expectations, rules, and rule systems existed in the past and exist in the present. Outcomes do not yet exist—but expectations, not outcomes, are the basis for "rules" approaches to human communication.

Of the four arguments we have mentioned so far, the last, the argument from freedom, is the most difficult to answer. If human behavior is amenable to scientific explanation, then, in principle, human behavior is perfectly predictable. If that is so, then human behavior is not a function of will, of choice, or of freedom, and such notions as blame and guilt, praise and pride, are meaningless. If people cannot help doing what they do, then they should take neither credit nor discredit for their behavior.

The answer to this argument may be difficult to assimilate because it probably will violate many of the generalizations you have come to accept in your own socialization. You *know* that you have freedom, that you have exercised choice, and that you have experienced guilt as a consequence of some activities and pride as a consequence of others.

Our answer to this argument will be facilitated considerably if you can pretend for a few minutes that human behavior is fully explainable and, in principle, predictable— that each of your acts is a consequence of directly or indirectly observable causes or systems. This position should not be impossible to take, for much of your experience leads you to it (though you may not have thought about it in this way before). Every time you make a prediction about your own behavior or another's behavior, you take this position to some degree. Certainly, you have made many such predictions in a lifetime: "If I cry, my parent will feed me." "If I go to school late, the teacher will scowl at me." "Mother gave me a blue shirt and a red one. If I wear the blue one, she'll ask me why I don't like the red one." "The boss is in a bad mood. If I ask for a day off, he'll refuse." "If I put transitions in this paper, the professor will give me an A in the course." "If I cook her a meal, she will propose marriage." "Did you notice how Kay and Victor talked to each other? That marriage won't last long." "If I get Smith elected, she will lower the interest rate." "If I quit smoking, I will live longer." These predictions are based on assumptions of system in human behavior. They assert that human behavior depends, at least to some degree, on antecedent events. If human behavior were *perfectly* free, *totally* unconstrained, then human behavior would be *perfectly* random, *totally* unpredictable. These kinds of predictions, then, commit you to at least a probabilistic (if not a deterministic) view of human behavior. Human beings may be free, but they are not completely free.

Actually, a probabilistic position is all that is necessary to justify a science of human behavior, but some social scientists go further, asserting that, in principle, *every* event in human behavior can be fully explained. This position, unlike the probabilistic one, leaves *no* place for choice, for human freedom. But if people do not make choices, why do they experience guilt and pride?

People who take the extreme position (determinists) would provide a resolution to this introspective paradox that goes something like this: Human beings learn that some behavior is likely to be followed by punishment, other behavior by reward. Most internalize generalizations about the kinds of behavior in which punishment and reward are likely to occur—codes of "morality." In other words, they learn to anticipate punishment as a function of certain behaviors and to anticipate reward as a function of other behaviors. They learn to call the anticipation of punishment "guilt," the anticipation of reward, "pride." With maturation, people learn to anticipate these very anticipations—they expect to be "guilty" if they behave in certain ways, to be "proud" if they behave in other ways. The anticipation of these feelings becomes one of the inhibitors of guilt-producing behavior and one of the facilitators of pride-producing behavior. The behavior itself is, in principle, fully predictable if the individual's code of "morality" is part of the predictor formula. Human behavior is not free, but human beings have the illusion that it is free.

This extreme position brings up two interesting questions: (1) Does a determinist experience guilt and pride? (2) Should society continue to punish those who violate its normative laws and reward those who are in some socially desirable way exceptional?

The answer to the first question is that determinists probably would not label their postbehavioral feelings (although they have learned to have those feelings, of course) with the nouns *guilt* and *pride*. A determinist might admit to feeling remorse about some past behavior by saying, "I wish that I had done otherwise" or "I will behave differently if similar circumstances occur again." A determinist will not say, "I should have done otherwise" or even "I could have behaved differently." Similarly, a determinist might say about a past behavior "I'm glad I did that" in circumstances in which most people might say "That makes me feel proud."

The deterministic answer to the second question is, "It depends." Certainly, the anticipation of punishment inhibits some kinds of behavior, and the anticipation of reward facilitates other kinds. If punishing "criminals" and rewarding "heroes" has the consequence of inhibiting crime and facilitating heroism, then these kinds of social punishment and reward increase society's control over its members. Possibly, other more effective and efficient methods of control could be found. For the determinist, the question is an empirical one.

The fifth (and final) argument against sciences of human behavior is anticlimactic compared with the argument from freedom. B. F. Skinner (1953, pp. 20–21) related the argument and his answer to it this way:

> Still another objection to the use of scientific method in the study of human behavior is that behavior is an anomalous subject matter because a prediction made about it may alter it. If we tell a friend that he is going to buy a particular kind of car, he may react to our prediction by buying a different kind. The same effect has been used to explain the failure of public opinion polls. In the presidential election of 1948 it was confidently predicted that a majority of the voters would vote for a candidate who, as it turned out, lost the election. It has been asserted that the electorate reacted to the prediction in a contrary way and that the published prediction therefore had an effect upon the predicted event. But it is by no means necessary that a prediction of behavior be permitted to affect the behaving individual. There may have been practical reasons why the results of the poll in question could not be withheld until after the election, but this would not be the case in a purely scientific endeavor.

Other anecdotal evidence can be added to Skinner's to bolster the case that predictions about behavior, if they are known to the person who is to do the behaving, may alter the behavior. One professor (Becker, 1953) did a study in which he tried to discover the effect of speaking position in a forensics contest. He examined the records of the Northern Oratorical League throughout its long history and discovered that the first speaker in the national contest had never been awarded a first-place judgment. He published his results. Presumably, the judges of the following year's contest read his report, and, that year, the first speaker won the contest. As in the 1948 poll, knowledge of a prediction may have affected behavior.

Skinner's answer to this objection is that knowledge of such predictions need not be made available outside the scientific community. This answer is unsatisfactory for two reasons: (1) It seems to advocate suppression of information, a practice repugnant to science; (2) it fails to deal with the behavior of scientists themselves—if knowledge of the scientific laws governing human behavior affects that behavior, then those who know the laws (the scientists) will not behave in accordance with those same laws.

Another answer (though not a perfectly satisfactory one) is that knowledge of the science of human behavior does *not* affect that behavior, even for scientists themselves. This answer appears to be valid at least for certain kinds of behavior. Percy Tannenbaum (1980, pp. 111–12) reported his reaction to a film in which members of the audience were given the perspective of the driver of the second car in a wild chase scene:

> All 300 people, myself very much included, issued an involuntary screech at [one] point, and I sensed a distinctly uncomfortable feeling in the pit of my stomach—literally a gut response.

When the film was over some minutes later, the memory of . . . my uncontrolled reaction lingered on and bothered me. I was annoyed that I had so readily succumbed to a film's obvious manipulations. After all, if I knew it was a film, that I was not actually in the car, why did I react as I did?

Determined not to be seduced again, I stayed on for the next showing. Now forewarned, I was presumably forearmed to avoid screaming out. As the car went into the slanting turn, 299 souls did scream while I in fact did not. But I was still very much bothered: Although I could control the overt response, I had the same sickening visceral feeling in the stomach. Being a dedicated researcher . . . I stayed on for six more showings of the same film, waiting for the critical moment to see if I could fully control the gut response but never fully succeeding, although the effect did diminish somewhat with time.

Tannenbaum's experience may indicate that knowledge of certain generalizations about behavior does *not* affect the knower's behavior to any great extent. Certainly, a physicist's experience of matter is not greatly affected by knowledge of the laws of physics. The physicist A. S. Eddington in 1929 (cited in Webb & Roberts, 1969, p. 332) described his dual experience of a table. The physicist as physicist knows the table as:

. . . numerous electrical charges rushing about with great speed. . . . Their combined bulk amounts to less than a billionth of the bulk of the table itself. I need not tell you that modern physics has by delicate test and remorseless logic assured me that my . . . scientific table is the only one which is really there. . . . On the other hand, I need not tell you that modern physics will never succeed in exorcising that [other] table—strange compound of external nature, mental imagery and inherited prejudice—which lies visible to my eyes and tangible to my grasp.

But knowledge clearly does affect at least some kinds of behavior. If it does not, why bother to learn things? And a better answer than either of those already given to the objection that knowledge of the laws of human behavior affects human behavior is to proudly claim that indeed it does—but to add the proviso that such knowledge itself can be considered a cause of behavior. In fact, whole theories have been expounded using such knowledge (or its absence or its distortion) as an explanatory variable.

One such theory is that of the "self-fulfilling prophecy," a theory to explain "how one person's expectation for another person's behavior can quite unwittingly become a more accurate prediction simply for its having been made" (Rosenthal & Jacobson, 1968, quoted in Williams, 1970, p. 382). This theory has been used to explain such disparate events as the outcomes of experimental studies (the "demand" effect) in which the predictions of the experimenter become known to experimental subjects and the academic performance of children in elementary schools (the "Pygmalion" effect) when teachers are led to expect exceptionally good or exceptionally poor performance from particular children. Knowledge of regularities in behavior (though for the Pygmalion effect the "knowledge" was erroneous) *does* affect behavior—but the effects can be predicted and explained.

Another theory that uses expectations of behavior to make systematic predictions about behavior is "reactance" theory (Bem, 1972, cf. Bowers, 1974). This theory is based on the proposition that, whether people actually are "free" or "independent," they value the *illusion* that they are not controlled by others, and they behave accordingly. The salesperson who points out a minicomputer to you by saying "This is a great model, but you probably can't afford it," is using reactance theory. That salesperson expects you to use your knowledge of your own financial independence (and your pride in it) to refute his or her claim, and to talk yourself into the purchase via that refutation. If you know about reactance theory and recognize the salesperson's strategy, you are *less* likely to buy the computer—and we have used your knowledge of reactance theory as an element in our explanation of your refusal to buy.

To the extent that you accept the arguments we have just made, you are justified in pursuing the scientific study of communication, of symbol-using behavior, even though such behavior may be uniquely human. Even if you do not accept the position that human behavior can be *fully* explained, your own experience must have led you by now to the conclusion that many fruitful generalizations are possible at least in a probabilistic sense. For our purposes, that conclusion is sufficient.

Thinking and Acting in Communication Research

As you probably have inferred from our two parables, a scientist tries to *explain* or *account for* or even *predict* variations in one or more classes of characteristics or events by relating those variations to variations in one or more other classes of characteristics or events. Isaac explained the boiling or tranquillity of water (a class of events) by relating it to distance from fire (a class of characteristics). Bernard and Gordon tried to explain the temperature at which water boils (a class of characteristics) by relating it to latitudinal position on the American continent (another class of characteristics). Joan explained the temperature at which water boils by relating it to altitude at which it is heated (still another class of characteristics). In science, any class of characteristics or events whose values may change (as in boiling/tranquil, close/far, east/west, high/low, hot/cold) is called a *variable*. If a variable is to have scientific recognition, its variations must be *observable*, so that Marie's "fire god" and "fire god's baby," for example, should never find a place in science. Variables whose variation the scientist hopes to explain are called *criterion* or, sometimes, *dependent* variables. (In studies where a causal relationship is assumed, these variables may be called *consequent* variables.) Variables used to explain criterion (or dependent) variables are called *predictor* or, sometimes, *independent* variables. (In studies where a causal relationship is assumed, these variables may be called *antecedent* variables.) For Isaac, the criterion variable was the boiling or tranquillity of water, and the predictor variables were, in various studies, nearness to fire, nature of vessel containing the water, location of the fire, and source of the water. (Isaac's studies led him to the conclusion that only one predictor variable, nearness to fire, explained variations in the criterion variable.) For Bernard and Gordon, and for Joan, boiling temperature was the criterion variable. Bernard and Gordon's predictor variable was latitudinal position, and Joan's was altitude.

Science claims to be a cumulative, self-correcting enterprise, so the scientist's studies must be *public* and *replicable* by other scientists. In order to make studies replicable, scientists define variables *operationally*—that is, they describe (sometimes in great detail) the methods they used in order to observe or produce the variables of interest to them. For Isaac, Bernard, Gordon, Charlotte, and Joan, the definition of "boiling" was not especially problematic. But Isaac must carefully define "nearness to fire." Bernard and Gordon went to considerable trouble to define latitudinal position, as did Charlotte to define altitude.

When scientists think that they detect a pattern among variables that has not been detected before, they propose a *theory*. Theories, then, are sets of statements asserting relationships among classes of variables, not all of which have yet been tested. A successful theory explains the behavior of a significant criterion variable or group of criterion variables. To be considered a theory, such a set of statements must be *corrigible*—capable of being *disproved*. Bernard and Gordon's theory was corrigible, because it could be disproved by any researcher who found that water boiled at a temperature not predicted by their chart. Joan's theory was corrigible because it could be disproved by any researcher who found that water boiled at a temperature not predicted by her altitudinal generalization. (Theories in social science, from Freud to Festinger, most often have been attacked for their incorrigibility.)

When a science reaches a certain maturity, its practitioners frequently must choose among two or more theories, each of which purports to explain the behavior of the same criterion variables. (For examples, see Eysenck, 1961; Hansel, 1966.) When that happens, the science ideally employs a combination of three criteria in its choice among the competitors: *validity, scope,* and *elegance.* One theory is more *valid* than another to the extent that it provides more accurate or more exact explanations than the other. If theory A predicts that "most" individuals will lie under particular circumstances, and if theory B predicts that "people low in self-esteem but not people high in self-esteem" will lie under those same circumstances, then theory B has greater validity than theory A (assuming that both are accurate). One theory has greater *scope* than another to the extent that it explains a greater range of behavior in a criterion variable or to the extent that it explains a larger domain of criterion variables. A "theory of planetary motion" has less scope than does a "theory of gravity," for the theory of gravity explains not only planetary motion but also a very large domain of the motion of other bodies. Finally, one theory is more *elegant* than another to the extent that it explains the same domain of criterion variables with statements or formulas that are simpler in form. We already have mentioned that Joan's theory was superior to Bernard and Gordon's in this respect. (It was also superior in its validity and scope.)

In their quest for theories that are valid, elegant, and substantial in scope, communication researchers use various methods, often classified according to the degree of manipulation exercised over the predictor variables.

Some studies simply attempt to *define, order,* or *categorize* variables, without asserting relationships among them. We will call these *descriptive* studies. A list of the 10,000 most commonly used words in English (Thorndike & Lorge, 1927) might result from this kind of study, for example. Many surveys are of this type, as are many studies whose purpose is to develop a new test or measurement instrument. Such studies sometimes result in variables defined in such a way that they can be more easily used in later scientific work when relationships among variables *are* of interest. Zipf's (1965) Law, which in a simplified form asserts that length of words is inversely related to their frequency of use, cannot be tested without a descriptive ranking of frequency of use, for example.

Other studies involve careful observation of predictor and criterion variables in their natural settings, with no attempt to manipulate the predictor variables. We will call such efforts *case studies* or *field studies.* A researcher carrying out such a study might draw conclusions about the psychological and communicative behavior of end-of-the-world cults (Festinger, Riecken, & Schachter, 1956) or about the relationships among settings and communication in a particular community or kind of community (Philipsen, 1975). Often, contemporary researchers begin such studies in a frame of mind that deliberately avoids preconceptions about what they might find. As a particular study progresses, the scientist progressively identifies variables, defines them, and perceives predictor-criterion relationships among them. A researcher involved in that kind of study uses *ethnographic* methods and seeks to develop what he or she might call *grounded* (because it has firm roots in data derived from direct observation) *theory.* For a justification of this method, see Glaser and Strauss (1967). For a good example of its operation in communication research, see Browning (1978).

Sometimes, a researcher is interested in the operation of predictor variables that are impossible or very difficult to manipulate. Gender, socioeconomic status, age, and most personality variables, for example, cannot be manipulated by a scientist. A researcher might then select individuals for study because of their placement on the variable. Such studies are called *quasi-experimental*. A host of studies in communication have used sex as a predictor variable (e.g., Janis & Field, 1959), and a few have used psychological gender as a predictor (e.g., Montgomery & Burgoon, 1977). Socioeconomic status has been used as a predictor variable in communication by Bernstein (1971) and many others. Similarly, a number of personality variables have been used in quasi-experimental ways, especially self-esteem (Manheimer, 1981).

Finally, communication researchers sometimes find it possible to *manipulate* variables, as Isaac did with nearness to fire, source of water, and location of fire, and as Joan did with the various altitudes at which she boiled water. Students of communication enjoy performing such manipulations on the content and form of symbolic messages. When a scientist manipulates a variable's level (or its presence and absence), the resulting study is called an *experimental* study. For many examples of such studies, see recent issues of such journals as *Communication Monographs* and *Human Communication Research*.

Field methods, quasi-experimental methods, and experimental methods sometimes are mixed in a particular study. (For example, see Courtright, Millar, & Rogers-Millar, 1980; Shimanoff, 1980.) Hence, you might hear about a *field experiment* in which a scientist, observing phenomena of interest in a natural setting, deliberately (but unobtrusively) introduces experimental messages from time to time, then observes what happens to criterion variables as a result. A scientist might also mix quasi-experimental and experimental variables, as in a study of the effects of the same experimental message variables on men and on women (sex being a quasi-experimental variable).

Most scientists seek experimental verification of theoretical statements as the ideal, because experimental methods can be used to efficiently winnow out theoretical statements that are erroneous. Other kinds of studies may (1) fail to take into account variables operating coincidentally with the predictor variables, or (2) involve confounded variables. You may have been the victim of the first kind of error if you have ever tried to learn the rules of a game simply by observing it being played. Because of the coincidence of variables in the particular instance of the game you observed, you might have arrived at such (potentially disastrous) theories as "a pair of red aces always wins in poker" or "a black king paired with a black jack always wins in blackjack." Experimental testing of these statements, of course, would induce you to discard them. A scientist confounds variables when he or she attributes a prediction to one variable when it actually is attributable to another unnoticed variable that always accompanies the first. You might, for example, observe that you always get good service at a particular restaurant on Saturday night but not on Thursday night. You might fail to observe that your appearance is always neat on Saturday night and sloppy on Thursday night. You could easily arrive at the conclusion that quality of service (the criterion variable) is a function of day of the week (the predictor variable). But it may well be a function of neatness of dress (a predictor variable confounded with day of the week). A perceptive experimenter could quickly resolve the ambiguity.

Neither variables nor research methods are scientific straitjackets. Both, in a sense, are the creations of the scientist, and scientists may create them with greater or lesser ingenuity. Like all human beings, scientists invent *concepts*, which, if they are designed to serve a particular scientific purpose, are called *constructs*. (Cf. Kerlinger, 1973, p. 28.) Physically, you may stand higher, when erect, than does the person who sits next to you in class. Somebody sometime invented the concept "height" (which is also a variable) so that this relationship could be thought of generally. Communication researchers, both professional and amateur, have invented such concepts as "meaning," "attitude," "communication apprehension," "language intensity," and "rhetorical sensitivity" to represent variables of interest to them, and have called these concepts "constructs." Dear to the hearts of contemporary communication theorists are such constructs as "rules," "constructions," "purpose," and "intention."

Using the concepts available (and sometimes inventing constructs when the available concepts do not serve well), communication theorists assert the existence of relationships among predictor and criterion variables. They test these theoretical assertions with as much rigor as they can devise, given practical limitations. The tests often require prior scientific descriptive work. Scientists' efforts may take the form of field studies, quasi-experimental studies, or experimental studies.

Communication Research as a Social/Rhetorical Activity

We may have given you the idea that science is a "pure" method, used by selfless people anonymously working to produce relational generalizations, some of which achieve the status of theory. You may perceive that individual scientists, their social and professional networks, and their rhetorical skills, are irrelevant to the enterprise.

If you have such a concept of science, it is an inaccurate one, of course. Scientists are human beings, and they usually behave like human beings, even when they are doing science.

First, *scientists tend not to discard a theory, even in the face of contradictory facts, until it is replaced by a better theory.* This reluctance is not unique to scientists, though it may retard the scientific enterprise more than it retards most enterprises. Human beings like to generalize. In spite of the dangers of oversimplification and inaccuracy, generalizations make people efficient. The only substitute for a generalization is a catalog of unsorted facts, and even people with exceptional memories dislike remembering catalogs. James Conant (1951, p. 173) (cf. Kuhn, 1970) expressed this tendency as it applies to scientists:

> *A conceptual scheme is never discarded merely because of a few stubborn facts with which it cannot be reconciled; a conceptual scheme is either modified or replaced by a better one, never abandoned with nothing left to take its place.*

Second, *scientists vary in their credibility among other scientists, and this variation partially accounts for the acceptance and longevity of some theories.* Scientists sometimes hesitate to discard the theories of a prestigious colleague during his or her lifetime, even when the theory is obviously faulty. According to Edwin Boring (1963, p. 8):

> *Many commentators have remarked the difficulty with which scientists abandon a theory, once important but now outmoded, until its author dies, for the author's prestige may maintain the authority of the Great Man even in the face of contradictory evidence.*

Scientists also may have negative credibility, which may adversely affect the chances that their theories will be accepted by the scientific community. Boring (1963, p. 69) wrote of how Mesmer, an "egotistic, opinionated" person, discovered hypnotism and how his discovery was rejected by scientists in the eighteenth century. Mesmer's activities were completely observable, and his explanations for his results were, at the time, scientifically respectable. He even found a Swiss priest who was practicing hypnotism as medical treatment, thus replicating Mesmer's results and, presumably, buttressing Mesmer's theory. Yet, his discoveries were rejected by the scientific establishment for about two centuries. Even sixty years after Mesmer, a British physician (also, according to reports, a rather aggressive man) was castigated for using hypnotism as an anaesthetic. Boring summarized his interpretation of the case:

> *If science is, as is so often claimed, quite impersonal, Mesmer's personality ought to have nothing to do with the question of his demonstration of [hypnotism]. Nobody knows whether Mesmer in his young manhood was more conceited than the average of men who later became famous. . . . In fact, conceit was involved in his scientific theory, since the theory had to do specifically with Mesmer. Yet nobody in the various investigating committees . . . was objective enough to see this crucial point. They denounced Mesmer, largely, so it seems to me, because of his personality, and thus mingled their own personalities with their scientific criticism.*

Third, *scientists increase their chances of devising, of publishing, and of obtaining acceptance for their theories as a consequence of social and professional networks.* Zuckerman (1977), in her analysis of Nobelist American scientists, very clearly establishes the power exerted by certain research centers in attracting, in motivating, and in politicking for future Nobelists in science. (You may be interested in knowing that, as a communication scientist, you are ineligible for a Nobel Prize. The only social science recognized by such a prize is economics.) In fact, probably the best predictor of winning a Nobel prize in science (other than having been born male) is to have had a mentor who already was or soon would be a Nobelist.

Finally, *the rhetorical skill of a scientist may affect the fate of a theory.* Some scientists are extremely skillful at presenting evidence and expressing concepts in such a way that the perceived importance of and support for their theories are enhanced. John Angus Campbell (1970) analyzed Charles Darwin's *Origin of Species* as a case in point. Jeanine Czubaroff (1974) showed the rhetorical strategies (some most *unscientific*) of Noam Chomsky, the linguist, and B. F. Skinner, the psychologist, in a dispute that was supposedly theoretical.

We need not cite all these reasons for believing that scientists have all the foibles of other human beings, of course. If science were an impersonal process, scientists would not care about such things as credit for discoveries. The discoveries would constitute their own rewards. But in fact scientists are extremely jealous of what they call "primacy" (credit for the *first* discovery of a relationship). One of the Nobelists interviewed by Zuckerman (1977, p. 188n), discussing scientists' concealment of their findings until "official" publication under their names could occur, spoke to her of "the presence of sharp elbows in science."

Dominant Models in Contemporary Communication Research

Social scientists in communication, like other human beings, operate from a set of assumptions, sometimes tacit and sometimes explicit, that guide their work. They call these sets of assumptions *models* or *paradigms*. These paradigms constitute frames of reference, perceptual filtering systems that guide what a social scientist seeks to discover and the means the social scientist employs in the process of discovery. They often also determine what a researcher will "see" in the results of a particular study as well as what he or she will fail to see.

In communication research, three such paradigms dominate the contemporary scene. We will call these the *covering law model,* the *rules approach,* and the *pragmatic paradigm,* and we will discuss each of them briefly. You may find one or another of them particularly appealing as a frame of reference from which to approach your own research. But all are respectable, and you may want to move among paradigms, experimenting informally with your own perceptual systems. Or you may eschew all three and explicitly devise or tacitly be trapped by other paradigms.

The Covering Law Model

Various theorists and philosophers have referred to the covering law model with a variety of different labels: determinism, the received view, positivism, the classical paradigm, logical empiricism. Whatever it is called, we agree with O'Keefe's (1975) conclusion that the covering law model is the most widely accepted perspective in contemporary communication research.

An important assumption of this approach is that the reasons for the occurrence of some communicative behavior *exist in the past.* The covering law model assumes that (1) a certain condition or conditions existed prior to the event of interest, and (2) these conditions were both necessary and sufficient for the event of interest to take place. Put more formally, this model asserts that the existence or occurrence of certain *antecedent conditions* (conditions which existed before the event) bring about or are the reason for certain *consequent* conditions. Accordingly, the search for explanation centers on describing and explaining the relationship or regularity among these antecedent and consequent events.

Advocates of the model seek to discover and articulate the *laws* that govern these regularities. The perspective assumes that the behavior of all objects—plants, planets, electrons, and human beings—is not random or chaotic. Rather, such behavior is under the control of or is governed by a set of natural laws, laws that actually exist in nature. Hence, the regularities or patterns observable in human behavior are "determined" by these laws. Unlike prescriptive traffic laws, scientific laws are descriptive—they cannot be bent or violated.

Such a perspective, of course, views human beings as essentially similar to other entities in the universe. As a consequence, this view has evoked criticism from theologians, philosophers, and some scientists who argue that the deterministic framework denies the existence of free will. We dealt with these arguments earlier in this chapter.

Types of Laws.   A thorough but succinct treatment of issues involved in the covering law model can be found in Berger (1977). We will rely to some extent on his essay.

The laws at the core of the covering law model can be classified into two groups—universal laws and statistical laws. Universal laws are thought to be unrestrained by time, space, cultural differences, or personal characteristics. They explain regularities that have existed, that presently exist, and that will exist in the future. Moreover, by the very fact that they are laws and not norms, habits, rules, etc., they cannot be broken. If the specified antecedent condition exists (e.g., if water is taken to sea level and heated to 100° Celsius), then the consequent condition *will* occur (water will boil). In fact, if a situation is observed where the regularity stated by such a universal law does not occur (e.g., water does not boil), then the law has been shown to be false and, according to the logic of this paradigm, should lose its status as a law. (But, as we indicated earlier in this chapter, scientists are human and sometimes fail to perceive facts that make them uncomfortable.)

Statistical laws are different from universal laws in that they do not suggest that a consequent event or condition will always follow a given antecedent. Rather, they assert that a specified antecedent condition will by followed by a given event a certain percentage of the time, and they predict the percentage within specified limits. Perhaps the best known example of such laws comes from genetics: If a man and a woman conceive a child, that child will be a female about 50 percent of the time. Note that before conception no prediction about the sex of a particular child is possible. No universal law is available at the moment to predict whether the child will be a male or female. The best that science can do is to state the probability that the child will be of one sex or the other.

As the genetic example shows, universal laws but not statistical laws allow specific predictions about particular events. Using universal laws, one can specify and explain why *this particular* pan of water boiled or why *this particular* chemical reaction took place. In contrast, statistical laws only allow predictions about larger groups or collections of events—about the sex of *all* babies who are born, or about the attitude change of *most* audience members who received a persuasive message. Hence, even though we might predict that 43 percent of the audience members who heard a persuasive message will change their attitude in a particular direction, we *cannot* predict with any certainty that John Smith, who sat in the fifth seat of the fourth row, will do so.

Conditional Logic. Despite the differences between these types of laws, they have an important feature in common. Together, they allow the covering law perspective to adopt and use a very formal and rigorous form of logic, often called *conditional logic*. Conditional logic is typified by the use of "if . . . , then . . ." propositions. We have used this type of logic several times in our description of these laws. Conditional logic is essentially a truncated form of the deductive syllogism studied in elementary logic classes. In its complete form, it would read:

1. IF: Certain antecedent conditions, A, exist
2. AND: A scientific law exists which states that A brings about the subsequent condition B,
3. THEN: Subsequent condition B will occur.

Two qualities of this type of logic are worth noting. First, both statements (1) and (3) refer to conditions or events that are *observed*. That is, they refer to the antecedent and consequent conditions that have been quantified and measured by some accepted set of rules or operations. For example, if A referred to a person's "height," then an acceptable rule for quantification would be to use a yardstick to measure the person's height in inches.

The conditions A and B in statement (2), by contrast, are theoretic or conceptual descriptions of these conditions. Hence, what connects the "meaning" of A with the observation of A are the operations used by scientists to measure A. These are alternatively called *correspondence rules* or *operational definitions*. An important assumption of the covering law model is that the rules for observation and measurement employed in (1) and (3) do indeed "correspond" to the conceptualization of A and B in statement (2). In

other words, it is assumed that the correspondence rules "exhaust" the theoretic meaning of the antecedent and consequent conditions. Since researchers would agree that no
method of measurement "exhausts" the meaning of a concept (Kerlinger, 1973), this
notion of absolute correspondence has received serious criticism from opponents of this
perspective. (See O'Keefe, 1975.)

A second important quality of conditional logic is that it strongly implies cause
and effect relationships (i.e., the occurrence of A *causes* the subsequent occurrence of B).
While most covering laws probably express such causal relationships, they need not
necessarily do so. Antecedent and consequent events may consistently appear together
but not be causally related. For example: *If* it is Sunday afternoon, *then* Sam will take a
nap. Even though Sam may nap *every* Sunday afternoon, without fail, it would make no
sense to postulate a law asserting that "Sunday" "caused" Sam's nap-taking behavior.
Rather, one would suggest that these two conditions regularly *coexist*.

Rules Approach

The rules approach rests on a set of assumptions about human beings and
their communicative behavior much different from those underlying the covering law
model. These differences are described succinctly (although evaluatively) by Miller
(1976, p. 11):

> *A rules centered approach stresses the communicator as an active agent who makes choices about
> the way to communicate in various episodic encounters. Such a position represents a radical break
> with prevailing mechanistic views of human behavior, which often picture communicators as
> relatively passive, helpless, automatons at the mercy of antecedent genetic and environmental
> forces impinging upon them. Stated differently, people are not always at the mercy of immutable,
> deterministic laws that despotically dictate their communicative transactions; instead they
> themselves play a role in creating the rules that govern their various message exchanges.*

Proponents of a rules perspective accomplish this "radical break" by positing that all
forms of human behavior *cannot* be explained by the same model or perspective. Rather,
they argue that social science must be "pluralistic"—that is, it must adopt different
explanatory models for different types of human behavior. Accordingly, rules theorists
maintain that human behavior should be divided into two classes or groups of activity.
As we will show shortly, the primary criterion for this division is whether the behavior
involves "choice" by the individual.

The first category of human activity has been labeled "controlled" behavior
(Pearce, 1976). This category includes a wide variety of activity for which a person's
intentions, desires, or purposes have no effect or relevance.

For example, if a person trips on the top step and falls headlong down a flight of
stairs, that individual's intentions or desires will do little to determine whether he or she
is seriously injured. A covering law model offers the best explanatory framework for such
events. The antecedent condition of "tripping on the stairs" when combined with
natural laws about gravity, mass, velocity, etc., will do an excellent job of explaining the
presence or absence of injuries in the hapless stair descender.

Having made the admissions (1) that controlled behavior exists and frequently
occurs, and (2) that it is most appropriately explained by the covering law model, rules
theorists advance their argument by maintaining that such instances of behavior have
little relevance for human communication. On the contrary, the rules perspective maintains that human communication falls into a second and distinct category of activity
labeled "influenced" behavior (Pearce, 1976). In contrast to controlled behavior, in-

fluenced behavior is *teleological*. It is behavior designed to *accomplish a specific purpose* (e.g., to indicate one's disgust, apologize for one's transgressions). Rules theorists assume that influenced behavior involves human choice. People are free to choose not only which purposes they wish to pursue, but also the means by which they wish to pursue them.

Influenced behavior is assumed to be primarily guided by the cognitive *meanings* people hold. As people enter into social, communicative situations, they attach meanings to the situation itself, to the other people involved in the situation, and to their attributed purposes for entering into it. The meanings are primarily influenced by the nature of the situation, or what rules theorists often term "episodes." As Pearce (1976, p. 20) suggests, "Communicators do not perceive their conversations as an undifferentiated stream of experience. Rather, they punctuate them into units." These units or episodes, then, are crucially important, for they provide a frame of reference that communicators use in assigning meanings. In turn, these personal meanings ultimately decide the purposes chosen, as well as the means chosen to fulfill them.

This set of assumptions constitutes the "radical break" to which we alluded earlier. Activities that fall under the heading of influenced behavior cannot be properly explained by a covering law model for two reasons. First, the concept of choice implies that an individual is free to break what in the covering law model would be a natural law. In fact, Cushman (1977, p. 35) characterizes teleological behaviors as "interfering with a cause in nature." Since a natural law by definition cannot be broken (that is, the consequence *will follow from* the antecedent), the concepts "choice" and "natural law" are incompatible.

Second, the idea of purposive activity implies that the "reason" for a person's behavior resides in the person's predictions about the future and not in some past antecedent condition. Consequently, the answer to *why* questions involves a statement something like, "because he or she intended to accomplish something in the future." Such an explanation is not only incompatible with the covering law model, it is a complete reversal of its logic. A teleological explanation uses the future to explain why something happened in the past.

To accommodate this reversal of logic, advocates of a rules approach have devised an alternative form of explanation that they call the "practical syllogism." This type of logic is designed to provide answers to *why* questions, while at the same time explicitly incorporating the concept of teleological behavior. As described by Von Wright (1971), the practical syllogism takes the form:

(1) A person, Jane, intends to bring about event or condition, "P." (2) Jane considers that she cannot bring about "P" unless she does behavior "B." (3) Jane sets herself to do "B."

The basic tenets of the rules perspective are illustrated by this syllogism. The explanation or reason for performing a certain behavior is to bring about a certain event or condition in the future. Jane's behavior is performed with the purpose of bringing about "P."

What are rules? How do they function? Are there different types? We will answer these questions in reverse order. A discussion of rules which fits nicely with the concept of episodes has suggested that there are two distinct types of rules (Sanders & Martin, 1975). These are labeled "regulative rules" (Rules$_r$) and "constitutive rules" (Rules$_c$). These two types of rules are thought to operate in much different ways. (For a dissenting view, see Shimanoff, 1980.) At least one theorist (Tompkins, 1982, p. 71) adds "prudential rules" (Rules$_p$) to this paradigm, but we will include this class of rules in Rules$_r$.

Rules$_r$ may be thought of as societal norms or standards. Accordingly, they include both implicit norms or standards for correct conduct, and explicit, publicly-stated legal statutes. They may be understood by considering the consequences that follow the violation of such rules—namely, some form of censure or disapproval. If one violates an implicit social Rule$_r$ (e.g., do not audibly belch in public), one is thought to be rude, boorish, etc., and will upon repeated violation of this Rule$_r$ be excluded from "polite" or "well-socialized" company.

The censure associated with the violation of an explicit, legal Rule$_r$ (e.g., do not take the life of another human being) is obvious. Usually, in fact, when these explicit Rules$_r$ are formulated a form of censure or punishment is attached.

The concept of a regulative rule is one with which we are relatively well acquainted in our culture. Some such rules are expressed in legal codes. Others find their way into books of etiquette, and others, more subtle, are not explicitly expressed anywhere.

A second class of rules—constitutive rules—are not usually associated with formal or legal codes. Rather, Rules$_c$ define a frame of reference within which certain behaviors may appropriately and coherently take place. In other words, Rules$_c$ are inherently associated with episodes. Earlier, we suggested that communicators punctuate their experience into episodic units, and that these units provide a framework for making choices about communicative behavior. Once experience has been framed into an episode, Rules$_c$ define the set of behaviors that *makes sense* within that episode.

In general, violations of Rules$_r$ bring about censure. Violations of Rules$_c$ bring about concern for the violator's social competence or mental health.

When we combine the concept of Rules$_r$ and Rules$_c$ with the notion of the practical syllogism, our description of the rules approach becomes relatively complete. The initial statement of the syllogism includes the following: "Jane intends to bring about 'P'." As we have seen, Jane's punctuation of her experience into an episode governed by Rules$_c$ serves to define the intentions or purposes that are appropriate and coherent. The second part of the syllogism indicates that, to bring about "P," Jane must perform behavior "B." This facet of the logic incorporates Rules$_r$. Jane has been socialized by her culture to know the rules regulating a communicative episode. Accordingly, she might exploit the rules in an episode called "personal quarrel" by shouting and slapping in order to bring about an apology.

Unlike laws, both Rules$_r$ and Rules$_c$ can be broken. People do belch in public, people do not always say "I'm sorry" when they should, and frequently people do behave in bizarre ways. Rules theorists argue that such communicative behaviors cannot be determined by natural laws, and that, therefore, the concept of rules, which explicitly recognizes an individual's ability to make choices and to follow intentions, is a more satisfactory explanatory mechanism than is the covering law model.

The rules approach, probably because of its reliance on mental rather than behavioral constructs, is the most controversial of the three we are discussing. Bochner (1978), Miller (1978), and Miller and Berger (1978) have criticized its conceptual and theoretical foundations. But it is also a very appealing approach, given the phenomenological human experiences of purpose, choice, and intention in everyday life.

Pragmatic Perspective

We call the third orientation toward human communication the pragmatic perspective. Pragmatics is the most recently developed approach to communication. In addition to its newness, pragmatics differs from the covering law and rules approaches in a fundamentally important way. Covering laws and rules offer radically different philosophies about how the universe of communication functions. In contrast, the pragmatic perspective presents itself not as a philosophy of science, but as an interesting and fruitful model for the study of human communication. Consequently, it is not incompatible with either laws or rules.

Although the original use of the term *pragmatics* is often attributed to Morris (1946), the use and development of this approach in communication research can be directly attributed to the work by Watzlawick, Beavin, and Jackson (1967), *Pragmatics of Human Communication*. These writers are psychiatrists and psychologists who have developed and practiced a relatively unique approach to the treatment of psychological pathologies—including marital and family relationship problems. Their approach de-emphasized the treatment of the individual person and his or her problems, focusing instead on the larger social unit of which the individual is a member (e.g., the marital dyad, the entire family, etc.). They have found that knowledge of the communicative *context* was extremely important for both understanding and treating a person's psychological problems. When they observed the communicative behavior of these larger social units, they frequently discovered characteristic *patterns* of interaction which recurred time and time again. Moreover, they found that these recurrent patterns of interaction actually facilitated the continuance of individuals' psychopathology. Accordingly, the main thrust of their diagnosis and treatment involved breaking the cycle of these communicative patterns and substituting a nonpathological communication environment. (See Watzlawick, Weakland, & Fisch, 1974.)

As communication researchers we are primarily interested in normal rather than pathological patterns of interaction. Various researchers have interpreted and extended the theoretic principles suggested by Watzlawick, Beavin, and Jackson. The pragmatic perspective involves the joining of two communication theories—systems theory and certain aspects of information theory.

Systems theory is that aspect of pragmatics which suggests the importance of the social, communicative context. It assumes that communication does not take place in isolation, but rather necessitates a communication system—the smallest of which may contain two members. Hence, to study the individual communicator and his or her behavior in isolation is to ignore the systemic processes characterizing this human activity.

Information theory, on the other hand, implies that as people communicate over time, they inevitably develop "patterns" of interaction. Communicators are constantly faced with a number of alternatives, and over time some become more likely than others. The messages sent and received in the immediate past, however, serve to "constrain" the probability of these choices. For example, the most likely response to a question for most communicators in most contexts is an answer. As similar sequences of messages occur, characteristic patterns develop, and redundancies in interaction can be observed.

When combined, these two modes of thinking form the foundation of the pragmatic perspective.

Systems Theory.   Detailed discussions of systems theory appear elsewhere, and we refer you to work by Mongé (1977) and especially by Fisher (1978a). For our purposes, we will confine the discussion to three basic principles: wholeness, openness, and hierarchical order.

The principle of *wholeness* is alternatively referred to as the principle of *nonsummativity*. This characteristic is so fundamental to a systems perspective that it has frequently been phrased as a maxim: "The whole is greater than the sum of its parts." This suggests that when people communicate, their messages make up a system in which the component parts (that is, the individual messages) become *interdependent* as a result of the message exchange. Stated differently, the behavior of one member of the system affects and is affected by the behavior of all other members. These interrelationships among the behaviors make the system a separate entity, which cannot be recreated by the simple adding together of the individual behaviors. Accordingly, to observe and study a single communicator in isolation is to arbitrarily discard this person's linkages to or interdependencies with the other members of the system.

A useful way to understand the wholeness principle is to describe a nonsystem, or what is commonly referred to in systems' jargon as a "heap." A heap is an aggregate or collectivity of individuals that has no basis for interdependence. Because the members are independent, their behaviors *do not* affect the other members of the collectivity. For example, you may have had the experience of going to a restaurant for a quick lunch and being forced to sit at a table completely filled with strangers. In this instance, being at the same table usually does not constitute membership in a system. You may eat as fast or as slowly as you want, you may read a book, write a letter, or daydream if you want, and you may leave the table without consulting the other people present. Hence, except for table manners and common courtesy, your behavior is independent of the collectivity. You may behave as if you were alone.

Contrast the situation where you go to lunch and sit at a table with friends, perhaps to compare class notes or to plan social activities. As you sit around the table in this context, you and your friends form an interacting social system. Because you are communicating with some purpose, your behavior affects and is affected by the other members of the system. You take turns speaking; you probably excuse yourself before leaving the table; and you probably find some means of asking permission to read, write, or daydream. Given this kind of interdependence, systems theorists would argue that observing your behavior and ignoring your companions' would be inappropriate and probably misleading. Since your behavior is intrinsically linked to the behavior of others, it would be almost impossible to explain your behavior without the context.

Openness refers to the degree to which a system exchanges information or energy with the environment around it. All living organisms are open systems. They must take in nutrients, water, and oxygen from the environment, and in turn they must expel waste products. The term *ecological balance* is a systems term referring specifically to the natural and unimpeded (by pollution, civilization, etc.) exchange of energy among various living, open systems and their environments.

All human communication systems also are open, although the commodity of exchange in this instance is information, not energy. All normal people belong to various open systems—family, class at school, friends, church choir, and so forth. As people enter and leave these various systems, they take information with them. In addition, even when people are not in an immediate, personal system, they gain information by reading, watching television, or personally experiencing nonsocial aspects of the environment.

As you might imagine, the concept of an open system has an opposite, the "closed" system. A closed system has impermeable boundaries and thus is unable to exchange either information or energy with its surroundings. Everything that is needed for its functioning is internally contained by the system. While the concept of a closed system makes an ideal contrast to openness, actually there is probably no perfectly closed system, no perpetual motion machine. All systems must be open to their environment to some extent, or they eventually will disintegrate. (In systems jargon, this tendency to disintegrate is called "entropy.") Hence, rather than label systems as either open or closed, we agree with Fisher's (1978a) recommendation that all systems be characterized by their *degree* of openness.

The primary reason for introducing this distinction between open and closed systems is to suggest that human communication systems, because they are open and thus exchange information with their environment, are capable of *self-regulation*. The eventual fate of a closed system is disintegration, and this process can never be reversed. In contrast, the open system can sometimes restore itself by drawing resources from the environment. People constantly restore their bodies by eating and resting. Similarly, they regulate and restore social systems by communication. If you have ever had a serious argument with a friend, spouse, or family member, and if your relationship is still intact, then you have experienced the self-regulating process of an open system.

Systems theorists assume *hierarchical order*. Almost every system is a component of a larger *suprasystem*, while simultaneously comprising a number of smaller *subsystems*. As an example, we will use the open communication system we usually call the family. As we move up the systems hierarchy, the family is part of the neighborhood, which is part of the city, which is part of the state, and so on until we reach the universe. If we move down the hierarchy, the family comprises its individual members, who, in turn, comprise various biological systems (the cardiovascular system, the digestive system, etc.), which comprise various organs, which comprise various cells, and so on.

This concept of hierarchical order implies that each system is a component in a vast set of interdependent linkages. Moreover, recall that the concept of wholeness suggested that we cannot appropriately and accurately study a member of a social system in isolation. Consequently, the appropriate study of any system involves locating it in its appropriate suprasystem.

Implications of Information Theory.   As we suggested earlier, physical systems and social communicative systems operate by similar processes. They differ, however, in the means by which their component parts are linked. Physical systems operate via energy, while social systems operate via information. Hence, certain implications of what is called "information theory" are an important aspect of the pragmatic perspective. We will discuss two fundamental applications that capture the essence of information theory: uncertainty reduction and redundant patterns.

Information theory, like the rules approach, begins with the proposition that people have the ability to choose from among a range of alternative behaviors. That is, as people enter into social interaction (more specifically, as they enter into each message exchange *within* a social interaction), they possess a set of alternative communicative behaviors from among which they may choose. Through a selection process, they reduce the number of available alternatives until they finally choose a single behavior.

Information theory can be applied to show that this selection process is not a random, haphazard, guessing game. Rather, people make purposeful choices. Hence, what allows them to systematically reduce the number of alternatives and eventually select a single behavior is *information*. People make choices about their behavior based on the information they possess. In the absence of any usable information, the choice becomes a random selection, and people are required to "guess" which behavior to perform.

The situation in which no information exists is one of maximum uncertainty. If the individual has no information by which to reduce the number of alternatives, then each of the choices has exactly the same probability of being selected, and the person is totally uncertain about which to choose. As information is received and processed, however, certain alternatives can be eliminated, thus making some choices *more* probable and others *less* probable. As this happens, the individual's uncertainty has been reduced. As even more information is received, the probabilities of selecting various options again change, and uncertainty is reduced further until a single behavioral alternative is selected.

Information theorists have coined a term for the basic quantitative unit of information: the *binary digit* (often abbreviated as a "bit") of information. A binary digit is defined as that amount of information necessary to reduce uncertainty by 50 percent. Information theorists do not consider the *quality* or *nature* of information—only its *quantity.*

To illustrate a la Broadhurst and Darnell (1965): Imagine that you are asked to guess which single playing card a friend of yours is holding on the basis of his or her yes/no answers to questions. Before asking the first question, you would be faced with maximum uncertainty. Each of the 52 cards in the deck is equally likely to be the one your friend is holding. At this point, your most efficient first question would be one that halves the possibilities, "Is it a red suit?" The answer to this question, regardless of its actual content, gives you one bit of information. Assuming that your friend has told the truth, you can immediately eliminate 26 cards from consideration. Your uncertainty has been reduced by 50 percent. Probably, your best strategy would be to continue to ask questions that eliminate half of the remaining possible cards ("Is the suit spades?") until your uncertainty has been reduced to zero.

Information theory assumes, therefore, that people are constantly seeking to reduce uncertainty by a process (albeit frequently implicit and unconscious) of asking questions. "Was that remark intended as an insult or a compliment?" "Was that a serious question or was she just wondering out loud?" Consequently, communication is seen as an ongoing process in which people are constantly seeking and obtaining information about which communicative behavior they should next perform.

An important concept of pragmatics which comes from information theory is that communicative events occur in a sequence that extends across time—that they exhibit *redundant patterns.* An appropriate analogy would be a steel chain in which each link represents a message in the overall sequence. (This analogy is especially apt because it suggests that each message in the sequence is directly linked to both the message that precedes it and the one that follows it, and is indirectly linked to all other elements in the system.)

Information theory assumes that each of these messages involves a rational choice based on the process of uncertainty reduction. Hence, the student of communication may be able to infer specific processes of uncertainty reduction from repetitive sequencing of messages. As the interaction continues, various sequences of messages may occur again and again. When this happens, information theory maintains that past choices have an impact on or "constrain" future choices. In other words, people tend to habitually process information, to repeatedly reduce uncertainty in the same way. Hence, communication systems exhibit *redundant patterns* of interaction across time. Because people tend to make the same choices in similar situations, certain sequences of messages repeat themselves and patterns become identifiable and, within limits, predictable. Moreover, the more redundant the patterns become (that is, the more often certain sequences are repeated), the smaller and more limited the range of alternatives available to the individual is thought to be. The system may become rigid, the chain in our analogy rusted.

Until recently, the pragmatic perspective has been applied principally in descriptive studies (to answer *what* questions). Some current thinking, however (Courtright, 1979; Hewes, 1979), implies that the perspective might also be used to answer more theoretical (*why*) questions.

Paradigms and Research Methods

All three of the paradigms we have discussed are well within the methodological rules of social science. Hence, the research methods that are the subject of this book are equally applicable to all three of these perspectives as well as to any emerging new perspective that would be called scientific. All three perspectives require that the researcher/theorist associate (or relate or account for) variables in terms of other variables. Hence, in the covering law perspective:

Variable (usually behavior) *A* is associated with variable (usually behavior) *Y*.
Variable (usually behavior) *B* is associated with variable (usually behavior) *X*.

In the rules perspective:

Variable (usually a rule or set of rules) *A* is associated with variable (usually behavior) *Y*.
Variable (usually another set of rules) *B* is associated with variable (usually behavior) *X*.
Variable (for example, censure) *C* is associated with variable (usually violation of Rules$_r$) *U*.
Variable (for example, attributions of incompetence) *D* is associated with variable (usually violation of Rules$_c$) *V*.

And in the pragmatic perspective:

Variables (usually behavior) *A, B, C, D*, and *E* are mutually associated.

The words that all of these kinds of statements have in common are *variable(s)* and *associated*. Our purposes in this book are to provide you with methods for conceiving and operationalizing *variables* and for specifying and generalizing *associations* among those variables. Although our general goal is to enable you to use these methods to construct *theory*, the methods may also be used for atheoretical purposes.

■ *Conclusion*

Science is a method of explaining events that depends on observing variables and conceptually relating the variation in and among those variables. The method is not esoteric, nor does it depend on esoteric apparatus or arcane vocabulary.

The scientific enterprise depends on freely available information. It cannot exist where investigators are permitted to plead private knowledge or methods. To insure free access, science employs operationism, a method of description that enables complete, independent replication of observations and scientific studies. Given this openness in its methods, science is a self-correcting process. Idiosyncratic errors in observation and inference are arrested as they fail to provide a replicable basis for future studies that attempt to build on them. Scientific discovery requires publication so that the enterprise can be cumulative and so that inaccurate observations, unjustified inferences, and invalid or incorrigible theories can be challenged.

Scientists seek their goal—improvements in theory—through various kinds of studies. Variables may be subjected to descriptive studies, as in the development of taxonomies, tests, and measurement instruments. Predictor and criterion variables might be related to each other through studies bearing such labels as "surveys," "field studies," "quasi-experimental studies," and "experimental studies."

Science is a human enterprise, and scientists have human foibles. Personality, credibility, social networks, and rhetorical skill all affect the progress of science. For scientists, the method is not its own reward. Like others, they seek fame, prestige, fortune, and even affection both inside and outside the community of scientists.

In communication, contemporary social scientists are likely to identify themselves with one of three models, or paradigms, or perspectives, or frames of reference. These are the covering law model, the rules approach, and the pragmatic perspective. All operate by the epistemological assumptions of science. Hence, the subject matter of this book is applicable to all three.

Experiments and Quasi-Experiments

Because of their advantages in efficiency and their ability to establish a single interpretation for the effects of various predictor variables, experimental and quasi-experimental methods are still the most popular among scientists who study communication (though the popularity of these methods probably is dwindling). In Chapter 1, we described Isaac's, Bernard's and Gordon's, and Joan's experiments in physics to illustrate various scientific concepts. In this chapter, we will not desert those intrepid researchers, but we will extend the epistemology they exemplify to research in communication. We also will introduce several new considerations for the design and execution of experiments and quasi-experiments in communication.

Though we will limit the discussion to experimental and quasi-experimental methods, the basic mode of thought exemplified in these methods can easily be extended to other studies designed to relate predictor and criterion variables in survey studies, field studies, and mixed studies. And the methods may be used in historical and critical studies of certain kinds to "predict backwards" (Bowers, 1968) or, as some writers have put it, to "postdict." That is, if you have a theory you want to test, and if that theory relates predictor and criterion variables as they are thought to have operated in past events, you can express your "predictions" using the mode of thought described here, and test those "predictions" by searching for previously uncovered evidence that the predictor and criterion variables of interest to you were present and behaving in conformity with your theory.

In spite of our best efforts in Chapter 1, you may still find the idea of experimenting with human communication a bit repugnant. But, informally, without replication and publication, you participate in communication experiments both as subject and as experimenter every day of your life. Consider the following short dialogue:

Mother: Johnny, eat your spinach.
Johnny: I don't like it.
Mother: You need spinach to get big and strong.
Silence.
Mother: Don't you want to grow up to be like Daddy? Look, he's eating his.

Johnny: I don't like it, Mother.
Mother: Spinach is good for your bones. You could get really sick without spinach.
Silence.
Mother: It tastes good, Johnny. Just try it. You'll like it.
Johnny (smelling the spinach): I can't eat it.
Mother: If you just take one bite, I'll give you a piece of candy after supper.
Johnny: I can't.
Mother: If you don't at least try it, you can't have any dessert.
Silence.

Both participants clearly are experimenting with communication, the mother in an attempt to exercise social control, Johnny in an attempt to resist it. We will analyze only the mother's experiments. She manipulates a number of predictor variables in order to change the state of one criterion variable, Johnny's ingestion of his spinach. At least eight predictor variables from the mother's point of view are detectable:

1. The mother's first response to the situation, a simple request, is an exercise of what might be called her referent power (French & Raven, 1960). She knows that Johnny sometimes does things that he otherwise would not do simply because she asks him to.
2. In her second utterance, she holds out to Johnny the distant reward of good health. She assumes that this is one of his goals, and she makes it salient for him by relating it to the ingestion of spinach. In a word that has an unfortunate double meaning in this context, she tries to get Johnny to *internalize* (Kelman, 1961) health as a reason for eating spinach.
3. When manipulation of this variable fails, she attaches to it what she thinks might be a stronger motive for Johnny, identification with his father. If Johnny has brothers and sisters, she might also at this point employ a little sibling rivalry: "Look, even the baby eats his spinach."
4. When even exercises of power and promises of remote rewards fail as predictor variables, the mother resorts to anticipation of remote punishment, the possibility of a mysterious bone disease.
5. Next, the mother tries the promise of immediate pleasure, the good taste of the spinach. Here, Johnny does a little testing of his own. The smell of the spinach, to him at least, fatally damages the credibility of his mother's claim. He prefers to base his action on the physical reality of the smell rather than the social reality proposed by his mother.
6. The mother knows that Johnny likes candy. She uses the anticipation of receiving candy as a relatively immediate reward. And by coaxing Johnny to take only a bite, she uses the "foot-in-the-door" technique (Freedman & Fraser, 1966).
7. When the promise of immediate reward fails, the mother resorts to anticipation of immediate deprivation (no spinach, no dessert).
8. Finally, the mother might perceive the very length of the dialogue as a relevant predictor variable. That is, she uses a strategy of *persistence* (Bowers & Ochs, 1971). If Johnny does eat his spinach in this instance, she probably will undertake a similarly long exchange on the next similar occasion (possibly with broccoli). (If Johnny tries the same strategy on his parents, he probably will be told to "stop pestering us.")

This analysis indicates that the mother is using (though not in a published and possibly not in a replicable way) experimental methods. Although her control over the conditions of the experiment (or, rather, the series of experiments) may not be ideal, although she sometimes confounds predictor variables, and although any results she derives will be narrow in the scope of their generalizability, the case serves as an introduction to the method with which you may be able to identify.

The Basic Design

John Stuart Mill (1930) systematized the definition of *causal relationship* from which the basic elements of the experimental method are derived. (But note carefully that contemporary experiments often are conducted to identify relationships thought to be other than "causal.") This thought can be reduced to the following proposition:

> If a variable thought to be a criterion variable occurs when a variable thought to be a predictor variable has preceded it, but if the variable thought to be a criterion does *not* occur, other things being constant, when the variable thought to be a predictor has *not* preceded it, then a causal relationship can be said to exist between the predictor and the criterion variables.

The condition requiring that the suspected predictor variable be *present* is called the *experimental* condition. The condition requiring that the suspected predictor variable be *absent* is called the *control* condition. Abstractly, these conditions can be represented in a successful experiment as follows:

(Experimental condition)   If P, then C.
(Control condition)   If non-P, then non-C.

(P and C stand for "predictor" and "criterion," respectively.)

In Chapter 1, Isaac was an example of this basic design. He was trying to explain variation in boiling, measured at two levels ("present" and "absent"), by variations in "nearness to fire," also measured at two levels ("near" and "not near"). He also conducted experiments to test alternate possible predictors for the criterion, including source of water, location of fire, and type of container. The predictor variables in Isaac's studies, then, included nearness to fire, source of water, location of fire, and type of container. Isaac had only one criterion variable—boiling and not boiling.

Contemporary communication research often employs experimental, quasi-experimental, and mixed designs that are much more complex than Isaac's, though they are no different in principle. For the moment, however, we will note only one inadequacy in the basic design. It proceeds from an all-or-nothing assumption, a premise that predictor and criterion variables are either present or absent. Contemporary science, including social science, often requires more precise quantification than the simple observation that something is either present or absent. Therefore, the basic experimental design is often considered one by means of which corresponding differences are detected in the *quantities* or *levels* of criterion variables as functions of differences in the *quantities* or *levels* of predictor variables. This method is called *concomitant variation*.

Three kinds of concomitant variation are frequent subjects of experimental study. The first hypothesizes a *direct* relationship, in which increases in the level or quantity of the predictor variable are thought to be accompanied by corresponding *increases* in the level or quantity of the criterion variable. The second hypothesizes an *inverse* relationship, so that increases in the level or quantity of the predictor variable are thought to be accompanied by corresponding *decreases* in the level or quantity of the criterion variable. Joan hypothesized and tested an *inverse* relationship from which she concluded that the criterion variable "boiling temperature" *decreases* as altitude *increases*. (Both direct and inverse relationships are *linear* relationships.) The third hypothesizes a *curvilinear* relationship between predictor and criterion variables, in which increases (or decreases) in the predictor variable to a certain point are accompanied by increases (or decreases) in the criterion variable, beyond which point the nature of the relationship changes. The relationship between *psychological drive* as a predictor variable and *lexical diversity* as a criterion variable, for example, probably is a curvilinear one (Bradac, Bowers, & Courtright, 1980). When drive is very low, so is diversity. As drive increases to a moderately high level, diversity also increases. But as drive approaches extremely high levels, diversity *decreases*. We have graphically illustrated a *direct,* an *inverse,* and one of the many kinds of *curvilinear* relationships in Figure 2.1.

The Problem of Random Fluctuation

Designing experiments in communication is not quite as straightforward as this discussion of the basic design might imply. As a social scientist, you usually cannot ascribe all variations in your criterion variable to variations in your predictor variable because social scientific theories are far from perfect. Thus, you will learn to expect some variation in criterion variables from experiment to experiment as the result of influences other than those emanating from the predictor variables you are manipulating or controlling. All the variation from uncontrolled variables is commonly lumped together and called *random fluctuation* in the criterion variable. An illustration will be useful.

As an experimentalist in communication, you might be interested in the following question: Does the presence of other people facilitate vocalization in very young (pre-language) children? You design an experiment to test for a relationship between "presence of others" (the predictor variable) and "vocalization" (the criterion variable).

For this first experiment, you direct your attention specifically to the caretaking parent as a facilitator of vocalization in young children. Your hypothesis is a simple one: The presence of the caretaking parent is related in a direct, linear way to the vocalization of the child.

Now you must operationalize the variables referred to in the hypothesis. To this end, you solicit the cooperation of two families that you consider normal, each of which has an eight-month-old child. The two children, Jeanne and Tommy, become your experimental subjects. For both children, the caretaking parent is the mother, so in this particular study, "caretaking parent" is operationalized as "mother."

Next, you must operationalize "vocalization." You have a number of options available. For example, you might count the number of detectable syllables the child utters, or you might measure in seconds the output generated by a voice-activated microphone (compare Cappella, 1980). If you accepted the second alternative, you would have to count even crying as "vocalization." You finally decide that the best operationalization, for your interests, would be time (measured in seconds) of noncrying vocalization. If you encounter instances on the tape recording where you cannot decide whether a vocalization is "crying" or "noncrying," you will refer the decision to the mother.

FIGURE 2.1. Three Kinds of Relationships Between a Predictor Variable and a Criterion Variable.

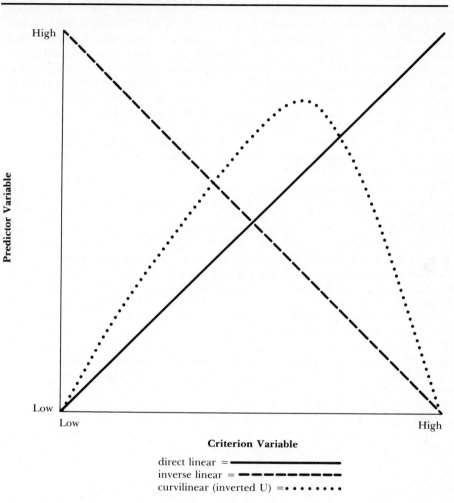

direct linear = ▬▬▬▬▬
inverse linear = ▬ ▬ ▬ ▬ ▬ ▬
curvilinear (inverted U) = • • • • • • • •

The predictor variable, presence or absence of the mother, is relatively easy to manipulate, given her cooperation. However, you face the problem of other possibly relevant variables, and you would like to avoid confounding these with the predictor variable. You would like to make your tests as natural as possible. A strange environment may affect the vocalization of one child differently from the way it affects the vocalization of another, or it may affect both in ways that would prevent generalization to a natural environment. (The problem of generalizing to a natural environment is sometimes called the problem of *ecological validity*, and we will discuss it in Chapter 6.) Therefore, you decide to conduct the experiment in the subjects' homes.

Time as a possibly confounding variable is also obviously relevant. You discover from the parents that the children are normally awake simultaneously between 11 A.M. and noon. You decide to conduct your studies between 11:00 A.M. and 11:30 A.M. You also note that family patterns of behavior may produce more vocalization on some days of the week than on others, and that this also may be a confounding variable. (For example, after an exciting weekend one child may be abnormally quiet on Mondays.) Because you obviously cannot control family patterns of behavior, you decide to design your experiment in such a way that both levels of the predictor variable ("alone" and "with mother") occur at least once during each day of the week. You then can feel safe that whatever irregularities occur because of the day-of-the-week variable affects both levels of the predictor variable equally. If you wanted to be even more sophisticated, you could analyze the data in such a way that day-of-the-week would be treated as a quasi-experimental predictor variable, so that whatever effects were attributable to it would be extracted from the test of the more critical alone-or-with-mother predictor.

Finally, you recognize that eight-month-old babies sometimes cry for inordinately long periods. When babies cry, they cannot simultaneously vocalize normally. Therefore, you decide to adjust the measure of the criterion variable to allow for crying behavior. You can make this adjustment by using a ratio of seconds spent vocalizing to seconds of noncrying behavior (vocal and quiet) in each of your half-hour periods. (Ratios are often useful to make sets of data comparable when, without adjustment, they would be incomparable. That explains why so many things are expressed in proportions or percentages. We will say more about this in Chapter 4.) For example, if on a given day Tommy cried for three minutes, vocalized for eight minutes, and did not vocalize for the remaining 19 minutes of his half-hour period, you would calculate his criterion "score" for that day as follows: 1800 seconds (time of the test) minus 180 seconds (time crying) equals 1620 seconds (noncrying behavior). And 480 seconds (time vocalizing) divided by 1620 seconds (noncrying behavior) equals .296. This last number, .296, is the ratio of Tommy's vocalizing behavior to all of his noncrying behavior during the test period that day. In effect, using this ratio makes Tommy's time spent crying irrelevant to the analysis. Crying neither hurts nor helps the child's vocalizing score.

You now give your final instructions. You have decided to run your tests over two weeks, because during that period you can schedule each child in the "alone" and the "with-mother" condition on each day of the week. You elicit each mother's commitment to the schedule and induce her to run all tests in the same room of the house at the same time of the day. During the "with-mother" tests, the mother is simply to sit where the child can see her (difficult as she may find it to be nonresponsive). She is to respond minimally or not at all to anything the child does, either vocally or nonvocally. Her mere presence is the experimental condition, so she is to read a book, knit, or engage in some other tranquil activity. Your tape recorders are installed; the playpens are ready for occupancy.

As a result of your measurements and calculations, you arrive at the scores shown in Table 2.1. These are your data. (You might note that *data* is a plural noun; the singular form is *datum*. If you find it awkward to say "the data are . . . ," try "the set of data is . . . .")

Your problem now is to make sense from the set of data, to analyze it. When you first glance at the table, you notice hopefully that in many cases each child's "with-mother" score is higher than the "alone" score. But as a social scientist, you are reluctant to admit that any conclusion you draw is based on a mere subjective glance at the data. Somehow, you must summarize the data.

One way to condense the data is simply to add up all the "alone" scores, then do the same with all the "with-mother" scores for the two children. Because you observed the children in each of the two conditions the same number of times, the two sums should

TABLE 2.1. Vocalization Ratios for Two Children "Alone" and "With Mother"*

Day of Week	Tommy		Jeanne	
	Alone	With Mother	Alone	With Mother
Sunday 1	.328			.550
Monday 1		.462	.536	
Tuesday 1	.228			.699
Wednesday 1		.284	.640	
Thursday 1	.418			.584
Friday 1		.349	.414	
Saturday 1	.475			.640
Sunday 2		.374	.622	
Monday 2	.324			.451
Tuesday 2		.500	.426	
Wednesday 2	.237			.692
Thursday 2		.263	.685	
Friday 2	.310			.475
Saturday 2		.382	.494	

*Hypothetical data.

be comparable. When you perform that calculation, you notice that the "with-mother" sum is higher, as you had hypothesized:

"Alone" sum	6.137
"With-mother" sum	6.705

This difference makes you think that you might be on your way to confirming a hypothesis. But you would like to be able to talk about the difference in terms other than sums. A comparison of the average vocalization ratio "alone" with the average vocalization ratio "with mother" would be desirable, so that you could say: "On an ordinary day, the 'alone' ratio is X, the 'with-mother' ratio, Y." To find this average (in this and most studies an average called the *arithmetic mean*), you divide each of the sums by the number of observations it represents (14). You find:

"Alone" average	.438
"With-mother" average	.479

You still are not confident that the difference you found is a systematic one, relating predictor variable to criterion variable, rather than one based on random fluctuation. You know that many uncontrolled variables might have affected the children's vocalization, even though you did your best to keep constant or otherwise control the obvious ones. One child's father may have left the house at an unusual time, thereby upsetting the baby and affecting vocalization. One child may have had a restless night, depressing noncrying vocalization the following day. These random variables may have affected your data at least as much as your predictor variable did. You would like to have some assurance that the difference you found is not easily attributable to such random variables.

The formal statistical techniques available to test the operation of random fluctuation in an experiment of this kind will be discussed at length in Chapters 8–14. However, Jeanne and Tommy can be used as a basis for the discussion of some of these techniques.

You reason that if your predictor variable is systematically related to your criterion variable, then the "with-mother" condition should yield higher scores at least fairly consistently. That is, most of the time, the children should vocalize more in the "with-mother" than in the "alone" condition. Thus, if you chart your data, you should find the "with-mother" ratios clustered at one end and the "alone" ratios clustered at the other. This clustering does not occur in Figure 2.2, where A stands for "alone" and M stands for "with mother."

At this point, your hypothesis does not appear to be tenable. As Figure 2.2 shows, the two distributions have much more space in common than would be expected if the relationship between predictor and criterion is direct and linear. The entire range of scores covers 471 units (the highest score, .699, minus the lowest score, .228).

You may have noticed that your hypothesis might fare better if you introduced a quasi-experimental variable, and we have not overlooked that variable. But we will reserve discussion of it for the section on "Repeated Measures Designs" later in this chapter.

FIGURE 2.2. Distribution of Vocalization Rates "Alone" and "With Mother."

M M		M MM		M MM M		M	M	M		M M
AA	A AA		AA A		A A A			A A	A	
.200	.250	.300	.350	.400	.450	.500	.550	.600	.650	.700

More Complex Designs

So far, we have been concerned with simple experimental designs, in which only one predictor variable and one criterion variable are employed.

Most contemporary communication experiments make use of more efficient designs that simultaneously test the effects of a number of predictor variables, sometimes on more than one criterion variable.

Suppose that, as a communication scholar, you and your research group are concerned with the problem of recruiting volunteers, especially women, for experiments. This problem is a real one for many social scientists for two reasons: (1) Volunteers are simply hard to obtain, and (2) unless everybody in a potential sample volunteers, those who do cannot be considered a random sample from a population. Your group sees in the problem a chance to do research that might have practical as well as theoretical value.

One member of your group, a first-year graduate student, has an extremely attractive, intelligent, socially adept 23-year-old brother who is a dentistry student at your university. In a brainstorming session on the female volunteer problem, she says, "I'll bet almost any unmarried female in school would volunteer to be an experimental subject if she were offered a dinner date with Brian." This statement impels a series of experiments.

Because your department has a standing policy of permitting appeals for volunteers in all its classes and because it offers courses required of all students at all levels, getting a representative sample of subjects for these particular studies is no problem. (Note the paradox: Your criterion variable will be "volunteering/not volunteering." Hence, a member of each class used will be a subject in this experiment by the very fact of his or her *not* volunteering to be in an experiment. This kind of study is the bane of university committees governing "informed consent" in the use of human subjects for social science research.)

Your group is now ready to compose the experimental messages. The message you have customarily used to recruit subjects in classrooms is as follows:

> As all of you know, this is a research as well as teaching department. We try to discover new knowledge about communication as well as to teach what we already know. Very often, research in communication requires human subjects for experimental work.
>
> Because this university has a policy against *requiring* students to participate in experiments, we must depend on volunteers whenever we cannot afford to pay experimental subjects. But graduate students are notoriously poor and seldom have money to pay subjects for participating in thesis and dissertation research.
>
> In any research for which you volunteer, your anonymity will be protected. And no study using volunteer subjects will involve any physical or psychological stress beyond the levels you habitually experience in everyday life.
>
> We hope that you will want to help add to the store of knowledge available to future generations of students (and, incidentally, help our graduate students progress toward their degrees) just as former students have added to the store of knowledge available to you. We are now going to pass around an "Experimental Volunteer Sign-up Sheet." If you sign, you will be committing one hour of your time, arranged to fit your schedule, to this valuable work. If you do *not* sign, your instructor will not hold it against you, of course.

You decide to use this message as the persuasive appeal in one of your conditions, to serve as a "control" or comparison point for the effects of other messages.

For an experimental condition in your first study, you decide to use exactly the same message except that you add the following paragraph between the second-to-last and last paragraphs:

> This semester, we are offering an added inducement for female volunteers. We will put the name of every female student who volunteers in a lottery. In about a month, when all the experiments are completed, we will draw the name of one of these volunteers and will fully support her financially for a dinner date with Brian, seated here on the right, at a local night club.

So far, this study is an example of the simple experimental design, with one predictor variable ("Brian/No Brian") and one criterion variable ("volunteer/ nonvolunteer").

You select randomly six sections of students enrolled in the department's large freshman course. You arrange for your speaker, Brian's sister, to appear in all six sections at the beginning of the class period for each section. (You will use the same speaker in all six sections so that "speaker" as a variable does not become confounded with the "Brian/No Brian" predictor variable.) Although no reference is made to Brian in the control ("No Brian") sections, you require his smiling and charming presence, so that his presence or absence will not be confounded with the appeal in the message.

On the day of the experiment, 20 female students attend each of the six sections. You break them down in terms of frequency of volunteers, and your results appear in Table 2.2.

A glance at the table shows that your manipulation failed to produce the desired result. Even the class with the highest proportion of volunteers reached only 50 percent—and that was a section *without* the Brian paragraph.

To provide a visual check on the overlap between the experimental ("Brian") and control ("No Brian") conditions, you arrange the data as shown in Figure 2.3 and find that the two distributions overlap substantially. Therefore, any apparent differences could easily be the result of random fluctuation, and you can attribute no effects to the experimental manipulation.

Your study now begins to attract the attention of others in your department. When your research group meets to discuss your results, a senior member of the faculty sits in and gives a short speech:

> I've had experience with quite a lot of work on persuasion, and unexpected results seem to be the norm rather than the exception. I've evolved a way of thinking about the process that might be helpful.
>
> Now, our first impulse is to consider persuasion as a very simple process. We think that if we appeal to a motive we know to exist, our persuasion will automatically be successful. And we know that those young women in those classes— or at least many of them—would like to have a date with Brian. Yet, they didn't sign up as volunteers.
>
> This situation indicates to me that we're thinking about persuasion in an

TABLE 2.2. Number and Percentage of Sign-ups "With Brian Paragraph" and "Without Brian Paragraph"*

Class	With Brian Paragraph		Without Brian Paragraph	
	Number	Percent	Number	Percent
A	4	20		
B			5	25
C	7	35		
D			6	30
E	9	45		
F			10	50

*Hypothetical data.

FIGURE 2.3. Distribution of Proportions for "Brian" *(B)* and "No Brian" *(O)* Conditions.

	O	*O*			*O*
B			*B*	*B*	

.20   .25   .30   .35   .40   .45   .50

inadequate way, that our implicit theory isn't a valid one. I think that in almost every case of persuasion various forces are working—some facilitating action, others inhibiting it. Clearly, the prospect of having a date with Brian should facilitate action for many of these subjects. But something else in the situation must inhibit it just as strongly.

My hypothesis, for the moment, is that freshman women, in general, have very fragile social self-esteem. For that reason, they hate to admit to social frustrations. But consider the situation you put them in. You ask them, in front of their peers of both genders, to take a chance on getting a date with an admittedly attractive young man. If they sign up, they see themselves as admitting, both to themselves and to their peers, that they can't get dates *for themselves* with young men as attractive as Brian, that they have to depend on a lottery. Their social self-images can't tolerate that admission. This perception, I think, inhibits them from volunteering. I'm surprised you got as many volunteers as you did from the classes with the "Brian" appeal.

To check my interpretation, I suggest that you do a second study in which you have two predictor variables instead of one. Senior women, I think, won't show this self-esteem effect. Brian's attractiveness will facilitate persuasion as much with them as with the freshman women, but the inhibiting effect of fragile self-esteem won't be nearly so strong for the seniors. So I think you should do the same study, this time using the date with Brian as an experimental variable and maturity (freshman/senior) as a quasi-experimental variable.

You decide to take the professor's advice. The study's design is shown in Figure 2.4 (p. 40). Researchers refer to a design like this in general as an "*A* × *B*" design, *A* standing for one predictor variable, *B* for the other.

This design has more advantages over the simple design than you might at first suppose. You could consider it merely to be two simple designs incorporated into the same study. This point of view would lead you to consider the effects of maturity (seniors versus freshmen) and motive appeal ("with Brian paragraph" versus "without Brian paragraph") separately. But in this study you are interested in more than that. You are looking for ways in which the two predictor variables *combine* to produce an effect on the criterion variable—that is, you are looking for an *interaction*. You think that motive appeal will have an effect for mature persons but not for immature ones.

To test the hypothesis, you follow exactly the same procedures you used in the simple study, only this time you follow those procedures with six classes of seniors as well as with six classes of freshmen. Again, 20 female students are present in each class. Table 2.3 (p. 41) shows the results, which seem to indicate that Brian may have some appeal after all. The results are summarized as arithmetic means in Table 2.4 (p. 41).

FIGURE 2.4. *A* × *B* Design.

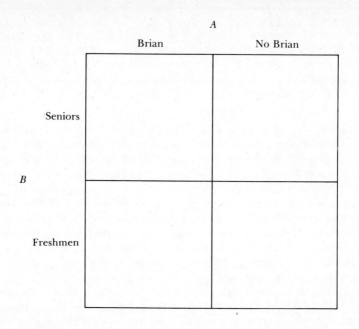

If you interpret the data in Table 2.4 as two simple experiments, you are led to the conclusion that both maturity and motive appeal had effects. Considering only the mean total *column*, you note that only 34 percent of the freshman women volunteered, whereas 53 percent of the senior women did. Considering only the mean total *row*, you note that with Brian as a motive appeal 61 percent of the students volunteered, whereas without him only 27 percent did.

While neither of those statements is inaccurate, they fail to reveal the best interpretation of the results. Maturity, *by itself*, did not have a positive effect on volunteers. In fact, within Table 2.4, you see that the seniors "without Brian" have the *lowest* proportion of volunteers. Further, the motive appeal, *by itself*, had no positive effect on volunteers. In fact, among freshmen, the motive appeal made no appreciable difference. The effect is an *interaction*—enhancement of the effect of one predictor variable by the effect of another.

To understand this relationship more clearly, consider Figure 2.5 (p. 42), where *FB* stands for "freshmen with Brian paragraph," *FO* stands for "freshmen without Brian paragraph," *SB* stands for "seniors with Brian paragraph," and *SO* stands for "seniors without Brian paragraph."

You should be able to observe from Figure 2.5 the following results of your experiment:

1. As in the first experiment, the freshman classes overlap considerably in the "with Brian paragraph" and "without Brian paragraph" conditions.
2. The seniors in the "without Brian paragraph" condition apparently are even more reluctant to volunteer for experiments than are the freshmen in either

TABLE 2.3. Number and Percentage of Sign-ups "With Brian Paragraph" and "Without Brian Paragraph" Among Freshmen and Seniors*

Class	With Brian Paragraph		Without Brian Paragraph	
	Number	Percent	Number	Percent
Freshmen				
A	10	50		
B			7	35
C	5	25		
D			9	45
E	6	30		
F			4	20
Seniors				
G	16	80		
H			4	20
I	19	95		
J			3	15
K	17	85		
L			5	25

*Hypothetical data.

motive-appeal condition. The overlap between the seniors in this condition and the freshmen in general is relatively slight.

3. The senior group in the "with Brian paragraph" condition clearly is more willing to volunteer than is any other group.

These results cannot be accounted for by the effect of either variable alone or by the effects of the two variables simply added together. Therefore, an interaction exists between the two predictor variables, maturity and motive appeal.

After celebrating your scientific success, your research group meets again to consider further the implications of the results. You now have a way of inducing large

TABLE 2.4. Mean Number and Percentage of Sign-ups "With Brian Paragraph" and "Without Brian Paragraph" Among Freshmen and Seniors*

Class	With Brian Paragraph		Without Brian Paragraph		Mean Total	
	Number	Percent	Number	Percent	Number	Percent
Freshmen	7.00	35	6.67	33	6.83	34
Seniors	17.33	87	4.00	20	10.66	53
Mean total	12.16	61	5.33	27	8.74	44

*Hypothetical data.

FIGURE 2.5. Distribution of Proportions for "Freshmen with Brian Paragraph" *(FB)*, "Freshmen Without Brian Paragraph" *(FO)*, "Seniors with Brian Paragraph" *(SB)*, and "Seniors Without Brian Paragraph" *(SO)*.

												SB	SB			SB
SO	SO	SO														
		FB	FB				FB									
	FO			FO		FO										
15	20	25	30	35	40	45	50	55	60	65	70	75	80	85	90	95

numbers of *senior* women to volunteer for your experiments, but you still have no way of recruiting an adequate proportion of *freshman* women. Again, the senior faculty member has something to say:

> The experiment we've just conducted indicates that our theoretical position, in which we balance facilitating forces with inhibiting forces, is a useful one. Brian does facilitate volunteering, and the reason he doesn't work for the freshman women is an inhibition effect he carries with him. That is, our appeal puts the freshmen in an approach-avoidance conflict, and we know what effects such a conflict has.
>
> We'd like to bring the level of freshman women who volunteer up to the level of our seniors. I suggest that the easiest way to do that would be to try some things that might lower the inhibition level—the avoidance motives—of the freshmen.
>
> I have two things in mind. First, I think that part of the inhibition comes from having men present in the class when the appeal is made. I suggest that when we make the appeal we excuse men from the class. Second, we've already talked about the probable reason for the freshman reluctance. These freshman women, most of whom are just past adolescence, say to themselves: "If I sign up, I'm admitting I can't get a date on my own." I therefore suggest that we make a confederate of the most attractive woman in each class (this mixed-gender research team can be the judge), privately induce her to volunteer first, and see if many of the others don't follow. I think the others will then say to themselves: "If *she's* willing to admit she'd like a date with Brian, I'm willing to admit it also." In other words, we'll plant a little opinion leadership in each class.

Approving this advice, you decide to design a third experiment that will serve as a check (a *replication*) on your previous results as well as a test of the new hypotheses. The design (see Figure 2.6) is a three-dimensional one, an $A \times B \times C$ design, in which predictor variable A is maturity, predictor variable B is motive appeal, and predictor variable C is counterinhibition (in which the conditions are men present, men absent, and men absent plus opinion leader). Each of the twelve blocks (or *cells*) in Figure 2.6 represents three classes.

Your previous research, together with your rationale, permits predictions about the proportion of volunteers from each cell relative to all other cells. These predictions

FIGURE 2.6. $A \times B \times C$ Design.

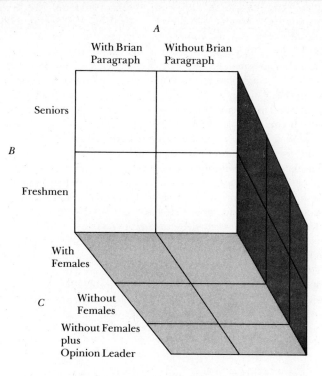

are expressed in the statement below, where F stands for "freshmen," S stands for "seniors," B stands for "with Brian paragraph," O stands for "without Brian paragraph," M stands for "men present," X stands for "men absent," and L stands for "opinion leader acting as confederate." The symbol $>$ means "will be greater than."

$$SBXL = SBX = SBM = FBXL > FBX > FOXL > FBM =$$
$$FOM = FOX = SOXL > SOX = SOM$$

You will find it easier to interpret this concise set of predictions if you notice certain features. It is arranged in such a way that everything to the left is either greater than or equal to everything to the right. Term by term, your predictions are as follows: The women in all senior classes in which the "Brian" appeal is made will volunteer in about equal proportions. (In the first experiment using seniors you managed to recruit about 87 percent by using the "Brian" appeal. You cannot expect to improve that very high proportion much by removing men from the sign-up session or by providing an opinion leader.) The fourth term *(FBXL)* stands for "freshmen/with Brian paragraph/ without men present with opinion leader." You expect women in this condition to volunteer at a level approaching or reaching the high sign-up proportion Brian achieved for seniors in the earlier experiment, and you expect this condition to be superior to all other freshman conditions. The fifth term *(FBX)* represents "freshmen/with Brian paragraph/without men present." You expect the absence of men to reduce the inhibitions of some of the freshman women, so this condition should be superior to all remaining freshman conditions. The sixth term *(FOXL)* represents "freshmen/without Brian paragraph/without men present with opinion leader." The fact that you make this condition superior to conditions the freshmen have undergone in previous experiments simply indicates that you expect the opinion leader to have some effect in her own right, regardless of Brian. The seventh, eighth, and ninth terms all represent freshman classes that you consider equivalent to those manipulated in the first experiment. You have no theoretical reason to expect that any of these cells will be superior to any other or superior to the freshman conditions tested in the first experiment. The tenth term *(SOXL)* stands for "seniors/without Brian paragraph/without men present with opinion leader." You expect the opinion leader to have some effect in her own right for seniors as well as for freshmen, so you predict that these classes will produce a higher proportion of volunteers than will the senior cells that have neither the "Brian paragraph" nor an opinion leader (the cells represented by the last two terms).

Table 2.5 shows the results of the study. Because the data are invented, we will pretend that the proportions in this study are identical to comparable proportions in the earlier study whenever cells represent identical conditions. (In real life, random fluctuation would make such identical proportions highly improbable.) The array of numbers in Table 2.5 is more confusing than helpful. Therefore, you construct Table 2.6, which summarizes the data. As usual, assume that 20 women attended each of the classes represented in the design.

TABLE 2.5. Number and Percentage of Sign-ups in Twelve Experimental Conditions*

	Freshmen With Brian Paragraph		*Freshmen Without Brian Paragraph*		*Seniors With Brian Paragraph*		*Seniors Without Brian Paragraph*	
	Number	Percent	Number	Percent	Number	Percent	Number	Percent
Men Present								
Class A	10	50	7	35	16	80	4	20
Class B	5	25	9	45	19	95	3	15
Class C	6	30	4	20	17	85	5	25
Men Absent								
Class D	15	75	6	30	18	90	2	10
Class E	13	65	9	45	17	85	6	30
Class F	14	70	5	25	19	95	4	20
Men Absent, Active Opinion Leader								
Class G	20	100	12	60	18	90	3	15
Class H	18	90	15	75	19	95	4	20
Class I	16	80	16	80	20	100	5	25

*Hypothetical data.

TABLE 2.6. Mean Number and Percentage of Sign-ups in Twelve Experimental Conditions*

| | Freshmen | | | | Seniors | | | |
| | With Brian Paragraph | | Without Brian Paragraph | | With Brian Paragraph | | Without Brian Paragraph | |
	Number	Percent	Number	Percent	Number	Percent	Number	Percent
Men present	7.00	35	6.67	33	17.33	87	4.00	20
Men absent	14.00	70	6.67	33	18.00	90	4.00	20
Men absent, opinion leader active	18.00	90	14.33	72	19.00	95	4.00	20

*Hypothetical data.

To make sure that you do not mistake randomly determined differences for real ones, you construct Figure 2.7 (p. 46) to show relative overlap among the various conditions, using the same notation scheme you employed in making your predictions.

On the basis of your theory, you had predicted that the optimum conditions would be *SBXL, SBX, SBM,* and *FBXL.* Examination of Table 2.6 and Figure 2.7 bear out this part of the hypothesis. The four conditions are far toward the high end of the proportion scale. They overlap considerably with each other but not much with the other eight conditions. Second, you predicted that the next best condition would be *FBX.* Again, the data confirm this part of the hypothesis. Your third prediction was that the next best condition would be *FOXL.* The data do not confirm this part of the hypothesis. The *FOXL* condition was equal, not inferior, to the *FBX* condition. You will have to consider revising your theory as it applies to the operation of an opinion leader among freshman women—and, probably, do another study to test your revised theory. You also predicted that the next four conditions *(FBM, FOM, FOX, SOXL)* would be equivalent. Depending on how you interpret your data, this part of the hypothesis may or may not be confirmed. The *SOXL* condition does share much of the distribution of the other three conditions. However, it seems to be more closely clustered with the following conditions, *SOX* and *SOM.* Apparently, for the seniors, the opinion leader had very little effect. Therefore, you might decide that only the first three conditions are equivalent, and that *SOXL* is more properly grouped with the two definitely inferior conditions, *SOX* and *SOM.*

Complex designs are not limited to three dimensions, though you will find it difficult to picture more than three in one diagram. In fact, the design you used has an implicit fourth dimension that, with the addition of four more cells, could have been made explicit. You chose to confound the "opinion leader present/absent" conditions with the "men absent" condition. But you could have made the opinion leader variable a fourth dimension of the design, so that it would have acted in all combinations with *all* other variables. (Or you could do a new study of the conditions missing from this one and analyze the resulting data with the data you already have.) In the four-dimensional

FIGURE 2.7. Distribution of Proportions in Twelve Experimental Conditions.

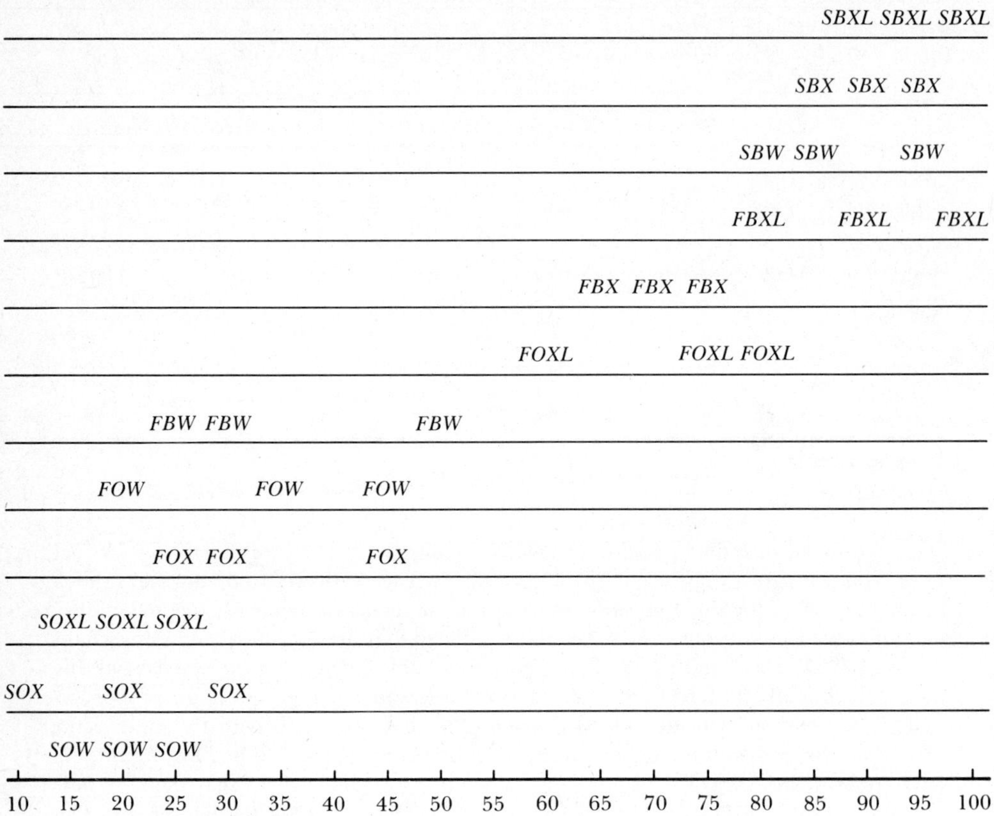

SBXL SBXL SBXL

SBX SBX SBX

SBW SBW   SBW

FBXL   FBXL   FBXL

FBX FBX FBX

FOXL   FOXL FOXL

FBW FBW   FBW

FOW   FOW FOW

FOX FOX   FOX

SOXL SOXL SOXL

SOX   SOX   SOX

SOW SOW SOW

10 15 20 25 30 35 40 45 50 55 60 65 70 75 80 85 90 95 100

study, you would have two levels of the freshman/senior variable X, two levels of the Brian/no Brian variable X, two levels of the males present/males absent variable X, and two levels of the opinion leader/no opinion leader variable, for a total of 16 cells. In short, you can design experimental and quasi-experimental studies to test the effects of variables and of their interactions with as many dimensions as the theoretical problem demands.

Repeated Measures Designs

One kind of complex design, because of its advantages and its frequency of use, deserves special mention. Recall the experiment with Jeanne and Tommy, when you measured their vocalization "alone" and "with mother." Given your method of analysis, in which you pooled the vocalization ratios of the two children in only the two conditions "alone" and "with mother," you failed to detect differences between the two conditions.

Suppose that instead you had treated the two subjects, Jeanne and Tommy, as *another* variable (a quasi-experimental one, of course), so that you could have concluded that part of the variation in the results originated in differences between the two children while another part originated in the "alone/with mother" variable. Table 2.7 shows what the means would have been in such an analysis, and Figure 2.8 displays visually the overlap between the "alone" and "with-mother" conditions if each child's *own* arithmetic mean is used as the midpoint of the scale. Obviously, if you had used this kind of design, you would have been considerably more encouraged about the validity of your hypothesis about social facilitation and vocalization rate.

TABLE 2.7. Means for Jeanne and Tommy "Alone" and "With Mother"*

	Alone	With Mother
Jeanne	.545	.584
Tommy	.331	.373

*Hypothetical data.

FIGURE 2.8. Vocalization Rate "Alone" and "With Mother" for Jeanne and Tommy Considered Separately.

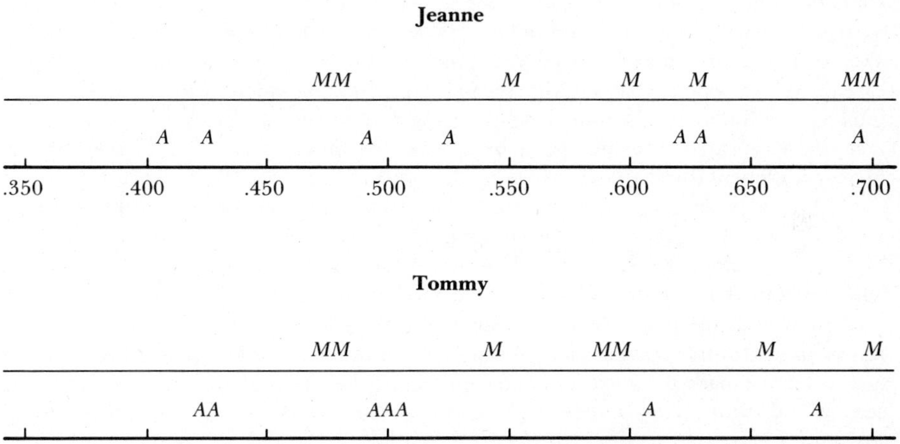

Jeanne

```
                MM              M      M   M          MM

        A   A         A     A              A A        A

.350    .400    .450    .500    .550    .600    .650    .700
```

Tommy

```
                MM          M       MM          M       M

            AA          AAA             A           A

.150    .200    .250    .300    .350    .400    .450    .500
```

This kind of design—where the same subjects generate criterion variables in more than one condition of the experiment and where "subjects" is employed as a quasi-experimental variable—is called a *repeated measures* design. This kind of design is contrasted with the more conventional *completely randomized* design, in which each subject generates criterion scores in one and only one cell of the design. Variables for which subjects generate scores at more than one level are called *within-subjects* variables. Variables for which subjects generate scores at one and only one level are called *between-subjects* variables. Many designs, and sometimes even a single variable, mix between-subject and within-subject effects. In general, within-subject predictor variables have a considerable advantage in social science research, for they remove from the criterion variables that part of the variation that can be accounted for by idiosyncratic characteristics of particular subjects. They are not always appropriate, of course, because for some variables the first exposure (among repeated exposures at other levels) systematically affects reactions to later exposures.

Earlier, we discussed *random fluctuation*. You may find it easier to understand the advantages of repeated measures designs and their associated within-subjects variables if we explain what elements make up random fluctuation.

All measurement is subject to some degree of error. Operational definitions and theories are never perfect. To put it more technically, predictor variables in a study never explain, account for, or predict, 100 percent of the variation in criterion variables.

Scientists often think of three kinds of forces as accounting for the leftover, residual, "error" variation. The first is actual errors in measurement. Measurement instruments, from yardsticks to IQ tests, are imperfect, as are those who employ them. Second, predictor variables unaccounted for by a particular theory may be at work to affect the criterion variables. The theory is incomplete or partly inaccurate, or the researcher finds it impossible or impractical to control or manipulate a particular variable or set of variables. Finally, some part of the residual variation is attributable to *idiosyncratic subject variables,* sometimes called *subject bias.* Jeanne *habitually* vocalizes more than Tommy. In another study, teacher A's ratings of student speakers is *systematically* more generous than teacher B's. In another, student M *always* uses more adverbs than student N. And so on.

All we will say at this point to help you control the first type of error is "operationalize your concepts, develop your instruments, and use those instruments with great care." All we will say about the second type is "read more widely and be more intelligent." But about the third type we can say "whenever your variables are appropriate, use a repeated measures (or partial repeated measures) design. Make *subjects* a quasi-experimental variable."

You may appreciate an example. Courtright and Courtright (1979) were interested in the best pedagogy for teaching grammatical rules to children who had been diagnosed as language disordered. Courtright and Courtright used action pictures to stimulate language production, and tested three methods of instruction.

The first method, one used widely by speech clinicians, required the child to repeat in parrot-like fashion each grammatical utterance of the experimenter immediately after she made it. Courtright and Courtright labeled this the *mimicry* condition. The second and third methods were derived from recent theory on cognitive processes and learning. The second method (the *modeling* condition) required the child to attend to an entire series of grammatical utterances without interruption. Only after the entire series was completed was the child asked to produce an utterance. In the third method (the *other modeling* condition), the child attended while the experimenter presented the entire series of grammatical utterances to a third person, who then produced a grammatical utterance.

In all three methods, learning (the criterion variable) was operationally assessed by showing the child a second series of action pictures, to which he or she was asked to respond by producing an entirely new set of grammatical utterances without additional help from the experimenter.

The hypothesis was that the *modeling* and *other modeling* methods would more successfully produce learning than would the *mimicry* method. The researchers were also

FIGURE 2.9. Design of the Courtright and Courtright Study.

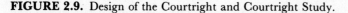

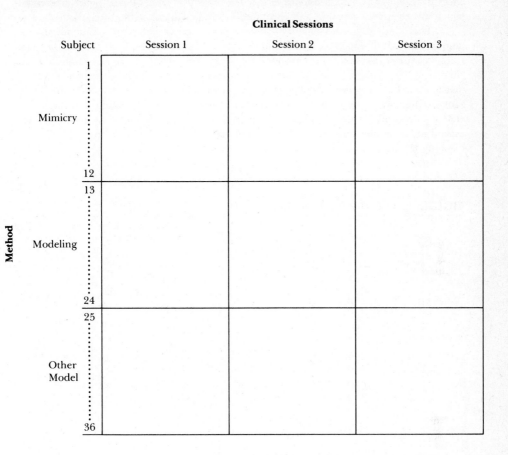

curious about whether the *modeling* and *other modeling* methods would differ in their effects. Assuming that the *other modeling* method was superior, would the extent of its superiority justify the time and effort necessary to include a third person in clinical learning situations?

The researchers realized that children (especially children diagnosed as "language disordered") probably carry with them many idiosyncratic influences that would, if ignored, add large amounts of variability to their performance on the learning task. Among many others, these might include intelligence, motivation, severity of disorder, and influence of parents. Therefore, Courtright and Courtright employed a repeated measures design in which each child participated in three clinical sessions which allowed the effects of idiosyncratic influences to be tracked across time. This design is illustrated in Figure 2.9.

This design, using "subjects" as a quasi-experimental variable, permitted the researchers to remove the idiosyncratic (but, presumably, constant) effects of each child.

(Exactly how this is done must await a later chapter.) It separates *within-subject* differences in learning as a consequence of the three methods from *between-subject* differences which are relatively constant and (presumably) independent of the three methods.

This kind of design removes "subject" as a source of "error." Individuals are unique, and this design takes that fact into account by making "subjects" a variable. The results of the study, with the "subjects" effect removed, were relatively straightforward (Figure 2.10). Both *modeling* and *other modeling* were superior to *mimicry* as methods of instruction. Furthermore, while *other modeling* was slightly superior to *modeling* for this sample, the overlap between the two conditions was substantial enough that the difference could easily be attributable to random fluctuation. The fact that all three lines ascend across *sessions* shows that the children learned something over time regardless of teaching method.

FIGURE 2.10 Profile of Means for Method.

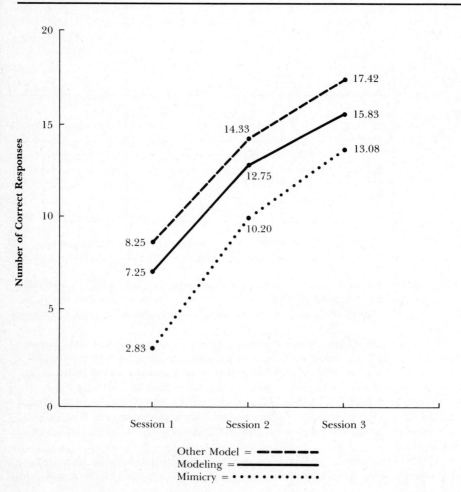

■ *Conclusion*

This chapter has introduced you to the logic and, in a conceptual way, to the method of experimental and quasi-experimental studies in communication. This method, as a logic, can be applied far beyond what are often referred to as "laboratory" studies of communication. If you can conceptualize explanations for events, and if you can operationalize the variables used in those explanations, you should be able to test those explanations by thinking experimentally and by analyzing data in experimental and quasi-experimental designs.

Subsequent chapters will be considerably more specific. In Chapter 3, we will introduce survey methods, and in Chapter 4 we will discuss observational analysis. Chapter 5 will concern the use of rating scales and other paper-and-pencil measurement techniques.

3 Chapter

Survey Methods

Using survey research, students of communication attempt, with interviews or questionnaires, to ascertain characteristics, opinions, or behaviors of a population, usually by sampling from, then generalizing back to, that population.

Most often, communication researchers use survey methods in attempts to *describe*, rather than to *explain* events. Linguists, for example, use survey methods to map the geographical distributions of various dialects. Students of mass communication use surveys to discover answers to such questions as "How do people use television?" On a more applied level, such organizations as Nielsen, Gallup, and Harris use surveys to discover the immediate popularity of television shows and the momentary opinions of voters.

Surveys may also be used to explain events, and sometimes they are even used in experimental and quasi-experimental studies, as when one sample is asked a question phrased in a particular way and another sample is given an alternative phrasing (the phrasing being an experimental variable) or when different samples are drawn from different social classes, age groups, or neighborhoods (social class, age group, and neighborhood being quasi-experimental variables). Survey methods sometimes are used to test extremely sophisticated hypotheses, as in Stark, Foster, Glock, and Quinley's (1971) study of prejudice among the Protestant clergy or Kim's (1980) study of the role of communication in the process of socializing Korean immigrants to Los Angeles.

Regardless of their purpose, survey researchers face common problems. These include (1) generating questions that, when answered, will fulfill the researcher's goals and that are not *biased, vague,* or *ambiguous;* (2) selecting a sample that is *adequate* in size and *representative* of the population to which the researcher hopes to generalize; (3) *organizing* the questionnaire (including the composition of a cover letter or introduction) so as to inflict minimal mental strain on the respondent and provide maximal efficiency to the interviewer; (4) deciding on the *method* by which the survey will be carried out, when the choice usually is among *door-to-door, telephone,* and *mailed questionnaire;* (5) deciding on a *design* for the study, a decision involving considerations that go beyond the survey itself depending on the nature of the research question; and (6) conducting a *pilot study*.

To illustrate the nature of these issues, we will consider at length a survey study conducted by a class of seniors in communication studies at the University of Iowa during spring semester 1982. The students in the class decided to conduct a survey in order to assess recognition of, use of, and attitudes toward a funded program called the "Academic Career Clusters Project," a project that had been in operation for two years and that had been designed to supplement the normal academic advising system in ways that would make apparent the career values of liberal education.

Generating Clear, Unbiased Items

Students in the class decided that their questions would elicit information that would indicate (1) the extent to which the project was recognized *(recognition)* among the University of Iowa students to whom it was directed; (2) the depth of *knowledge* of the project among those who recognized it; (3) the first *source* of information about the project among those who recognized it; (4) *use* of the project and of materials and activities generated by the project among those who had knowledge of it; and (5) because of a history of controversy surrounding the project, especially within the faculty of the College of Liberal Arts, *academic adviser attitude* toward the project. The University of Iowa has an advising system in which some students are advised by staff advisers (who were not expected to be divided in their attitudes) and some are advised by faculty advisers (who were expected to be divided in their attitudes), so the class also needed an indication of whether a particular student's adviser was a staff or a faculty adviser.

Small groups in the class were assigned the task of composing clear, unbiased questions for each of the areas of inquiry. All groups quickly realized that a particular item might be either of two types: *open-ended*, in which the respondent was asked to supply an answer without constraints; and *closed-ended*, in which the respondent was asked only to choose from among a set of categories supplied by the interviewer. All groups also quickly realized that, if a question were *open-ended*, the interviewer needed a set of categories into which any response could be coded. (Otherwise, responses could not, without undue effort, be meaningfully analyzed.) Hence, even though an item might be open-ended from the respondent's point of view, the responses should be codable into a finite, discrete set of categories from the interviewer's point of view.

The first temptation in composing a questionnaire or interview schedule is to try to get too much information with a single item. Hence, for the first task, to discover scope of *recognition* of the project, the group was tempted simply to ask: What do you know about the Academic Career Clusters Project? Analysis by group members showed that this question was both vague and biased. To test for vagueness, the group members each imagined responses that might appropriately be supplied to the item. They included "not much," "plenty," "that it's a project of the College of Liberal Arts," "that it's controversial," "that it's useful," "that my friend doesn't like it," "that it's a supplement to academic advising," etc. The possible appropriate responses are so varied in content and form that they would be virtually impossible to code. To test for bias, each group member examined the question for assumptions it made, either about the knowledge of or the attitude of the respondent. The form "What do you know about . . ." assumes *some* knowledge, and therefore puts some psychological pressure on the respondent to supply a response other than "nothing." That is, the question *assumes* recognition, whereas the group's purpose was to *discover* the presence or absence of recognition. The item is biased: It indicates to the respondent what response (or what kind of response) the interviewer desires.

After considerable discussion, the group settled on a closed-ended question in which the categories implicitly supplied were "yes" and "no." The item they ultimately agreed on for *recognition* was:

> *Have you heard of the "Academic Career Clusters Project" (sometimes called the "Clusters Project" or "Clustering")?*
>
> _____ 01. No
>
> _____ 02. Yes

The depth of *knowledge* group faced similar problems. They were tempted to gather a great deal of information about the project, then to write a multiple-choice test that could be scored. That method would have resulted in a *very* long questionnaire, of course, and they soon discarded it because they anticipated that very few respondents would stand for it. As you might guess, this group's first attempts were at least as vague as were those of the recognition group. Ultimately, the group decided on two questions, the first of which was open-ended: What do you understand the "Academic Career Clusters Project" to be? Since the question is open-ended, the group had to decide how individual interviewers should categorize responses to it. On the basis of their research into the project, they stipulated that responses combining the idea of *course selection* with the idea of *preparation for the future* would be coded as *accurate;* most other responses would be coded as *inaccurate;* and responses the interviewer considered difficult to code into one of those two categories would be written out verbatim and judged accurate or inaccurate by a consultant to the Academic Career Clusters Project.

Knowing that the *recognition* item would precede this item, they also revised it (as would other groups) so that the "Academic Career Clusters Project" became simply "project." Hence, the interviewer's version of this item became:

> *What do you understand the project to be?*
>
> _____ 01. Inaccurate
>
> _____ 02. Accurate
>
> _____ 03. Possibly accurate (specify answer) _____

The group also stipulated, of course, that this and succeeding questions would not be asked of respondents who had not recognized the project, but deferred action on that until organization of the instrument became a matter for discussion.

Because the project had been a matter of some public controversy, in which a frequent spokesperson for the project had been its director, the group decided that an item about her identity might be a simple and unobtrusive measure of depth of knowledge about the project. They therefore supplied as another *knowledge* item an open-ended item with instructions to interviewers for coding:

Can you tell me who the director of the project is?

——————— 01. Accurate [Nancy Harper]

——————— 02. Partly accurate ["Somebody in the Liberal Arts office." "A woman whose name I can't remember." "Somebody on the Communication faculty." "Somebody on the Journalism faculty."]

——————— 03. Inaccurate or don't know.

Note that both questions supplied by the *knowledge* group are *softened* rather than *blunt*. That is, the form of the questions ("What do you understand . . ." "Can you tell me . . .") implies that an inability to answer is nothing to be ashamed of. Such softening helps to maintain *empathy* with a respondent. Blunt questions ("What is the project?" "Who is the director?") may strike the respondent as too directive and may cause antagonism toward the interviewer and the interview. Note also that the *recognition* question has no such softening; the class later regretted that, for some interviewers thought, after all interviews had been conducted, that some respondents had been reluctant to supply an answer other than "no" because they perceived that they were to undergo an examination on the subject. Note also that these questions are cast in what might be called an "oral" mode, for the groups were assuming that the study would be conducted by telephone (with good reason, as we will indicate in a later section). Softening can also be accomplished in a "written" mode. Instead of "Can you tell me . . . ," the question might be "Indicate, if you can, . . ."

The *source* group was to identify, for each respondent who recognized the project, the information source of which that recognition was a function. Like the *knowledge* group, this group wanted responses to be a matter of *recall*, not simple *recognition*. Therefore, their question or questions must also be open-ended in form with a set of categories into which interviewers could classify responses. When the source was "academic adviser," the group wanted to be able to specify whether the adviser was "staff" or "faculty." On the basis of their research, the group made a list of likely sources consisting both of those directly generated by the project and of those indirectly possible. Ultimately, the group settled on the following item, with bracketed instructions to the interviewer:

From what source did you first hear of the project? [Fit response(s) into one or more (if respondent is unsure) of the following categories. (List continues on p. 56.)]

——————— 01. Academic adviser (faculty) [If in doubt, ask where adviser's office is. If Burge, Quadrangle, or 116 Schaeffer Hall, adviser is "staff" (2). Otherwise, adviser is "faculty" (1).]

——————— 02. Academic adviser (staff)

——————— 03. Faculty member (other than academic adviser)

——————— 04. Staff member (other than academic adviser)

——————— 05. *Daily Iowan*

——————— 06. Public media other than *Daily Iowan*

——————— 07. Direct mail brochure (or *Guide to Academic and Career Planning*)

——————— 08. Fellow student(s)

_____ 09. Orientation Program representative

_____ 10. Project-sponsored presentation in residence hall or fraternity or sorority house

_____ 11. Project director (or Nancy Harper)

_____ 12. Relative(s)

_____ 13. High school adviser (or counselor)

_____ 14. Other

(specify) _____

_____

_____ 15. Can't remember

The _use_ group, after analysis, decided that the project actually could be used in either of two ways and that their questions should be answered only by those who had accurate _knowledge_ of the project (a matter for our section on organization). First, the project might have stimulated some students to use a different _conceptual strategy_ for planning coursework than they otherwise might have adopted. Second, some students may have used _actual materials and activities_ generated by the project. This group therefore decided that they would write two items, one about each type of use.

The project had distributed materials, held meetings, consulted with academic advisers, and sponsored other activities to call students' attention to the possibility of adopting a "clustering" strategy for their college years. Such a strategy implied that students would consciously plan some of their actions (including the selection of some courses) in order to acquire certain competencies that (the project's research had shown) were the same competencies required in certain classes of careers. Students might have adopted this strategy without ever having had any "official" contact with the project. The _use_ group wrote their first question, a closed-ended item with the implicit "no" and "yes" options, to identify these students.

Have you used the approach advocated by the project in planning your course schedules here at the university?

_____ 01. No

_____ 02. Yes [includes "a little," "kinda," etc.]

The second question of the _use_ group was the extent to which publications and activities sponsored by the project had actually been used. The group decided that the question should not be a leading one ("Which of the publications and/or activities sponsored by the project have you used?"). Usually, leading questions (a kind of biased question) are appropriate only when the interviewer strongly suspects that the respondent would be embarrassed to give a true answer if the question were _not_ a leading one ("How often do you cheat?"). Therefore, the group divided the question into two parts. The first part gave the respondent the opportunity to say "no" with no embarrassment. The second part, the options for which were based on the group's research, identified specific publications and activities used by those who said "yes." Remember, at this point only those who had been able to characterize the project accurately were being asked the question at all.

Have you used any materials or participated in any activities sponsored by the project? [If "yes" or "I think so"] Which? [Fit responses into one or more categories below. If respondent asks to be cued, feel free to read the list or appropriate parts of it.]

——————— 01. No

——————— 02. *Clusters Sourcebook*

——————— 03. *Guide to Academic and Career Planning* (or "brochure" or "pamphlet")

——————— 04. Computerized advising program *Computerized Career and Academic Planning* or *C-CAP*

——————— 05. Presentations in residence halls, fraternity/sorority houses, alumni center

——————— 06. Publishing careers seminar

——————— 07. Political professions careers seminar

——————— 08. Corporate communication careers seminar

——————— 09. Arts and entertainment careers seminar

——————— 10. Personnel training and consulting careers seminar

——————— 11. International affairs careers seminar

——————— 12. Environmental professions careers seminar

——————— 13. Other

(specify) ——————————————————————————

—————————————————————————————————————

The last group (the *adviser* group) probably had the most difficult task. They were to discover to what extent the project had influenced academic advisers, and what the attitudes of academic advisers were toward the project. (You may wonder why they did not survey academic advisers directly. They had three reasons. First, the project administration politically preferred not to *arouse* attitudes toward the project among advisers at this particular time. Second, another project was planned to interview a few academic advisers about this and other matters. Third, adviser attitudes *as inferred by advisees* were actually as interesting to the class as were adviser attitudes assessed directly.) In addition, the group was to ask their questions in such a way that they could compare the behavior and attitudes of staff advisers with those of faculty advisers.

The group knew that some respondents had already identified their advisers as "faculty" or "staff" in answer to the question generated by the *source* group, and that some had indicated discussion of the project with an academic adviser in response to the *source* group's question. Hence, the *adviser* group wanted to call interviewers' attention to this possible redundancy and to avoid asking any respondent a repetitive question.

Ultimately, the group decided that a clear, unbiased sampling of opinion on *advisers* would require five items. Note that the group divided the *inferred attitude* topic into two: (1) adviser's attitude toward the particular respondent's use of the clustering approach, and (2) adviser's general attitude toward the approach. Note also that the group did not ask *directly* whether the adviser was "faculty" or "staff," for they suspected that many students would not unambiguously know the answer. Instead, the question asked the physical location of the adviser's office, and interviewers inferred from that answer an answer to the question "faculty" or "staff."

The five questions from the *adviser* group were:

Have you ever discussed the project with your academic adviser? [If respondent has already indicated in an earlier item that he or she has done so, don't ask this question, but record 02 as the response to this item.]

_____ 01. No or can't remember [skip to final item]

_____ 02. Yes

Where is your adviser's office? [If Burge, Quadrangle, or 116 Schaeffer Hall (Liberal Arts Advisory Office), mark 01. Otherwise, mark 02. Respondent may have already responded to this in an earlier item. If he or she did so, skip the question but mark the appropriate answer.]

_____ 01. Staff

_____ 02. Faculty

When you discussed the project with your academic adviser, did you bring it up, or did your adviser?

_____ 01. I did

_____ 02. My adviser did

_____ 03. I can't remember

Did your adviser encourage you to use the approach advocated by the project, discourage you, or express no opinion about your using it?

_____ 01. Encouraged me to use it

_____ 02. Discouraged me

_____ 03. Expressed no opinion

_____ 04. I can't remember

In general, do you think that your adviser is positive, negative, or neutral about the project? [If respondent asks you to be more specific, say "When I say 'in general,' I don't mean as it applies to you specifically or to students in your major specifically." If you can very easily infer the answer to this item from the way the respondent answered the previous item, do not ask the question, but record the appropriate answer below.]

_____ 01. Positive

_____ 02. Negative

_____ 03. Neutral

_____ 04. Don't know or can't remember

The class as a whole decided to generate one more item, because they thought that use of the Clusters project might be related to academic major. They therefore generated an item, open-ended in form but closed-ended in coding, to identify respondents with certain broad classes of academic interests:

What is your major? [Fit the response into one of the following categories.]

———— 01. Communication (journalism, communication, broadcasting and film, communication studies)

———— 02. Social science (psychology, sociology, anthropology, political science, economics, etc.)

———— 03. Humanities (English, history, philosophy, American studies, classics, foreign languages, etc.)

———— 04. Natural science (mathematics, zoology, physics, computer science, etc.)

———— 05. Education (elementary education, special education, etc.)

———— 06. Fine arts (art, music, theatre, dance)

———— 07. Interdepartmental ("Bachelor of General Studies," "Bachelor of Liberal Studies")

———— 08. Other (write out specific response for later coding) ————

The class also decided to use university records to record each respondent's classification (as junior or senior, for example) and sex on the chance that these variables might predict recognition, knowledge, and use of the clustering strategy.

At this point, the class thought that they had clear, unbiased substantive items that would solicit the facts and opinions they had decided to gather. They had learned (as you should) that, in general, *closed-ended* items are easier to code than are *open-ended* ones, but that, often, an item might be open-ended in form but closed-ended in fact (for the interviewer has a comprehensive set of discrete categories into which responses can be fit). They had learned (as you should) that a good test for *vagueness* or *ambiguity* is to imagine all possible appropriate responses to an item. If the range of such responses is too great, the question is vague or ambiguous and needs to be made more specific or directive. ("Sex?" "Yes, please." "Never." "None." "Sinful." "Female.") They had learned (as you should) that an item is *biased* if it seems to imply, in form or content, the answer desired by the interviewer, or if its form eliminates the possibility of certain response(s) ("Is Ford or Chevrolet the best American automobile?" "Are you a conservative or a pinko radical?" "When did you last vote in a student election?"). They had learned (as you should) that such items should only be used with great caution (if at all), when strong evidence exists that the true answer is one most respondents would be embarrassed to give if the item were *not* biased in form. They had learned (as you should) that items often can be *softened* in order to establish *empathy* between interviewer and respondent, so that the respondent does not feel defensive, as though he or she is being examined or cross-examined. And they learned (as you should) that no item should be required to do too much work, that often a research concern requires several items to do it justice.

They had not yet finished generating items, for they would require others when they began to think about *sampling* and the generalizations they wanted to be able to make.

An Adequate and Representative Sample

Adequacy

How large must a *sample* be in order to justify generalization to a *population*? What is an *adequate* sample? We will attend to this question again in later chapters, but at this point the question is an immediate one. It is a source of controversy for many nonscientists (though not for scientists). The controversy takes the form of biased questions such as: "How can the Nielsen organization generalize to millions of television viewers from a sample of only about 1600? How can Gallup or Harris predict an election from a sample of fewer than 2000? Why, that's only one out of every 25,000 or so voters."

The objections are beside the mathematical point. Assuming that a sample is reasonably representative of a population (a subject for the next section) and assuming that the interview or questionnaire items are clear and unbiased (that is, assuming that the answers given are "true" answers), the adequacy of a sample does *not* depend on its *proportion* of the population it comes from. (In fact, the "population" for many scientific studies is infinitely large—for example, all "learners," past, present, and future. How does one sample a proportion of infinity?) A sample is *not* to be conceived as a collection of entities each of which stands for a particular number of other entities. The *entire sample* stands for the *entire population*.

Sampling theory is a branch of probability theory, and we will not try to explain all the mathematics on which it relies. And, for any sample that is smaller in number than the entire population, some element of uncertainty exists. If you want to be certain on a survey question, you must ask everybody, not a sample. But sampling theory permits you to keep the uncertainty within limits. A scientist who has sampled carefully (and who has asked clear, unbiased questions) can say such things as: "I am 95% certain that the proportion of the population who would answer question X with a 'yes' is between .45 and .55." Or even: "I am 99.9% certain that the proportion of the population who would answer question X with a 'yes' is between .45 and .55."

The formula by which a scientist can set those limits is a simple one, and we will present it here. If the sample is to be a "large" (say, larger than 200) one, and if the data are to be treated as proportions (as in 45% or .45 say "yes"), then the 95% margin of error is established by the formula:

$$1.96\sqrt{\frac{p(1-p)}{N-1}} \tag{3.1}$$

where p stands for the proportion discovered in a sample and N stands for the number of entities in the sample. Note that *nothing* in the formula stands for the number of entities in the population. That number is literally irrelevant. From a sample of 1600, a scientist can generalize with as much confidence to a population of 200,000,000 as to a population of 10,000.

Students in the class doing the "Academic Career Clusters Project" survey, for example, decided that they could easily do by telephone a sample as large as 400. They asked the question: "If our sample is 400, what will be the 95% margin of error for a question like 'Have you heard of the Academic Career Clusters Project'?" Imagine that 50% of the sample would answer "yes," so $p = .5$. (Actually, in making this kind of estimate, you would be wise always to use .5 as the estimated proportion, for it is the most conservative possible estimate. The margin of error *narrows* slowly but progressively as the proportion goes above and below .5.) The proposed sample is 400, so substitute 400 for N in the formula. The 95% margin of error, then, is:

$$1.96 \sqrt{\frac{.5(1 - .5)}{400 - 1}}$$

The class worked the formula and discovered that with a representative sample of 400 the 95% margin of error would be .049. That is, having completed the survey, they should be able to say something like: "We are 95% certain (or it is 95% probable) that .5 (or 50%) plus or minus .049 (or 4.9%) of the population would report having heard of the Academic Career Clusters Project. Therefore, we are 95% certain that the proportion in the population who would report having heard of the Academic Career Clusters Project is between .451 (or 45.1%) and .549 (or 54.9%)." The students decided that this 4.9% margin of error at the 95% level was acceptable to them, and they decided to sample about 400 students from the population of interest.

If you experiment with Eq. 3.1, you will discover (for good mathematical reasons) that as a sample becomes larger the margin of error narrows, but that the margin of error does *not* narrow *in direct proportion to* increases in the size of the sample. That is, a sample of 800 (double our 400 example) does not cut the margin of error in half. (In fact, a sample of 800 cuts the 95% level margin of error from .049 to .035.) To cut it in half (to .025), you would need a sample of 1600. As samples become large beyond 1600, reductions in the margin of error grow ever more slowly, so that most survey and polling organizations have settled on 1600 as a reasonable number. With samples of 1600, they can say that they are 95% sure that their samples are within 5% (2.5% on either side of the sample proportion) of the population proportion.

Representativeness

If estimating margin of error from sample size is as simple and as mathematically "pure" as we have represented it, then how do we explain survey "failures," as in the *Literary Digest* poll of 1936 when Alf Landon, who ultimately carried only two states, was picked as a winner over Franklin D. Roosevelt? Or many polls of 1948, when Thomas E. Dewey was picked to defeat Harry S. Truman? Or various polls of 1980, when the contest between Jimmy Carter and Ronald Reagan was declared "too close to call" though in the election itself Ronald Reagan won very decisively?

We think that those "failures" were *not* the result of *inadequacy* of sample size. Rather, they were the result of *unrepresentativeness* of samples vis-à-vis populations. We accept as axiomatic the proposition that people change, that a decision today may be reversed tomorrow and that what is undecided today may be decided tomorrow. Therefore, to some degree *any* sample of people today is unrepresentative of a population of people tomorrow. Polling *for the purpose of prediction*, therefore, always runs the risk of great or small changes in the population between the time of sampling and the time when the prediction is tested by a real event (for example, an election). To demonstrate this to yourself, observe that the television networks, on election night, also generalize to a population (the electorate) from results already in (that part of the electorate whose votes already have been counted). They do so with an extremely high success rate. But they are generalizing from a sample to a population of which it is *representative*, not to another population (the same people polled the previous day).

The notorious *Literary Digest* poll of 1936 had another problem in representativeness, one which has been pointed out often since. It was a telephone poll. Voters in 1936 were in an economic depression, and only the prosperous were likely to have telephones. The prosperous were likely to be Republicans. Therefore, the *Literary Digest* had a highly unrepresentative sample, one systematically selected (by the "telephone" decision) to favor Alf Landon's party.

We do not claim that all polling "errors" are a result of shifts in the population between the time of the poll and the event that they are supposed to predict. A sample adequate in size might nevertheless lead to an erroneous generalization—in fact, it is expected to be "wrong" beyond the margin of error about 5 percent of the time. Therefore, five out of a hundred "failures" can be accounted for by the theory of probability. And many "failures" probably can be accounted for by the inability of pollsters to ask clear and unbiased questions. Nevertheless, we think that the most notorious "failures"—in which careful organizations mispredicted events or were unable to predict events—are a function of people's (or human populations') dynamic, changing (and therefore interesting) character. A sample of today's opinions is not from the same population of opinions, often, as is a sample of tomorrow's opinions.

In order to obtain a representative sample, you must first carefully *define* the population to which you expect to generalize as a result of the survey. Once you have defined that population, ideally, you would *obtain a list* of each individual in that population. (In the real world, you nearly always find it impossible to obtain such a complete list, and you will do the best you can with what you can find.)

Once you have the list, you must decide whether to do *completely random* sampling or to do random sampling with some qualifications (usually called *stratified random* sampling). In a *completely random* sample, each individual in the population has an equal chance of being selected for the sample. In a *stratified random* sample, the population list is first broken down into sublists according to some variable on which you want to insure equal or proportional representation. These subpopulations are then randomly sampled according to the number of respondents you want from each part of the sublist. For example, you might want "gender" to be equally distributed by male and female. If you did, you would first break down the population list by gender, then randomly sample in equal numbers from the "male" and the "female" sublists.

Generally, a completely random sample will show representation of any and all levels of any and all variables that is approximately proportional to the representation of those variables in the population. For example, if the population consists of 50% males and 50% females, a large random sample drawn from that population would almost certainly contain about 50% males and 50% females. Hence, you probably will not often find it necessary to stratify your sample if your wish is to have the sample's proportions on a particular variable comparable with the population's proportions on that variable. But you may want your sample on a certain variable to be *disproportional* with the population on that variable. For example, if "intelligence" were an important predictor variable in your study, and if you knew that only 3% of your population of interest was "highly intelligent," you might want to *overrepresent* that 3% in your sample in order to have an adequate number of "highly intelligent" individuals to make conclusions about.

The procedure to be followed in random sampling is a simple one. Many lists of random numbers are available, and we have included one of them as Appendix F in this book. First, you give every individual a number consisting of the same number of digits. (In a population of 10,000, these digits conventionally would go from 00001, 00002, 00003 . . . to . . . 10,000. Next, you close your eyes and place your finger at a random place in the table of random numbers. If the five-digit number you are pointing to is between 00001 and 10,000, you identify that individual in the population as a member of your sample. If not, you run your finger across the page, or down it, or diagonally in it (it doesn't matter which, for the numbers are randomly assorted in any direction) until you come to a five-digit number that is within the range 00001–10,000. Having identified one member of the sample, you continue moving your finger until you come to a number that identifies a second, and so on, until you have identified as many members of the sample as you want. As you proceed, you will sometimes come to a number specifying an individual who has already been chosen for the sample. When that happens, simply skip that individual and keep going.

You probably will find various ways to simplify this procedure. If your list is in pages that have columns, for example, you might first randomly select a page, then randomly select a column number on that page, then randomly select a name from that column, repeating this procedure until your sample is complete.

Now we will return to the "Academic Career Clusters" survey as an illustration. Students in the class decided that their sample would be a *completely random* one. They saw no reason to insure overrepresentation of any particular group, and they knew that a completely random sample almost certainly would result in a sample distributed in important respects proportionally with the population distribution.

They identified the population of interest as "students in the College of Liberal Arts at the University of Iowa who had been on campus for all fall and spring semesters during the two-year life of the project." Without available money to identify all members of this population from the registrar's computer, they looked for other means by which to get such a list.

They had available to them the *Student/Staff/Faculty Directory*, published the preceding semester. This directory identifies students by the college in which they are majoring and by class. For example, a student identified as "A3" was during that semester a junior majoring in one of the liberal arts departments, while a student identified as "B1" was during that semester a freshman in the College of Business Administration. In the interests of practicality, students in the class decided to confine their search for a sample to students identified as "A3" or "A4" in that directory. They would eliminate from the sample students who were no longer in liberal arts or who had not been on campus throughout the life of the project through questions asked in the survey itself.

The student listings in the directory took up 110 pages, each page consisting of four columns of names. The 35 students in the class divided up these 110 pages, most taking three pages, a few taking four. Each student randomly sampled pages and columns within his or her pages. (This procedure violated the assumptions of random sampling slightly. Actually, the class was doing a random sample stratified by the pagination of the directory. This qualification seemed unlikely to affect the results.)

Members of the class, having randomly drawn pages and columns, might then have randomly drawn names from the selected columns. But, considering the process by which the directory was printed, they realized that this last step was unnecessary. The first "A3" or "A4" entry in a column of the directory had that placement by a random process, for printers do not systematically decide which name will appear first in a column (with the exception of the first name in the first column of the first page). To save time and effort, then, these researchers used that first name in the randomly selected column as a potential member of the sample.

The *Directory* was not ideal as a listing of members of the population to which the class wanted to generalize. It had been published in the fall semester, but the survey was being conducted in the spring semester, and some students may have changed majors (and hence not fit the "liberal arts" criterion), and some may have been recent transfers to the university (and hence not fit the "all fall and spring semesters during the two-year life of the project" criterion). Although not ideal, the *Directory* was the only listing available to a group of researchers with no access to funds. For this reason, the class decided to eliminate nonpopulation members from the sample with a series of two questions. In the first, the potential respondent was asked:

In what college of the university are you majoring?

01. Business (accounting, finance, industrial relations, management, marketing), dentistry, engineering, graduate, law, medicine, nursing, pharmacy. [If response is 1, apologize for the bother, say goodbye, and hang up.] [If response is "economics," find out whether in liberal arts (2) or business (1).]
02. Liberal arts (or a major you know to be in liberal arts). [Go on to the next item in the survey.]
03. Education. [Go on to the next item in the survey.]

Like many other items, this one was open-ended in form but was coded in a closed-ended manner, since the interviewers had a complete and discrete list of categories into which they could fit responses. Option 03 was counted as "liberal arts" because, at the University of Iowa, the undergraduate College of Education is wholly contained within the College of Liberal Arts, and students in education receive liberal arts degrees.

Members of the class had some trouble deciding how to phrase the question about length-of-stay at the university. Their first impulse was simply to ask, "Have you been a student at the university during each of the last four semesters?" But when they tested this question's ambiguity and vagueness, they found it unacceptable. They could easily imagine that some respondents would include the current semester in the four, while others would not and they could easily imagine that some respondents would include the eight-week summer session as a "semester," while others would not. Ultimately, they decided to break the question into two items:

Were you a student here at the university during spring semester 1980?

01. No [apologize for the bother, thank the respondent, and hang up].
02. Yes [go on to the next item].

Have you been enrolled here at the university every fall and spring semester since then?

01. No [apologize for the bother, thank the respondent, and hang up].
02. Yes [go on to the next item].

Each of the 35 students in the class agreed to try to reach each sampled name at least twice (at different times of the day) and to eliminate from the sample respondents who indicated that they were not majoring in liberal arts or that they had not been at the university for all of the four semesters constituting the life of the Clusters project. They agreed to replace the "lost" respondents by randomly sampling new names from their assigned *Directory* pages until each had gathered 12 usable responses from respondents who met the criteria defining the population of interest. If all had fulfilled the agreement, a sample of 420 members of the population would have resulted. Because of a few illegible or otherwise unusable responses, the actual sample was 415.

The sample was not perfect on the representativeness criterion, though the class did as well as it could given certain limitations. The decision to sample only from among those classified in the *Directory* as juniors and seniors meant that sophomores in liberal arts who had been at the university throughout the life of the project were eliminated from the sample. This weakness was exacerbated by the fact that the *Directory* was a semester out-of-date, so that even some juniors (who had attained that status as of the semester when the survey was conducted) were eliminated. Also, the decision to try each sampled respondent only twice may have biased the sample to exclude many hard-to-reach people—a variable that might conceivably have been related to use of a career-conscious strategy for academic planning. (In fact, the class discovered later that the sample included women in a slightly higher proportion than their proportion in the population would have warranted. Apparently, at least in 1982, women students were slightly more likely to be at home than men students were.) The fact that it was a telephone sample meant that students without telephones (or without listings during the previous semester) were excluded from the sample. Finally, the class decided not to pay for toll calls, so that students not living in Iowa City (or not living in Iowa City during the previous semester) were excluded.

As things turned out, none of these weaknesses apparently affected to any great extent the validity of the study. The slightly disproportional representation of women was unimportant, for gender was not systematically related to any other variable of interest. And a later, separate study (this one based on transcripts for the entire population) verified the most important substantive results of the survey study.

In a responsible survey study, the sample must be adequate in size and representative of the population about which the researcher wants to generalize. Adequacy can be assured by use of a simple formula—a formula that tells the researcher the probable limits within which he or she is likely to err. Representativeness is a more difficult problem, and it usually is solved by sampling randomly—a procedure in which every member of the population has an equal chance of appearing in the sample. Because of practical limits, perfectly random sampling is seldom possible, and researchers should recognize (and, if possible, test the effects of) biases in their sampling methods.

Organization

Your purposes in *organizing* a questionnaire or interview schedule are to (1) draw the respondent into the experience, and (2) keep him or her involved until you have gathered responses to all items. In other words, your problem is to motivate response. Conventionally, this problem is solved by means of a *cover letter* in a questionnaire or an *introduction* in an interview and by *conceptual grouping* of items within the questionnaire or interview schedule. We already have alluded to another means for motivating response: *avoiding offensive and confusing items* by refining and sometimes *softening* the wording of items, so that the respondent does not get the impression that he or she is being evaluated by the interviewer.

The Cover Letter or Introduction

In the cover letter or introduction, you should first establish the auspices of the study—the sponsoring agency or organization. Often, you will have a number of options. When you have more than one option available, you should adopt the one most likely to appeal to the members of your particular sample, assuming that your choice will not bias your sample's responses. Remember, an item—or an entire instrument—is biased if it gives any indication that the interviewer (or the sponsoring organization) would prefer certain responses.

Next, the cover letter or introduction should very briefly supply a reason or two for responding. Usually, this section appeals to the respondent's sense of the value of time by minimizing the time and effort required. (But you should always be honest about that time and effort.) Sometimes, it also appeals to the respondent's altruistic impulses by indicating the value to "education" or to "society" that the results of the survey will have. Occasionally, the sponsoring agency will promise and deliver some material return on the time and effort invested: cash, a coupon, a copy of the results, for example.

Then the introduction or cover letter should guarantee personal anonymity to the respondent. This is both to encourage the respondent to participate and to facilitate *honest* participation.

Finally, in a telephone or face-to-face survey, the introduction should seek the implicit or explicit commitment of the respondent to participate.

In the survey study we have been discussing, the introduction the class decided on was simple but very effective (fewer than one in fifty potential respondents refused to participate). The bracketed material is directed to the interviewer. The unbracketed material is the introduction to the survey.

> [*Note:* Conduct yourself in a professional, businesslike manner. You need not give your last name. If the respondent makes personal overtures, you would be well advised to put him or her off in a friendly way. *If the respondent seems reluctant, do not exert pressure.* Just thank him or her and conclude the call. If anyone has questions about the survey, refer him or her to the Chair of the Communication Studies Program at 353-____.]
>
> Hello. May I speak with [name of respondent]?
>
> My name is [first name], and I'm helping to conduct a survey for a communication research class. I'll be asking you to answer about a dozen short questions. It probably won't take more than ten minutes—and it may only take a few seconds.
>
> I had to identify you by name in order to get a random sample. But I'll protect your anonymity by tearing your name off my list and throwing it away as soon as the call is completed, so I won't have a record of your name or the names of any of the other eleven people I'm calling.
>
> You're free to decline, of course, and to refuse to answer any particular question. But I'd appreciate your participation. Are you willing to participate?
>
> [If "no," apologize for the bother, say goodbye, and hang up.]
>
> [If "what's it about?" say "academic planning and advising here at the university."]
>
> [If "yes," proceed to the first item.]

Grouping Items

Like any good message, a survey instrument is organized. You should group together items that are related conceptually in order to minimize mental strain for the respondents, just as in an essay you group thoughts together in paragraphs and sections in order to minimize mental strain for a reader. In a complex interview schedule or questionnaire, you should even provide organizational markers—section headings and transitions ("now I'm going to ask you a few questions about . . .") for major shifts in concept.

But considerations of topical coherence need to be balanced with considerations of efficiency. If the answer to one or two questions will eliminate the respondent from your sample, for example, that question or those questions should come first in the instrument, so that you do not waste your time (and the respondent's) gathering data that you have no intention of using. And if a particular response to one item implies that another item or series of items should be skipped, then obviously the screening item should come before the other items.

Finally, you should use the principle of *commitment* in organizing your survey instrument. Once a respondent has answered a few questions, he or she is likely to complete the instrument, for people dislike unfinished tasks. Therefore, no items that are likely to be "difficult" or otherwise distasteful should come early in the instrument. If possible, the instrument should begin with items that nobody in the sample would have a problem answering.

To illustrate: In the senior seminar survey we have been considering, the first item was the one most likely to eliminate potential respondents from the survey.

> *In what college of the university are you majoring?*

A response to this question other than "Liberal Arts" or "Education" implied that the potential respondent was not a member of the population to be sampled. Hence, interviewers were instructed to politely conclude the call at this point if the response eliminated the potential respondent from the sample.

Two items that also would eliminate potential respondents from the sample were those to establish the person's length of residence at the university. Nevertheless, the class decided that the question about the respondent's major within liberal arts was so closely related, conceptually, to the question establishing liberal arts as the "home" college that the item about the major should follow immediately:

> *What is your major?*

Then the class inserted the items that would eliminate some respondents from the sample:

> *Were you a student here at the university during spring semester 1980?*
>
> *Have you been enrolled here at the university every fall and spring semester since then?*

A negative response to either of these items would imply that the respondent was not a member of the relevant population and hence that the call should be politely concluded.

Next came the items about recognition and knowledge of the Clusters project. The recognition item as the candidate for next position was an obvious one, for nonrecognition implied that all other questions were impossible ones. A negative response, therefore, would prompt the interviewer to terminate the interview:

> *Have you heard of the "Academic Career Clusters Project" (sometimes called the "Clusters Project" or "Clustering")?*

Following the recognition item (for respondents who had not been terminated by a nonrecognition response) came two "knowledge" items and an "information source" item, all closely related to the recognition item and therefore coherent:

What do you understand the project to be?

Can you tell me who the director of the project is?

From what source did you first hear of the project?

The "knowledge" items led easily into the two "use" items:

Have you used the approach advocated by the project in planning your course schedule here at the university?

Have you used any materials or participated in any activities sponsored by the project? [If "yes" or "I think so"] Which?

Finally, the survey instrument concluded with the slightly more difficult (because they called for some judgments) "adviser" items:

Have you ever discussed the project with your academic adviser? [If respondent has already indicated in an earlier item that he or she has done so, don't ask this question, but record "yes."]

Where is your adviser's office?

When you discussed the project with your academic adviser, did you bring it up, or did your adviser?

Did your adviser encourage you to use the approach advocated by the project, discourage you, or express no opinion about your using it?

In general, do you think that your adviser is positive, negative, or neutral about the project?

At the end, of course, interviewers must be given a way to close the interview. It can be very simple:

Those are all my questions. Thanks (or thanks very much) for helping me out. Goodbye.

Method of Administration

Survey researchers usually consider three possible methods for administering a survey instrument: the *personal interview* (sometimes called the *door-to-door* or *face-to-face* method), the *telephone* survey, and the *mailed questionnaire*. Each method has its advantages and disadvantages, of course.

If you have unlimited time and funds, if your survey instrument is long and complex, or if your sample consists of well-protected or very busy people, the *personal interview* is the preferred method. Zuckerman (1977), for example, used this method in her study of American Nobelists, as did Stark et al. in their study of the Protestant clergy. Typically, the researcher selects the sample very carefully, writes and/or telephones potential respondents or their representatives for an appointment, then interviews them in their homes or offices.

This method has decided advantages over other methods. The respondent knows that the researcher is strongly committed to the project and is likely to reciprocate that commitment. Hence, if the auspices of the study are appealing and if the motivational appeals are strong, response rate both in general and to particular items is likely to approach 100 percent. Furthermore, a competent interviewer in the personal context has nearly total control of the situation. Social rules define the interviewer role rather clearly, and the interviewer can probe unclear or ambiguous answers, can detect nonverbal signs that the respondent is dodging questions (and can reword or repeat questions to test for and resolve inconsistencies), and can elicit and record spontaneous comments that may, upon analysis, illuminate certain results.

Balanced against these clear advantages are time and expense. The researcher must travel to the respondents according to their schedules, sometimes door-to-door and sometimes, as in Zuckerman's study, city-to-city. If the sample is a large one, the researcher must hire or otherwise recruit other interviewers, who, as individuals, carry their own sources of error around with them. That is, interviewers' personal characteristics may turn some respondents on and turn others off, producing unanticipated and unanalyzable effects. The interviewers must be extensively trained to minimize their individual effect—but the training is costly.

The *telephone* survey usually is relatively efficient. When time and resources are limited and the survey instrument is relatively straightforward (it obviously cannot require visual aids), it often is the preferred method. If the introduction to the study is constructed well and if the sample is accessible by telephone, response rate can approach 100 percent. The interviewer has less control than in the personal interview, but social rules of telephone usage govern most respondents so that, once started, they will finish. (Telephone solicitors, unfortunately, know this fact—and may be altering it.) Interviewers must be trained for a large sample, but not to the same extent, usually, as for personal interviews. Clues to dishonest responses are present to some extent in a telephone survey, though they are not as evident as in the personal interview. The telephone survey probably should not be used if dishonest answers to some items are likely. But if dishonest answers are likely, the researcher probably should revise the items.

The telephone survey imposes important biases on some samples. Very poor people are unlikely to have telephones, and very rich people are unlikely to be accessible by telephone (for they have unlisted numbers and/or batteries of gatekeepers). Therefore, the telephone method probably should not be used when socioeconomic status might be an important variable.

One further caution about telephone surveys: Some researchers, instead of sampling individuals, sample telephone numbers. In most cities, this is an easy thing to do. The researcher simply randomly draws one of the exchanges (first three digits), then randomly draws a series of four more numbers. This method can easily introduce very substantial biases into a sample. (1) A single telephone number may serve one individual or (as in a university fraternity or sorority) fifty or sixty. Hence, every individual in the population does *not* have an equal chance of being chosen for the sample, and the sampling method is not truly random—unless "telephone numbers" is the population of interest. (2) In many housing units and in most businesses, one or two individuals adopt or are assigned the task of answering the telephone. Therefore, a sample of telephone numbers is likely to be biased in favor of "habitual telephone answerers" and not representative of the population (unless the population is "habitual telephone answerers").

Given the variety of functions the *mailed questionnaire* has been asked to fulfill, you should not be surprised that such methodologists as Bailey (1978) and Kerlinger (1973) disagree about its utility. We find no fault with a well-constructed questionnaire, with appropriate auspices and cover letter, as a research tool. The questionnaire should be accompanied by a stamped (preferably hand-stamped, a trifle crookedly, to show human involvement) envelope addressed to the researcher.

The principal advantage of the mailed questionnaire is that very large samples can be reached by it at the cost of only slightly more than double the current first-class postage rate for each potential respondent. A secondary advantage of a mailed questionnaire is that the stimuli to response (the items themselves) are completely standardized. Individual interviewers cannot impose their own personal styles on the items in a mailed questionnaire.

The principal disadvantage of the mailed questionnaire is that, unless respondents are very strongly motivated, many will not bother to fill out and return it. Many will not even read the cover letter. Unlike the personal interview and the telephone survey, the mailed questionnaire has no system of social rules that, in a sense, require response. You can discard a questionnaire more easily than you can hang up the telephone or slam the door in response to a potential interviewer. Even with follow-up letters to nonresponders (conventionally sent about three weeks after the original wave of questionnaires), some researchers have considered themselves fortunate to achieve a 50 percent response rate.

A secondary disadvantage of the mailed questionnaire is that no nonverbal clues are available to signal difficult items or dishonest responses. Hence, respondents can more easily give inaccurate but socially desirable responses than they can in the personal interview or in the telephone survey.

When you choose a method of administering your survey instrument, you must balance the advantages and disadvantages of each method against those of the others. The nature of the research problem often implies the method of administration. If a response rate approaching 100 percent is required, the mailed questionnaire probably should be eliminated as the method of choice, even if repeated follow-up letters are to be used. With rapid developments in electronic methods of communication (e.g., teleconferencing, interactive cable television, computer networks) and increases in postage costs, the mailed questionnaire may even become obsolete, for it may lose its principal advantage—low cost.

Survey Design

Usually, surveys are used to describe variables and their relationships in a particular population at a particular time, rather than to test theory. Nevertheless, a good survey study *can* test theory, especially given the existence of powerful new techniques for statistical modeling, such as in what is usually called "path" analysis. Examples of such theory-testing studies are those by Stark et al. (1971) and by Kim (1980). A survey study may even be an experimental one in which the predictor variables are, for example, systematic variations in the conditions under which the survey is administered or alternate forms or wordings for the items in the instrument.

Methodologists usually distinguish among survey designs according to *who* is surveyed and *when*. Most survey studies, including the senior seminar one we have been using as an example, employ a *cross-sectional* design. That is, each member of one sample is questioned once. Variables in such a design (or in any of the others) may be measured simply for descriptive purposes ("What proportion of students used resources provided by the project?") or for quasi-experimental purposes ("Were women more likely than men to use the resources provided by the project?" "Were communication majors more likely than natural science majors to have accurate knowledge of the project?"). However, developmental (or other time-dependent) variables are difficult (though not impossible) to test with a cross-sectional design.

Designs that do take time into account are sometimes called *longitudinal* designs. Methodologists distinguish among three types of longitudinal designs.

Using a *trend study,* the researcher administers the same survey instrument at different times to samples from the same population. For example, if the senior seminar had administered its survey to a sample drawn from juniors and seniors in liberal arts (1981), again to a sample drawn from juniors and seniors in liberal arts (1982), and again to a sample drawn from juniors and seniors in liberal arts (1983), conclusions could be drawn about *trends* in recognition, knowledge, and use of the project among juniors and seniors in liberal arts, 1981–83.

A second longitudinal alternative is the *cohort* design. Using this design, a researcher administers the same survey instrument to different samples drawn from the same population (defined by age grouping) as that population moves through time. For example, the senior seminar might have sampled from among freshmen in 1981; from among sophomores in 1982; from among juniors in 1983; and from among seniors in 1984. The focus of research concern in such a design almost by necessity is change in the population (in the example, change in the population who were freshmen in 1981) as the population ages.

Finally, a popular longitudinal design, especially during political campaigns, is the *panel study.* In a panel study, the researcher surveys (with the same or different instruments) the *same* sample at various times. The panel study can be most straightforwardly used as a way to infer the influence of particular events (e.g., a presidential debate) on, for example, opinions. The panel can be surveyed immediately before such an event and again immediately afterward. Changes in responses to the survey can then be attributed to the influence of the event, at least if a control panel, which does not experience the event, shows no change between the two administrations of the survey.

Pilot Study

Most students of communication research are plunged into survey studies as their first experience with data. In the old movies, a juvenile Mickey Rooney or a precious Shirley Temple would say, "*Hey,* kids! *I've* got an idea! *Let's* put on a *show!*" In the contemporary research methods class, the instructor or a student is likely to say, "*Hey,* kids! *I've* got an idea! *Let's* conduct a *survey!*"

Like a good show, a good survey is relatively rare. For the same reason that a good show has a dress rehearsal, a good survey (and most other good examples of research methods) has a pilot study.

In a pilot study, the survey instrument is tried out on a few members of the population of interest. This tests the mechanics of the procedure as well as the workability of the items and their organization. During the course of designing the survey and devising the instrument, researchers become ego-involved in items, their wording, and their organization, and this involvement may blind them to sources of vagueness, ambiguity, bias, and faulty grouping. The pilot study is a shakedown flight: Analysis of the pilot study should identify problems before they become costly (or even fatal) ones.

■ Conclusion

Researchers using survey methods may use those methods to do experimental studies, quasi-experimental studies, or mixed studies. Most often, however, surveys are used simply to describe certain aspects of a population by sampling an adequate and representative subset of that population.

A survey study is likely to be defective unless the researcher seriously attends to problems in *generating items,* in *sampling,* in *organizing* the survey instrument, in choosing among the *administrative methods* available, in appropriately *designing* the study, and in *piloting* the instrument. The solutions to all of these problems depend—and should be considered in the context of—the specific research hypotheses or questions to be investigated and the practical limitations of the researcher's circumstances. Typically, especially in sampling and administrative method, the ideal cannot be achieved, and the researcher must choose among compromises.

The Observation of Communicative Behavior: Content Analysis (Tabular and Contingency)

Using observational methods, a researcher focuses on the *content* and/or the *style* of communicative behavior. Often, observational methods are used descriptively. But nothing prevents them from being used for theory construction and testing, in the contexts of field methods, quasi-experimental methods, and experimental methods.

In the chapter on survey methods, we frequently referred to *populations* and *samples* of individuals. The same logic of generalization governs observational studies, but the focus of analysis, instead of a *person*, is a *behavior* (or, more accurately, the *selection* of a behavior from among a *set* of behaviors). Hence, for example, an observational study might focus on expressions of the achievement motive in Thematic Apperception Tests (McClelland, Atkinson, Clark, & Lowell, 1953); on mentions of dialect in written evaluations of a persuasive speech (Bowers, 1970, pp. 309–13, reporting on Houck & Bowers, 1969); on the lexical diversity manifested by interviewees in situations of varying stress (Bradac, Konsky, & Elliott, 1976); manifestations of "groupthink" in cohesive and less cohesive group discussions (Courtright, 1978); or on indicants of stress in suicide notes (Ogilvie, Stone, & Schneidman, 1966; Osgood & Walker, 1959).

In this chapter, we divide such studies into two types: *tabular*, in which messages are analyzed without regard to the sequencing of their parts; and *contingency*, in which sequencing (or the dependence of one part of a message or interaction on earlier parts) is a major focus of attention. We will first discuss "units" and "categories" in tabular content analytic studies, their operationalization, and their further use in contingency studies, with a note on the ubiquitous utility of ratios; then briefly outline the issue of "structure" in category systems with reference to what is sometimes called "grounded theory"; and finally describe a number of examples, both of tabular and contingency studies.

Units, Categories, and Their Operationalization

Communication occurs in a relatively uninterrupted stream. An observer of communication who wants to generalize about this stream must *segment* it in order to reliably count or measure the parts. These segments or *units* are then counted as belonging (or not belonging) to one or another of the *categories* in a set of categories.

A *unit,* then, is an element to be *categorized.* In communication studies, a unit might be an element such as an individual word, a duration of talk measured in seconds, a length of talk measured in number of words, a string of words identified by their function (e.g., a newspaper headline, a picture in an advertisement), a syntactic unit (e.g., a sentence, an independent clause, a paragraph, an adjective), a turn at talk (that is, an uninterrupted utterance by one individual in conversation or group discussion), a frame or shot in a film, a scene in a television show, a "speech act," a "complete thought"— and the list could go on and on.

Each unit is then counted as a member of a category that is theoretically or practically interesting to the researcher. A word as the unit, for example, might be counted as belonging to the category "substantive word" or the category "function word," or the category "verb" or the category "nonverb"; each 25 seconds of talk as a unit might be counted as belonging to the category "metasubstantive" or the category "substantive"; each newspaper headline as a unit might be counted as belonging to the category "page 1," the category "page 2," the category "page 3," and so on; each shot in a film as a unit might be counted as belonging to the category "two seconds long," the category "three seconds long," the category "four seconds long," the category "five seconds long," and so on. You get the idea. Deciding what your *units* will be and what your *categories* will be depends completely on the research question you want to answer. These decisions are crucially important, because once you have committed yourself to a system of units and categories you will be unable to switch to another, more refined system except by starting all over.

If all of this seems a little strange to you, recall the survey study we discussed in Chapter 3. At a fundamental level, some of the procedures used in that study were content analytic procedures. For example, each answer to the question "What is your major?" was considered a *unit.* Each of these units was then placed by the interviewer into a *category:* communication, humanities, social sciences, etc.

The difference between that survey study and observational studies is that in the survey study the segments (or units) were given a priori, by the careful process of constructing the interview schedule. In an observational study, units and categories must be decided a posteriori, *after* messages have already been encoded by one or another source. Thus, the problems of deciding on units and categories for an observational study are considerably more difficult.

Unfortunately, a researcher can find very little help with the problems of unitizing and categorizing observational data in the literature of communication research. Hatfield and Weider-Hatfield (1978) compared various types of units for their usefulness in the study of communication in small groups. Their results suggest that for certain purposes "complete thoughts" (rather than, for example, "15-second segments" or "utterances") are the most useful units for analyzing such discussions.

Unitizing

Decisions about unitizing observational data should be guided by the need to strike a balance between two concerns. The unit needs to be *inclusive* enough to manifest whatever item or items are of interest to the researcher. Yet, the unit needs to be *manageable*—not so inclusive that it is simply general or vague, not so inclusive that it manifests an indeterminate number or mixture of the item or items that are of interest to the researcher. Hence, the unitizing decision must be a clear one, so that other individuals (including coders who might assist the researcher) can replicate unitizing judgments reliably.

For example, if you were interested in studying the frequency with which solutions are proposed in group discussions, your unitizing problem would be to designate units of content (probably contained on an audiotape or a videotape or in a written transcript), each unit of which would be placed in the category "a proposed solution" or in the category "not a proposed solution." For that research problem, a short unit of time (e.g., ten seconds) probably would not be sufficiently inclusive. Many proposed solutions would involve more behavior than would be included in a 10-second segment. On the other hand, such a unit as the "utterance" (the time for which a speaker holds the floor before being interrupted by another speaker who then holds the floor) (Gouran, 1969) probably would be unmanageable, for many utterances probably exhibit more than one proposed solution (as, for example, when a speaker compares the advantages and disadvantages of several proposed solutions in one utterance). If you were trying to solve this problem, you might settle on such a unit as the "speech act" (Searle, 1969), a unit that designates a communicative function or intent to segments of content.

In contrast, if you were interested in identifying units of "language intensity" (the degree to which a speaker's language about a concept deviates from attitudinal neutrality) (Bowers, 1963), the 10-second segment as a unit would probably be unmanageable, *too* inclusive, and the speech act or utterance clearly might manifest more than one instance of intense language. For this problem, you might decide that "the noun phrase" and "the verb phrase" are appropriate units, each to be categorized as (for example) "intensely positive," "neutral," or "intensely negative." Or, you might isolate the "substantive word" (generally, a verb, a noun, an adjective, or an adverb) as the appropriate unit.

Categorizing

The researcher's best chance to exhibit ingenuity in an observational study is in devising the category system. Categories may be thought of as cubbyholes into which units are placed (and, ultimately, counted). The various niches in a cash register drawer are categories called pennies, nickels, dimes, quarters, half-dollars. Each coin is a unit.

In tabular analyses, category systems generally tend to be one of two types. *Descriptive* systems categorize units in terms of what they *are* (e.g., masculine pronouns, statements denoting violence, negative depictions of women). *Functional* category systems, on the other hand, categorize units in terms of what they *do* in a communication context (e.g., ask questions, propose solutions, give information). (In contingency analyses, category systems may be *structural*, categorizing units in terms of the way they "fit together" in a communication context, and this structure may be either descriptive or functional. We will deal with this complication later in this chapter.)

The category system you adopt has the effect of imposing structure on the "reality" of the text you analyze. The only "meaning" your category system can help you discover must be inherent in the system itself; any elements not accounted for in the category system will be lost to you forever (or until you devise a new system). The imposition of structure on naturally-occurring behavior has stimulated some controversy and criticism among communication theorists (Delia, 1977; Folger & Sillars, 1977; O'Keefe, 1975), and we will return to the topic in a separate section.

In general, category systems for observational analyses should be *finite* and *exhaustive,* and the categories within the system should be *mutually exclusive.* However, a category system may include more than one *dimension* of coding. If it does, the three criteria apply to each dimension rather than to the system as a whole. Gouran (1969), for example, in his analysis of problem-solving discussions, analyzed each utterance in a finite, exhaustive, and mutually-exclusive category system on each of eight dimensions such as "orientation," "opinionatedness," and "provocativeness."

The requirement that the set of categories be *finite* in number might (and probably should) be taken a step farther: The set must not only be finite; it must also be manageable. A category scheme that included 5000 categories would be finite, but (unless it were made into a complex hierarchy) it would not be manageable for most human coders. As with unitizing, categorizing must strike a balance between inclusiveness and manageability. Given too few categories, coders will be forced to fit observations into categories that are either inappropriate or vague, and important insights might be lost. Given too many categories, decision processes will become impossible. Nevertheless, given a choice between too few and too many categories, we would usually opt for too many. You can always collapse categories to get rid of useless or redundant ones at a later stage of analysis. But if your categories are vague, you *cannot* subsequently refine them except by starting all over.

The requirement of *exhaustiveness* implies that each and every unit of behavior be assignable to a category. You should not have several units of behavior left over. Sometimes, a system has only two categories, one for the units of interest (e.g., "metaphors") and one for all other units (e.g., "nonmetaphors"). Generally, however, all categories are substantive (that is, classify something of interest to the researcher), and the residual or "other" category is small, containing only units (1) of absolutely no interest to the researcher and hence not worth classifying, or (2) actually unclassifiable (e.g., incomprehensible utterances on an audiotape, uncodable intrusive sounds). This residual category then is simply reported for its informational value; it is *not* used in the analysis of substantive results.

Finally, at least for researchers relatively new to observational analysis, categories should be *mutually exclusive*. That is, each unit of behavior should be assignable to *one and only one* category. To put it still another way: Categories should not overlap. To help yourself visualize the problems that might arise from a category system that does not satisfy this criterion, imagine that you were trying to functionally analyze conversation. Imagine further that your category system had in it *both* the category "asks question" *and* the category "requests information." What would you do with such strings as: "What's *wrong* with you today?" "Are you kidding?" "Are you crazy?" "Nice day, isn't it?" You should now be convinced that the category system needs more work.

In spite of our recommendation that young researchers employ mutually exclusive categories, we acknowledge that Hewes (1979) has made a persuasive case for employing multiple category systems for certain kinds of functional analyses, specifically analyses of dynamic human interaction. He argues that in conversation a particular behavior can simultaneously function in more than one way. For example, the utterance, "What do you think about the second issue?" may serve both to seek information and to change the topic. If such an utterance is permitted to be assigned only one functional classification, the richness and complexity of human interaction will be masked by the simplicity of the category system. (Our recommendation for the example given would be to increase the dimensionality of the coding system, so that "requests information" would belong to an "informational" or "substantive" dimension, while "changes the topic" would belong to a "topical metacommunicative" dimension, possibly.) To his credit, Hewes has offered a solution to the statistical problems often attendant on multiple classification schemes, though the complexity of that solution places it well beyond the scope of our introductory treatment.

From Conceptualization to Operationalization

In the sections on unitizing and categorizing, we have given some guidelines to be used in constructing a formal category system for observational analyses. In this section, we will sketch some practical suggestions for operationalizing those guidelines—for actually applying the principles of observational analysis.

The recommendations listed below were originally proposed in a slightly different form by Bowers (1970, p. 303). Although he designed them specifically to aid the researcher engaged in a subcategory of observational analysis, content analysis, we believe that they are applicable to observational analysis generally. Several of the suggestions have already been made, but we hope that repeating them here will serve to reinforce their importance. To facilitate the reliable and efficient application of a formal coding scheme, the researcher should:

1. Define his or her categories with words whose common meanings denote the variable of interest.
2. Define his or her units carefully, so that coders will know, for example, whether they are to make judgments of words, sentences, thought units, or time periods.
3. Survey material similar to that which is to be analyzed in order to discover the relative difficulty of the judgments to be made.
4. Prepare a list of instructions as explicit as possible for the coders to use in assigning units to categories. (These instructions sometimes are called *decision rules*.) This list of instructions should include illustrative material and possibly a dictionary specifying certain types of units for certain categories.
5. Test these instructions by having coders attempt to use them on material similar to that which will be coded in the main analysis.
6. Then check the coders' reliability on this "pilot" material. (We will tell you how in Chapter 6.)
7. If necessary (and it probably will be necessary), revise his or her units, categories, and decision rules, and test reliability again.

All aspects of an observational analysis should be subject to rigorous conceptualization and thorough pilot testing. The appropriate time to discover problems in a coding system is *before* extensive coding begins.

Sampling in Observational Studies.   Like the survey researcher, the observational analyst confronts problems of sampling. But whereas for the survey researcher membership in a population probably is defined by status as an individual, for the observational analyst membership in a population may be defined by status as small as "word," "phrase," or "speech act." The observational analyst, therefore, is well advised to define his or her "population" with great care: Does it consist of people? Of words? Of sentences? Of utterances? Of utterances (or words or sentences) in a particular kind of situation?

Our general advice (though, practically, you may be forced to violate it) is that you should *not* sample from among a coherent set of symbolic material but that instead, once you have chosen such a set, you should analyze it all. Sampling, by definition, excludes a large body of data from the analysis. The excluded part may contain important or unique information, especially in contingency (or structural) analyses. Often, the most interesting patterns of behavior occur infrequently (see Stech & Goldberg, 1972). Using a sampling approach, you have a very high probability of excluding these interesting but infrequent events (or combinations of events).

But sampling is frequently necessary, though undesirable. Suppose, for example, that you were interested in analyzing the portrayal of women on prime-time commercial network television. Prime time consumes three hours a night, seven nights a week, 52 weeks a year, on each of three networks. Thus you would be faced with 3276 hours (or 136.5 days) of data available for analysis in a single year.

If you must sample, you should proceed in the same manner as in survey research. First, identify and number members of the population to be sampled. Second, select from among that population a sample adequate in size and representative of the population, either by random selection or stratified sampling.

To continue the portrayal-of-women example: Assume that enough women are portrayed in 100 hours of programming to permit generalization to the population of prime-time commercial programming, so that 100 hours is a sample adequate in size. If you decided to sample randomly, you would (1) label each hour on each network with a discrete four-digit number between 0001 and 3276, and (2) using a table of random numbers, select 100 of those hours.

An alternative (and possibly better) way would be to stratify the population (and randomly sample in a certain proportion from among the strata) according to some criterion that makes sense for these data. For example, if you were interested in comparing the portrayal of women among the three commercial networks, you might stratify the population in three tiers, by network. If you were interested in comparing the portrayal of women between action/adventure shows and prime-time serials (soaps), you might stratify the population by program content rather than by network hours.

The concept of stratified sampling can easily be generalized to other observational arenas. Obviously, creativity is called for in the process of connecting the kind of generalization desired as a result of the research to the kind of sampling that would most efficiently permit that generalization. But in the abstract, principles governing sample selection for observational studies do not differ from those governing sample selection for survey studies. For observational studies, you must break out of the mind-set that equates the concept "human being" with the concept "member of a population." In observational studies, populations consist of behaviors, not people. Behaviors, like people, are subject to adequate and representative sampling.

Contingency Studies.   In contingency studies, an important focus of attention is the relationship *among parts* of the set of data—structural relationships. Often (but not always), the relationship sought is a temporal one, characterized by such words as *follow, precede, before,* and *after.* Hence, the contingency analyst might ask such research questions as: How probable is it that a question will be immediately followed by an answer? How probable is it that, in conversation among siblings, a threat will be followed within the next three turns at talk by a counterthreat? How probable is it that an utterance characterized as "dominant" in a conversation will be followed by an utterance characterized as "submissive"? Or by another utterance characterized as "dominant"? How probable is it that a drinking episode on a prime-time television show will be followed in the same show by alcohol-related harm to a drinker? How probable is it that a particular typeface will appear as the headline for a particular type of magazine article?

One kind of contingency analysis, which we will use to illustrate the concept, is called *interaction analysis,* and a modification of it is called *lag sequential analysis.* These are not the only kinds of contingency analysis, and you should not let your thinking be limited by the fact that we use them as examples.

In contingency analyses, as in tabular analyses, the researcher first defines carefully the *units* and *categories* to be used in the study. He or she then codes the data, but, unlike the tabular analyst, he or she *scrupulously preserves the order of events.* For the contingency analyst, "units" then become "sequences of units."

To illustrate: Suppose that you were interested in "dominance" and "submissiveness" in conversations among children as presented in elementary reading textbooks. Your interests extend beyond the simple tabulation of "dominant" and "submissive" statements in these textbooks, for you suspect that these conversations exhibit a subtle form of sexism.

You decide to sample from among the most widely used elementary reading textbooks, and, within those textbooks, you do a stratified sample of conversations, sampling equally from among boy-girl, girl-girl, and boy-boy conversations. Your initial unit of analysis is the "utterance" or "turn at talk," and you categorize each of the units as exhibiting dominance (a *D* unit—for example, "Let's play ball"), submissiveness (an *S* unit—for example, "What shall we do?") or neither (an *N* unit—for example, "Mother said we can have a cookie now"). For an elaboration of this kind of category system, see Ellis (1979). Like Ellis's, your coding of any particular utterance depends greatly on its context. You can imagine, for example, contexts in which "Mother said we can have a cookie now" might be a dominant statement—as when the previous speaker has suggested another activity now.

Now assume that one of the boy-girl conversations shows the following pattern, in which the number indicates the utterance number in temporal sequence, *B* indicates "boy," *G* indicates "girl," *D* indicates "utterance characterized as dominant," *S* indicates "utterance characterized as submissive," and *N* indicates "utterance characterized as neither dominant nor submissive":

1. *BD*
2. *GS*
3. *BN*
4. *GN*
5. *BD*
6. *GS*
7. *BD*
8. *GS*
9. *BN*

We have represented these results as an interaction analyst might represent them in Figure 4.1 (p. 80). The *rows* in the figure represent the first (or *antecedent*) utterance in each series of two utterances. The *columns* in the figure represent the second (or *subsequent*) utterance in each series of two utterances. (A series of two utterances sometimes is called a *digram.*) The numbers in the figure represent a tally of the number of times a particular kind of subsequent utterance followed a particular kind of antecedent utterance and the percentage this number represents of the total number of utterances that were subsequent to this particular kind of antecedent utterance (the row total in the figure).

You should note that, even though the conversation consisted of nine utterances, the total in the figure is only eight. This is because your unit of analysis has now become

FIGURE 4.1. Lag-1 Analysis of a Hypothetical Conversation.

	BD (%)	BS (%)	BN (%)	GD (%)	GS (%)	GN (%)	Row Total
BD					3(100)		3
BS							
BN						1(100)	1
GD							
GS	1(33)		2(67)				3
GN	1(100)						1

an antecedent-subsequent *pair* of utterances, and, because the first utterance has no utterance antecedent to it and the last utterance has no utterance subsequent to it, each of those utterances is counted (in a manner of speaking) as only half a unit. To put it another way: The second utterance is counted as part of two units, the first-second and second-third pairs. So are all other utterances, except for the first one and the last one, each of which is counted as part of only one unit.

Inspecting Figure 4.1, you might begin to take considerable satisfaction in your hypothesis about subtle sexism in elementary reading textbooks. Every time the boy makes a dominant utterance, the girl makes a submissive one. (That sentence expressed a *contingent* relationship.) And the girl makes no dominant utterances at all. (That statement expressed a *tabular* finding.) If these results held up across all boy-girl conversations, and if the contingencies were significantly different in girl A-girl B and in boy A-boy B conversations, you would have successfully demonstrated the tenability of your sexism hypothesis. And, in fact, one of our students, Arlene Badger, in a study much like this one, has done so.

The kind of analysis we have just described deals with contiguous antecedent-subsequent contingencies, or digrams. In the language of *lag sequential* analysis, it was at the "lag-1" level. A lag-2 analysis would plot in the rows antecedent utterances and in the columns subsequent utterances *plus one,* disregarding the intervening utterance. We have plotted this analyses in Figure 4.2 for the hypothetical boy-girl conversation under consideration.

You should be able to understand this figure by referring to the coded conversation, and we will refrain from explaining it. This analysis results in a total of only seven units because the first two and last two utterances do not enter into as many lag-2 units as do the intervening ones.

A more complicated kind of sequential study (Markov process analysis) may also be done of three-unit contingencies *(trigrams)* at the second order level, of four-unit contingencies *(tetragrams)* at the third order level, etc. We will illustrate this for the hypothetical conversation under discussion at the second order (trigram) level. Figure 4.3 represents this analysis (see p. 82).

The rows in the figure represent antecedent *digrams.* Note that, since each digram represents a *pair* of utterances, certain combinations of categories are impossible and are not shown. A *B* utterance by definition can never immediately follow another *B* utterance, nor can a *G* utterance immediately follow another *G* utterance. The columns in the figure represent the single utterance subsequent to the digram—the utterance that will

FIGURE 4.2. Lag-2 Analysis of a Hypothetical Conversation.

	BD (%)	BS (%)	BN (%)	GD (%)	GS (%)	GN (%)	Row Total
BD	1(33)		2(67)				3
BS							
BN	1(100)						1
GD							
GS					1(50)	1(50)	2
GN					1(100)		1

complete the trigram. In this analysis, as in the simpler lag-2 analysis discussed earlier, you have a total of only seven units, and by now you should be able to figure out why that is true.

To reinforce the difference between tabular analyses (in which the unit is a single occurrence) and contingency analyses (in which the unit is a structural combination of two or more occurrences, often arranged temporally), we will quote from Fisher (1978b, pp. 216–17):

> *Interactional analysis inherently involves temporal analysis of categorized actions, so that the single act is not the primary unit of quantitative analysis. Rather, the fundamental unit is the interact (a recurring sequence of two contiguous acts) [which we have called the digram], the double interact (a recurring sequence of three contiguous acts) [which we have called the trigram], a triple interact (four acts) [which we have called the tetragram], and so forth.*

But interactional analysis is only one kind of contingency analysis, and contingencies need not always be defined temporally. You should try to keep your mind open to all the possibilities for analyzing contingencies, in spite of our stress on interaction analysis.

The Ubiquitous Utility of Ratios

An observational researcher often must compare bodies of text that are not the same size. One newspaper is larger than another; one speech is longer than another; one movie is longer than another; one conversation is longer than another. The effects of these disparities often can be eliminated by the use of ratios. Usually, a ratio in an observational study is the quotient obtained by dividing instances of the category of interest by the total number of instances (including those in the category of interest) in that text. If you were interested in instances of the first-person singular pronoun, for example, you could compare texts of different length by dividing, in each, the number of first-person singular pronouns by the number of all personal pronouns. Such a ratio is a simple proportion. If each text has the *same* number of units in it, you have no reason to use it. But texts to be compared seldom have the same number of units in them. Whenever they do not, you probably will find it useful to think in terms of proportions or other kinds of ratios. One kind of ratio that has been used to measure the active (as opposed to passive) style of English prose, for example, divides the total number of nouns and verbs in a passage by the total number of adjectives and adverbs.

FIGURE 4.3. Second-Order Markov Analyses of a Hypothetical Conversation in Trigram Form.

	BD (%)	BS (%)	BN (%)	GD (%)	GS (%)	GN (%)	Row Total
BD-GD							
BD-GS	1(33)		2(67)				3
BD-GN							
BS-GD							
BS-GS							
BS-GN							
BN-GD							
BN-GS							
BN-GN	1(100)						1
GD-BD							
GD-BS							
GD-BN							
GS-BD					1(100)		1
GS-BS							
GS-BN						1(100)	1
GN-BD					1(100)		1
GN-BS							
GN-BN							

Some ratios, however, are systematically affected by the length of a text. A commonly used ratio in communication research is called the *type/token ratio,* a measure of lexical diversity. To arrive at the type/token ratio (TTR) of a text, the researcher (or, more likely, the researcher's computer) divides the number of *different* words in the text by the *total* number of words in the text. But the TTR is systematically affected by the length of the text. The longer an individual speaks or writes, the more likely he or she is to reuse the same words and thus to depress the TTR. Researchers have solved this problem by making a further ratio of the ratio in what is called the *mean segmental type/ token ratio* (MSTTR). To calculate this ratio, the researcher first divides the text into passages of a given length (often, 50 or 150 words). He or she then calculates a TTR (or segmental TTR) for each of these passages. Finally, the researcher adds up all of the segmental TTRs and divides by the number of passages to calculate a mean (thus "mean segmental" TTR or MSTTR). This ratio is not affected by the length of the text, for each passage is treated as a new, short text.

The purpose of this brief exposition is to help you become sensitive to ratios as ways of solving problems attendant on texts or sets of observations that are unequal in size. But you should also be aware that certain kinds of ratios can themselves be affected by text size and that your ingenuity can help you to find a solution to problems in comparison even when that happens.

On the Issue of Structure

The covering law model, which we discussed in Chapter 1, dominated communication research and theory for many years, and it continues to be the dominant paradigm. That model and some of the statistical techniques used by its practitioners demand rather rigorous, well-defined steps leading to the scientific acceptance of its laws and theories. These demands, in turn, lead to a demand for exact planning of methods and exact *initial* unitization and categorization schemes for observational studies. (We might add that observational studies have only rarely emerged from practitioners of that model.) The researcher begins with relatively narrow, specific hypotheses or research questions and specifies *in advance* the precise methods by which those hypotheses will be tested or those questions will be answered.

In the quintessential structured approach, the researcher specifies (and thereby controls) in advance not only the unitization and categorization scheme and the method of analysis, but also the environment and, often, the selection of message sources. The result is a rigorously designed observational experiment. Such a study usually results in relatively clear tests of the hypotheses proposed or relatively clear answers to the research questions asked. But the approach also has the effect of inhibiting the appreciation of unanticipated phenomena or patterns in the data, some of which, if they were appreciated, might be more theoretically interesting than the highly structured findings themselves. That is, the approach not only structures the methods used in the study, it also structures the reality of communication as perceived by the researcher.

We have nothing against structure, and we hope that many researchers will continue to use a structured approach. The approach is most strongly justified when "strong" theory is available to be tested in the area of concern. For example, Bradac, Konsky, and Elliott (1976) had a strong theory relating strength of drive to verbal behavior as a guide to their structured investigation. They manipulated the expectations that potential interviewees would have about the personality and demeanor of their potential interviewers. (Actually, the interviewers were trained *not* to vary indications of their personality or demeanor across expectation conditions.) The interviews, given this prior manipulation and control, were audiotaped and transcribed. The analysis was carried out using a highly structured unitization and categorization system—so structured that a computer could do it without human intervention. The study revealed significant differences in the verbal behavior of interviewees, depending on the type of person they were led to think their interviewer would be. And the results generally supported the theory that the study was designed to test.

In another highly structured observational experiment, Courtright (1978) tested the theory known as "groupthink" (Janis, 1972). (Briefly, groupthink is thought to occur in highly cohesive groups as a function of their desire to maintain harmony at the expense of rational decision-making processes.) Courtright experimentally manipulated both the cohesiveness and another aspect of the mental set experienced by the problem-solving groups in his study. A highly structured analysis of the communication occurring in those groups offered some support for the groupthink theory and indicated a central role for one of the categories, disagreement, in effective group decision making.

Under the influences of the rules paradigm and the pragmatic paradigm, and especially under the influence of such methodologists of social science as Glaser and Strauss (1967), many researchers to some degree have liberated themselves from the demand for structure required by the covering law paradigm. The approach to observational studies among some researchers is determined less by an "I predict that X will happen" spirit and more by a "What might happen if . . ." spirit.

No researcher's investigation can be *completely* unstructured. The researcher must specify in advance, even if only implicitly, at least the kind of phenomena to be investigated. Furthermore, like all human beings, researchers wear various kinds of blinders as a function of their capabilities and previous experiences, in research and otherwise. Nevertheless, many recent studies in communication have begun with fewer theoretical and methodological assumptions than have been customary.

In these less structured studies, the range is wide, both in the structure of the study itself (so that field studies are becoming relatively more frequent and experimental studies relatively less frequent) and in the unitization and categorization schemes imposed on the data. Some even impose less a priori structure on the statistical techniques to be employed or on the mental set in which statistical results might be interpreted.

Such studies are appropriate especially when no "strong" theory is available to explain the phenomena of interest. Hence, less structured studies are designed (to the extent that they *are* designed) for the purpose of beginning the process by which theory is constructed rather than for the purpose of testing theory.

Among studies in the middle range of structure are the interactional observation studies of Rogers and Farace (1975) and a series that followed (e.g., Courtright, Millar, & Rogers, 1980; Courtright, Millar, & Rogers-Millar, 1979; Millar, Rogers-Millar, & Courtright, 1979; and Rogers-Millar & Millar, 1979). In these studies of relational communication, husbands and wives are interviewed in their homes (so that the environment is not the structured one of a laboratory). The couples are asked to "spontaneously" discuss topics provided by the researchers (so that interactions are not structured, but topics are). The coding system for the conversations is relatively structured, but this group of researchers has been relatively open to making adaptations in it as unanticipated phenomena have occurred. Finally, each couple fills out a rather lengthy questionnaire, and various items from this questionnaire may be compared with the results from the observational data in the hope (but not necessarily the expectation) of finding (or finding hints of) systematic relationships (so that the method of analysis and rules of interpretation of results are relatively unstructured).

The least structured of observational studies, in general, are those proceeding explicitly from a "grounded theory" (Glaser & Strauss, 1967) approach. These studies start by defining the unit of analysis, but deliberately *avoid* defining the category system. In fact, in a sense, defining a category system is a principal objective of these studies.

Once the unitization method has been defined, the researcher compares each unit with each other unit, deciding as he or she goes along which of the units fit together (that is, might be considered to belong to the *same* category) and which do not (that is, might be considered as belonging to *different* categories). When this process is complete, the researcher reexamines the categories to decide whether some should be collapsed or combined. This process of categorizing and critically recategorizing is called the *constant comparison* technique. Finally, the researcher hypothesizes for future testing possible theoretical relationships among the categories as he or she has defined them.

Researchers using a grounded theory approach face severe problems in establishing the reliability of their units and of their categories. Both the researcher and the coders must be exceptionally perceptive—that is, must have an exceptionally acute sense of what in a unit might be theoretically interesting in a category or in a combination of categories. We do not recommend this technique to you as a relatively inexperienced researcher. But for a good example of the use of the technique in communication research, see Browning (1978).

Examples of Observational Studies

The Raders Study

Mary Lou Raders, while an undergraduate student at the University of Iowa, had a strong interest in what is called "popular culture," the system of beliefs and behavior in which most ordinary cultural members participate. Raders suspected that an element in American culture had undergone a significant change between the mid-1950s and 1977 (the year she did her study). Specifically, she thought that the culture had become less tolerant of violence and less oriented toward physical action than it had been formerly. She wanted to find evidence to support this idea through tabular observational analysis.

Raders decided to use as her population the Sunday comic section of the *Des Moines Register,* the largest daily newspaper in the state. As samples from that population, she chose the immediately preceding Sunday's comics (this was in the spring of 1977) and a Sunday as near as possible to the same date in 1955.

She decided that the individual frame would be her *unit* of analysis. (Because frames can be identified with perfect reliability, Raders did not have to be concerned with unitizing reliability.) She assigned each frame to one of two *categories:* (1) an *action* frame involved "quick and/or great movements" and/or "intense and startling violent acts and their direct repercussions"; (2) *nonaction* frames included all other frames, or conceptually, frames that showed "verbal action only" or "stationarity or minor acts of movement."

The results of the study showed that, in the 1955 sample, 47% of the 300 frames were in the action category, whereas in the 1977 sample only 33% of the 197 frames were of the action type. Using appropriate statistical techniques such as those we will describe in a later chapter, Raders determined that this difference was too large to be easily accounted for by chance. Did the American culture become less physical and more contemplative between 1955 and 1977? To the extent that the Sunday comics reflect or project the popular culture, and if Raders's sample was adequate and representative of the Sunday comics, it probably did.

The Courtright Study

In another relatively straightforward application of tabular methods for observational analysis, Courtright (1974) addressed the question of possible changes in the rhetorical appeals of the Black Panther Party. During the late 1960s and early 1970s, the Black Panthers had been noted for their militancy, manifested in appeals to "arm yourselves and shoot to kill" racist oppressors. Probably as a result of such appeals, the Black Panthers came under constant and intense police scrutiny. Several armed skirmishes between police and Black Panthers resulted in the killing or wounding or imprisonment of a number of party leaders and members. Militant rhetoric and tactics had proven to be costly to the party.

Courtright's review of the literature on social movements and agitation uncovered several theories to suggest that these costs would soon engender a change in rhetorical appeals. (See especially Gurr, 1970.) An organization cannot maintain a publicly militant stance in the face of numerous and consistent setbacks. Also, some statements from the leader of the Panthers indicated that the party had forsaken the "rhetoric of the gun" and instead was concentrating on community relief and education programs.

To test the theory that Panther rhetoric changed during the period of interest

(1968 to early 1972), Courtright performed a content analysis of the party's principal publication, the *Black Panther Inter-Communal Newsletter*. Because this was a weekly newspaper consisting of a dozen pages or more, and because Courtright's resources in time were limited, he decided to sample. Accordingly, he analyzed only the second page of the first issue of each month for certain months that were critical to the test of the theory. The unit of analysis was linguistic and reliably identifiable: the complete sentence. Each of the units was placed in one of two categories: (1) an *aggressive* category, in which units contained "the idea of nonaccidental harm to another person or object"; or (2) a *nonaggressive,* residual category for those units *not* containing the idea of nonaccidental harm to another person or object.

The results of the study provided empirical evidence supporting the theory being tested. Furthermore, Courtright was able to apply additional theory, given this support, and to predict probable subsequent changes in the style and content of the Black Panthers' rhetoric.

The Annenberg Studies

George Gerbner and his colleagues at the Annenberg School of Communication, University of Pennsylvania, are engaged in a long-term "cultural indicators project" to "monitor the world of television drama." We will briefly describe part of that research—the part concerned with violence on television (Gerbner, Gross, Jackson-Beeck, Jeffries-Fox, & Signorielli, 1978). You may have occasionally seen some of the reports of this research reported in *TV Guide*.

One of the goals of this project is to develop a "violence index"—a single descriptive indicator of the amount of violence on television. Such an index can be used to compare violent programming across time, among types of programs (e.g., comedy versus drama), or according to any other criterion decided on by the researchers (e.g., among networks during prime time).

As we have indicated, television offers a massive volume of material. Gerbner et al. sampled from among this volume for their research. They recorded for analysis a full week of prime-time and weekend-daytime (8 A.M. to 2 P.M.) programs for all three commercial networks during the fall of the year. By comparing such samples to other kinds of samples, these investigators have provided evidence supporting the validity and reliability of this sampling method for the kinds of research problems that interest them.

The unitization method for this research is somewhat more complicated than is that of any study we have presented previously. The analysis employs three different kinds of units, which are considered simultaneously. One kind of unit is the *program*—"a single fictional story presented in dramatic form." A second is the *episode*—"a scene . . . confined to the same participants." The third kind of unit is the *character*—both major characters ("the principal role essential to the story") and minor characters.

The category scheme into which the units are placed is a simple dichotomy. Each unit is judged either *violent* or *not violent*. Each year the researchers recruit about twenty coders and train them for three weeks to reliably recognize and record units of violence. The definition of *violence* confines it to "clear, unambiguous, overt physical violence," including such phenomena as "murder, 'natural' catastrophes, or 'accidents.' " Apparently, then, violence can be either intentional (which we would call "violent aggression") or unintentional. Furthermore, the coders record it whether it is presented in a realistic, serious, fantasy, or humorous context.

Using the three kinds of units as categorized, the researchers calculate a rather complicated "violence index," which we will not explain. They claim that this index is highly reliable, so that "prevalence, rate of incidence, and character involvement in violence must all change in the same direction to register a substantial change in the index."

As we indicated earlier, the calculation of this index facilitates answering any number of research questions. An analysis across time (1967–77), for example, comparing children's weekend programs with adults' prime-time programs, shows a considerably higher violence index for the children's programs. This difference between children's and adults' programs is considerably greater than are the year-to-year differences for either type of program.

You may consider it strange that children's programs are calculated to be more violent than prime-time programs, and it seems likely that the violence index will be the subject of close scrutiny by critics. Gerbner and his colleagues have provided a rationale for the violence index, but perhaps some aspects of that rationale need to be tested.

The Breed and De Foe Study

You may be tired of reading about action, aggression, and violence, and we will now divert your attention to drinking—or, rather, "The Portrayal of the Drinking Process on Prime-Time Television" (Breed & De Foe, 1981). This study sampled "ten episodes of each of the [top-rated by Nielsen] situation comedies and five episodes of each of the [top-rated] fifteen dramas" between November 1976 and February 1977. All of the situation comedies (e.g., "All in the Family," "Barney Miller") were half-hour shows, and all of the dramas (e.g., "Baretta," "Bionic Woman") were one-hour shows.

Breed and De Foe selected for analysis from among these programs scenes with what they called a "significant" relation to alcohol or drinking. They used seven criteria to define the relation of the scene to alcohol as "significant":

> (1) portrayal of heavy drinking; (2) a purpose in drinking that went beyond sociable sipping; (3) a consequence that probably would not have occurred if a nonalcoholic beverage had been ingested; (4) some response to drinking activity by another person; (5) an evaluation of drinking as good or bad; (6) a contribution of drinking behavior to plot or characterization; or (7) humor that reflected on any of the above six criteria.

Each character in each of these scenes was considered a unit of analysis.

The researchers used a number of dimensions in their category system. Each character was categorized as a "drinker" or a "disapprover" as well as being categorized by sex, socioeconomic status, moral character, importance of the role to the show, and age. "Disapprovers" were also categorized by their relationship to the drinker. (Friends were most likely to express their disapproval, followed by family members other than a spouse.) The consequences of drinking were categorized into twenty types, one of which was disapproval. In the analysis, Breed and De Foe collapsed a number of these consequences into five negative consequences, ranging from embarrassment and a hangover to harm to self and others. The most likely negative consequence of drinking was strained relationships.

Seven conclusions from the study relate drinkers, drinking, and the consequences of drinking on prime-time television to "accepted cultural norms or standards of public health." We will report them (in paraphrase) not only because they indicate the social potential for observational studies of this type, but also because they might encourage you to be skeptical about the social reality presented by drinkers on prime-time television:

(1) Minors almost never drink on television, and young adults seldom do (15% of the drinkers were young adults). But their attitudes toward drinking "sometimes suggest an eagerness to start." (2) On television, characters often drink "to face a crisis or to escape from tension." In reality, alcohol above a small amount decreases the ability to solve problems. (3) Most often, no serious consequences of drinking are shown on prime-time television. Serious consequences are considerably more likely in real life than their portrayal on television implies. (4) Disapproval of heavy drinking on prime-time television is infrequent and usually ineffectual. That is, the consequences of heavy drinking for those close to the drinker are not clearly shown. (5) Prime-time characters "infrequently decline the offer of a drink." (6) Characters whose roles are important suffer consequences from drinking less often than do nonregulars on the series. "The stars seem to be given near-immunity." (7) The "sheer frequency" of drinking on television is much greater than it is in the culture generally.

You should note that the Breed and De Foe study involves both tabulations (e.g., of drinkers by age) and contingencies (e.g., the likelihood of disapproval following drinking). Furthermore, the study, more clearly than most, documents an unfortunate social situation: The portrayal of drinking and its consequences on prime-time television is distorted in such a way that it could unjustifiably encourage (or fail to discourage) drinking among viewers.

The Pingree, Hawkins, Butler, and Paisley Study

And now to sexism. Pingree, Hawkins, Butler, and Paisley (1976) devised a general "scale for sexism" and applied it to pictured portrayals of women in advertisements occupying at least one-sixth of a page in *Ms., Time, Newsweek,* and *Playboy.* Units in the study, then, were advertisements of the size specified containing the picture of a woman.

Pingree et al. sampled by randomly selecting ten such advertisements from each issue of each of the four monthly magazines published between July 1973 and June 1974. The resulting sample resulted in 120 advertisements each from *Time, Newsweek,* and *Playboy.* From *Ms.,* only 87 advertisements meeting the criteria were available during the one-year period. You might figure out for yourself, in light of our earlier discussion of the ubiquitous usefulness of ratios, how Pingree et al. coped with the problem of the smaller sample from *Ms.*

The "scale for sexism" consists of five "levels" (roughly analogous to "consciousness levels" in "consciousness raising"), proceeding from Level 1 ("Woman is a two-dimensional, nonthinking decoration") to Level 2 ("Woman's place is in the home or in womanly occupations"), Level 3 ("Woman may be a professional, but first place is home"), Level 4 ("Women and men must be equals"), and finally Level 5 ("Women and men as individuals"). Level 5 images, as the researchers note, occur rarely, possibly because, requiring as they do "women and men [who] are viewed as superior to each other in some respects, inferior in other respects," they are difficult to display in a single photograph or drawing.

The five "levels" constituted Pingree et al.'s category system. The researchers reported a very high level of coder reliability, in which, among 447 ads and 19 coders, only 15 disagreements about consciousness level occurred.

Among all four magazines, 27% of the advertisements were at Level 1; 48% were at Level 2 ("Woman's place is in the home"); 4% were at Level 3; 19% were at Level 4; and only 2% were at Level 5. Testing contingencies between consciousness level and magazine, Pingree et al. found that, as predicted, *Playboy* had the most advertisements at Level 1 and *Ms.* had the most at Levels 4 and 5. *Time* and *Newsweek* were similar to each other and had more status quo advertisements (Level 2) than did *Playboy* or *Ms.*

A later study (Skelly & Lundstrom, 1981) applied an analogous consciousness scale to the images of men in magazine advertisements, sampling from general interest magazines *(Reader's Digest, Time, New Yorker)*, magazines designed to be of interest to men *(Esquire, Field & Stream, Sports Illustrated)*, and magazines designed to be of interest to women *(Cosmopolitan, House Beautiful, Redbook)*. Besides sampling systematically from among the nine magazines, Skelly and Lundstrom stratified their sample by year of publication (1959, 1969, and 1979).

As might be expected the researchers report various contingencies among magazine type, year, and consciousness level. Among the more interesting (and unexpected) findings was that the number of advertisements portraying men at the lowest level of consciousness (as two-dimensional sexual objects) increased significantly between 1959 and 1979 in all types of magazines, but especially in magazines of interest to women (from 12.5% in 1959 to 55% in 1979).

The Ellis Study

The final observational study we will summarize was a contingency study of "relational control in two group systems" (Ellis, 1979). The two "systems" comprised a "problem-solving" or "decision-making" system (two groups of students who met weekly for three months on "university related problems" which directly affected the group members") and a "women's consciousness-raising" system (one group from Reno, Nevada and another from Salt Lake City, Utah, each of which met occasionally during a three-month period). Ellis sampled four complete one-hour sessions of interaction from each group.

The study used methods closely analogous to those we described earlier for the hypothetical study of interaction in children's reading textbooks. First, Ellis recorded for each act or utterance (an uninterrupted turn at talk) a notation of its relational control (in general, dominating, submissive, or neither, though Ellis's system was more complicated). In the first run-through, then, the turn at talk was the unit of analysis.

But since the study was of *interaction* rather than *action*, a contingency study rather than a tabular one, the important unit of analysis for Ellis was the relationship between contiguous turns at talk and the relationship between turns at farther removes than one. Furthermore, Ellis was concerned with *phases* in the two kinds of systems—repetitive patterns of interaction that might occur in one part of a session, to be replaced by another pattern in another part.

Ellis's interpretations of the results take up six pages in his report of the study. Generally, the decision-making groups were strongly characterized by interactions of *equivalent symmetry* (an utterance neither dominant nor submissive followed by another of the same type). But this type of interaction is not characteristic of all phases in the decision-making groups. The early phase is characterized by competition for control, and mildly dominating utterances are relatively frequent in response to neutral ones. And the final phase is more strongly characterized than are other phases by mildly submissive utterances in response to neutral ones, as the members coalesce in relation to preferred solutions.

The interaction patterns in the two consciousness-raising groups differed substantially from each other. In one group, very little relational control was attempted, and Ellis wrote that the group "simply spins out long chains of relational equality with only sporadic transitions to other modes of control." The other group operated in a way similar to the decision-making groups, where mild dominance attempts were frequent, most often followed by neutral extensions.

Among the studies we have attended to, the Ellis study is the most complex. Probably, it is also the one most closely and directly concerned with communication per se.

■ Conclusion

Observational methods may be used in field studies, in quasi-experimental designs, and in experimental designs. They may be used to describe phenomena, to generate theory, or to test theory. Like survey methods, observational methods sometimes require sampling. They always require decisions on unitization and on categorization schemes. Tabular observational studies display frequencies of units among categories. Contingency studies display relationships of units among categories, often over time (as in interaction studies). Ratios are frequently useful in observational studies as a means of compensating for unequal size of various texts or other inequalities among bodies of material to be analyzed. Of all research methods, observational methods are probably most to be desired in studies where the principal focus is *communication itself,* rather than its antecedents and its consequences.

Paper-and-Pencil Tests and Rating Scales

Measurement scales and paper-and-pencil instruments in general are heavily used in the social sciences, including communication research. Such instruments have several advantages. They are an efficient way to gather data. Respondents usually find them easy to interpret and thus simple to complete. And the data obtained are almost instantly available for statistical analysis. Given the proper forms and formats, scales in machine readable form can be fed into computer statistical packages with virtually no human coding or other intervention.

But such instruments are also subject to misuse and abuse. The ease with which they can be prepared facilitates atheoretic fishing expeditions—"quick and dirty" research, in the jargon of the game. Somehow, the availability of an array of scales often has the effect of encouraging researchers to use them (even though they may be only tangentially related to the variables of interest) rather than to thoroughly search for and, if necessary, to devise operational scales that have a coherent relationship to conceptual variables.

Scales attempt to obtain information about subjects' perceptions by means of self-report. Normally, of course, such information is not observable in any other way. The logic of this method of measurement might be called "backward inference" (see Miller & Berger, 1978, p. 49). The act of marking a scale is overt, observable behavior. The researcher assumes that the behavior is influenced by ("is the result of," "is caused by") cognitions the subject had at the moment the marking took place. Therefore, the researcher infers backwards from the marks to the cognitions or cognitive processes that brought them about.

Scales are also used to detect *changes* in cognitions and cognitive processes. If, for example, a subject filled out evaluation scales on a product before viewing a commercial for the product and immediately after viewing the commercial, and if the earlier evaluation was less favorable than the later one, the researcher would infer that the subject's attitude toward the product had changed. (The researcher might be tempted to assert that the commercial "caused" the change, but, as we indicated in Chapter 2, such an attribution should not be made in the absence of a control condition.) Such changes are not *directly* observable, and scales represent an efficient, indirect way of reasonably inferring their existence.

We will not try to survey the very extensive domain of self-report scales. Appendix A indexes many that have been used recently in communication research. In this chapter, we will categorize their uses broadly as encompassing (1) the study of cognitive states and traits, (2) the study of attitude formation and change, and (3) the rating of others' communicative behavior.

Cognitive States and Traits

Currently, social scientists are pursuing a hot controversy about cognitive *states*, cognitive *traits*, and the distinction between them. Cognitive *states* are situationally dependent and of relatively short duration. Their existence is intrinsically bound to a particular person, object, context, or situation, or to some combination of these elements. When the element or combination changes, the state disappears or changes. Some examples of cognitive states that have been used as variables are fear, anger, test anxiety, trust (or the judgment of another person as trustworthy), empathy, judgments of communicator credibility, and feelings of interpersonal solidarity.

Cognitive *traits* are thought to be relatively enduring attributes or characteristics of an individual. Traits, then, are thought to operate and influence behavior in many situations the individual encounters (Bem & Allen, 1974; Hewes & Haight, 1979). As Parks (1980, p. 220) has suggested, traits "reflect, or perhaps impose, regularity on human behavior. Their explanatory power is derived from their ability to parsimoniously summarize behavioral or cognitive responses in diverse situations." Recent research has cast into question the assumption of cross-situational consistency (for example, between apprehension in a public speaking situation and apprehension in an intimate conversation), thereby raising doubts about the utility of traits as explanatory mechanisms.

Examples of traits that have been used to explain communicative behavior include self-esteem, social introversion, machiavellianism, dogmatism, and locus of control ("externality/internality"). One trait that has received a great deal of attention is "communication apprehension" or "an individual's level of fear or anxiety associated with either real or anticipated communication with another person or persons" (McCroskey, 1977, p. 78). Another is "androgyny" or psychological gender (Bem, 1973). (On an androgyny scale, members of any biological sex can be classified as primarily masculine, primarily feminine, or androgynous—a combination.) Two other relatively recent entries in the list of measurable traits are rhetorical sensitivity (Hart, Carlson, & Eadie, 1980) and interaction involvement (Cegala, Savage, Brunner, & Conrad, 1982).

Both states and traits usually are measured by self-report, paper-and-pencil instruments. Almost always such instruments consist of multiple scales or items. Remember that operational definitions should exhaust conceptual meanings as fully as is possible. Because anything deserving the name *state* and especially *trait* has many aspects to its conceptual meaning, an instrument to measure it must also have multiple aspects or "dimensions" or clusters of items.

A recent "state" study by Wheeless and Grotz (1977), for example, was designed to develop a self-report instrument to measure one individual's "trust" in another. Among the fifteen scales included in the instrument by which one individual expresses trusting or suspicious perceptions of another are trustworthy/untrustworthy, confidential/divulging, candid/deceptive, reliable/unreliable, and faithful/unfaithful. Each scale is related to the core of meaning associated with the concept "trust." But each measures the perception of a subtly different aspect of that concept. When the fifteen scales were combined into a single index, that index provided a relatively exhaustive measurement of "trust" as a state.

Students of communication, of course, seldom are interested in states or traits for their own sake. Most often, they are interested in the relationships among states, traits, and communication. The state of "trust," for example, is significantly and directly related to self-disclosive communication. Similarly, many other aspects of an individual, measurable by paper-and-pencil instruments, have been found to have systematic relationships with various aspects of communication. But people whose interest is in communication should keep in mind that the study of cognitive traits and states is a means to an end—understanding communication—not an end in itself.

Attitude Formation and Change

Attitude formation and change via communication (persuasion) has been a staple of communication research for almost half a century. In this research, self-report measurement scales have been the norm for assessment of attitudes.

Attitudes have been considered important because, like states and traits, they are thought to mediate behavior. That is, messages received are thought of as filtering through an individual's attitudes, and hence the attitudes (or filters) must be taken into account in any explanation of the individual's subsequent behavior. Moreover, certain types of messages have the potential to change the attitudinal structure, and therefore to change the individual's behavior in a remote sense. Although much research in communication has focused on attitudes, then, that research is important only insofar as it can be related to behavior, especially communicative behavior.

In the past few years, the popularity of attitudes as predictor or criterion variables has declined noticeably (Miller & Burgoon, 1978). This decline probably is not the fault of self-reports as measuring instruments. Rather, the cause probably is a conviction partly based on research that attitudes are *not* very directly related to behavior, or that they are related to behavior only in very trivial or very complex ways.

Attitudes are thought of as evaluative cognitions, involving judgments of the "goodness" or "badness" of attitude objects (Fishbein & Ajzen, 1975). You might think that this evaluation would straightforwardly affect behavior: If a person's attitude toward an attitude object is positive, that person should behaviorally tend to approach the object; if the attitude is negative, the person should behaviorally tend to avoid the object.

But if you consider your own behavior, you will quickly perceive that the relationship is *not* straightforward. Do you sometimes avoid people you like very much (possibly because you are afraid they will reject you if you approach them)? Do you sometimes seek out people even though you dislike them (possibly because they and only they can do for you things that you must have done)? These kinds of inconsistencies between attitudes and behavior have shown up in some studies, thereby calling into question the usefulness of attitudes as predictors of behavior. Other studies have shown problematic connections among attitudes and behaviors. You might have a very positive attitude toward religion—yet never attend church. You might have a very positive attitude toward the Democratic party—yet never campaign for one of its candidates. You might conclude from this that attitude toward an *object* is not the same thing as attitude toward a *behavior* (Seibold, 1975). And your conclusion would be right.

Some research and theory (Ajzen & Fishbein, 1980; Fishbein & Ajzen, 1975) has attempted to overcome these problems of attitude-behavior inconsistency and still retain the practical advantages of self-report measurement scales. These theorists argue that a psychological construct in addition to "attitude" must be measured if the "attitude" construct is to relate systematically to behavior. They call this additional construct "intention" to behave.

Basically, these researchers argue that global attitudes toward objects, such as those conventionally measured by self-report scales, are not very predictive of *single, specific* behaviors. Hence, if behavior is the criterion variable of interest, the individual's intention to perform that particular behavior should be measured via self-report scales. In effect, then, the researcher would be measuring attitude toward a behavior rather than attitude toward an object.

They divide this attitude toward the behavior (or behavioral intention) into two parts. The first is a rather direct evaluation of the perceived consequences of the behavior, and might be measured as follows:

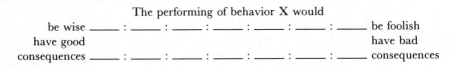

The performing of behavior X would
be wise ____ : ____ : ____ : ____ : ____ : ____ : ____ be foolish
have good
consequences ____ : ____ : ____ : ____ : ____ : ____ : ____ have bad
consequences

The other component of a behavioral intention is what Fishbein and Ajzen call the person's "subjective norm"—the perception of whether salient others (e.g., family, friends, workmates) would approve of the behavior. This component might be measured by:

Most people who are important to me think I
should ____ : ____ : ____ : ____ : ____ : ____ : ____ should not
perform behavior X

The two components can then be combined (though not necessarily with equal weights) into a single index of a person's intention to behave.

Research relating behavioral intention to actual behavior has had promising results. Ajzen and Fishbein (1980) reported successful prediction of behaviors as disparate as weight loss, women's occupational orientations, family planning, consumer activity, drinking among alcoholics, and voting.

Another promising approach to increased utility for self-report scales in persuasion research is somewhat similar. This approach, called the "expected value" approach (Bowers, 1974; Tedeschi, Schenker, & Bonoma, 1973), predicts behavior on the basis of two kinds of self-report measures: (1) the perceived values associated with various kinds of outcomes of the potential behavior; and (2) the perceived probability that each outcome *will* be achieved by the potential behavior. Each perceived value is then multiplied by its associated probability, and the products are added up to index the behavior's "expected value." If the expected value of *performing* a behavior is greater than the expected value of *not* performing it, then the individual should perform the behavior.

These approaches, and one or two others, have infused new energy into research on persuasion. They have also added conceptual clarity to the role of self-report scales in that research.

Rating the Communicative Behavior of Others

In the two sections immediately preceding this one, we have been concerned with subjects' descriptions of their *own* cognitive constructs. Rating scales also frequently are employed to obtain information about the communicative behavior of others. This is probably the kind of rating scales Becker (1970) had in mind when he defined *rating* as "describing an individual, group of individuals, behaviors, or artifacts of behaviors in terms of one or more numerical scales" (p. 213). Although this kind of rating provides some information about the cognitive-perceptual framework of the person doing the rating, this information is secondary to (and sometimes interferes with) the primary purpose—to describe the object or behavior being rated.

You may have first encountered this kind of rating scale in a communication classroom. Instructors frequently devise (sometimes borrow) and use rating scales to evaluate the communicative performance of their students. These instruments may not have the physical appearance of scales as we have been describing them, but to assign to a communicative performance one and only one category from a series of ordinally ranked categories (such as A, B, C, D, F) is to use a rating scale. In fact, much of the early research on rating scales and their application to communication behavior originated with scholars whose purposes were primarily pedagogical.

But our concern is with communication research methods, not with communication pedagogy. And rating of the behavior of others is eminently useful as a method, especially when, as Becker (1970, p. 214) says, "the subject of study is inadequate as a direct source of information or . . . some other measurement technique would disrupt the process being studied."

Now consider explicitly the two conditions under which this kind of rating is especially appropriate. Communicators frequently are *not* the best sources of information about their own behavior. They become immersed in the situation, fail to monitor behavior carefully, and forget and distort when they are asked to recall it. Or they perceive a personal stake in their self-reports, become ego-involved, and bias their own reports, usually positively but sometimes negatively. Raters uninvolved in the behavior normally provide much more reliable and unbiased descriptions and judgments.

Second, Becker says that ratings of others are appropriate when other methods might "disrupt the process being studied." To illustrate: Suppose that you were interested in the degree of consensus exhibited by a discussion group from one minute to the next during the discussion. You would almost certainly "disrupt the process being studied" if you stopped the group after each minute of discussion, distributed to and had the members fill out self-report scales, then instructed them to resume the discussion. In general, measurement is better the more unobtrusive it is (Webb, Campbell, Schwartz,

& Sechrest, 1966). Rating scales, especially if what is being rated is on tape or in transcripts, provides very unobtrusive measurement.

We would add to Becker's two conditions that this kind of rating is also especially useful when, third, the variables of interest can be only vaguely defined ("attractiveness," "language intensity," "friendliness," "metaphoric quality"), or, fourth, the cost of more direct means of measurement (which often involves taping and transcribing material) exceeds the theoretical or methodological benefit to be gained by such laborious and time-consuming procedures.

Researchers have not been slow to recognize the appropriateness and efficiency of rating scales in certain kinds of research. Standard instruments have been devised for investigating such topics as qualities of feedback (Leathers, 1971), group productivity (Leathers, 1972), quality of group communication (Gouran, 1978), and communicator style (Norton, 1977), among many others.

Types of Scales

In this section, we will present some properties and assumptions of various types of scales, attending most closely to the types you are likely to use (Likert scales, and, especially, semantic differential scales), giving only passing attention to others.

Likert Scales

This type of scale is named for the psychologist, Rensis Likert, who introduced it as an alternative to the more tedious and time-consuming methods of rating then in use (Likert, 1932). Basically, a single Likert scale consists of a statement (usually—though not necessarily—of value or opinion rather than of fact), followed by a scale, usually consisting of five levels, on which the subject can indicate his or her agreement or disagreement with the statement. For example:

Current government policies are effective in curbing inflation.

_____ Strongly agree

_____ Agree

_____ Neither agree nor disagree

_____ Disagree

_____ Strongly disagree

You can add a "Very strongly agree" option to one end and a "Very strongly disagree" option to the other if you want a seven-level rather than a five-level scale. The format of such scales (e.g., whether the options are arranged vertically, as in our example, or horizontally) has very little effect on the validity and reliability of the measurements obtained.

Conventionally, these scales are scored by assigning "1" to one end of the scale (consistently so that, for example, if "Strongly disagree" indicated the same attitude on one item that "Strongly agree" indicated on another, "Strongly disagree" would be scored "1" on the first and "Strongly agree" would be scored "1" on the second) and "5" to the opposite end ("7" if you use seven-level scales), with those in between assigned in ascending order scores from 2 through 4 (or through 6 for seven-level scales). Then the scores from the set of scales representing all aspects of the attitude, judgment, or opinion, are summed. This sum represents the subject's position on the cognitive continuum of interest (probably, "attitude toward the current administration" for the example given).

The use of a sum from a number of scales as an index of cognitive state involves some assumptions, and you should test the accuracy of these assumptions in pilot studies if you can. First, the method assumes that all items on the test are *relevant* to the cognitive construct of interest. If any are irrelevant, the validity and reliability of the entire instrument will be damaged. Second, the method assumes that *each* item is *equally* representative of the cognitive construct being measured (Kerlinger, 1973). If you sum, you weight all items equally. If they should not all be weighted equally, then you should use a method other than summing. Third, the method assumes that the cognitive construct being investigated justifies the use of a number of summed scales. This assumption can be simply illustrated. If you were to measure a subject on a single five-level Likert scale, the score obviously would be between 1 and 5—and your maximum discrimination for a given subject would have only five levels. If you measured the same subject on the same cognitive construct with ten Likert scales, the score would be between 10 and 50, so that the potential for discrimination among positions on the continuum would have increased eightfold—from 5 for one scale to 41 for 10 scales.

We will not try to explain the procedures by which Likert scales are developed and tested. To discover those procedures, you should refer to Emmert (1970), Kerlinger (1973), and/or Nunnally (1978). You can find an account of Likert scaling in addition to interesting comparisons with other methods of scaling in Fishbein and Ajzen (1975). The last source named gives an excellent but succinct treatment of self-report measurement techniques generally.

Semantic Differential Scales

The most complete description and explanation of semantic differential scaling is located in Osgood, Suci, and Tannenbaum (1957). These researchers and various of their colleagues at the University of Illinois were interested in the concept "connotative meaning"—the affective or emotional meanings of words and other symbols.

To analyze the concept, Osgood and his associates carried out tests over a number of years. In these tests, subjects would be asked to rate a wide variety of concepts on a wide variety of bipolar adjectival scales. Examples of such scales are:

```
    good ____ : ____ : ____ : ____ : ____ : ____ : ____ bad
    tall ____ : ____ : ____ : ____ : ____ : ____ : ____ short
   sweet ____ : ____ : ____ : ____ : ____ : ____ : ____ sour
 sincere ____ : ____ : ____ : ____ : ____ : ____ : ____ insincere
```

By employing many scales, the researchers thought that they could come close to "exhausting" (or fully describing) the connotative meaning of the concepts tested.

Over the series of tests, Osgood et al. decided that the best form for a single scale was like the form just illustrated. A semantic differential scale, then, is a seven-level scale bounded by bipolar adjectives. Such a scale conventionally is scored by assigning "1" to what is often the "bad" end, "7" to what is often the "good" end, "4" to the middle (neutral or irrelevant) position, and "2," "3," "5," and "6" to other positions, following the same scheme.

Over many tests, using a statistical technique called factor analysis, the Illinois researchers discovered that, regardless of the concept being rated, the semantic differential scales tended to cluster together in predictable ways. Osgood et al. rather consistently isolated three factors, or dimensions of connotative meaning. They labeled these dimensions *evaluation, potency,* and *activity.* Examples of the particular scales characterizing each of the three dimensions follow:

> *Evaluation:* good/bad, fair/unfair, positive/negative, kind/cruel
> *Potency:* strong/weak, brave/cowardly, heavy/light, hard/soft
> *Activity:* vibrant/still, active/passive, hot/cold, tense/relaxed

Of the three dimensions of connotative meaning, evaluation accounted for by far the greatest variations in scales across concepts. In fact, in a later close look at Osgood et al.'s methods, Darnell (1970) cast serious question on the three-dimensional theory and argued, in effect, that *all* scales are evaluative but that for some scales the evaluative polarity shifts from concept to concept. For the concept "Mother," for example, "warm" probably would be the positive end of the scale "warm/cold." But for the concept "Ice Cream Cone," the "good" end of the same scale would probably be the "cold" end.

In spite of Darnell's and others' reservations about the theoretical foundations of semantic differential scaling, it has been and continues to be most useful in communication research (Snider & Osgood, 1969). Kerlinger (1973, p. 579) rightly asserts that the method is "flexible and relatively easy to adapt to varying research demands, quick and economical to administer and score." Nunnally (1978) describes the method as a "workhorse" for the social sciences.

The semantic differential's heavy weighting on evaluation makes the method a natural for the measurement of attitude. You can also choose adjectives to measure various other important constructs: intention to behave (likely/unlikely, probable/improbable); attitude toward one's own or another's behavior (wise/foolish, prudent/imprudent, cautious/foolhardy); and many others.

The Camille Benton Rowe Studies.   In one series of studies, Camille Benton Rowe, while an undergraduate at the University of Iowa, used the method to measure the connotative dimensions of selected display typefaces and to test the appropriateness of various typefaces in the headlines above articles with different kinds of content. (These studies are partially reported in Rowe, 1982.) Rowe asked subjects to rate ten different typefaces, highly varied in density and form, on 26 semantic differential scales. Factor analysis resulted in her decision to discard eight of the scales and to cluster the others in five dimensions. She named the dimensions (1) *potency,* characterized by scales including hard/soft, constrained/free, strong/weak, dark/light, masculine/feminine, rugged/delicate, tight/loose; (2) *elegance,* characterized by scales including rich/poor, beautiful/ugly, expensive/cheap, meaningful/meaningless; (3) *novelty,* characterized by scales including simple/complex, legible/illegible, usual/unusual; *antiquity,* characterized by the scales old/new and old-fashioned/modern; and (5) *evaluation,* characterized by the scales good/bad and dirty/clean.

As a result of this first study, Rowe was able to chart the position of each of the ten typefaces tested on each of the five dimensions of connotative meaning. She could then characterize the connotative meaning of each typeface. For example:

"Excelsior Script" was perceived as the least potent of the typefaces. It also connotes elegance, slight novelty, slight antiquity, and a slightly positive evaluation. Next to Cloister Black, Excelsior Script was the most connotatively distinguishable of the typefaces.

She was also able to assert that five of the ten typefaces tested did *not* differ significantly in their connotations.

In a second study, using the sum of the same semantic differential scales (now organized into dimensions), Rowe had subjects rate the "most appropriate and least appropriate headline typefaces" for each of two magazine articles—one with "romantic" content, the other with "practical" content. In this study, subjects marked *two* blanks on each scale, one for the position that they thought represented the *most* appropriate headline for a particular article, the other for the position that they thought represented the *least* appropriate headline for that article. This procedure is analogous to that recommended by Darnell (1970).

Rowe was able to conclude that different typefaces were considered appropriate (and inappropriate) to the two kinds of content. An appropriate headline for a romantic article would be in a typeface that is slightly elegant, more usual than novel, and neither potent nor impotent. For a practical article, the appropriate typeface would be potent, slightly elegant, and definitely not novel.

The Gouran, Brown, and Henry Study. For a much different purpose, Gouran, Brown, and Henry (1978) used the semantic differential method as a tool in an investigation of the relationship between communicative behavior and "quality" of discussion in policy groups. They devised seventeen semantic differential scales, somewhat different in format from Rowe's.

Eight scales were used to measure the "quality" of the discussions:

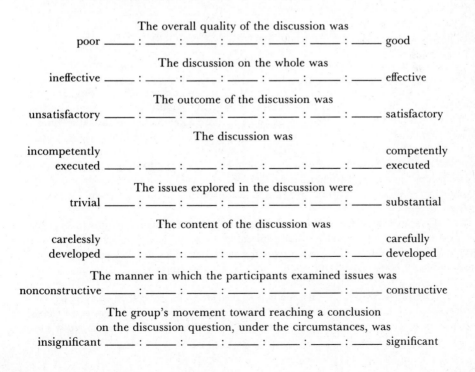

The overall quality of the discussion was

poor ____ : ____ : ____ : ____ : ____ : ____ : ____ good

The discussion on the whole was

ineffective ____ : ____ : ____ : ____ : ____ : ____ : ____ effective

The outcome of the discussion was

unsatisfactory ____ : ____ : ____ : ____ : ____ : ____ : ____ satisfactory

The discussion was

incompetently executed ____ : ____ : ____ : ____ : ____ : ____ : ____ competently executed

The issues explored in the discussion were

trivial ____ : ____ : ____ : ____ : ____ : ____ : ____ substantial

The content of the discussion was

carelessly developed ____ : ____ : ____ : ____ : ____ : ____ : ____ carefully developed

The manner in which the participants examined issues was

nonconstructive ____ : ____ : ____ : ____ : ____ : ____ : ____ constructive

The group's movement toward reaching a conclusion
on the discussion question, under the circumstances, was

insignificant ____ : ____ : ____ : ____ : ____ : ____ : ____ significant

Gouran et al. used nine scales in the same format to measure behavior (or, rather, *perceptions* of behavior) in the discussion groups:

The behavior of the group was

not goal
directed ___ : ___ : ___ : ___ : ___ : ___ : ___ goal directed

The participants initiated discussion on

irrelevant
issues ___ : ___ : ___ : ___ : ___ : ___ : ___ relevant issues

The participants' contributions were

poorly
amplified ___ : ___ : ___ : ___ : ___ : ___ : ___ well amplified

The participation in the discussion was

unevenly
distributed ___ : ___ : ___ : ___ : ___ : ___ : ___ evenly distributed

The positions taken in the discussion were

undocumented ___ : ___ : ___ : ___ : ___ : ___ : ___ documented

Ideas expressed in the discussion were

uncritically
examined ___ : ___ : ___ : ___ : ___ : ___ : ___ critically examined

The participants dealt with issues

unsystematically ___ : ___ : ___ : ___ : ___ : ___ : ___ systematically

The interpersonal relationships among the participants appeared to be
unhealthy ___ : ___ : ___ : ___ : ___ : ___ : ___ healthy

The functions of leadership in the discussion were

poorly
served ___ : ___ : ___ : ___ : ___ : ___ : ___ well served

You may have noted that, although the Gouran et al. scales are "bipolar," they are not all "adjectival." This illustrates the very great flexibility of the semantic differential method. Not all descriptive words and terms are adjectives. You should feel free to use the method (as many researchers have) in ways that go beyond its original intent.

You should also note that, ideally, "behavior" ought to be analyzed by observational methods. But to operationalize such behaviors as "healthy interpersonal relationships" in an observational framework would be very laborious (though it probably ought to be done by someone sometime). Rating scales provide a viable, informative alternative.

Gouran et al. concluded from their study that the behavioral measures as predictor variables did a reasonable job of explaining "quality" in the policy discussions. In their particular sample, the best predictors were the scales for "relevance of issues," "handling of issues," "amplification," and "goal directedness."

The Liska Study.   In a methodological study, Liska (1978) used the semantic differential method to provide evidence that the criteria people use to assess the "credibility" of a communicator change from situation to situation. We cite the study as an excuse for providing an extensive array of semantic differential scales. We do not present the array because we advocate that you use these particular scales. Rather, we hope that the length and variety of the list will convince you that you can think of scales appropriate to your particular research problems. Following is a *partial* list of the scales Liska employed:

> absolute/relative, open/closed, probable/improbable, suave/gauche, large/small, active/passive, ugly/beautiful, loud/soft, sociable/antisocial, straight/crooked, affectionate/distant, enthusiastic/bored, concerned/unconcerned, rough/smooth, fast/slow, good/bad, usual/unusual, grateful/ungrateful, gullible/skeptical, educated/uneducated, amusing/serious, hysterical/calm, contented/discontented, positive/negative, random/systematic, certain/uncertain, safe/risky, clean/dirty, hard/soft, mature/immature, sweet/sour, eccentric/conventional, long/short, feasible/not feasible, kind/cruel, elegant/sloppy, early/late, wise/foolish, authoritarian/democratic, rash/cautious, happy/sad, empty/full, concise/diffuse, pursuing/avoiding, miserly/generous, personal/impersonal, dependent/independent, hot/cold, sensitive/callous, important/unimportant, consistent/inconsistent, light/dark, outgoing/reserved, orderly/disorderly, motivated/unmotivated, experienced/inexperienced, sophisticated/naive, clever/dull, male/female, black/white, complex/simple, awkward/graceful, stable/changeable, rich/poor, overstated/understated, theoretical/practical, articulate/inarticulate, abstract/concrete, overt/covert, sharp/dull, private/public, severe/lenient, fact/fiction, proud/humble, impulsive/deliberate, plain/ornate, high/low, fortunate/unfortunate.

The semantic differential method is indeed a workhorse for communication research. It is a flexible, elegant, easily used tool that can fit virtually any research problem in which perceptions, cognitions, and judgments are important variables. Although it may not map semantic space in as simple a way as its authors first proposed, it probably constitutes the best way to assess the connotative meaning of a concept to a person. As with all other measuring instruments, of course, the validity of any particular set of semantic differential scales depends on the fidelity with which the conceptual definition of a variable is matched with its operational definition.

Other Scaling Methods

The Likert and semantic differential methods of rating are the most widely used in communication research. Many alternative methods exist, however, and have from time to time been used to investigate human communication. We will discuss briefly four of these alternatives: Thurstone scaling, Guttman scaling, multidimensional scaling, and Q-technique.

Thurstone Scaling.   This method was first proposed in Thurstone and Chave (1929), but you can find additional details on its development in Thurstone (1931), Fishbein and Ajzen (1975), and Bailey (1978). The basic goal of the Thurstone method is to develop an "equal-appearing" interval scale. The initial step is to generate a large number of belief and intentional statements about a given attitude object. These items should be varied highly in their degree of presumed favorableness toward the object. A group of judges then considers the set of items, placing each item in one of eleven categories, ranging from "quite favorable" to "quite unfavorable." Once the judging is completed, the researcher discards all items about which the judges expressed disagreement or which are apparently irrelevant to attitude. From this "scaled" (from quite favorable to quite unfavorable) pool of items, a smaller number, usually about twenty, is selected. If the procedure is properly performed, the researcher assumes that the result is a unidimensional attitude scale for that particular attitude object. In scoring, each item is weighted by its judged degree of favorableness or unfavorableness toward the attitude object.

The obvious disadvantage of the Thurstone method is the excessive time and effort required to develop one scale for one attitude object. In other words, the effort is costly, and the cost is often unjustified by the outcome. This drawback to the method prompted Likert to develop his method of summated ratings.

Guttman Scaling.   Guttman's basic idea was to develop a perfect "cumulative" scale (Edwards, 1949; Guttman, 1949). The researcher tries to array a set of belief or intentional items according to their degree of favorableness toward an attitude object. If the items are arrayed cumulatively, every subject will agree with the items up to a certain point (representing his or her attitude) and will disagree with all items beyond that point.

To illustrate by analogy: Imagine that you were trying to develop a Guttman scale of physical strength. You might arrange various weights, similar in size and shape, weighing 30, 50, 100, 120, and 200 pounds, respectively. (Notice that this scale—like all Guttman scales—is ordinal, not interval. We will explain this distinction in Chapter 6.) You would then ask subjects to lift each weight, starting with the lightest, until they came to one that was too heavy. If a subject were unable to lift the 100-pound weight, you could legitimately assume that he or she had reached a limit—that the same subject would be unable to lift the 120-pound weight or the 200-pound weight. You could also assume that the same subject would be able to lift any weight *under* 100 pounds that you might want to add to the scale of weights.

If you substitute belief statements for weights, you can similarly construct a Guttman scale for attitude. The process is somewhat like Thurstone scaling, for a group of judges initially scales the items. The researcher then arrays the items in order of favorableness, and subjects make a dichotomous choice—agree or disagree—on each item. The scale assumes that subjects will agree with items up to a certain point (e.g., item number 5), and then will disagree with the remainder. The subject in the example would receive a score of "5" on the scale.

Like the Thurstone method, the Guttman method requires large amounts of time and effort with the result being only one attitude scale for one attitude object. Also, mistakes during scale development, especially in the judging phase, will render the scale less than cumulative and therefore, given its assumptions, useless.

Multidimensional Scaling (MDS).   Traditionally, theorists have thought of attitudes as unidimensional, and many of the methods of rating them have proceeded from that assumption. Some researchers, especially recent ones, have conceived of cognitive concepts and constructs, including attitude, as multidimensional. Furthermore, the multiple perceptions involved in cognitive concepts and structures may be related to each other in any number of complex ways. The availability of computers has enabled these researchers to operationalize their multidimensional assumptions.

Again, we will illustrate by analogy. Imagine a clear plastic ball filled with a clear gelatinous substance. Suspended in the substance are ten marbles. These marbles can move inside the ball, but only if an outside force is exerted. Shake the ball and allow the substance and the marbles to settle. You will see that the marbles have formed patterns within the ball. If you rotate the ball slowly, you will be able, by constantly comparing your perceptions of the patterns, to settle on one description of them that you think is most complete and elegant. What you are viewing and interpreting are ten marbles suspended in multidimensional (or Euclidean) space.

Assume that the space within the ball represents a person's attitude toward birth control. Assume that each marble represents a salient perception by an individual relevant to that attitude. Some of the concepts about which the individual has perceptions might be: birth control pill; spouse's attitude; religious beliefs; doctor bills; money; babies; health; law. And one marble represents "me" as a concept. (See Woelfel, Cody, Gillham, & Holmes, 1980.)

Once the salient concepts are defined, you can meaningfully interpret the array within the space. Each perception can be distanced from each other perception, and the relative distance can be taken to define the degree of relatedness of the perceptions. A crucial distance is that between the concept "me" and each other concept. These distances are taken to represent the salience of a given perception to the individual's attitude. With this approach, you can interpret an individual's attitude as the entire multidimensional array of perceptions relevant to that attitude rather than as a single score on a unidimensional scale.

Many of the concepts involved in MDS (multidimensional scaling) are too complex for treatment in an introductory book like this one. We encourage you to consult Fishbein and Ajzen (1975) for a fairly elementary introduction, Nunnally (1978) for a thorough but nonmathematical account, and Woelfel and others (Gillham & Woelfel, 1977; Woelfel, 1980; Woelfel, Cody, Gillham, & Holmes, 1980; Woelfel & Danes, 1980) for applications of MDS in communication research.

Q-Technique. Q-Technique (Stephenson, 1953) is a method by which individuals sort themselves (with the help of statistics) into cognitive types.

First, the researcher generates a large number of statements relative to a concept or attitude object. Then each subject sorts the statements according to some criterion specified by the researcher (often, extent of agreement or disagreement). Commonly, the individual is required to sort the statements into some particular distribution specified by the researcher.

For example, as a subject in such a study you might be given, in random order, a set of thirty evaluative statements about "situation comedies on prime-time television." You might be asked to sort the statements as follows: two in the "strongly disagree" pile; five in the "disagree" pile; seven in the "slightly disagree" pile; eleven in the "neutral or irrelevant" pile; seven in the "slightly agree" pile; five in the "moderately agree" pile; and two in the "strongly agree" pile.

The researcher would then assign each item a score, depending on which pile you put it on. A rather elaborate statistical program, which normally requires the use of a computer, would then process the sorting patterns of all subjects in the study and define "types" of sorters—groups who cluster in the strength of their agreement and/or disagreement on certain items. One type, for example, might be "those who agree with favorable statements about situation comedies with female stars and disagree with unfavorable statements about situation comedies starring young children." Typically, the researcher would then invent an interpretive label for each type isolated. We leave it to you to invent a label for the type described in the example.

■ *Conclusion*

In what way is the relationship of the semantic differential to communication research similar to the relationship of this chapter to this book? . . . Right. Both are workhorses. We have here been concerned with paper-and-pencil tests, self-report measures of other kinds, and rating scales. These matters are of interest to social science generally. We have from time to time indicated that many of these kinds of measures are not central to research on communication. Personality traits and situational states, for example, interest communication theorists only to the extent that they can be related systematically to communicative behavior. But some of the measures we have discussed *are* of central interest, for reliable ratings provide one efficient way of describing communicative behavior.

Chapter 6

Levels of Measurement, Reliability, and Validity

Much of what interests researchers in communication has to do with what goes on in people's heads—their conceptual schemes, their perceptions, and their judgments. To the extent that these internal events influence the way people use symbols, the communication theorist must take them into account. This point has been made persuasively by Delia (1977).

But internal events are not accessible to direct observation and measurement. They are matters for inference. In the preceding chapters, we have discussed a number of methods by which such internal events may be inferred. In this chapter, we will attend to certain concepts of measurement that are especially important to these methods. We will assign space to concepts roughly in proportion to our judgment about the importance of the concepts. Some distinctions (for example, among "Levels of Measurement") have been important to the history of communication research and theory, but are less important today. We introduce these distinctions because you probably would be unable to participate in some conversations among literate social scientists if you were unaware of them. But you probably will not make direct use of the distinctions in your own work.

A restroom philosopher once scribbled: "Any idea that can be put in a nutshell probably deserves to be there." The idea of "measurement" may be one of the exceptions to the rule. Although hundreds of books and articles have been written on the concept, it can be put in a nutshell. Measurement consists of the rule-governed process of "assigning numbers to objects in such a way as to represent quantities of attributes" (Nunnally, 1978, p. 3).

Certain terms in the definition deserve amplification. The phrase *rule-governed* refers to the kinds of "correspondence rules" we discussed earlier, when we were concerned with operationalization. These rules are designed to connect the conceptual meanings of variables to the empirical (or operational) observations of those variables. They comprise sets of directions for measuring something in such a way that its conceptualization is not violated. In reports of research, these correspondence rules are more often implicit than explicit.

These rules are used to assign numbers that represent "quantities of attributes" of objects. Researchers do not measure objects. They measure characteristics or qualities, or, globally, *attributes* of objects. Unfortunately, in everyday talk this fact is sometimes overlooked. You probably would say about a friend, "She is intelligent" or "She is charming," not "She possesses quite a lot of the attribute of intelligence" or "She rates high on the charmingness scale." This discrepancy between everyday talk and the reality of social science sometimes results in unwarranted criticism of social scientists. They do *not* reduce human beings to a set of numbers. They *do* sometimes try to develop ways to measure certain conceptually defined attributes of human beings.

And what sorts of things might we mean by "quantities" of attributes? We are very liberal in response to the question: What is a quantity? Some methodologists are conservative. They might distinguish between "qualitative" and "quantitative" research. In "qualitative" research, they would say, numbers are not used to represent "quantity" but rather to represent mere presence or absence of a "quality." In a quasi-experimental study, for example, you might assign a "0" to "biological males" and a "1" to "biological females." A conservative would say that these numbers are merely used as labels, not as quantities.

We liberals would reply that "presence" and "absence" are, at a rudimentary level, measurements of quantity. "Something" is different quantitatively from "nothing," and the difference can be indicated by the difference between "0" and "1" or by the difference between any other two numbers. (Sometimes the definitions of *something* and *nothing* are arbitrary, as when "femaleness" is assigned a score of 1, "maleness," a score of 0.) Numbers used like labels can enter into statistical regularities, can sometimes be averaged, and can often be used to predict numbers measuring other attributes. Whether such "qualitative" numbers are used appropriately or not depends on individual researchers and the way they operationalize their particular research variables. But we fail to see any very important difference, insofar as research methods are concerned, between "qualitative" variables and "quantitative" ones. In our extended example of survey methods, for example, "academic major" would have been labeled by some a "qualitative" variable. But the students who did that study were able to use the variable to predict the probability of various other variables that were more clearly "quantitative"—including extent of knowledge about clustering, extent of use of the clustering strategy, etc.

Other levels of measurement are more precise about quantity, so that the question becomes *how much* of some attribute is present, not merely *is* the attribute present. In the section that follows, we will discuss this distinction in more detail; then we will return to the liberal-conservative controversy. Other sections will describe characteristic uses of scales and of other paper-and-pencil instruments, outline traditional distinctions among types of scales, and discuss the important concepts "reliability" and "validity."

Levels of Measurement

A conservative methodologist, S. S. Stevens (1951), among others, asserts that four basic levels of measurement can be distinguished. Each level is "higher" than the level that precedes it in that each includes all the mathematical properties of the previous (so-called) lower level, while adding some new properties of its own. We will discuss these traditional levels sympathetically, but we will be unable to resist an expression of our liberalism from time to time.

Nominal Level

As its name suggests, nominal measurement is concerned with naming things. It places objects into mutually exclusive and exhaustive categories according to some characteristic of the objects. As we indicated earlier, "0" for "male" and "1" for "female" are nominal measurements. The numbers mean no more than "M" or "F" would. In many of our examples of observational studies, measurement was nominal. A statement might be "dominant" (1), "submissive" (-1), or "neither" (0). A frame in the Sunday comics might show "action" (1) or "nonaction" (0). A sentence in the Black Panther publication might be "aggressive" (1) or "nonaggressive" (0).

Other examples of the nominal level include social security numbers, numbers on athletic uniforms, indications of marital status, etc. Categories are named and thereby distinguished from each other. Sometimes, we substitute numbers for names. But the numbers, if used nominally, merely indicate the presence or the absence of some quality. They do not represent *amount* of that quality.

Conservatives therefore deny nominal variables the status of "quantitative." They claim that numbers used as labels do not behave like numbers at all. Technically, any attempt to add, subtract, multiply, or divide them would result in nonsense. (What does the difference between two social security numbers *mean?*)

The liberal position, as we will show later, accepts the conservative position for numbers that have *only* a naming function, as a social security number has. But many numbers used to name categories can also enter into meaningful relationships. For example, if you think that women are more likely to use eye contact when listening than men are, you might assign each woman in your sample the number *1,* each man the number *0,* measure "eye contact while listening" in seconds, and test for a direct relationship between "womanness" (measured at two "levels," 1 and 0) and "eye contact while listening." Although, strictly speaking, the numbers *1* and *0* are nominal as we have used them here, they are also something more than nominal if they can be used as quantitative predictors. The liberal feels free to use nominal numbers, recognizing their limitations, as though they were "real" numbers whenever necessary in the search for "quantitative" relationships that are theoretically interesting.

Ordinal Level

Ordinal measurement is analagous to ranking. Its categories go beyond the nominal in that they imply "more" or "less" of the attribute of interest, not merely the "presence" or "absence" of that attribute. In ordinal measurement, however, the researcher cannot say *how much* more or *how much* less of the attribute is represented by the various categories.

Communication research abounds with ordinal measurement. Credibility, attractiveness, homophily, etc., are routinely categorized as "high" and "low," or, sometimes, "high," "medium," and "low." If categories can be rank-ordered in terms of an attribute, the researcher can claim to have an ordinal "scale" of measurement.

But is it a "scale"? The concept "scale" implies that underlying the rank-ordering is a continuum of quantity of the attribute being ranked. Hence, if you categorize communicators as more or less "attractive," you must assume that these two categories ("more" and "less") lie *somewhere* on a scale by which "attractiveness" is scored. (What is a single unit of attractiveness? Of cohesiveness? Of credibility?) In ordinal measurement, the researcher either claims that the attribute in question has no such scale or that the units of the scale cannot be ascertained. Therefore, if an ideal kind of scaled continuum exists, the researcher has no way of discovering for his or her categories their exact position in relation to each other—except for "more" or "less."

These limitations of ordinal measurement produce some problems for communication research. Perhaps the most important group of problems stems from the fact that ordinal measurement does not permit knowledge about the size of the *intervals* among ordinal categories. Groups that are "high," "medium," and "low" in cohesiveness are different—but *how much* different? When a theorist tries to generalize from one study to another, those theoretical efforts might be stymied by ordinal measurement. Categories from one research report to another may shift their positions on the underlying scale but not change their names, so that one study's "low" credibility might be another's "medium" credibility. This kind of shifting definition can be a theorist's nightmare. For example, such shifts have been problematic in the study of proxemics (the effects of distances on communicative behavior), where "near" and "far" have been defined in widely differing ways and the consequences for generalizations about interpersonal distances and maintenance of eye contact have been confusing, to put it mildly.

Conservatives claim that, because the intervals among levels of an ordinal variable are unknown, certain mathematical operations do not make sense. Liberals recognize the danger but use the mathematical operations anyway for the purposes of doing certain kinds of statistical analyses.

Interval Level

Interval measurement, like ordinal measurement, asserts that various categories represent "more" or "less" of an attribute. But interval measurement also asserts that, in units of some kind, *how much* more or *how much* less can be specified. That is, interval measurement asserts the existence for practical purposes of a scale of measurement in which level 1 is as much less than level 2 as level 2 is less than level 3, etc. The intervals among units on the scale are equal. For interval measurement, the zero point may be arbitrary (zero does not necessarily represent "none of" the attribute), so that values of the attribute on the scale may be negative.

Probably the most easily available and understood example of interval measurement is temperature, conventionally measured. The measurement is in degrees, arbitrarily defined as the expansion of mercury (or some other substance) as it is heated a certain amount. The zero point is also arbitrary, and certainly does not imply "no temperature." But the numbers can be manipulated meaningfully as numbers. They can be added, subtracted, multiplied, and divided. Most social scientists find this kind of manipulability useful and assume that their measurements, somehow or other, meet the requirements of an interval scale. As we will try to show later, no good reason prevents them from making that assumption.

Ratio Level

The "highest" level of measurement is ratio measurement. Ratio scales, like interval scales, possess a common and constant unit of measurement, and thus the distance between any two points on the scale can be calculated in such a way that the same distance between any other two points has the same meaning. In addition, a ratio scale's zero point is not arbitrary. Zero literally means "none of" the attribute being measured.

The existence of a "true" zero point gives a ratio scale two properties. First, entities measured on the scale cannot have negative values. (How can something have less than "none" of something?) Second, no matter what unit of measurement is used, the ratio between two particular points on the scale will not change. For example, "age," a ratio scale, can be unitized in terms of years or months. The ratio of ten years to five years is two—the same as the ratio between the same points specified as 120 months and 60 months. More generally, any mathematical operation (adding, subtracting, multiplying, dividing) of points on the scale by the same positive number will leave unchanged the properties of the *scale* (that is, the relation of the points to each other).

Two types of data qualify unquestionably as ratio data. Tukey (1977) calls these types "amounts and counts." *Amounts* are ratio measures of "how much" of something an object possesses. Familiar examples are age, weight, height, income, and so on. *Counts* are frequencies: How often has something occurred? Measurement of frequencies is fairly common in communication research: number of smiles in a given period of interaction; number of solutions to a problem proposed by a group; number of disfluencies by a speaker. And the list could go on indefinitely. What these variables have in common and what qualifies them as ratio scales is that zero means no behavior of the type in question and that each unit, a single occurrence, is common and constant as a unit of measurement.

The "Weak" Versus "Strong" Measurement Controversy

You should understand that the controversy between conservatives and liberals has a basis in logic, though many researchers pay little attention to it in practice. You might violate certain assumptions about the appropriate use of numbers and of certain statistics—but you should do so from a basis of information, not ignorance.

To briefly extend the argument: Conservatives hold that the four levels of measurement constitute "weak" and "strong" measurement. Nominal and ordinal numbers are "weak"; interval and ratio numbers are "strong." "Weak" numbers operate more like labels than like numbers; "strong" numbers and only "strong" numbers should be manipulated with the use of normal mathematics and of certain kinds of statistics.

The dichotomy is problematic for researchers because, given the conservative position, most common statistical procedures could not be applied to data that, in a purist's view, would be nominal or ordinal. (These statistics are called "parametric" statistics, for they include assumptions about "parameters," or, in a sense, idealized distributions of numbers given an infinite set of numbers.)

An example will illustrate the point. Assume that, for whatever reason, you want to ascertain attitudes from a certain sample toward "the president of the United States." An easy, efficient way to get an indication of such attitudes is to ask respondents to check a scale like the following:

the president of the United States

bad _____ : _____ : _____ : _____ : _____ : _____ : _____ good

You decide to "score" the scale by assigning "1" to the leftmost blank, "7" to the rightmost, and "4" to the middle (or "neutral") blank, and "2," "3," "5," and "6" appropriately to the other blanks.

These data depend on perceptions, including evaluations. You cannot *prove* that the interval between "1" and "2" is the same distance as that between "4" and "5," so you cannot be confident that what you have is an interval scale. You cannot prove it because perceptions, including evaluations, are not susceptible to direct physical measurement. But you probably would not encounter much argument if you called it an ordinal scale. All you would have to do is give evidence that your respondents considered rightward marks on the scale to indicate more favorable attitudes than leftward marks.

Now suppose that you request 100 people, selected at random, to fill out this scale. When you began to analyze these data, your first question probably would be: What is the average attitude of the people in this sample toward the president of the United States? The most common way to answer this question, and the way that is most useful statistically, is to calculate as "average" the arithmetic mean of the scores in the sample: to add the 100 scores together and divide the sum by 100. But a conservative would not permit you to do this. Because you do not *know* that the data fit the requirements of interval measurement, you cannot appropriately add them together, much less divide into them.

You could find alternative averages that are appropriate for ordinal measurement. In ordinal measurement, a common average is the median (the "score" with an equal number of scores above or below it). In nominal measurement, a common average is the mode (the most frequently marked "score"). But the mean, and certain assumptions about the distribution of scores around the mean, are at the heart of most traditional and familiar statistics. If you are not permitted to calculate a mean, then you must settle for alternate statistics. And these alternative, "nonparametric" statistics, tend to be less powerful means of generalizing, especially for complex experimental, quasi-experimental, and mixed designs, than are their parametric counterparts.

Liberals use parametric statistics unless their data provide them with very strong reasons *not* to. Anderson (1961) seriously and Lord (1953) wittily have given detailed defenses of the liberal position. Liberals tend not to demand proof that a scale has properties of an interval scale if the numbers resulting from that scale look anything like the distribution assumed by parametric statistics. Liberals recognize that statistics, like numbers and other concepts such as "scales," are human inventions for human use. No divine statistician marked an infallible boundary between nominal and ordinal or between ordinal and interval scales. Furthermore, empirical studies have shown that even rather serious violations of the assumptions of interval measurement and of parametric statistics do not unduly affect the outcome—the accuracy of generalization—of those statistics. Parametric statistics are "robust," strong enough to handle many kinds of scales.

We will have much to say about parametric statistics in subsequent chapters. When you have read those chapters and tried to apply the procedures described, you will understand better the conservative-liberal controversy. We encourage you to be liberal—but to recognize *what* liberal things you are doing and *why* you are doing them.

Reliability and Validity

Until this point, we have referred to the important concepts "reliability" and "validity" only in passing. We have reserved a more complete discussion for this chapter partly because commonsense explanations seemed to suffice for earlier chapters and partly because these two concepts make a rather neat bridge between the conceptual material we have covered up to now and the more technical, statistical operationalizations of those concepts we will discuss in Chapters 8–14.

Both concepts require full and explicit treatment if their importance is to be adequately appreciated. The treatment we offer, though it might be too simple for the tastes of a highly sophisticated methodologist, is, we hope, adequate to the purposes of an introductory book. The task of writing such a treatment requires the synthesis of literally hundreds of books and articles on these topics. We have tried to make the synthesis particularly relevant to communication research.

Our discussion will be nonmathematical, in the main, although we will introduce a few formulas relevant to reliability. Candidly, our attempt to be nonmathematical raises an explanatory obstacle or two. Discussions of reliability often depend heavily on the "theory of measurement error," and that theory has a decidedly mathematical flavor. Sometimes, a formula can be worth a thousand words, or at least a few hundred. If you consider yourself ready for a more technical explanation, we encourage you to read Guilford (1954) and Nunnally (1978).

Reliability

Every discussion of reliability like this one is based on a premise: *Measurement in the social sciences is subject to a certain degree of error.* The particular degree of error, of course, depends largely on the type of measurement attempted. If measurement procedures are simple and the things to be measured are relatively concrete, errors are likely to be so small that they will not affect either statistical tests or the generalizations based on those tests. If you are simply counting the frequency of the pronoun *I* in a number of texts, nobody is likely to worry much about the reliability of your measurement.

But conversely, as concepts or constructs to be measured become more abstract, as measurement procedures increase in complexity, and/or as respondents are asked to make more subjective or complicated judgments, the error component of measurement tends to increase. You must attend to this as a problem, for, as Kerlinger (1973, p. 473) writes:

> There is growing understanding that all *measuring instruments must be critically and empirically examined for their reliability and validity. The day of tolerance of inadequate measurement has ended.*

We will return shortly to the concept of reliability as degree of error. For the moment, we will take a more commonsense view. When we attach the adjective *reliable* to a measurement instrument or procedure, we generally refer to one of two related meanings (Kerlinger, 1973). The first is that the measurements obtained by the use of a given instrument or procedure are *stable*—consistent across *time*. Hence, an instrument or procedure would be stable if, for example, the same attribute of the same subject were measured by it at various times and if those various measurements were consistent. The instrument or procedure would also be stable if the various measurements were inconsistent but the inconsistencies could be shown to have been caused by actual changes in the concept being measured rather than by random fluctuation in the performance of the instrument or procedure.

The second meaning frequently attached to reliable measurement is that it is *accurate* measurement. At any given time, the instrument or procedure exhibits little error. Stated differently, an instrument or procedure can be said to be reliable in the sense of accuracy if the several items or several observers used to measure it can be shown to be *internally consistent*—which constitutes evidence that they are measuring the same phenomenon.

Of the two meanings, the second is most important. If measurement of an unchanging construct at a given time is accurate, it follows that measurement at various times will be stable. Accordingly, estimates of reliability in communication research have tended to stress accuracy rather than stability.

Now we will return to the more technical concept, "degree of error." If measurement implies some error, then the score that a rater or procedure assigns a subject or phenomenon for a given instrument consists of two parts: the "true" score and an "error" component. Note that we do not imply by the word *error* that the *subject* or the *phenomenon* has committed an error. The word refers to imperfection in the measurement instrument or procedure.

A very simple equation in which X represents a score models this concept:

$$\text{Total } X = \text{True } X + \text{Error } X \tag{6.1}$$

The error component is a random component. It does not vary systematically with the attribute or phenomenon being measured. It may be a function of any number of forces over which the researcher has no control: weather, health of the rater or respondent, emotional state of the rater or respondent, fatigue, idiosyncratic definitions or odd use of language, etc. Over a large number of measurements of the same attribute or phenomenon, these random forces tend to balance themselves out so that their effect becomes negligible. In fact, the average or mean value of many repeated measures is sometimes taken to be a reliable estimate of an attribute or phenomenon that in a single measure is prone to considerable error.

The "true" score is assumed to be the score which would be obtained if all conditions were perfect. Such a score would be obtained if (1) the measurement instrument were internally perfect in all respects, and (2) no external forces caused fluctuation in the behavior of a particular subject or phenomenon. In practice, these conditions apparently are an unattainable ideal.

In fact, evidence of reliability cannot be deduced for a single score obtained on a single occasion. Instead, social scientists work with entire samples of scores.

The first step is to calculate the total *variance* of the sample of scores. The formula for calculating variance will be presented in Chapter 8, and for the moment we will continue to define it as the "spread" or "dispersion" of scores around a center point, usually the arithmetic mean. Unless each member of the sample has exactly the same score (in which case no variance exists), you will be able to calculate variance as a statistic.

In actual practice, variance will always be a real positive number (e.g., 6.73 or 22.87). For some purposes, this number will be useful, but for the present explanation it is not. For the moment, we will simply refer to the overall, total dispersion of scores around the mean as total variance.

Now we are in a position to define reliability more technically. Reliability is that proportion of the total variance that is "true" variance—that is, reliability is that proportion of the total variance that is a function of actual variation in the attribute or phenomenon being measured. In the formulas that follow, we will refer to this part of the Total Variance as True Variance. The rest of the variance, we will call Error Variance.

The information in all these words can be reduced greatly in a basic formula, where "rel" stands for "reliability":

$$\text{rel} = \frac{\text{True Variance}}{\text{Total Variance}} \tag{6.2}$$

Eq. 6.2 represents reliability as a simple proportion or ratio of the true variance to the total variance. If we include one additional fact about variance, this formula can be expanded in some meaningful ways. Recall that in Eq. 6.1, we asserted that a subject's total score was the result of adding together two other scores: the True Score (True X) and the Error Score (Error X). Similarly, the total *variance* of a *sample* of scores is the combination of the variance of the true scores and the variance of the error scores. Because the formulas will now begin to be awkwardly long if we continue to spell everything out, we will now begin to abbreviate "variance" as "Var":

$$\text{Total Var} = \text{True Var} + \text{Error Var} \tag{6.3}$$

Eq. 6.3 suggests that the total variance is the sum of two independent (that is, unrelated or uncorrelated) components. The sum of two independent parts equals the whole.

By a few simple algebraic manipulations using Eqs. 6.2 and 6.3 as a basis, we can devise two more ways to calculate reliability. Recall Eq. 6.2:

$$\text{rel} = \frac{\text{True Var}}{\text{Total Var}}$$

But recall also that, algebraically manipulating Eq. 6.3:

$$\text{True Var} = \text{Total Var} - \text{Error Var}$$

Therefore,

$$\text{rel} = \frac{\text{Total Var} - \text{Error Var}}{\text{Total Var}} \tag{6.4}$$

Also, if we assume that perfect reliability would be indicated by a reliability of 1.00 (that is, the true variance and the total variance are identical), then Eq. 6.5 models still another method for obtaining the reliability of a sample of scores:

$$\text{rel} = \frac{\text{Total Var} - \text{Error Var}}{\text{Total Var}}$$

$$= \frac{\text{Total Var}}{\text{Total Var}} - \frac{\text{Error Var}}{\text{Total Var}}$$

$$= 1 - \frac{\text{Error Var}}{\text{Total Var}} \tag{6.5}$$

The bottom line of Eq. 6.5 suggests that reliability is the difference between perfect reliability (1.00) and the proportion of error variance that exists in the obtained measurements. Thus, the smaller the proportion of error, the higher (and for reliability, higher is better) the reliability. Although Eqs. 6.3, 6.4, and 6.5 look different, you can easily prove (either through algebra, as we have done, or by playing with various numbers) that each produces exactly the same reliability coefficient.

From this description and these formulas, we can make an important point. Earlier, we equated "reliability" with "accuracy." This equivalence is vividly (well, . . . convincingly) illustrated in Eq. 6.5, where reliability is explicitly defined as discrepancy from perfect measurement. Precise, careful, accurate measurement, therefore, will result in variance due to the dispersion of *true* scores rather than to the dispersion of uncontrollable, random, *error* scores. We have repeatedly asserted that statistical procedures are intended to account for the variance among scores. If a large part of each score is "error"—and therefore random, by definition unexplainable—no theory of communication, no matter how conceptually accurate, can explain the variance in a distribution of those scores. Hence, reliable measurement is basic to the responsible testing of theory.

This description of reliability should serve as the foundation for understanding how the concept is used in communication research. The concept is frequently applied to two domains of measurement: (1) the reliability of paper-and-pencil instruments, and (2) the reliability of observations of behavior by raters and coders. The fundamental concept does not vary between these two domains, but conventional differences in procedures require separate treatments.

Reliability of Self-Report Instruments.   Our discussion will proceed from a few assumptions about measurement instruments. First, we will assume that the instrument *as a whole* is designed to measure a single concept or construct. Such a concept or construct is conventionally called a "factor." In practice, one instrument might measure more than one factor, but to consider such extensions would unnecessarily complicate this discussion. Second, we will assume that each item forming a part of the instrument is intended to operationalize a slightly different aspect of that single underlying factor. When the items are combined (usually, but not necessarily by means of summing), we assume that the resulting index exhausts the conceptual meaning of that underlying factor as completely as possible.

Hence, our concern is not with the reliability of a single item but with the reliability of the total score—the index of the factor—that results from combining scores of the single items. Each item should be positively related to that index. Hence, our concern in this section is with the *internal consistency* or *homogeneity of measurement* exhibited by the instrument.

Our earlier, more general discussion of reliability can be straightforwardly applied to the total or combined reliability of a measurement instrument, and we will not repeat that discussion here. But we will make an important point about measurement instruments.

Several times in preceding chapters, we have emphasized the desirability of multiple-item rather than single-item measurement instruments. The conceptual rationale for our preference is this: Multiple-item instruments are more likely to exhaust the conceptual meaning of a variable than are single-item instruments. The technical definition of reliability with which we are now concerned, however, allows us to demonstrate the importance of that preference from a more technical point of view.

Simply stated: You cannot calculate the reliability of a single item. The calculation of reliability requires variance—dispersion of scores around a central point—and variance cannot be calculated from a single score. Reliability is the proportion of the variance that can be explained by variance in "true" scores divided by the total variance.

Here we are concerned with the consistency or homogeneity of single items in relation to the total score from a multiple-item instrument. If the instrument consisted of only one item, we would be left with the impossible questions: Consistency with what? Homogeneity among what?

To make this same point mathematically, we will introduce one of the most important and basic formulas for calculating the reliability of a multiple-item instrument. The formula is usually credited to Cronbach (1951), and the reliability coefficient derived from it is frequently called "coefficient alpha" or "Cronbach's alpha."

$$\text{rel} = \frac{N}{N-1}\left(1 - \frac{\Sigma V_i}{V_t}\right) \tag{6.6}$$

where N represents the number of items or scales in the instrument; V_i represents the variance of an individual item across the sample (i is a general symbol which stands for "any item," or the ith item); and V_t is the total variance across the sample of the summed or otherwise combined scores of the individual items. The capital Greek letter, sigma, Σ, is a conventional symbol that says "sum what follows." Hence, in the formula it tells you to sum all n of the individual i variances, or, in other words, to sum the variances of the individual items: $\Sigma V_i = V_1 + V_2 + V_3 + V_4 + \cdots + V_n$. Obviously, capital sigma is a valuable shorthand tool, and we will use it frequently in subsequent chapters.

If you study Eq. 6.6 carefully, you may perceive that it is not substantially different from Eq. 6.5. Eq. 6.6 takes into account the size of the instrument *(N)* and designates the sum of the individual item variances (ΣV_i) as the error component. (See Cronbach, 1951, pp. 302–305 for a more complete explanation of the relationship of this formula to reliability more generally defined.) As we indicated, reliability cannot be calculated for a single item, and this formula makes that fact very explicit. You may have noticed that, if $N = 1$, then $N - 1$ must be 0 and the first term in the formula would have 1 divided by 0, which is undefined. Furthermore, with only one item the parenthetical part of the formula also reduces to zero. You should be able to figure out why, and we will refrain from helping you. Cronbach's alpha, then, explicates a technical problem with single-item instruments. Because you have no way of calculating their reliability, you have no way of determining whether what is being measured is a "true" score for an attribute or phenomenon or an "error" score for the operation of random, unexplained forces. When researchers refer to the reliability of a measurement instrument, they mean the *entire* instrument. The reliability coefficients they supply (or should supply) in their reports indicate what proportion of the variance resulting from their measurement is "true" variance resulting from variation in the attribute or phenomenon being measured.

Cronbach's alpha may be used across coders (analogously to across items) for purposes of assessing the reliability of observers, but other methods of estimating reliability for observational data are more conventional.

Reliability of Observations. In our early discussion of reliability, we said that it was sometimes conceptualized as (1) stability across time and sometimes as (2) accuracy at a single time. We also noted that, for good reason, the second criterion is the one most often adopted in communication research.

But observational analysis introduces problems that self-report instruments do not have. In self-report measures, you need to consider only two sources of error in the measurement process: the individual being measured and the instrument or procedure doing the measuring. In observational analysis, these two sources of error also are present. But a third source of error lies in the person of the coder. And, to complicate matters further, multiple coders of the same observations frequently are used in observational analysis.

Methodologists have broken down these sources of error into three types of reliability for observational analysis. Stability in measurement across time is inferred from *intraobject* reliability and (2) *intraobserver* reliability. Accuracy at a single time (or a series of times) is inferred from (3) *interobserver* reliability. As with self-report measures, the principal concern has been with accuracy, here inferred from agreement among observers. Stability has been given little theoretic or empirical attention.

Intraobject reliability.   Many forces influence communicative behavior, and most of these forces are extraneous to the concerns of a given researcher doing a given study. Such extraneous forces might include the person's health, the weather, recent communication (e.g., a recent argument with the person's employer), recent other experiences (e.g., a speeding ticket received on the way to work), drug use, etc. These forces themselves might be the subject of study, in which case, of course, they are not "extraneous." But researchers cannot attend to all variables at the same time. Those not attended to are sources of error—random, unexplained variance.

From day to day these random forces can be assumed to vary: They appear and disappear, increase and decrease. In this sense, the reliability of a communicator's (or a communication system's) behavior is analagous to test-retest reliability on a self-report instrument. If the subject or system is observed on many occasions, the random forces tend to balance out, and a relatively "true" overall picture of the behavior can be obtained.

This account assumes that a communicator or communication system will exhibit stable, consistent patterns of behavior when the effects of extraneous forces are taken into account. We must emphasize, however, that this assumption has seldom been empirically tested, and *inconsistency*, rather than consistency, in communicative behavior may be the norm (see Courtright, Millar, & Rogers, 1980). One reason for the paucity of research on this matter is the difficulty inherent in separating variance attributable to the behavior of the communicator or communication system from variance attributable to the coding behavior of the observer (Becker, 1970). Typically, the only access a researcher has to the behavior of communicators is through the units and categories reported by observers. Hence, the observed and the observer are completely confounded, and sorting who is responsible for what is impossible.

As a result, most researchers assume, rather than assess, intraobject reliability. We would not be surprised to find that this state of affairs would change soon, as ingenious methodologists begin to attend to the problem.

Intraobserver reliability.   Intraobserver reliability has been defined by Becker (1970, p. 223) as "the degree of agreement of a rater [or observer] with himself when he judges [or unitizes or categorizes] the same object at different times." (Notice that, in the phrase "the same object," Becker assumes intraobject reliability.) The observer's reliability can be affected by all the same extraneous forces that influence the communicator's reliability. Observers occasionally have headaches, engage in disputes, and get depressed on a cloudy day. As with communicators, over repeated observations these random forces balance out.

Unlike communicators, observers are engaged in a very specific task: to apply a coding system to segments of behavior based on a set of decision rules. While random forces can affect the performance of that task, the researcher can take steps to minimize those extraneous disturbances. As we mentioned in Chapter 4, the clarity of the coding system and the explicitness of the decision rules are critically important in reducing inconsistency. Well-trained observers are significantly more reliable than are untrained ones (Becker, 1970).

Interobserver reliability. Interobserver reliability is defined as "the degree of agreement among different raters [or observers] judging [or unitizing or categorizing] the same object" (Becker, 1970, p. 223). Since the various observers attend to the same segment of behavior, this form of reliability assesses accuracy rather than stability. And if accuracy is high, stability must also be high. Hence, this is the most common form of observational reliability assessed in communication research.

Generally, researchers doing observational studies are required to (1) use multiple observers for at least a sample of the observations under investigation, and (2) report interobserver reliability. Several procedures are available for calculating that reliability. For the simplest case, where only two observers are categorizing behavior in a nominal system, Cohen (1960, 1968) provides a straightforward approach. Reliability is calculated as the degree (or proportion) of agreement between the two observers beyond what would be expected by chance (as calculated from probability theory). If, for example, two observers were assigning behaviors in a two-category system, and if any particular behavior were as likely to appear in one category as the other, chance (or probability theory) would dictate that the observers should agree .25 of the time. If *only* that proportion of agreement were found, then the intercoder reliability would be zero: *no* proportion of the observations could be attributed to "true" codings.

Cohen's Kappa is calculated by the following formula (Crow, 1982):

$$\kappa = \frac{P_o - P_c}{1 - P_c} \qquad (6.7)$$

in which P_o is the observed proportion of agreement (agreements divided by total number of observations coded), and P_c is the chance proportion of agreement. The researcher creates a matrix so that observer 1's codings are entered in the columns, and observer 2's codings are entered in the rows. Complete agreement between the coders would result in all tally marks occurring in the diagonal cells. Once all observations are entered in the matrix for both observers, the researcher calculates P_1 and P_2. If observer 1 coded 5 observations of 50 as "one-up," for example, the proportion of "one-up" codings for observer 1 (P_1) would be .10. P_1 is calculated for each coding category by dividing the row total by the grand total (50 in the example). P_2 is calculated by dividing each column total by the grand total. P_c then can be calculated by multiplying each P_1 by its corresponding P_2 and summing the products. This sum (P_c) is the amount of agreement between observers 1 and 2 that can be easily accounted for by chance.

More complicated procedures are available for more complicated systems. Guetzkow's (1950) method is applicable both to systems using more than two observers and to those where observers both unitize and categorize behavior. Krippendorff (1980) has an entire chapter on reliability and its calculation in observational studies. Finally, when behavior is recorded on rating scales rather than placed into nominal categories, Ebel's (1951) method is appropriate. Although all three of these procedures differ from each other and from the alpha coefficient we introduced earlier, all have the same purpose: to separate "true" variance from "error" variance and to calculate the proportion of the total variance that is "true."

We have indicated that a precise coefficient of reliability can and should be calculated in any study where abstraction or complexity might make measurement reliability questionable. This includes nearly all studies in communication research. We have not yet indicated what might be an "acceptable" level of reliability for a measurement instrument or procedure. How much (or what proportion) of the variance must be "true" if an instrument of procedure is to be considered adequately reliable?

One answer is in the results of the study itself. If relationships are discovered between predictor and criterion variables that could not easily be explained by chance (in the jargon of the game, "statistically significant" relationships), then the reliability for measuring all variables entering those relationships is extremely likely to be adequately reliable. Recall that "error" variance is randomly distributed. A variable with a high proportion of error variance, then, is randomly, unsystematically, unpredictably distributed. Such a variable would have a very low probability of entering into a systematic (one that could not easily be explained by chance) relationship with another variable. If *both* variables in a relationship contained a high proportion of error variance, the probability of their exhibiting a systematic relationship would be even further reduced. In fact, some researchers apply formulas to "correct" for acceptable unreliability in their measurements. These formulas, in effect, take out the effects of unreliable measurement (within limits), and hence allow a closer approximation of "true" relationships among variables. We will not discuss such formulas further, and we urge you to seek reliable measurement rather than to rely on such formulas.

But most researchers prefer to calculate reliability directly rather than to infer that it is acceptably high from the results of their overall studies. With direct estimates of reliability, acceptability varies from situation to situation. If, for example, a measurement instrument or procedure has been used repeatedly in the past with very high reliability (say, .95), and if a set of scores using the same instrument or procedure achieves a considerably lower level (say, .80), the lower level may be considered unacceptable. It may indicate that the researcher was careless in his or her research procedures, that at least one of the coders employed was remarkably idiosyncratic, that the paper-and-pencil test employed was blurry, or something of the sort. In the absence of such established standards for an instrument or procedure, however, researchers generally have established .70 as the minimum acceptable index of reliability.

Validity

Social scientists use the concept "validity" in two rather distinct ways. The first has to do with the validity of a measurement instrument or procedure. The second has to do with the validity of an entire study. We will deal with them both.

Validity of Measurement Instruments and Procedures.   *Validity* as the term applies to measurement instruments may be the most misunderstood concept in the social sciences. We will discuss two sources of confusion.

First, the term is often used in conjunction with "reliability." As we have just explained, empirical indexes exist for assessing reliability. No such indexes exist for validity. No investigator can say, "In this study, variable X is .90 valid." Rather, the validity of a measurement instrument is assessed by the accumulation of evidence across various studies and various investigators. Such evidence comes from many sources, and, for a "valid" instrument or procedure, it tends to indicate that the instrument or procedure measures operationally what it was designed to measure conceptually. The demonstration of a measure's "validity," then, is a highly rhetorical enterprise. The researcher must gather evidence from a variety of sources and use it skillfully if other researchers are to be convinced that a particular measure is a valid one.

Second, many researchers and most other people are confused about what it means for a measure to be "valid." Frequently (and unfortunately) validity is defined as the ability of instrument to measure what the investigator says it measures. As Becker (1970) argues, this is nothing more than operational definition in reverse. And clear operational definition does *not* insure validity. More important, the circular definition implies that a measure can be valid in only one sense, that it is valid or it is not. Validity is, to some degree, situational: It depends on the researcher's purpose. Hence, whenever you encounter the word *valid*, you might inquire: Valid *for what?* As purposes change, so does the nature of validity and so does the nature of the evidence required to establish validity.

An example will indicate that measures invalid for one purpose might be valid for another. The measurement of intelligence quotients (IQ) has been a controversial subject both among social scientists and in the public at large. Many people have convincingly argued that tests operationalizing the concept intelligence (IQ tests) largely measure formal educational attainment and require for success socialization in white, middle-class norms and values. Consequently, children from other backgrounds are disadvantaged by the assumptions implicit in the tests. Some critics have invented IQ tests based on the norms and values of other subcultures, and have demonstrated that individuals with high IQs as measured by the established tests have low IQs as measured by the subcultural tests. Are IQ tests valid for measuring intelligence? Almost certainly not, unless *intelligence* is oddly defined as "what an IQ test measures."

Now assume that a researcher is interested in predicting the academic success of children who will be enrolled in schools dominated by white, middle-class teachers embodying white, middle-class norms and values. The researcher demonstrates that, among other measures, performance on a standard IQ test is a very successful predictor. Is the IQ test valid for predicting academic success in that kind of school? It is, though you still might prefer not to call what is being measured "intelligence."

A measure is valid, then, to the extent that it is useful in achieving the researcher's purpose (Becker, 1970; Nunnally, 1978). And, depending on purpose, different types of evidence are useful in demonstrating validity. Conventionally, methodologists discuss three types of such evidence: content validity, predictive validity, and construct validity.

Content validity.   In the research literature, content validity sometimes is called face validity, intrinsic validity, or, occasionally, representativeness. It is the easiest type to understand and the easiest for which to provide supportive evidence. And it comes closest to the unfortunate definition, that an instrument is valid if it measures what the investigator says it measures.

A measure has content validity if the items or procedures that make it up seem to represent the concepts that the researcher is trying to operationalize. Kerlinger (1973, p. 458) defines it formally:

> Content validity is the representativeness or sampling adequacy of the content—the substance, the matter, the topics—of a measuring instrument. Content validation is guided by the question: Is the substance or content of this measure representative of the content or the universe of content of the property being measured?

Often, when content validity is the only criterion, the concept or construct being measured is not expected to enter into meaningful relationships with other concepts or constructs. No instruments measuring "similar" or "opposite" concepts or constructs may be available for comparison. In fact, the measure under consideration may be the *only* operationalization of the conceptual variable of interest.

One example might be taken from classroom settings. Assume that your instructor has devised a final examination for the course in research methods. As Nunnally (1978) suggests, such a test would not be designed to predict some other concept or construct, nor would it be designed to fit into a larger theoretic network. Its purpose would be to measure as directly as possible your level of achievement in one particular course. Accordingly, your instructor's principal concern would probably be with content validity: Do the items on the test adequately represent the material you were supposed to have learned in the course? Is your score representative of your knowledge?

Like your instructor, researchers in communication usually consider content validity. A measure of "communicative competence" must adequately represent the cognitions and behaviors of which such competence is comprised. If it does not, the researcher's critics will question the content validity of the measure.

The degree to which a measure has content validity depends on the judgments of informed critics (Kerlinger, 1973, p. 458). The researcher gives evidence of content validity by providing a rationale for the inclusion of some items and the exclusion of others. Nunnally (1978, p. 93) writes that attempts to establish content validity "rest mainly on appeals to reason regarding the adequacy with which important content has been sampled and on the adequacy with which the content has been cast in the form of test items."

Predictive validity. Predictive validity is the degree to which a measurement instrument or procedure estimates or forecasts in systematic ways variables which are external to it (Nunnally, 1978). The external variables are sometimes called *criterion* variables, and this type of validation is sometimes called "criterion-related validity." The IQ test in our earlier example, to the extent that it failed to sample items relevant to all subpopulations, did *not* have content validity—its items were *not* representative of the concept "intelligence" for all groups. But it *did* have predictive validity, at least in the example given. It was valid for systematically predicting a measure external to itself— academic success in a certain kind of school.

In a pure sense, then, predictive validity is independent of the content of the measure. Regardless of its content, if it predicts accurately it is useful and therefore valid for the purpose of making those predictions. An individual's height is a fairly good predictor of his or her chances of being assigned leadership roles in organizations. But nobody would say that part of the "content" of "leadership" is "height." This independence from content explains why predictive validity most often is appealed to in applied, rather than theoretic, research. It is likely to be the principal form of validation to help the people who must answer such questions as: Should I admit X to graduate school? Should I hire applicant A or applicant B to sell my product? Which form of treatment should W receive for his communicative disorder? How likely is it that Z will have a heart attack? Should I marry F or G? As Nunnally writes: "The word *decision* should be kept in mind, because this is what predictor tests are all about."

Construct validity. For theory, the most important and certainly the most difficult type of validity to establish is construct validity. This kind of validity addresses the *why* questions involved in measurement. Stated technically, a researcher concerned with construct validity seeks to understand what underlying constructs account for patterns of relationship between the measure in question and other variables. If one variable predicts others successfully, it has predictive validity. If the researcher can give convincing theoretical reasons for those successful predictions, the measure also has construct validity.

The search for reasons involves a highly integrated blend of theory and empiricism. First, the researcher must convincingly establish the content validity of the measure, that is, define the domain being measured and demonstrate that the instrument or procedure representatively and adequately samples that domain. This often requires a theoretical/empirical investigation of the internal structure of the measure—a discovery of what groups of items go together and what that clustering means conceptually. Second, the concepts or constructs isolated in the determination of internal structure must be used to predict the occurrence or magnitude of other concepts or constructs external to the measure in a theoretically meaningful way. That is, a rationale must be provided in which aspects of the measure in question are asserted to have specific, systematic relationships to other measures. Third, these predicted relationships must be empirically tested.

To the extent that the rationale is shown to work, the researcher has established the validity both of the measure *and* of the rationale. To the extent that it does not work, (1) the instrument lacks content validity or (2) the rationale is in error. In either case, further research and theorizing are in order.

This discussion may seem familiar to you. If it does, it should. Construct validation is very similar to the scientific process in general. As Cronbach and Meehl (1955, p. 300) point out, "construct validity is not essentially different from the general scientific procedures for developing and confirming theories."

Construct validity is seldom achieved in the neat way we have outlined, and it is seldom achieved by a single researcher. It is usually the result of accumulated evidence over many studies by many researchers. Moreover, construct validation often lags behind empirical research. Researchers like to do empirical work. Only after such work has revealed a measure's interesting interrelationships with other variables is a theorist likely to attempt to make those relationships conceptually meaningful. (For a recent example of such post hoc theorizing, see Bradac, Bowers, & Courtright, 1979, 1980.) Research and the establishment of ad hoc relationships typically precede theory in the social sciences.

Validity of Research Studies: Internal, External, and Ecological Validity.
Validity, as the term is applied to an entire study, has a somewhat looser meaning than it has in its application to a particular measurement instrument or procedure. In general, its referents can be divided into three types: (1) *Internal* validity is the likelihood that, given the premises of the study, the explanation of the results is the one proposed by the researcher. (2) *External* validity is the likelihood that another researcher, using the same methods, would be able to replicate the results of the study. (3) *Ecological* validity is the likelihood that the results of the study would generalize to the "real world." A particular study can be internally valid but externally and ecologically invalid, or internally and externally valid but ecologically invalid.

All three kinds of validity are usually defined by negation. A study is thought to be internally, externally, and ecologically valid to the extent that a critic cannot identify sources of *invalidity.*

Issues of internal validity concern the relationships between method and explanation. Could the results of the study be plausibly explained in ways other than those proposed by the researcher? If two variables, either of which could explain the results, are confounded in an experimental study, for example, the study is internally invalid to the extent that the researcher attributes the explanation to one or the other of the confounded variables. Faulty sampling method, faulty instruments, and faulty research design all are grounds for questioning a study's internal validity. We refer you to Campbell and Stanley (1963) for a catalog of eight specific threats to internal validity.

Both external and ecological validity have to do with the ability of the study to be generalized outside itself, and we will discuss them together. Our friend Jim Bradac might do a faultless, internally valid experiment using as a subject his cat Chervil. If he tries to generalize his results to cats in general, a critic might point out that his cat Chervil has a unique learning history which is likely to invalidate attempts to replicate the study with other cats. Or the critic might point out that only Bradac seems to have the gift of communicating with cats, and that an attempt to replicate his results with the critic's cat Jenny did not succeed. Or the critic might ecologically point out that Bradac carried out his studies in antiseptic, highly insulated, laboratory surroundings, and that the relationships discovered would be nonexistent or trivial outside that setting. In short, any condition, manipulation, or measurement procedure which differs from what the researcher and/or the subjects might encounter in other environments is a threat to the external or ecological validity of the study.

In communication research, you might often encounter conflicts between internal validity and external/ecological validity. Your efforts to insure one type of validity might jeopardize the other types. For example, you might, in your quest for internal validity, design a very tightly controlled laboratory study in which you eliminate all possible explanations for the phenomenon of interest except the one you hypothesize. In the process, you might create such a contrived, artificial environment, or such implausible conditions, that others would find it ridiculous to generalize from your study even to other laboratories, much less to the "real world." But if, in your quest for external/ecological validity, you limited yourself to descriptive field studies in only the most mundane environments and using only the least obtrusive methods of measurement, you would simultaneously eliminate your ability to control *any* extraneous forces, and critics could therefore question the internal validity of your study by proposing plausible explanations of your results based on uncontrolled variables.

As with many other issues we have discussed, the solution usually lies in compromise. No study achieves both perfect internal validity and perfect external/ecological validity. The researcher must be guided by the strength of the theory being tested and the experience of others in working with that and similar theory. Frequently in recent years researchers have "triangulated" research problems, designing studies to test the same theoretical propositions both in tightly controlled, internally valid circumstances and in more loosely controlled, more natural, more externally/ecologically valid circumstances. We encourage this approach to the problem. A generalization gains power if it is tested and confirmed in multiple situations.

The Relationship Between Reliability and Validity

So far, we have been treating reliability and validity as independent concerns. They are not independent. A measurement instrument or procedure can be reliable without being valid. But an instrument or procedure cannot be valid without being reliable.

A simple example will make the point. Suppose that you were interested in exploring the relationship between physical attractiveness and leadership in problem-solving groups. You have difficulty finding a way to operationalize "physical attractiveness," and, because your assignment is due tomorrow, you decide to use "head circumference" as an index of "physical attractiveness."

Doubtless, you could obtain a stable and accurate measure of each individual's head circumference. The variable would be *reliable*. But we doubt that any critic would perceive that the index had content validity; we doubt that the predicted relationship would occur, so the measure would not have predictive validity; and you would be hard-pressed to justify it systematically in a theoretic framework, so it would lack construct validity.

If a measure is valid in any of the three senses of validity, on the other hand, then it must be adequately reliable. Any measure with high content validity, predictive validity, or construct validity necessarily must be measuring something other than the random operation of extraneous forces. Hence, if a measurement instrument or procedure is valid in any of the three senses, then it *must* be reliable.

In a sentence: Reliability is a necessary but not a sufficient condition for validity.

■ Conclusion

This chapter, with its discussion of levels of measurement, reliability, and validity, has done the work of bridging the earlier, more conceptual chapters with the later, more technical ones. We take, and we encourage you to take, a "liberal" position on issues about levels of measurement. Reliability and validity are crucially important concepts, and all respectable social scientists use them frequently.

Chapter

Finding a Researchable Idea and "Searching the Literature"

Until now, we have been assuming the existence of a research idea and have been explaining ways of investigating it. Where do research ideas come from?

Creativity is one of the least understood aspects of psychology, and we will not attempt to approach it as an abstraction. Probably, it can be learned, at least to some degree, and for some hints we refer you to Boring (1963), Koestler (1964), and Watzlawick, Weakland, and Fisch (1974).

In a mundane sense, ideas come from the mental activities called *analysis* and *synthesis*. *Analysis* breaks concepts down into their component parts. *Synthesis* combines and recombines concepts, sometimes in very useful ways. Neither activity can be conceived without the other, but analysis sometimes is thought of as logical activity, synthesis as creative activity. Analysis is "reasonable," synthesis "imaginative." In general, analysis precedes synthesis, for one must understand what parts make up a whole before one can understand how those parts act together as a system.

Koestler perceives that creative activity is likely to occur when an individual thinks of experience in two frames of reference simultaneously—when one way of thinking about experience collides (in a sense) with another. When Archimedes sat in his tub while thinking about the problem of measuring the size of the crown, one frame of reference (bath-taking activity) collided with another (measuring size), resulting in the idea of measuring volume by the displacement of water (Eureka!). Koestler calls these frames of reference "matrices," and characterizes the collision of two matrices as "bisociation." Watzlawick, Weakland, and Fisch refer to much the same phenomenon as "second-order" thinking.

Another way of thinking about it: You may encounter a theory in your reading, or you may hear about a theory from your teacher. Given a knowledge of this theory, your thinking might proceed as follows:

If variable B affects variable C the way this theory predicts, and if (as I think) variable D behaves in the same way as variable C in certain contexts, then variable B can be expected to affect variable D the same way it would affect variable C in those contexts.

This is an act of analytic thinking. You have deduced a hypothesis about the behavior of variable D from an extant theory. This kind of thinking can be made very systematic and can be expressed as postulates, axioms, theorems, and corollaries (for example, see Bradac, Bowers, & Courtright, 1979, 1980; Gurr, 1970).

If, on the other hand, you reasoned as follows, you would be exhibiting synthetic thinking:

> For many years, people have been trying to explain the behavior of variable C as a causal function of variable B. I think that they have failed to perceive the presence of variables A and D. Furthermore, I do not think that the behavior of any of the four variables can be explained as causal functions of any one of the others. They must be considered a system in which all of the four variables mutually influence each other. The "cause" is the whole system, not the behavior of one variable or another. They relate to each other according to certain functions, which I can express.

Researchable ideas may come either from analysis or from synthesis (probably more often from analysis), but you are more likely to become famous for your research ideas if they come from synthesis, from creative recombination of concepts or frames of reference for concepts. Not everybody exhibits genius as a synthesizer, but genius is worth investigating and nurturing.

Our treatment necessarily must be rather prosaic, because we must assume that you probably are not yet a genius. Hence, we will consider sources of ideas that are available to any reader of this book.

General Sources

We have frequently expressed the idea that all human beings are what might be called "naive" scientists. That is, people in their everyday thought and behavior exhibit curiosity, confront anomalies, invent hypotheses to satisfy their curiosity and explain the anomalies, and sometimes conduct informal experiments to test those explanations. This leads to the conclusion that one common source of research ideas is experience.

Experience alone and the kinds of hypotheses informally derived from it are unlikely to lead to very good research. Koestler (1964) and others have shown that the most likely research comes from experience in the context of a great deal of reflection about a specific problem. Experience probably will not be a prolific source of research ideas for you unless you consider that experience reflectively, preferably in the light of what others have written about the same kind of experience.

Necessity often leads to that kind of reflection on experience and to the investigation of the work of others. You are more likely to find a solution to a problem if you *must* find a solution. For you as a student, classroom assignments serve as a kind of necessity. You must find an idea if you are to fulfill the assignment. For other kinds of people, the requirements of a job serve as a kind of necessity. If a corporation has hired you to measure its "image," you must find ways to make that measurement. For many scholars, the "publish or perish" doctrine serves as a kind of necessity. If a scholar is to achieve tenure in a major university, he or she must do research and must publish the results of that research. Necessity generates obsession with a particular problem, and that obsession has the effect of prompting a person to perceive many of the phenomena of everyday life as potentially relevant to the problem. The person thus brings more different frames of reference to bear on the problem and increases the likelihood of Koestler's felicitous collision of matrices, of a Eureka! insight. What would otherwise be an ignored accident or mundane event might instead become a perception upon which discovery relies.

If you want to see the effects of experience, reflection, and necessity dramatically portrayed, read the popular novel by Jean M. Auel (1982), *The Valley of Horses*. In that book, the heroine, Ayla, and to a lesser extent her lover, Jondalar, continually confront problems during the Ice Age in Europe and solve them through synthesis. Furthermore, Auel does a plausible job of presenting the psychological dynamics leading to Ayla's and Jondalar's discoveries.

Experience need not necessarily be firsthand. It may be vicarious. The experience of others, including their formal research experience, can be a source of researchable ideas. In Appendix A, we have provided a catalog of such experience in the form of an index of variables employed in communication research during a three-year period. The compilation of that chapter required analysis of research during those three years into its parts—the variables—statically considered. We hope that it will prompt you to further analysis and ideally to some synthesis—to dynamic considerations of possible relationships among some of those variables. You might consider Appendix A to be a part of this chapter. Before you read further, scan it for possible researchable ideas.

One prerequisite for ideas leading to good research is unshakable confidence in your own abilities (1) to form the ideas, and (2) to do the necessary research. We think that more research is inhibited by lack of this kind of confidence than by lack of ability. Unfortunately, we have no way of quickly imparting this kind of confidence. You must discipline yourself to read critically, to use your time with discipline, and to do research persistently and habitually. In this book, we are supplying you with a tool to increase both your confidence and your ability. Discoveries based on the kind of thinking this book presents are occurring daily in communication, a field ripe for harvest. You will not become one of the reapers unless you have confidence in your ability to use the equipment—including your mental equipment.

Scholarly Sources

In this book, we are specifically concerned with ideas for the disciplined activity called communication research. While research based on experience, reflection, and necessity might be useful, it is not likely to be accepted by the community of scholars in communication unless it systematically takes into account earlier research done by others. In the rest of this chapter, we will explain how to "search the literature" to discover in a more or less efficient manner what has been done by others on the problem you have chosen as your own.

The literature search is important for two reasons. First, knowledge of what others have done on your topic will enable you to avoid needless repetition of earlier research. Second, knowledge of previous work will enable you to avoid the mistakes made by previous researchers. As we have stressed repeatedly, social science is a cumulative process resulting from the collective, public work of a community of scientists. Your search into previous studies allows your work to be a contribution to this community rather than a redundancy.

Central and Peripheral Journals in Communication Studies

Two organizations publish periodicals that regularly carry communication research studies. These are the Speech Communication Association and the International Communication Association.

The Speech Communication Association publishes four journals: (1) *Communication Monographs;* (2) *Quarterly Journal of Speech;* (3) *Communication Education;* and (4) *Critical Studies in Mass Communication.* The International Communication Association publishes (1) *Human Communication Research* and, in cooperation with the Annenberg School of Communication at the University of Pennsylvania, (2) *Journal of Communication.* You should become familiar with the kinds of research reports published by all of these journals. Each is published quarterly, and each is indexed by author annually, at the end of the last issue each year. The two most likely to carry full reports of studies done from a social science perspective are *Communication Monographs* and *Human Communication Research. Journal of Communication* carries short research papers, and, unlike the others, begins its pagination with each new issue rather than with each new volume number. Hence, for that journal, your references must include issue (the season of the year in which it was published) as well as volume number. *Quarterly Journal of Speech* seldom carries full research studies done from a social science perspective, but it often prints excellent syntheses of an entire stream of research and sometimes presents philosophical underpinnings of various research controversies.

Regional communication associations in the United States also publish journals that regularly carry research reports in communication. While important studies published in these journals are likely eventually to find their way into the references of the more prestigious national journals, a conscientious researcher will survey the regional journals to avoid the risk that he or she is missing something important. The four regional research journals in communication are *Southern Speech Communication Journal, Western Journal of Speech Communication, Central States Speech Journal,* and *Communication Quarterly* (published by the Eastern Communication Association). These journals are more likely than the national ones to devote entire issues to particular problems in research and theory.

Two of the journals mentioned so far regularly print reviews of books relevant to scholars in communication, though a lag of a year or more might intervene between the time the book is published and the time it is reviewed. The two that carry book reviews are *Quarterly Journal of Speech* and *Journal of Communication.* In addition, *Human Communication Research* sometimes carries "state-of-the-art" papers in which books relevant to a particular research problem might be incidentally reviewed.

A number of journals published by other associations or institutions are likely to carry articles of interest to researchers in communication. These include (and the list is not exhaustive, by any means) *Journal of Applied Communication Research, Communication Research, Journal of Verbal Learning and Verbal Behavior, Language and Speech, Journalism Quarterly, Public Opinion Quarterly, Human Relations, Journal of Conflict Resolution, Journal of Personality and Social Psychology,* and *Philosophy & Rhetoric.* Finally, because communication is a discipline that has implications for many other disciplines, journals of those other disciplines (sociology, psychology, anthropology, political science, linguistics, even economics, among others) sometimes report articles relevant to communication research. Communication scholars read widely, and the most important of those relevant articles are likely to appear with some time lag in the references to articles in the communication journals.

Finally, scholars whose interests are in a particular arena of communication (for example, the marriage arena) will find specialized journals available. If you decide to specialize in family communication, you will find indispensable such journals as *Family Process* and *Journal of Marriage and the Family*.

As we have implied, your literature search should be of the references to articles as well as to the articles themselves. Frequently, you will be able to identify by name a few scholars whose work has been especially important to a particular research problem. You can then search for other sources on the same problem by focusing on those few names.

The Matlon Index

Ronald J. Matlon of the University of Arizona has compiled an *Index to Journals in Communication Studies Through 1979* that is extremely useful to communication scholars. This index examines fourteen journals from their first publication through the 1979 issues.

The journals indexed by Matlon are *Quarterly Journal of Speech, Communication Monographs, Communication Education, Southern Speech Communication Journal, Western Journal of Speech Communication, Central States Speech Journal, Communication Quarterly, Association for Communication Administration Bulletin, Philosophy & Rhetoric, Journal of Communication, Human Communication Research, Journalism Quarterly, Journal of Broadcasting,* and *Journal of the American Forensic Association.*

The Matlon index is organized into three parts: a table of contents, in which article titles and authors are reproduced for each issue of each journal; an index of contributors, in which all authors are alphabetically indexed to appropriate volumes and issues of each journal; and an index of subjects, coded in a relatively complicated manner, but including a "key-word" index to the more complicated system.

You will want to extend your search beyond 1979, of course, but the Matlon index can give you an idea of what titles and even what authors and key words to focus on in your search of individual indexes in more recent journals.

Other Library and Computer Indexes

Libraries have compiled many scholarly aids for literature searches, and some of them have been computerized. Each of the aids we will consider in this section provides its own directions for use, and we will not duplicate those directions. But we will briefly explain the concept of "key words" for computer searches.

Many of the bibliographical aids we will consider have been computerized. This means that you can supply the reference librarian equipped to do computer searches with "key words" which should occur in any research report that is relevant to your problem. The librarian then will instruct the computer to supply you with bibliographic references in which your key word or your combination of key words appears.

Your key words may come from a thesaurus accompanying the particular bibliographical aid (a fairly economical procedure), or, more interestingly, it may be *any* word (for example, the name of a particular author), for which the librarian does an "on-line" search. The on-line search capability of computerized aids makes your search extremely flexible, so that, for example, you might recover all references in which both key words *communication* and *negotiation* appeared in article titles. Or you might recover all references to articles of which Researcher, My Favorite, is the author.

Furthermore, you need not procure *all* of the references indexed by your key word or combination of key words. The librarian can instruct the computer to supply the four (or six, or ten, or sixteen) references exhibiting those key words most recently entered in the system.

If you intend to do a computer search, your reference librarian probably will require you to fill out a form like this one:

> Please give in your own words a description of the problem to be searched. Be as specific as possible, including any synonyms, related concepts or terms, or alternative spellings. Since the computer searches for key words it is important that you analyze your topic as carefully as possible.

Limits to the search request:

1. What type of search do you need?
   _____ Retrospective—coverage of back years of the database
   _____ Current awareness—coverage of future updates of the database
   _____ Broad—a fairly long list, missing few relevant references but probably including many nonrelevant items
   _____ Narrow—a relatively short list containing mostly relevant references but probably missing some relevant items
2. Language:
   _____ English only
   _____ Any language
   _____ Other _____
3. Maximum cost _____ (Strict adherence to a maximum cost may limit results)

Please list two or three citations to relevant works dealing with the subject to be searched, if known, or any important authors, organizations or publications which have dealt with the subject. Indicate whether there are any authors whom you wish to exclude due to prior familiarity with their work.

All of the indexes that have been computerized also exist as library documents, and you may, of course, do more laborious manual searches instead of computerized ones. But if computerized aids are available to you, you will find it worthwhile to explore their capabilities.

Educational Resources Information Center (ERIC).   ERIC is a federally supported project, and it has a communication component. It is computerized, and can be used either with key words from its Thesaurus or for on-line key word searches. It is more likely than most other sources to report on material (such as papers read at scholarly conventions) that has not yet been published or referred to in the journals.

To find out more about how to use ERIC, ask your librarian for *Indexing and Retrieval in the ERIC System* by Lynn Barnett.

Social Sciences Citation Index.   The *Social Sciences Citation Index* indexes regularly over 1000 social science journals, including the national journals most likely to carry important social scientific studies in communication, and selectively about 2000 others. It is made up of what its editors call the Citation Index, the Source Index, the

Corporate Index, and the Permuter Subject Index. It carries a general introduction as a guide to its use. It is computerized.

Typically, you would begin using this index having first identified the names of a few authors who have previously worked on your problem. Used ingeniously, the index can answer many questions for the searcher. Among those listed by the editors of the index are:

> Has this paper been cited?
> Has there been a review on this subject?
> Has this theory been confirmed?
> Has this work been extended?
> Has this method been improved?
> Has this suggestion been tried?
> Is this idea really original?
> Where is the full paper for this preliminary communication?
> Have subsequent errata and correction notes been published?
> Where are the raw data for a review article on this subject?
> Who else is working in this field?
> Are there data to delineate this field of study?
> Has this theory or concept been applied to a new field?
> What are all the current works in which this person is primary author?
> What are all the current works in which this person is secondary author?
> What other works has this person written?

An example: On December 2, 1982, we asked SSCI to provide us with the most recent four articles whose entries contained both of two key words: *communication* and *conflict*. The system supplied us with a printout showing, among other things:

> Sillars, A. L., Parry, D., Coletti, S. F., Rogers, M. A. "Coding verbal conflict tactics: Nonverbal and perceptual correlates of the avoidance-distributive-integrative distinction." *Human Communication Research*, 1982, Vol. 9, No. 1, pp. 83–95.
>
> Holz, J. "Community conflict and the press." Other key words: Tichenor, P. J., Donohue, G. A., Olien, C. N. *Journal of Communication*, 1982, Vol. 32, No. 3, pp. 220+.
>
> Cobb, E. J., Leitenberg, H., Burchard, J. D. "Foster parents teaching foster parents." Other key words: communication and conflict, resolution skills training. *Journal of Community Psychology*, 1982, Vol. 10, No. 3, pp. 240–249.
>
> Pinxten, R. "Man and mankind: Conflict and communication between cultures." Other key words: Glenn, E. *Communication and Cognition*, 1982, Vol. 15, No. 2, pp. 264–265.

Other Indexes.   Besides the *Social Sciences Citation Index* and ERIC, other indexes frequently useful to communication researchers are available in both conventional and computerized form. These include *Language and Language Behavior Abstracts, Psychological Abstracts, Sociological Abstracts, Comprehensive Dissertation Index, Magazine Index, National Newspaper Index* (includes the *New York Times*, the *Wall Street Journal*, and the *Christian Science Monitor*), the *Newspaper Index* (includes the *Los Angeles Times*, the *Washington Post*, the *Chicago Tribune*, and the *San Francisco Chronicle*), and the *New York Times Information Bank*.

Other indexes specific to communication but, as far as we know, not computerized include *Communicontents*, a quarterly in which each issue contains roughly a hundred short abstracts of new books, and *Communication: A Guide to Information Sources*, published in 1980 and containing references to general communication studies and to work in interpersonal communication, group communication, international communication, political communication, and mass communication. It has author, title, and subject indexes.

■ *Conclusion*

This short chapter by no means exhausts reference and other sources of ideas that you may be able to exploit. It does refer you to experience in the light of reflection and necessity as one source of researchable ideas, to our own Appendix A and other vicarious experiences as another source, and to certain standard library aids as a third. We encourage you to practice synthesis, bisociation, second-order thinking, as well as conventional analysis, as you seek to develop and test communication theory. And we encourage you to find fuller explications of those creative processes, especially in Koestler (1964) and in Watzlawick, Weakland, and Fisch (1974).

# Chapter

The Description and Analysis of Data

At several points in earlier sections of this book, the construct of "communication apprehension" was employed to exemplify some methodological procedure or concept. From a variety of anecdotal and empirical evidence it has been concluded that a sizable number of people in our society experience severe, occasionally debilitating anxiety when faced with a communicative situation. In a similar fashion, educators have recently introduced the construct of "math anxiety." They have discovered that even their brightest, most intelligent students become extremely anxious when faced with (and thus do their best to avoid) any situation or experience which even hints at numbers, figures, or mathematical concepts.

This problem is lucidly described in a recent book by Erickson and Nosanchuk (1977, pp. 1–2). They write:

> Students are expected, and expect themselves to be able to read at very difficult levels. They read complex ideas as presented by difficult writers, and deal with ideas intelligently and critically. It may take time and even be painful but the reader, being confident, is spurred by his confidence and usually is successful. But suppose he or she is beginning to read a table of numbers, not a chapter of words. That's quite another story! Many students who are bright with anything but numbers freeze up when numbers come along. They don't even try to cope; instead they immediately succumb to "data-phobia." The symptoms of data-phobia are easy to spot when reading an article with tables in it. The poor victim of the phobia reads the text confidently, absorbing the argument and possibly taking issue with it. Then comes a table; and the data-phobe may avert his eyes, stare at the table helplessly without knowing what to make of it, or skim the table very quickly to see if he can find what the author says is there. . . . Unless there are really gross departures from this in the table, our data-phobe is likely to find the author's explanation acceptable, even though the reader agrees with nothing else in the paper. It may surprise some readers to learn that author's interpretations of tables are sometimes incorrect. . . . For all sorts of reasons the reader simply cannot rely on a paper's author to get everything out of the paper's data, and one certainly can't expect that he will always interpret the data the way the reader would like to do.

Before beginning the discussion of statistics and their application to communication research, we (and possibly you) must confront this very real problem. Although we have no delusions that the next few paragraphs can totally alleviate an aversion to math which has developed over many years of formal schooling, we will endeavor to reduce this anxiety just enough to allow the concepts presented in the next several chapters to sink in and be retained. It is our position that anyone with enough intelligence to be in college, and especially anyone who has read and understood the previous chapters of this book, possesses more than sufficient ability to comprehend the basic statistical concepts we will present.

First and foremost, the primary attribute needed to comprehend and use statistics is not mathematical training, but rather the ability to think logically. Statistics are nothing more than applied logic. Throughout this book, we have stressed that communication research is a matter of asking questions and then seeking their answers. It is very much a form of empirical detective work that involves inductive logic, deductive logic, a bit of substantive experience, and occasionally even playing a hunch. The use and application of statistics, therefore, is simply an agreed-upon method for formalizing that logic. If a researcher expects his or her answers to questions to be accepted by others as factual (i.e., a jury of scientific peers), then the methods for obtaining such answers must conform to certain logical standards. Most often, these standards are supplied by the logic of statistics.

At this point, the hard-core "data-phobes" are probably muttering, "These guys can't fool me. There's math involved in statistics." Of course, they are right; statistics require you to understand and perform some basic mathematical calculations and operations. Nevertheless, the statistics presented in the next several chapters will require no more than the ability to add, subtract, multiply, and divide. Hardly advanced mathematics! In addition, some basic, elementary algebra (e.g., how to rearrange the sides of an equation) would be helpful, but that too is logic which can be picked up easily without formal training.

Finally, the remaining diehards are no doubt saying, "I've looked at stat books before, and they're a maze of foreign letters and weird symbols." To this complaint we must, alas, agree. Statistics, like communication and all other disciplines, does have its jargon, and it does employ a number of symbols to express this jargon. Nevertheless, this obstacle is no different from that faced when learning any new skill, whether it be automobile mechanics or the growing of African violets.

There is an old saying, "Everything is hard until you know how to do it." So it is with statistics. At first glance, the novel symbols and the constant use of numbers seems formidable, if not insurmountable. There is, of course, a natural tendency to resist learning new, unfamiliar concepts. Once they become familiar, however, their meaning will be clear, and they will actually come to be viewed as both efficient and necessary.

Some Necessary Symbols

To aid the avoidance of this "symbol shock," we present below a few of the most frequently encountered symbols in statistics. We hope that by discussing them out of the context of various equations and formulas, we can facilitate familiarity. Moreover, the list which follows should provide a handy reference table to which you can return as you read subsequent chapters. We will not, of course, present all of the symbols and their definitions which will be used; this would serve to confuse rather than clarify matters. As we progress, however, we will define every new symbol before introducing it in the discussion. For the present here are a few basic symbols:

Y: an alphabetic symbol which represents an observed or measured variable. In the abstract it may represent any variable, but in calculation will be identified with a specific variable name. The other letter frequently used to symbolize such variables is X.

N: the number of observations of a variable in a data set. Depending on the context of the study, these observations may be individual people, families, groups, cities, etc.

Y_i: an individual observation of the variable Y; in this case, the ith observation. The subscript i refers to any observation between 1 and N. This letter may be replaced with a number, Y_1, Y_2, etc., thereby symbolizing a specific observation.

$\sum$: the capital Greek letter sigma. It is a direction to sum or add up the value of a variable which follows.

$\sum_{i=1}^{N} Y_i$: is an expression which directs that all of the individual values of Y from the 1st to the Nth be added together. The letter and number ($i = 1$) under the sigma indicate where to begin summing; the N (or number, if known) over the sigma indicates where to stop.

$$\sum_{i=1}^{N} Y_i = Y_1 + Y_2 + \cdots + Y_i + \cdots + Y_N.$$

$\overline{Y}$: is the arithmetic mean of the values of Y. The mean is the sum of the observations divided by the number of observations which were summed. Therefore,

$$\overline{Y} = \frac{\sum_{i=1}^{N} Y_i}{N}$$

Frequently, however, the specific variables to which $i = 1$ and N refer are understood and the subscripts are dropped, leaving,

$$\overline{Y} = \frac{\sum Y_i}{N}$$

These few symbols will suffice to begin this chapter. Additional symbols will occasionally be introduced, but they will be no more complicated, just new. If you simply approach the following chapters as an exercise in logic and not mathematics, they will be no more difficult or confusing than the ones you have just encountered.

Statistical Concepts—Describing Data

The primary purpose of employing statistics in communication research is to aid the researcher in drawing suitable scientific conclusions from the data. The data which have been obtained are arrayed and manipulated in a prescribed manner, and statistical "tests" are performed to determine whether the data conform to the hypotheses advanced by the researcher. If these tests reveal that the hypothesized relationships exist, the researcher has obtained evidence to support his or her theoretic predictions. If other results are obtained, the researcher must conclude that either (1) the hypothesized relationships do not exist, or (2) there have been serious flaws in the procedures and/or measurement of the study which have prohibited the detection of such relationships. Either conclusion requires additional theoretic and empirical inquiry.

The entire process of using statistics to test theoretic hypotheses or predictions involves the use of what have been labeled "inferential statistics." In other words, statistical tests allow the investigator to draw logical *inferences* from the data. They represent the formalization of the deductive logic which was mentioned earlier. Statistical inference is the primary and most frequent use to which statistics are put in communication research. Without such statistics, the field of communication could not operate as a social science.

Despite this heavy (and necessary) emphasis on hypothesis testing, the logic underlying statistical inference is *not* the place to begin the initial introduction to statistical concepts. That will come later. For the present, the discussion of a more common application of statistics is in order, namely, the *description* of data. Statistics are quite capable of providing a variety of basic descriptive information about the variables which have been observed or measured. Moreover, it is in this descriptive sense that statistics are most frequently encountered in everyday life: e.g., that the life expectancy of males in our society is 72.4 years; or that the average professional basketball player now earns (gulp!) over $100,000 a year.

The logic which underlies these statistical descriptions is the conceptual foundation for understanding and using inferential statistics. Just as children must walk before they can run, so must communication researchers be able to describe the relevant attributes of their data before they can draw inferences from them. The descriptive and inferential functions of statistics are not disjointed or independent. On the contrary, they are logically related in a straightforward hierarchical fashion.

This discussion of descriptive statistics will begin with a presentation of the two most important attributes of any "set" or "batch" of observed values of a variable. These attributes are labeled the "center" and the "spread" of the data (Tukey, 1977). Although several alternative statistics which represent these attributes will be presented, the desire to draw inferences from data will require a more detailed exploration of two: the *arithmetic mean* and the *variance* of the data. Finally, even though this chapter will concentrate on describing a single variable, the statistics to be presented are equally applicable to all other variables in the data set.

The Center of the Data

To illustrate the fundamental importance of this attribute of data, consider a seemingly macabre, yet extremely realistic example. Assume that you are a bookie of sorts who takes bets from both friends and strangers. You, however, are a rather unusual bookie in the sense that you only accept bets on a single "sporting" event: how long a person will live. You bet that a person will live to a certain, specified age, while that person bets that he or she will die before that age. The bettor puts down his or her bet in yearly increments. Hence, if you win the bet, you get to keep the money for as long as the person lives and use it to make more money for yourself. If you lose the bet (i.e., the person dies before the age you specify), you must pay off the bet in full out of your winnings and profits from other bettors.

In case you haven't yet recognized this method of wagering, such bookies in our society are formally recognized as life insurance companies. Moreover, the primary determinant of whether insurance companies succeed or fail is their ability to calculate accurately the average life expectancy of the people from whom they take bets (i.e., issue policies). Of course, some people will die sooner than average, while others will live longer than expected. Nevertheless, if these companies carefully calculate the center of the data for the variable called "life expectancy," they can balance off their losses against their wins and most likely make a profit in the process. One thing is certain: Few life insurance companies go bankrupt.

The point of this example is to illustrate the importance of obtaining a numerical index of the center of the data. Frequently, this index is referred to as the *central tendency* of the data. If a researcher knows nothing else about the people from whom these data are collected, the center becomes the *expected value* of their score. That is, other things being equal, the center of the data is the best prediction of the score an individual will provide. As in the life insurance example, the researcher who employs the central tendency as the sole predictor of a person's score will frequently be wrong—some people will score higher and some lower. More important, the goal of scientists is to obtain additional information about each person which will reduce the error of prediction. In the absence of such information, however, the center of the data becomes the expected value for each respondent, and hence the best bet for prediction.

Thus far, the center of the data has been presented as a relatively abstract concept. As indicated above, however, a number of alternative statistics operationalize this concept into a numerical index. Currently, only three such alternatives will be discussed: the *mode*, the *median*, and the *mean*. Each of these statistics is defined and calculated differently, and each possesses its own inherent strengths and weaknesses. Nevertheless, they all attempt to locate the center of the observed data. The order in which these three statistics are discussed reflects the amount of use and acceptance they have achieved in communication research.

The Mode.   The *mode* is simply defined as the most frequently observed value of a variable. In other words, when researchers refer to a "modal score," they are referring to that value of a score which was most frequently obtained from the participants in the study. The mode, therefore, is calculated quite easily by performing a *frequency count*. This is no more difficult than simply placing slash marks (/ / / / /) next to each possible score the respondents provide.

For example, assume the data have been obtained from 25 respondents on their attitude toward willow trees. (This example was purposely selected, for we assume that most people possess neither strongly positive nor strongly negative attitudes about willows.) These 25 scores were obtained by requesting each respondent to complete a 7-point semantic differential scale whose anchor points were "good-bad." If these hypothesized data are vertically arrayed and a frequency count is performed, the results might resemble those presented in Figure 8.1. Clearly, the mode of this set of scores is 4, because it was the most frequently chosen scale value. These data, then, correspond to the assumption that most people are "neutral" toward willow trees.

Another aspect of these data worth noting is that the center of the data (i.e., the mode) and the middle of the data correspond perfectly. Frequently, this will not be true. To illustrate this point, assume everything about the previous example is the same except that the respondents' attitudes toward increased federal taxes are now measured. It would seem reasonable to assume that most people would not have a positive (or even neutral) attitude toward this topic. Hence, a frequency count of these data might look

FIGURE 8.1. Hypothetical Data on Attitude Toward Willow Trees.

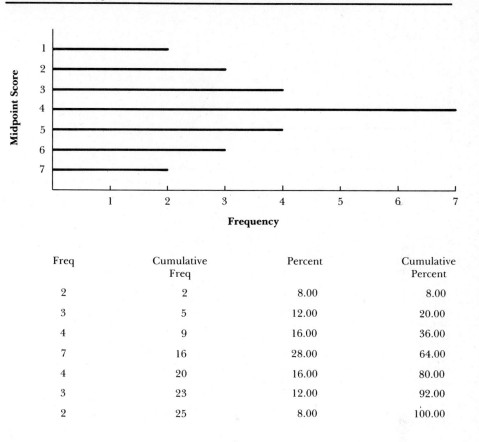

Freq	Cumulative Freq	Percent	Cumulative Percent
2	2	8.00	8.00
3	5	12.00	20.00
4	9	16.00	36.00
7	16	28.00	64.00
4	20	16.00	80.00
3	23	12.00	92.00
2	25	8.00	100.00

something like Figure 8.2 (p. 138). For these data, the mode is 7, which is far from the middle of both the scale itself and the values actually obtained from the scale.

This second example was designed to illustrate the primary weakness of employing the mode as a measure of central tendency. In many instances, it may give a very distorted picture of the center of the data. Because the mode is the most frequently obtained score, it is totally insensitive to the frequency or position of other scores along the measuring scale. To provide an extreme example, suppose that from these 25 respondents, 13 had marked a "7," and 12 had marked a "1." The mode, of course, would still be 7, even though all logic would suggest that the center was somewhere between these two extremes.

Given this weakness, it should not be surprising that communication researchers seldom employ the mode as an index of central tendency. More often than not, the mode would provide an inaccurate estimate of where the center actually was located. For example, suppose two scores had exactly the same frequency; or, even more extreme, suppose all of the scores had the same frequency. In such cases, the mode would not be a useful statistic.

This is not to suggest that the mode is a totally useless statistic. On the contrary, when an investigator's inquiry centers on questions of frequency (e.g., What is the most

FIGURE 8.2. Hypothetical Data on Attitude Toward Increased Federal Taxes.

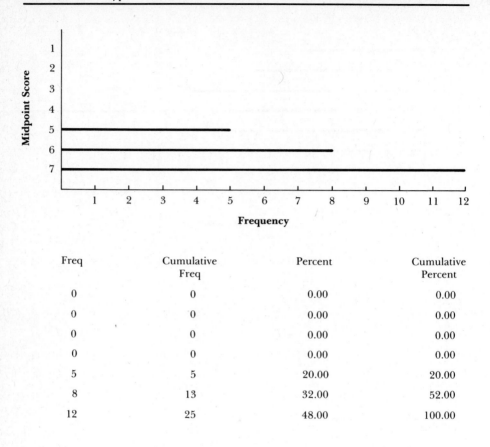

Freq	Cumulative Freq	Percent	Cumulative Percent
0	0	0.00	0.00
0	0	0.00	0.00
0	0	0.00	0.00
0	0	0.00	0.00
5	5	20.00	20.00
8	13	32.00	52.00
12	25	48.00	100.00

frequent type of nonverbal response to a message perceived as an insult?), the mode will be the statistic of choice. Be that as it may, the desire to draw inferences from the data makes the accurate depiction of the center of the data a necessity. The mode will frequently fail to provide this information.

   The Median.   The median of a batch or set of scores is both conceptually and mathematically a much more accurate index of central tendency. The median is defined as the 50th percentile of a batch of scores. In other words, one half of the scores are larger than the median and the other half are smaller. Consequently, the median is by definition the *middle* of the obtained values of a variable.

   Despite this increased precision, the calculation of the median is, in practice, as simple and straightforward as that of the mode. The first step is to array the scores vertically in rank order from highest to lowest (or vice versa). The next and final step is to begin at the top of the array and count down half way (i.e., $N/2$ scores). If the number of obtained scores (N) is odd, the median will be the discrete score exactly in the center of the arrayed data. If, on the other hand, N is even, *two* scores will be located in the "center." The median, therefore, is the arithmetic mean or average of these two scores.

To illustrate these procedures, return to the data set presented in Figure 8.1. Since there are 25 scores in this batch of data, the median will be the 13th rank-ordered score. In this example, therefore, the median is 4. For these data, the median and the mode happen to be exactly the same; the reason for that will be discussed later. If the same procedure is performed on the data in Figure 8.2, the median turns out to be 6. Recall that the mode for these data was 7. Moreover, it was suggested that the mode was not a particularly accurate description of this central tendency. Even a purely visual inspection of these data (called "eyeballing" by researchers) suggests that the center of the data must lie somewhere between 7 and 5. The median, therefore, is a much more intuitively satisfying index.

The strengths and weaknesses of the median tend to be one and the same. The median's primary strength is that it is an extremely *robust* descriptive index of central tendency. Because it is defined as the 50th percentile of the obtained data, the median is totally insensitive to extreme scores or (in more statistical jargon) "outliers." This insensitivity to extreme scores is achieved by the process of rank ordering described earlier. Simply put, each observation's actual score (whether, for example, it is measured in units of dollars, inches, or scale points) is replaced by its *rank* in the data set ranging from 1 to N. Hence, even though the difference between the Nth and the N-1th score may be quite large in terms of actual units, this difference is ignored in the process of rank ordering. As a result, when an investigator (1) is interested in describing a batch of data and (2) desires the center of the data to correspond as closely as possible to the middle of the data, the median is an extremely useful statistic.

As indicated above, this major strength of the median (i.e., robustness) is also its primary weakness. Whereas the median is especially suited for the description of data, these same properties render it considerably less useful for drawing inferences from those data. The detailed rationale for this must await the discussion of the "spread" of the data. For the present, suffice it to say that an index of spread (more specifically, the variance) of the data is indispensable for drawing inference. More to the point, the calculation of this spread must be based on the value of each score in its original units. Since the median transforms these original scores into unitless ranks, its usefulness for inferential statistics is more than a bit limited.

The Mean.   The arithmetic mean is the most important and most frequently used index of central tendency. Most students encounter this statistic in grade school (although it was usually called the "average") long before they have any concern about statistical description or inference. It may be of some comfort to know, therefore, that the calculation of the mean is no more difficult now than it was then. Our current interests, of course, require that we impart to the mean a few additional conceptual attributes that were not described by your grade school teacher.

Recall that the mean is defined as the sum of a set of scores or observations divided by the number of scores in the set. This verbal definition is symbolized in Eq. 8.1.

$$\bar{Y} = \frac{\sum\limits_{i=1}^{N} Y_i}{N} \tag{8.1}$$

Recall the $\bar{Y}$ (pronounced Y-bar) is the symbol for the mean of the observations and the Greek sigma (Σ) is the mathematical symbol for summation.

The data arrayed in Figure 8.1 can be used to illustrate the actual calculation of this statistic.

$$\bar{Y} = \frac{\sum\limits_{i=1}^{N} Y_i}{N} = \frac{7 + 7 + 6 + \cdots + 2 + 1 + 1}{25} = \frac{100}{25} = 4$$

It is worth noting that the mean as an index of central tendency for these data is exactly the same as the median and the mode. This equality will have important implications during the discussion of one of the major "parameters" of parametric statistics.

If these calculational procedures are applied to the data in Figure 8.2, a different set of circumstances arises: the mean equals neither the median nor the mode.

$$\bar{Y} = \frac{\sum\limits_{i=1}^{N} Y_i}{N} = \frac{7 + 7 + 7 + \cdots + 5 + 5}{25} = \frac{157}{25} = 6.28$$

Recall that earlier it was determined from eyeballing the data that an accurate index of the center of these data must fall somewhere between 5 and 7. A more detailed visual inspection of Figure 8.2, however, will suggest that because a score of 7 is more frequent than a score of 5, the center will be a bit closer to the larger number. In this instance, a mean of $\bar{Y} = 6.28$ corresponds to that expectation.

With these two examples in mind, a more conceptual (as opposed to mathematical) definition of the arithmetic mean can now be presented. Assume that the obtained scores are arrayed on a horizontal beam, much like the typical playground teeter-totter. The beam itself represents the original continuum of measurement in original units, and the frequency of each score represents the "weight" each score exerts on the beam. The data from the two previous examples have been arrayed in this manner in Figure 8.3. As can be seen from this figure, the mean represents the fulcrum or balance point along the beam; i.e., the point at which the teeter-totter would remain perfectly parallel to the ground. It is in this sense that the mean indexes the center of the data—the point at which the *obtained* scores are perfectly balanced on the scale of measurement.

This analogy can also illustrate the primary weakness of the arithmetic mean: The mean is very sensitive to extreme scores. If the mean is thought of as the balance point of the set of obtained measurements, then the inclusion of extreme scores will require the mean to shift—sometimes radically—in order to "rebalance" the data. For the purposes of description, only a few such outliers render the mean an inaccurate index of the center of the data. This is why the median, in contrast, is a more robust descriptive statistic. It ignores outliers by simply transforming them from original units to a rank.

Similarly, for inferential purposes the presence of outliers is also quite undesirable. As suggested, the mean is the primary index of central tendency for drawing inferences from data. Accordingly, to the extent that the mean is affected by extreme scores, the inferences which are drawn (and perhaps the substantive conclusions as well) will be mistaken. Equally important, the presence of outliers will also affect the second attribute of data necessary for the drawing of inferences, namely, the spread. Clearly, one or more extreme scores will make any index of spread much larger, with the result again being the potential for inaccurate conclusions. Given these realizations, you should not be

FIGURE 8.3. Illustration of Arithmetic Mean as Balance Point or Fulcrum of Obtained Scores.

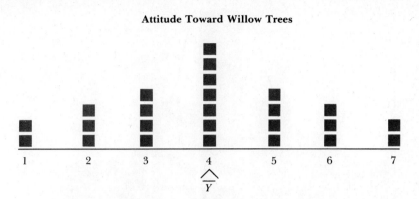

Attitude Toward Willow Trees

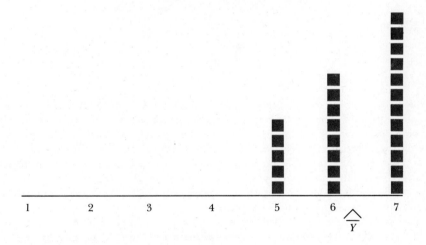

Attitude Toward Increased Federal Taxes

surprised that one of the basic assumptions of parametric statistics is the absence of extreme scores.

The Relationship of the Mean, Median, and Mode. Several times during the discussion of central tendency, we have mentioned that the mean, median, and mode for one of the data sets (see Figure 8.1) were exactly the same. Although such a situation is not especially frequent in the empirical analysis of actual data, there can be little doubt that it is extremely desirable. In fact, it is an *ideal* situation when all of these measures of central tendency correspond.

To illustrate the reasoning behind this desirability, Figure 8.4 presents these same data in a slightly different manner. First, the frequency count is transposed on its side and frequency is represented by solid bars. Occasionally such a visual representation will

FIGURE 8.4. Frequency Histogram Representing Normal Distribution.

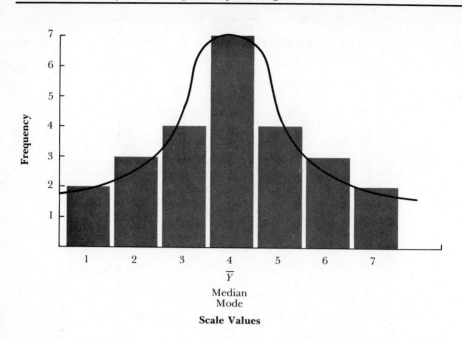

be called a vertical bar chart, but the technical name for this type of array is a *histogram*. Also notice that in Figure 8.4 the midpoints of the vertical bars have been connected with a smooth curved line. You may recognize the shape as the familiar bell-shaped curve. This type of curve and its relationship to central tendency will be discussed in some detail. First, however, it is necessary to emphasize one important fact: The bell-shaped curve is representative of frequency. All such curves are really shorthand depictions of a frequency histogram. Their entire purpose is to visually display the frequency of various scores along the continuum of measurement.

In statistics, the bell-shaped curve is an especially important concept which is synonymous with what is known as a *normal distribution* of scores. A normal distribution requires that (1) the score with the highest frequency of appearance be the mean score (i.e., the mean = the mode), and (2) as scores increase in their distance from the mean they decrease in frequency. Moreover, this decrease must be symmetrical for scores on both sides of the mean. Stated differently, the mean must be in the exact center of the obtained data (i.e., the mean = the 50th percentile = the median) and the scores on both sides of the mean must decrease in frequency in a perfectly "balanced" manner.

These requirements ensure that for data which are normally distributed, the mean, median, and mode will be exactly the same. The concepts of the middle of the data, the most frequent score in the data, and the balance point or fulcrum of the data are one and the same. Clearly, for the description of the center of data, whenever the three indices of central tendency are equivalent, a researcher's confidence in the accuracy of description is greatly enhanced.

For the purpose of statistical inference, a normal distribution assumes additional importance. The mean is the primary index of central tendency for statistical inference.

Further, it has been shown that the mean is very sensitive to extreme scores, and when they exist the mean tends to be a less accurate index. For data to assume a normal distribution, however, there can be no extreme scores. By definition, every score above the mean must be balanced by a score which is an equal distance below the mean. In addition, as these scores become further away from the mean, they must *decrease* in frequency. As a result, normally distributed data "protect" the mean against its major weakness by not allowing extreme scores which can unduly affect its performance as an index of central tendency.

To illustrate these relationships, Figure 8.5 presents a histogram and curve of the hypothetical data on attitudes towards increased taxes. Obviously, the normal, bell-shaped curve is not apparent. These data form a *skewed* distribution. The "hump" in the data (the mode) is skewed to either the right or the left of the middle of the scale of measurement. Notice further that the mean, median, and mode do not correspond. As is always the case with skewed data, the mean falls between the other two indices. This

FIGURE 8.5. Frequency Histogram Representing Skewed Distribution.

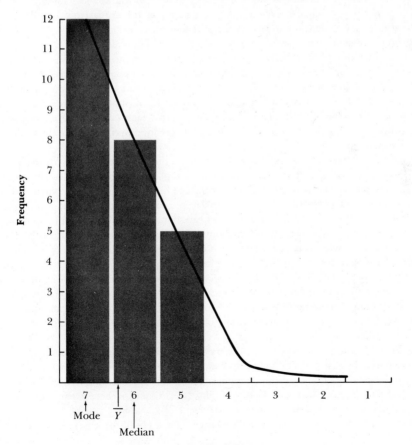

type of data creates problems in terms of accurate description. As for statistical inference, the difficulty inherent in such data (especially a skewed distribution with outliers) should also be apparent. Whenever the distribution of the data causes the mean to be numerically different from the median and the mode, the potential for inaccurate inference is unavoidable.

The result of this discussion is the ability to present a fundamental assumption of statistics. The data from which statistical descriptions and inferences are drawn are assumed to be normally distributed. A normal distribution is the best insurance of the accuracy of these various indices. It is important to realize, however, that this is indeed an *assumption*. A normal distribution must occur naturally; it cannot be imposed on data.

In the actual conduct of research, obtained data only infrequently exhibit a perfectly normal distribution. Data stray from this ideal distribution, and outliers are not uncommon, especially in observational data where certain behaviors are simply counted. As a result, when faced with such situations, the researcher must take special care to prevent inaccuracies from creeping into his or her descriptions and inferences.

The Spread of Data

The second important attribute necessary to describe data is its "spread." *Spread* refers to the dispersion of scores around the center of the data. How much do the observations vary around the index of central tendency? A numerical index of spread or dispersion is essential for both statistical description and inference. For descriptive purposes, an index of variability is a necessary supplement to the measure of central tendency. To be sure, the mean, median, and mode provide important information about the "average" observation—i.e., the center of the distribution. For a more complete description (at least as complete as can be obtained in summary form), it is also necessary to describe the distance and frequency with which the scores are distributed around that center. Without a numerical index of spread, descriptions of data would be woefully inadequate.

For the reasons stated previously, a thorough discussion of how the dispersion of data relates to statistical inference must await the presentation of the descriptive statistic. Nevertheless, that discussion may be prefaced by suggesting that the variability of observations is intrinsically linked to the basic purpose of science. Perhaps the most fundamental goal of science is to answer *why* questions—to explain how phenomena of interest are related. From a statistical point of view, the fundamental *what* of these explanations (i.e., what is it that science explains) is the variability of these phenomena. In other words, communication research seeks to explain *why* people vary in their communicative behaviors. Although the explanations per se are substantive communication theories, the variability which is being accounted for is very much a statistical attribute of data. Accordingly, a thorough knowledge of both the concepts and numerical indices of data dispersion is indispensable for understanding and performing empirical communication research.

Before turning to the various summary statistics which index spread or dispersion, we will pause briefly and ask a purely conceptual question. Specifically, what characteristic or attribute of data should a numerical index of spread capture? For the indices of central tendency, we had a fairly straightforward response: Where is the center of the observed data? In a similar manner, the concept of variability can be captured in a relatively direct question: What is the "average" deviation of the observed scores from the center of the data as indexed by the mean? Two statistics accurately and succinctly provide this information. Moreover, these two indices are the most informative and useful statistics for both description and inference.

Deviations from the Mean. At this point, we could simply describe the two statistics and present their calculational formulas. And most of you, like thousands of students before, would accept this presentation, dutifully memorize the formulas, and have no idea of the logic by which they were derived. This is an approach we wish to avoid. Instead, by using the basic conceptual question an index of variability is designed to answer, we will derive these formulas with a bit of logic and common sense.

Recall that the basic question is: What is the "average" deviation of the observed scores from the center of the data as indexed by the mean. For the moment, we will ignore the part about "average" deviation and concentrate solely on obtaining the total of the deviations of the observed scores from the mean. At first glance, this seems an easy problem to solve. It would require little effort or mathematical ability to simply subtract the mean from the value of each score and add those differences together. This should result in the desired total.

Table 8.1 (p. 146) displays a small data set on which this procedure can be performed. For the present, no substantive or theoretic interpretation will be given to these data. The focus will be exclusively on calculation. Notice that in the second column of this table the operation symbolized by $(Y_i - \bar{Y})$ has been performed. More important, the totals at the bottom of that column clearly illustrate the major drawback associated with this simple subtraction approach to calculating dispersion: The sum of the differences from the mean is zero:

$$\sum_{i=1}^{N}(Y_i - \bar{Y}) = 0$$

After a moment's reflection, this finding should not be a surprise. By definition, the mean is the center of the data in its original units. It is the balance point or fulcrum of the obtained data. Accordingly, if the value of the mean is subtracted from each score, the data should indeed "balance." Mathematically, such balance is operationalized by the fact that the sum of such differences will be zero. In addition to revealing the need for an alternative approach to describing dispersion, this result also provides additional insight into the meaning of the arithmetic mean as a measure of central tendency.

As for an alternative to calculating variability, another moment of reflection will reveal a second strategy. Recall that the initial attempt was foiled because the positive and negative deviation scores canceled each other and created a sum total of zero. The negative differences, however, could be eliminated by discarding the minus signs; i.e., by summing the *absolute values* of the deviation scores. (The absolute value of a number is symbolized by a straight line on each side of the number; for example, $|-8| = 8$.)

This approach is illustrated in the third column of Table 8.1 and is symbolized by $|(Y_i - \bar{Y})|$. Moreover, as the total at the bottom of the column indicates, a positive total (86) has been obtained. It is quite possible, therefore, to calculate the average deviation from the mean (3.74). Could it really be this easy?

Unfortunately, the answer is no. Although this approach to describing variability possesses the advantages of calculational ease and simplicity, it is seldom used by

TABLE 8.1. Listing of Raw Score and Various Attempts to Define Spread

OBS	Y	$(Y_i - \bar{Y})$	$\lvert(Y_i - \bar{Y})\rvert$	$(Y_i - \bar{Y})^2$	
1	23	2	2	4	
2	21	0	0	0	
3	15	−6	6	36	
4	27	6	6	36	
5	25	4	4	16	
6	29	8	8	64	
7	18	−3	3	9	
8	28	7	7	49	
9	21	0	0	0	
10	25	4	4	16	
11	23	2	2	4	
12	25	4	4	16	
13	19	−2	2	4	
14	17	−4	4	16	
15	24	3	3	9	
16	18	−3	3	9	
17	24	3	3	9	
18	21	0	0	0	
19	13	−8	8	64	
20	16	−5	5	25	
21	17	−4	4	16	
22	15	−6	6	36	
23	19	−2	2	4	
$\sum_{i=1}^{N}$	483	0	86	442	(SS)
$\bar{Y}$	21	0	3.74	20.09*	(VAR)
				4.48	($\sqrt{\text{VAR}} = sd$)

*This "average" was calculated by dividing by $N - 1$ instead of N.

researchers as an index of dispersion. The rationale, simply stated, is that this approach almost always underestimates the variability of the data set. As an index of dispersion, it is frequently too small.

Fortunately, a simple mathematical operation accomplishes the desired goal. This involves no more than simply squaring each deviation score and adding up all the squares. The fourth column in Table 8.1 illustrates this procedure. Symbolically, this approach is represented by Eq. 8.2.

$$\sum_{i=1}^{N}(Y_i - \bar{Y})^2 \qquad (8.2)$$

The process of squaring makes large deviation scores contribute more to the variability than small ones (e.g., 8^2 does not equal $4^2 + 4^2$). The farther away a score is from the mean, the more it proportionally contributes to an index of variability. Notice also that the total at the bottom of the column is considerably larger than that resulting from the absolute deviation method (442 versus 86). Finally, it should be pointed out that this total does have the potential to be zero—definitely a conceptual requirement. If all of the observed scores were the same (and thus equalled the mean), there would be no variability and this index would be zero.

This total represents one of the most important numerical indices in all of parametric statistics. Formally, it is called the *sum of squared deviations from the mean,* but most often its label is shortened and it is simply referred to as the *sum-of-squares.* It is usually abbreviated simply as *SS.* The importance of sum-of-squares is twofold. First and most obvious, it is the preliminary and most basic step in calculating any index of variability. Before the "average" deviation from the mean can be determined, a total which can be divided must be calculated. The sum-of-squares is this total. Second and perhaps most important, every test of statistical inference either directly or indirectly employs sums-of-squares in its calculational procedures. To say the least, it is a most widely used and most important statistical index.

Although Eq. 8.2 fulfills all of the conceptual requirements of an adequate index of variability, it is infrequently used in calculation. The need to calculate and square N deviation scores is simply too cumbersome and time-consuming. A more efficient method for calculating SS is:

$$SS = \sum_{i=1}^{N} Y_i^2 - \frac{\left(\sum_{i=1}^{N} Y_i\right)^2}{N} \tag{8.3}$$

Eq. 8.3 requires that each Y score be squared and these squares be added together. For the data in Table 8.1, $\sum_{i=1}^{N} Y_i^2 = 10,585$. Next, the sum of the Y scores is calculated (483) and this total is squared ($483^2 = 233,289$) and divided by N ($233,289/23 = 10,143$). When the latter quantity is subtracted from the former, the result will be exactly the same as that obtained from Eq. 8.2: $10,585 - 10,143 = 442$. Even though Eq. 8.3 offers no heuristic insight into the concept of variability, it provides a much easier method for calculating this important statistical index.

This conceptual understanding of sum-of-squares allows a straightforward presentation of the two statistics which describe the spread of data. To review, the conceptual goal is to obtain a numerical index which characterizes the "average" deviation of the obtained scores from the mean. Both of these statistics provide that information, but present it in a slightly different form. As a result, they are used for somewhat different purposes.

The Standard Deviation of Data.   The standard deviation *(sd)* of any variable *(Y)* containing N observations is symbolized by Eq. 8.4.

$$sd_Y = \sqrt{\frac{\sum_{i=1}^{N} (Y_i - \bar{Y})^2}{N - 1}} \tag{8.4}$$

Verbally, this formula directs one to (1) compute the sum-of-squares for the variable Y,

(2) divide that value by the number of observations minus one, and (3) take the square root of that entire quantity. The numerical quantity which results represents the amount in original units that a typical or standard observation deviates from the mean.

Given Eq. 8.4, it is a fairly simple matter to insert the appropriate values from the data in Table 8.1.

$$sd_Y = \sqrt{\frac{\sum\limits_{i=1}^{N}(Y_i - \bar{Y})^2}{N-1}} = \sqrt{\frac{SS}{N-1}}$$

$$= \sqrt{\frac{442}{22}} = \sqrt{20.09}$$

$$= 4.48$$

Simple enough, but what does 4.48 mean? This number indicates that the typical score in this batch of data deviates 4.48 units from the mean. Some individual scores deviate more and, of course, some deviate less, but this statistic represents the *standard* deviation of all scores in the data set. As such, it is highly descriptive of the spread of the data.

If you have been reading carefully, you have noticed a subtle shift in the terminology used to describe this statistic. Previously, the index of spread was conceptualized as the "average" deviation from the mean. Now, it is being described as "typical" or "standard." Recall, however, that whenever the term *average* was employed, it was set off in quotation marks. It was meant to describe a conceptual goal, not a mathematical reality. After all, to be technically accurate, the true average deviation from the mean is zero—that is what is meant by balance.

By first squaring the deviation scores and then finding the square root of the mean squared score, the standard deviation opts for an alternative mathematical approach. Although the standard deviation is not technically the "average" deviation from the mean, it does fulfill all of the necessary conceptual and logical requirements. As a result, it is universally accepted by scientists and statisticians as a valid descriptive index of the spread of data.

One last clarification is in order. In describing Eq. 8.3, we suggested that the value obtained by dividing the sum-of-squares by $N - 1$ was the "mean of the squared deviation scores," that is, the "average." In the past, the mean was obtained by dividing by N. Although we hesitate to sow the seeds of conceptual confusion, both accounts are correct. The quantity represented by $N - 1$ is referred to as *degrees-of-freedom (df)*. Whenever we are estimating the dispersion or variability of a *sample* of scores, the degrees-of-freedom of that sample are $N - 1$.

Degrees-of-freedom refer directly to the number of scores in the sample data set which are "free to vary." In other words, how many scores are free to assume *any* score? The reason that one score is *not* free to vary is that in order to estimate the standard deviation, the sum of the N scores was calculated and divided by N; i.e., we must calculate the mean. Once the sum of the N scores has been determined, the number of scores free to vary is reduced by one. To illustrate, assume the following set of scores: $5 + 3 + 7 + 1 + 6 + X = 26$. It requires no great mathematical genius to determine that the score designated by the X must be 4. It *must* be 4. It can assume no other value. Once the sum of the six scores and the values of the first five scores (any five scores!) are fixed, the sixth score possesses no freedom to vary (see Walker, 1940).

Throughout the remainder of this book, all of the indices and statistics presented will employ degrees-of-freedom to determine the "average" deviation from the sample mean. Because each of these statistics requires that the mean of the sample be calculated initially, only $N - 1$ scores remain free to vary. Hence, even though the conceptual notion of "average" deviation remains the same, the computation of this "average" must rely on one less than the complete set of scores.

The Variance of Data. The second and perhaps more frequently used statistic to represent the spread is called the *variance* (VAR) of the data. Eq. 8.5 presents the symbolic formula for calculating the variance.

$$\text{VAR} = \frac{\sum_{i=1}^{N}(Y_i - \bar{Y})^2}{N - 1} \tag{8.5}$$

In words, the variance is obtained by dividing the sum-of-squares by $N - 1$. When examined carefully, this formula is the same as that for standard deviation, except that the square root sign has been removed. In short, the variance is the square of the standard deviation. It represents the typical or standard deviation squared.

Moreover, the variance *must* be obtained before the standard deviation can be calculated. Hence, a researcher really gets two statistics for the price of one. For example, in the previous calculations on the data in Table 8.1, the variance was 20.09 (i.e., $\sqrt{20.09} = 4.48$). Conceptually and descriptively, the knowledge of the variance provides little information that was not already available from the calculation of the standard deviation. If anything, squaring the standard deviation makes it actually less descriptive.

The question, then, is: Why use it? What is the value of a "less descriptive" statistic? The answer, simply put, is that using the variance in any calculation or formula which employs an index of spread makes that calculation much easier to perform. Square roots are a nuisance. They make any number of formulas unnecessarily complicated and (especially prior to electronic calculators and computers) are relatively difficult to calculate. Long ago, mathematicians found that it was easier and more efficient to square *all* of the elements of a formula than it was to calculate the square root of even one. As a consequence, almost all formulas associated with inferential statistics use the variance instead of the standard deviation, not because the variance adds any conceptual or descriptive clarity, but because it makes the results of these formulas easier to obtain.

One final point. Because the variance is relatively uninformative as a descriptive statistic, researchers tend not to represent variance as a number (e.g., 20.09). Such a number simply has little conceptual meaning. Instead, they have developed the practice of presenting variance as a percent. All of the variance of any given variable is obviously 100% of the variance. In the discussion of reliability (Chapter 6), we suggested that 90% of the variance might be due to true scores and 10% due to errors of measurement. Similarly, in later chapters when statistical inference is discussed, a certain percentage of the variance will be identified as "systematic" (i.e., it can be explained or accounted for), while the remainder will be labeled as random or unexplainable.

The point of introducing this notion here is to emphasize that when researchers talk about variance as percent, they are always referring to a percent of "something"— that is, a numerical quantity to which that percentage can be referred. Moreover, that numerical quantity can be directly calculated from the data by applying Eq. 8.5. Consequently, when reports of research or textbooks (including this one) refer to variance as a percent, you should not be confused. Before that percentage can be determined, the variance must be calculated as a concrete and specific number. Discussions in terms of percent of the variance, therefore, are merely attempts to bring conceptual meaning and clarity to an otherwise uninformative statistic.

Standard Scores—Making Units Comparable

Thus far, the discussion of central tendency and dispersion has presented the logic and calculation of the various statistics in terms of the "raw" data. The mean, standard deviation, and so forth have employed calculations based on the metric or unit by which the data were originally obtained. For the statistical description of one or more variables treated individually, this is most often a necessary and desirable practice. It provides a conceptual benchmark for comparing individuals or groups in terms of the original unit of measurement. As long as all such comparisons are made with data having the *same* unit of measurement, the use of that common unit can actually aid substantive interpretation.

A problem frequently arises, however, when a researcher begins making descriptive or inferential comparisons about individuals or groups on several variables— variables which were obtained by employing different units of measurement. For example, if a researcher wanted to compare men and women on their level of education (measured in years), he or she would encounter little difficulty in interpreting such a comparison. In contrast, if the same researcher wanted to assess the relationship between education and income (measured in dollars), problems with interpretation could arise. The totally different units (years and dollars) by which these variables are measured would make meaningful descriptions difficult to provide.

To understand the nature of this difficulty and how it can be overcome, you must first understand an inherent attribute of units of measurement. In almost all instances, the unit in which a given variable is measured is a totally arbitrary decision of the investigator. Income, for example, can just as easily and accurately be expressed in francs, marks, or lire as in American dollars. Earlier, in fact, we argued that many of the variables of interest to communication researchers have no actual metric or unit—e.g., interpersonal attractiveness, nonverbal sensitivity, etc. Even though operationalization and measurement of such variables may be both valid and reliable, the unit selected for such measurement is an arbitrary decision.

The implication of this for data description and inference is that most statistical indices are affected by the unit of measurement. Their values increase or decrease depending on which unit is selected. It is important to realize that frequently such changes have nothing to do with substantive or theoretic interpretation. A person who has gone to school 12 years has also gone to school 24 semesters, 36 quarters, or (assuming 180 school days per year) 2160 days. All of these units of time contain the same information, even though the values of the statistics such units might produce would be vastly different.

As a result, it is apparent that what is needed is a procedure for transforming *any* variable with *any* metric into a common and comparable unit of measurement. This need not be a "real" unit—it can be an equally arbitrary choice—and it need not possess substantive or theoretic meaning. What is requisite, however, is that any and every variable can be transformed into it. To some extent, this problem was addressed earlier when it was suggested that a common practice among researchers is to refer to variance by percent rather than by raw units (technically, raw units squared). This practice avoids the problem of differing metrics among variables and allows researchers to make straightforward comparisons.

Similarly, in Chapter 9 the correlation coefficient will be introduced. It serves as a standard index for assessing the magnitude or strength of relationship between two variables. The relationship between any two variables, irrespective of their units of measurement, can be described and tested by this standard index.

For the present, however, the focus is on the need to transform the unit of measurement for a single variable into a common metric. What is required is that the mean and standard deviation of that variable are the same as all other variables which have been so transformed; a method which not only makes their metrics equivalent, but their central tendency and dispersion as well. This seems an unachievable goal until you realize that all variables already possess a common characteristic: namely, their standard deviation. Although the actual value of the standard deviation is directly affected by the original unit of measurement, conceptually all standard deviations are equivalent. Regardless of their actual numerical value, they conceptually represent the amount by which a standard or typical observation deviates from the mean. Consequently, a logical choice for this common and comparable unit or metric is the standard deviation unit. Any value of any variable can be reexpressed as the number of standard deviations it differs from its mean.

Traditionally, the scale onto which such converted or transformed scores are placed has been called the *z-scale,* and the transformed scores are referred to as *z-scores.* Moreover, the actual reexpression is frequently referred to as *standardizing* data. The formula for conducting this transformation is actually quite simple. It is expressed by Eq. 8.6.

$$z_i = \frac{(Y_i - \bar{Y})}{sd_Y} \tag{8.6}$$

This equation states that the mean value of the variable $(\bar{Y})$ should be subtracted from each individual score in the data set (Y_i). This will result in both positive and negative difference scores, whose total and thus mean are zero. Next, the equation directs that each deviation score be divided by the standard deviation of the variable (sd_Y). The result is that each score (z_i) is representative of the number of standard deviations it varies from the mean. Even though all of the calculations were performed in the original unit of measurement, all reference to that original unit is now gone. It has been replaced by a unit which is common to all variables: the standard deviation.

Table 8.2 (p. 152) illustrates the procedure on the data originally in Table 8.1. Several interesting and important attributes of z-scores can also be noticed in this table. First, notice that the mean of the z-scores is zero. This is true for any variable which has been so transformed, and results directly from the fact that the mean of the initial deviation scores $(Y_i - \bar{Y})$ is zero. If the "average" amount by which the scores deviate from the mean is zero, then that amount converted to standard deviation units is also zero.

In addition, note that the sum-of-squares for the z-scores is 22, or exactly $N - 1$. This, in turn, means that both the standard deviation and the variance (sd^2) of these z-scores is equal to 1.0. This characteristic also holds true for all variables which have

TABLE 8.2. Listing of Raw Score and Accompanying Standard Score   (z-score)

OBS	Y	z-score	z^2
1	23	0.4462	0.19910
2	21	0.0000	0.00000
3	15	−1.3386	1.79186
4	27	1.3386	1.79186
5	25	0.8924	0.79638
6	29	1.7848	3.18552
7	18	−0.6693	0.44796
8	28	1.5617	2.43891
9	21	0.0000	0.00000
10	25	0.8924	0.79638
11	23	0.4462	0.19910
12	25	0.8924	0.79638
13	19	−0.4462	0.19910
14	17	−0.8924	0.79638
15	24	0.6693	0.44796
16	18	−0.6693	0.44796
17	24	0.6693	0.44796
18	21	0.0000	0.00000
19	13	−1.7848	3.18552
20	16	−1.1155	1.24434
21	17	−0.8924	0.79638
22	15	−1.3386	1.79186
23	19	−0.4462	0.19910
$\sum_{i=1}^{N}$	483	0	22

$$(SS)$$

$$sd = \sqrt{\frac{22}{N-1}} = 1$$

$$VAR = sd^2 = 1$$

been standardized in this manner. Because each observation has been converted to standard deviation units, the typical or standard score must, by definition, deviate only one such unit from the mean.

When these attributes are combined, they indicate that *any* variable which is standardized into z-scores will have a mean of zero and a standard deviation (or variance) of 1.0. These universal parameters make z-scores more efficient and simpler to use when calculating additional descriptive and inferential statistics. This advantage is in addition to the fact that the statistics which are obtained are directly comparable because they have been calculated from scores possessing a standard metric.

It is important to reassert that transforming variables into standard or z-scores in no way alters the information those variables contain. Because the transformation involves only subtraction and division by a constant (i.e., $\overline{Y}$ and sd are the same for all observations of a variable), no important characteristics of the data are changed. The distance of each score from its mean—even though reexpressed in different units—is proportionally the same, and any relationships that the standardized variable had with other variables remain unaltered. The only change is the ease by which a researcher can make meaningful comparisons among variables.

■ *Conclusion*

This chapter has emphasized the importance of obtaining several basic statistics which describe the characteristics of each measured variable. First, the necessity of determining the "center" of the data was discussed and three alternative statistics were presented to achieve this goal: the mean, median, and mode. For most purposes, the mean would be the statistic of choice, although it was emphasized that the mean is especially sensitive to extreme scores. In fact, one of the primary reasons for so carefully exploring and describing individual variables is to ensure that such outliers do not unduly bias the estimate of the center of the data.

The second important attribute of univariate data was presented as their "spread" or dispersion around the central tendency. In this instance, the goal was to describe the amount by which a typical or "average" observation deviated from the mean—a goal which was fulfilled by calculating the standard deviation. In addition, two closely related statistics called the variance and the sum-of-squares were introduced. For various reasons of ease and efficiency, these latter two statistics are much more frequently used than the standard deviation in performing statistical tests of inference. In contrast to their calculational utility, their conceptual or substantive meanings were characterized as seldom useful for describing data.

Finally, this chapter introduced the concept of and procedure for "standardizing" individual variables by transforming them into z-scores. The scores of a standardized variable will be represented in standard deviation units and will have $\bar{Y} = 0$ and $sd = 1$. Admittedly, such reexpressions possess limited descriptive utility when considering individual variables in isolation; most often statistics based on the raw data are more informative. The true usefulness of z-scores will surface during the discussion of bivariate (and later, multivariate) relationships.

Bivariate Data Description

Throughout this book we have emphasized (perhaps to the point of redundancy) a single guiding principle: the discovery, description, and explanation of *relationships* is at the heart of every social scientific endeavor. Such relationships may be conceptualized in various ways, depending on the research perspective and the theoretic content. For our present concerns, the details of these differences are not important. All perspectives assume that relationships represent regularities which occur in the real world. Such regularities, in turn, form the basis for the construction and evaluation of communication theory.

As just described, the process of social science envisions its end result to be the theoretic explanation of behavioral regularity, and for communication researchers, regularities in communication behavior. Phrased in a manner we have used before, communication research attempts to provide theoretic answers to *why* questions. Given this process, the role of research methods and statistics assumes a subsidiary function. Empirical methods are simply tools which communication researchers employ in the process of answering *why* questions. This subsidiary role, however, should not be taken to mean that such methods are unimportant or trivial tools. On the contrary, they are perhaps the most important. Before relationships can be explained, they must be discovered, thoroughly described, and tested or confirmed to assure their existence is factual. These prerequisites fall largely in the province of empirical methods, especially statistics. This is a relatively large and crucially important territory. Nevertheless, as you increasingly come to understand and employ empirical methods, you should remind yourself continually that the sole reason for their use is to expand our understanding of communication behavior. For communication researchers, empirical methods are *not* an independent scholarly pursuit.

Conceptualizing Relationships

In order to fully grasp the logic which underlies the statistical description of relationships, we must begin once again by asking, at a conceptual level, what information we seek to obtain. What do researchers and theorists mean when they assert that two variables are related? First, it is clear that the concept of a relationship between two variables (i.e., a *bivariate* relationship) implies the absence of statistical or theoretic independence. These two variables (or more technically, the concepts or constructs they represent) are linked, attached, or associated for some reason. (Remember: this "reason" is totally the concern of theory, and is in no way addressed by statistics.) Accordingly, this means that observed changes in the values of one variable are accompanied by concomitant change in the other: As scores for one variable increase, the scores for the other variable exhibit a simultaneous or concurrent change. That is, they either increase or decrease accordingly. Implicit in this description, of course, is that *both* sets of scores must be obtained from the *same* sample of observations.

In statistical jargon, the term used to describe such concomitant change is *covariation*. Quite literally, covariation means to "vary together." As the values of variable X exhibit more or less deviation from the mean, $\bar{X}$, the values of variable Y exhibit a systematic tendency to deviate or vary from their mean, $\bar{Y}$, to the same degree or magnitude. Consequently, the conceptual question for which an answer is sought can be cast: To what extent do the two variables of interest exhibit concomitant change in their values? In other words, to what extent do they covary? From the point of view of statistics, the concept of a relationship is operationalized by the principle of covariation.

In these previous questions, the phrase "to what extent" suggests, not surprisingly, that few variables are perfectly related. They do not exhibit perfect covariation. Two explanations for this are readily apparent. First, all social science measurement is subject to some degree of error. All scores contain an error component or random variation. Since randomness, by definition, cannot be systematically related to anything, measurement error serves to attenuate or make smaller all observed relationships. As measurement becomes more accurate, the "true" degree of relationship can be more precisely determined.

The second reason for imperfect relationships is more substantive. Simply put, some variables are less than perfectly related in nature. Other substantive variables intervene to decrease their degree of covariation. To cite a simple example, assume that the number of minutes spent reading a newspaper each day increases with (covaries with, is related to) a person's years of formal education. Such covariation, no doubt, will be far less than perfect. Some highly educated people are too busy to read the newspaper on a regular basis; certain professionals spend their time reading specialized journals or magazines, while for many, the emergence of television news subtracts from the time they read the paper. As a result, while there may be a very real relationship between newspaper reading and education, any number of additional variables serve to explain why it is less than perfect.

To involve these additional variables in the process of description and explanation, however, requires the use of multivariate rather than bivariate relationships. We will discuss multivariate relationships, albeit very briefly, in subsequent chapters. For the present, assume that perfect, absolute covariation can occur only when two variables are measuring exactly the same phenomenon in exactly the same way. Because this seldom happens (except occasionally by mistake), the conceptual questions about relationships must almost always ask "to what extent" two variables covary.

Two additional aspects of this conceptual question are worth noting. First, it is important not to confuse the concept of relatedness or covariation with that of causation. The assignment of the label "cause-effect" to a relationship is primarily the concern of theory. Clearly, there are certain relationships in medicine and science where causation is almost inherent: the severity of a stroke and the loss of speech; or the measurement of an earthquake on the Richter scale and the dollar amount of damage done to buildings.

In communication research, however, it is far more common that causality is either indeterminate or nonexistent. For example, do TV portrayals of marriage cause people to be more aware of their own marital difficulties, or do one's own marital problems create an increased awareness of such TV portrayals (see Baran & Courtright, 1980)? Whatever the answer, it will not be provided by statistical description and analysis. Only a well-conceived and well-articulated theory can place causal ordering on such relationships.

Second, it is necessary to realize that relationships can assume either of two forms. Variables can exhibit direct covariation, or they can covary inversely. Direct relationships are usually symbolized by a ($+$) sign. This means that as the values of variable X increase, the values of Y increase also. Inverse relationships are most often symbolized by a ($-$) sign, signifying that as X increases in value, variable Y concomitantly decreases.

Direct covariation would be exemplified by the relationship between the communicator credibility of a persuasive speaker and the amount of attitude change in his or her audience. Other things being equal (an important qualification), the *more* credible a speaker is perceived to be, the *more* attitude change he or she will evoke in the audience. An example of inverse covariation would be the relationship between communication apprehension and the number of interpersonal interactions in which one participates: i.e., the *more* apprehensive about communicating a person becomes, the *less* he or she participates in interaction with others.

Despite these differences, the basic conceptual meaning of covariation remains unaltered. Larger or smaller deviations from the mean of X are accompanied by or associated with deviations of similar magnitude in Y. What distinguishes direct from inverse relationships is the direction of those deviations. If the direction is the same, either both positive or both negative, the relationship is direct. If the direction is opposite, an inverse relationship is implied. In either case, the concept of "varying together" is the basic operating principle.

Illustrating Relationships Graphically

Perhaps the simplest, yet most effective method of describing the relationship between two variables is to visually display that relationship in a two-dimensional graph. By simply plotting the values of one variable against those of the other, you can frequently see (literally) the direction and magnitude of a given relationship. As one becomes a more sophisticated and inquiring analyst of data, it is occasionally necessary to employ more advanced graphic techniques (see Tukey, 1978). Currently, however, a straightforward, two-dimensional "scatterplot" will be sufficiently descriptive.

Before offering several examples of such plots, we will again pause and conceptually ask what it is we would expect to see. First, what would a plot between two variables that were totally unrelated look like? The answer: random. The absence of relationship implies that the two sets of scores exhibit no systematic pattern of covariation. As a result, any plot of their scores will display complete randomness or absence of pattern. In contrast, the scores of two variables which are perfectly related (again, a rarity or a mistake) will exhibit a highly systematic and recognizable pattern. Depending on the nature of the relationship, this pattern may be a straight line or some form of a curve; the exact form is not important to this discussion. If a relationship between two variables is "perfect," then their plot will depict a very definite and discernible pattern.

In between these two extremes, scatterplots of moderate relationships will exhibit a little of both. That is, taken as a whole their plot will show a general or diffuse pattern, which is referred to as a "trend." The individual points of the plot will not all correspond to this trend. They will be scattered here or there in an unsystematic fashion, thus illustrating that at least part of the relationship is composed of random error.

Table 9.1 presents the hypothetical scores for two variables which were gathered from 15 subjects in a study. The first variable, Loneliness, represents the scores from an index designed to assess individuals' perceptions of how lonely they are. The possible scores on this scale range from 1 to 10. The second variable, TV Hours, represents the number of hours per week each individual watches television. The univariate descriptive statistics for each variable also appear in this table. In addition, the raw scores for each variable have been transformed into their corresponding z-scores.

From the data arrayed in Table 9.1, it is difficult, if not impossible, to detect whether these variables are related in any meaningful way. To examine their relationship visually, it is necessary to plot the values as displayed in Figure 9.1 (p. 158). The 10 possible values of the Loneliness index are arrayed on the horizontal axis (formally called the abscissa), while the hours of television watched are represented on the vertical axis (the ordinate).

A visual examination of this plot suggests that these two variables are moderately to strongly related. Notice that the scores tend to stretch out in something of a straight line which slopes toward the right-hand corner of the plot. This indicates that as scores along the horizontal axis increase, so, to some extent, do scores along the vertical axis. Consequently, a direct relationship between Loneliness and TV Hours is suggested.

TABLE 9.1. Hypothetical Data on Loneliness and TV Watched Per Week

OBS	Lonely	TV_{Hours}	z_{Lonely}	z_{Hours}
1	5	10	−1.4808	−1.7889
2	6	12	−0.4712	−0.8944
3	8	17	1.5481	1.3416
4	7	16	0.5385	0.8944
5	6	15	−0.4712	0.4472
6	7	15	0.5385	0.4472
7	6	14	−0.4712	0.0000
8	5	11	−1.4808	−1.3416
9	7	13	0.5385	−0.4472
10	7	14	0.5385	0.0000
11	5	12	−1.4808	−0.8944
12	7	14	0.5385	0.0000
13	6	13	−0.4712	−0.4472
14	8	18	1.5481	1.7889
15	7	16	0.5385	0.8944
Σ	97	210	0.00	0.00
Mean	6.47	14	0.00	0.00
SS	13.73	70	14.00	14.00
VAR	.981	5	1.00	1.00
sd	.990	2.236	1.00	1.00

FIGURE 9.1. Scatterplot of Loneliness Index and TV Hours.

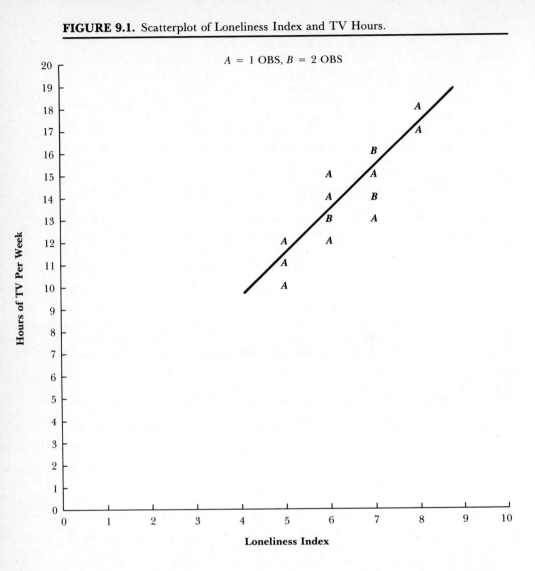

Figure 9.2 displays a plot between the same two variables, but in this instance their corresponding *z*-scores are graphed. Loneliness is still on the horizontal axis and TV Hours on the vertical. Notice, however, that the scaling of both axes is much different. Despite this difference, the plot looks much the same: the same general trend is depicted. Actually, the plot of the relationship is *exactly* the same. Earlier we emphasized that because standardization does not alter the distribution of the scores, it does not affect a variable's relationship with other variables. Figure 9.2 provides visual evidence of this very important property.

Both of these plots illustrate a direct or positive relationship. In contrast, Figure 9.3 (p. 160) shows a scatterplot of two variables whose relationship is negative or inverse.

FIGURE 9.2. Scatterplot of Standardized Scores for Loneliness and TV Hours.

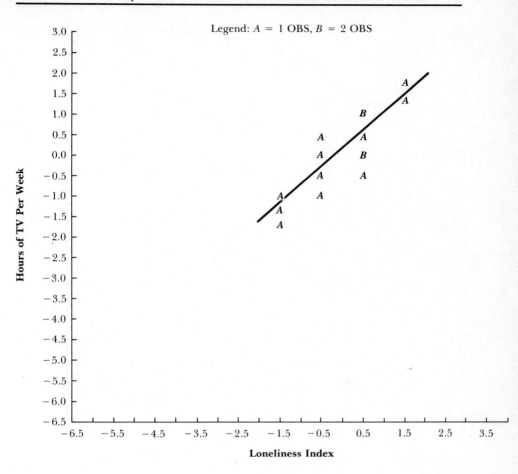

To remain consistent with our example, this figure depicts a plot between the number of dates a person has each month and the hours of TV they watch per week. The plotted scores still tend to exhibit a straight line or linear trend, but this time they slope downward, indicating that as scores on the horizontal axis increase, scores on the vertical axis tend to decrease. Substantively, this would suggest that people who date more frequently tend to watch less TV. It should be emphasized that inverse relationships are just as frequent and just as important to theory construction as are direct ones.

It would be unwise to conclude this discussion of visually examining relationships by leaving the impression that all relationships are linear, i.e., their scatterplots approximate the shape of a straight line. Such a conclusion would be false. Any number of relationships are actually curvilinear—their scatterplots assume the general shape of a curve. Such trends are still indicative of relationships, but they suggest that the relationships will be a bit more difficult to statistically describe and theoretically explain.

Figure 9.4 (p. 162) illustrates such a relationship between the variables of Com-

FIGURE 9.3. Inverse Relationship Between Dates Per Month and TV Hours.

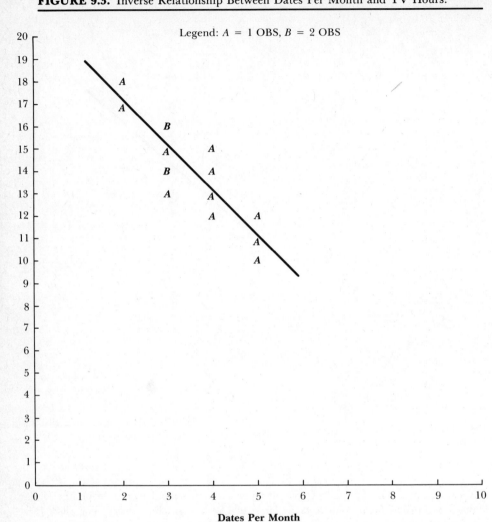

munication Effectiveness in small groups and Self-Esteem. Notice that the effectiveness scores tend to increase as Self-Esteem moves from low to moderate. After a certain point, however, effectiveness ratings begin to decrease as self-esteem scores continue to become larger. From this plot one might conclude that moderate levels of Self-Esteem are related to maximum effectiveness in small group situations. In contrast, group members who are either very high or very low in Self-Esteem tend to be much less effective communicators. Perhaps individuals who are low in Self-Esteem participate less in the discussion, while those extremely high in Self-Esteem tend to be egotistical and thus attempt to dominate the interaction. Whatever the explanation, it is clear that the relationship is not linear; it cannot be described as simply direct or inverse in the linear sense. Nevertheless, assuming that such a relationship is found to exist, an attempt must be made to explain it using the most appropriate theory at one's disposal.

A Numerical Index of Relationship—Covariance

As important as these various scatterplots are to an investigator, they can at best be described as both preliminary and exploratory. Their function is to provide a general picture of the relationship, to give a visual indication or suggestion of what information various numerical indices might provide. In fact, most research reports and articles present only numerical indices of a relationship. It is assumed that the reader can "imagine" the type of two-dimensional plot which would correspond to such an index.

One of the most basic and fundamental of these numerical indices is called the *covariance*. Frequently, it is abbreviated as either "COV" or "σ_{XY}." As you might surmise, the index of covariance between two variables attempts to numerically capture and represent the conceptual properties of covariance we discussed earlier. In short, it describes the concomitant variation between two variables. Stated differently, it represents as a single number the "average" amount by which deviations from the mean of one variable are associated with similar deviations in another variable.

Symbolically, covariance is presented as:

$$\text{COV} = \frac{\sum_{i=1}^{N}(X_i - \bar{X})(Y_i - \bar{Y})}{N - 1} \tag{9.1}$$

This equation directs one to first turn each X-score and each Y-score into a deviation score; i.e., find its difference in *raw units* from its mean. Each X deviation score is then multiplied by its corresponding Y deviation. When this is completed for all N observations, these products are summed. The label frequently applied to the entire numerator of Eq. 9.1 is "sum-of-products," which is abbreviated SP. Thus Eq. 9.1 can be re-expressed as:

$$\text{COV} = \frac{SP}{N - 1} \tag{9.2}$$

As a final step, one calculates the "average" product of these deviations by dividing the sum-of-products by $N - 1$. Again, the rationale for using $N - 1$ rather than N to compute this "average" revolves around the concept of degrees of freedom discussed in Chapter 8. It is the quantity which is always used when calculating the covariance from a sample of data.

If you examine Eq. 9.1 carefully, you will see that the sum-of-products and subsequently the covariance can assume either a positive or negative value. This property, of course, corresponds to the conceptual distinction between direct and inverse relationships. If a given X-score falls below its mean, its deviation score will be negative. If the corresponding Y deviation score is positive (i.e., Y_i is greater than $\bar{Y}$), then their product term will be negative. If both deviation scores are *either* positive or negative, direct covariation is indicated and the product term will be positive. Assuming that a sufficient number of these product terms take on negative values, the sum-of-products and the covariance will be negative also. How large this negative covariance will be depends on the magnitude of the respective deviation scores. Nevertheless, a negative sum-of-products can result only when the conceptual conditions for an inverse relationship exist—that is, increases in the value of one variable (positive deviations from the mean) are accompanied by decreases in the other (negative deviations from the mean). As a result, this numerical index fully captures all of the conceptual properties required to describe an empirical relationship.

The calculations required to obtain covariance can be illustrated by using the data on Loneliness and TV Hours presented earlier. Table 9.2 displays these data in their raw form, as well as their respective deviation scores and product terms. The sum-of-products is obtained by simply summing the product terms. Thus,

$$SP = 5.88 + .94 + 4.59 + \cdots + 6.12 + 1.06$$
$$= 27$$

As was true of the sum-of-squares for a single variable, SP can be obtained much more efficiently by employing a special calculational formula:

$$SP = \sum_{i=1}^{N} X_i Y_i - \frac{\left(\sum_{i=1}^{N} X_i \right) \left(\sum_{i=1}^{N} Y_i \right)}{N} \tag{9.1a}$$

FIGURE 9.4. Curvilinear Relationship Between Group Effectiveness and Self-Esteem.

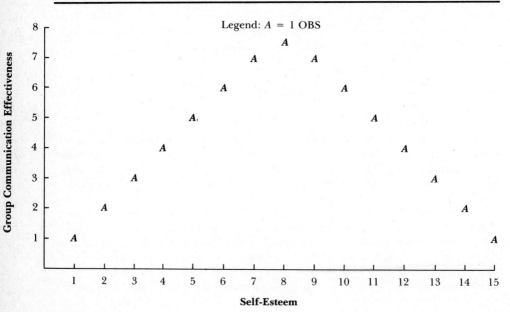

TABLE 9.2. Deviation Scores and Product Terms for Loneliness and TV Hours

OBS	X	Dev$_X$	Y	Dev$_Y$	Products
1	5	−1.47	10	−4	5.88
2	6	−0.47	12	−2	0.94
3	8	1.53	17	3	4.59
4	7	0.53	16	2	1.06
5	6	−0.47	15	1	−0.47
6	7	0.53	15	1	0.53
7	6	−0.47	14	0	0.00
8	5	−1.47	11	−3	4.41
9	7	0.53	13	−1	−0.53
10	7	0.53	14	0	0.00
11	5	−1.47	12	−2	2.94
12	7	0.53	14	0	0.00
13	6	−0.47	13	−1	0.47
14	8	1.53	18	4	6.12
15	7	0.53	16	2	1.06

For the present data,

$$\sum_{i=1}^{N} X_i Y_i = 1385$$

$$\frac{\left(\sum_{i=1}^{N} X_i\right)\left(\sum_{i=1}^{N} Y_i\right)}{N} = \frac{(97)(210)}{15}$$

$$= \frac{20{,}370}{15}$$

$$= 1358$$

Thus, $SP = 1385 - 1358 = 27$, which corresponds exactly to the value obtained from Eq. 9.1.

Finally, as directed by Eq. 9.2,

$$COV = \frac{SP}{N - 1}$$

$$= \frac{27}{14}$$

$$= 1.9285$$

These results indicate that the "average" amount by which Loneliness and TV Hours covary is 1.93. Moreover, the fact that this number is positive indicates that these two variables are directly related. This information, of course, corresponds to the preliminary suggestion obtained from Figure 9.1.

A "Standard" Index of Relationship—The Correlation Coefficient

These calculations for covariance give rise to several difficult questions. What does a covariance of + 1.93 mean? How does one interpret such a number? Is it indicative of a strong relationship? A weak relationship? We describe these questions as "difficult" because the index of covariance offers little assistance in answering them. Much like its companion index for a single variable (the variance), the covariance can be quite useful for performing subsequent calculations, but of little or no use for substantive interpretations.

The reason for this difficulty can be traced directly to a problem we have mentioned before: units of measurement. Because the sum-of-products and covariance are calculated from raw data, their values are directly affected by the units of measurement in which the two variables were originally obtained. Moreover, this problem is compounded by the fact that covariance is calculated by multiplying these raw scores. The result is a covariance metric whose units are the *product* of the values of the original variables. In the illustration in the previous section, for example, the covariance is + 1.93 units on the Loneliness × Hours scale. Clearly, this is not a readily interpretable number.

Perhaps more important, this value cannot be compared in any meaningful way to indices of covariance from other pairs of variables. Because covariance will be arbitrarily large or small depending on the units of measurement of the variables involved, such values cannot be used to compare the magnitude of two or more relationships. In short, it is impossible to draw conclusions about the relative "strength" of relationships.

The remedy for this problem is really quite simple. It requires that prior to calculating the covariance, all variables be standardized into a common metric by transforming them into z-scores. Not only would such standard scores possess a common mean and variance ($\bar{X} = 0$, VAR $= 1$), but they would possess a common metric as well. As a result, their standardized covariance could be directly compared to similar indices from other variables, and conclusions about their relative magnitude of relationship could easily be made.

The term used to label this standardized or z-score covariance is the *correlation coefficient*. Frequently named after its inventor, Karl Pearson, the Pearson correlation coefficient possesses several desirable properties. First, like the index of covariance, correlations can assume either a positive or negative value—obviously, a conceptual requirement for distinguishing between direct and inverse relationships. Second and perhaps more important, the correlation coefficient is "bounded" at both the upper and lower extremes. Unlike covariance which can take on extremely large positive or negative values, all correlation coefficients will fall between the range of + 1.0 to − 1.0. They can be no larger or smaller.

As a result of these bounds, a correlation of + 1.0 indicates perfect direct covariation, while a value of − 1.0 represents perfect inverse covariation. The third and final property of correlation coefficients is that a value of 0.0 represents absolutely no relationship; total independence between two variables. As the values increase between 0.0 and + 1.0 or decrease between 0.0 and − 1.0, relationships of larger magnitude are indicated. The result is that the magnitude of all relationships can be evaluated on a universal scale. This makes comparison and interpretation a much more straightforward task.

Recall that Eq. 9.1 directs the calculation of the covariance as follows:

$$\text{COV} = \frac{\sum_{i=1}^{N} (X_i - \bar{X})(Y_i - \bar{Y})}{N - 1} \tag{9.1}$$

When z-scores are entered into this formula, however, the calculation of difference scores is unnecessary because the mean of both variables is zero. Consequently, the formula for calculating the correlation coefficient (symbolized by r) can be reexpressed as:

$$r = \frac{\sum_{i=1}^{N} (Z_{X_i} - 0)(Z_{Y_i} - 0)}{N - 1} \tag{9.3}$$

$$= \frac{\sum_{i=1}^{N} Z_{X_i} Z_{Y_i}}{N - 1}$$

In words, the correlation is the sum of the z-score products divided by $N - 1$.

These calculations can be illustrated by returning to the standardized scores for Loneliness and TV Hours found in Table 9.1:

$$r = (-1.4808 \times -1.7889) + (-0.4712 \times -0.8944) + \cdots +$$
$$(1.5481 \times 1.7889) + (0.5385 \times 0.8944)/14$$

$$= \frac{12.1914}{14}$$

$$= .8708$$

This value provides two pieces of information about the relationship between Loneliness and amount of TV viewed per week. First, these two variables exhibit a direct relationship. This information, of course, corresponds to what has previously been learned from Figure 9.1 and the calculation of covariance. The coefficient of correlation, however, provides additional empirical evidence that this relationship is relatively strong. In fact, it could appropriately be described as very strong. Given that the upper limit for correlations is $+1.0$, the value of $r = .8708$ is much closer to a perfect relationship than to total independence. Obviously, it is not perfect, indicating that both variables contain some proportion of their variance which is random or unsystematic as far as the relationship is concerned.

Obtaining Correlations from Raw Data

The formulas thus far have presented a method for calculating the correlation coefficient when both variables have been transformed into z-scores. Such transformation, while not particularly difficult, is certainly time-consuming. It requires a large number of separate calculations ($2 \times N$, to be exact), and introduces equally many opportunities for simple mathematical error. Accordingly, it would be quite useful to possess a formula which allowed the correlation coefficient to be calculated directly from various indices of the raw data. Eq. 9.4 presents such a formula:

$$r = \frac{\text{COV}}{\sqrt{\text{VAR}_X \, \text{VAR}_Y}} \tag{9.4}$$

We have previously described the covariance as the index of relationship calculated in the original units of the variables. The denominator of Eq. 9.4, however, introduces a new concept. When two numbers are multiplied and their square root is obtained, this latter value represents a type of "average." It is referred to as the "geometric mean." In Eq. 9.4, the geometric mean is used to determine the "average" variance of the two variables, X and Y. The correlation coefficient, in turn, is expressed as a ratio of the covariance to this average variance.

To understand this formula, consider again the conceptual meaning of a perfect relationship. If two variables are perfectly related, all of their statistical characteristics will be the same, including their variance. Moreover, the covariance will equal the variance of either variable, which will be equal to each other. Finally, the geometric mean of the two variables will be:

$$\text{GM} = \sqrt{\sigma_X^2 \, \sigma_Y^2}$$

but if $\sigma_X^2 = \sigma_Y^2$

$$\text{GM} = \sqrt{(\sigma_X^2)^2}$$
$$= \sigma_X^2$$

As a result, the correlation coefficient will be $+/-1.0$, which it must be for a perfect relationship. However, because variables are very seldom perfectly related, it follows that the two variances will seldom be equal. Consequently, the geometric mean gives the best estimate of the "average" variation of these two variables.

From previous calculations, it is known that the covariance between Loneliness and TV Hours is 1.9285, while the variances are .981 and 5.0, respectively (see Table 9.1). If these values are inserted in Eq. 9.4,

$$r = \frac{1.9285}{\sqrt{.981 \times 5.0}}$$

$$= \frac{1.9285}{2.2147}$$

$$= .8708$$

Thus, within rounding error, Eqs. 9.3 and 9.4 produce exactly the same index of correlation.

For this particular example, Eq. 9.4 was easy to calculate because we had previously performed the preliminary computations. It is possible, nevertheless, to make this equation somewhat simpler, thus avoiding several computational steps. If Eq. 9.4 is expanded, it becomes:

$$r = \frac{SP/N-1}{\sqrt{(SS_X/N-1)(SS_Y/N-1)}} \tag{9.5}$$

but since N *must* be the same for both X and Y,

$$r = \frac{SP/N-1}{\sqrt{(1/N-1)^2}\,\sqrt{SS_X\,SS_Y}}$$

$$= \frac{SP/N-1}{1/N-1\,\sqrt{SS_X\,SS_Y}}$$

At this point, simple algebra will show that the two $N-1$ terms cancel, thus leaving:

$$r = \frac{SP}{\sqrt{SS_X\,SS_Y}} \qquad (9.6)$$

Once again, using the previous calculations from Loneliness and TV Hours:

$$r = \frac{27}{\sqrt{13.73 \times 70}}$$

$$= \frac{27}{31}$$

$$= .8709$$

The slight difference in the result is due solely to rounding error.

In summary, the correlation coefficient is designed to be a standardized index of the magnitude of relationship between two variables. Regardless of whether it is calculated from z-scores or directly from the parameters of the raw data, its interpretation is the same. Also, its interpretation is unchanged, regardless of whether the relationship is direct or inverse. The direction of the relationship is different, but not its meaning in terms of amount, strength, or magnitude. Finally, we described a method for calculating the correlation coefficient directly from raw data. This approach is clearly more expedient, as it avoids the large number of computations required to convert the data to z-scores. For most correlational analyses, this will be the preferred method of calculation.

Rank-Order Correlation Coefficients

The previous description of the Pearson correlation coefficient assumed that the variables whose relationship was being assessed were continuous; their scores represented some amount on a continuum. Unfortunately, the definition of "continuous" is somewhat different depending on whether one adheres to the "conservative" or "liberal" school of measurement and statistics (see Chapter 6). Fundamentalists, for example, would maintain that only those variables whose scores have been obtained from interval or ratio level measurement should be considered continuous. Thus, ordinal measurement in the form of ranks is precluded from description and analysis by Pearson r. Because we adhere to the liberal school, we will shortly argue that such an exclusion is unwarranted and can safely be ignored. For the present, however, we will accept the fundamentalist definition in order to introduce an alternative approach to calculating the correlation coefficient.

Occasionally in the course of analyzing social science data, one encounters variables whose values are in the form of ranks. Such variables might include: ranking in one's high school class; position in the hierarchy of an organization; or the listing of "most preferred" to "least preferred" options or positions in a public opinion poll. All data such as these would be classified as ordinal measurement. It is possible to determine that one observation has more or less of a particular characteristic than others, but not to determine exactly how much more or less. According to the fundamentalists, any attempt to calculate the mean of such ordinal data would result in nonsense. Because such ranks do not represent real numbers, their mean could not be interpreted in any meaningful way. Without an interpretable mean, it would be impossible to obtain any of the statistical parameters necessary to calculate correlation: specifically, either z-scores or sum-of-squares and sum-of-products.

Despite the fundamentalist prohibition against analyzing ordinal data by Pearson r_S, a relationship between two variables is not precluded simply because their values are in the form of ranks. On the contrary, such variables can certainly be related in any of the ways we have previously described, including complete independence. The argument is that their relationships cannot be assessed by statistics which employ the mean as the measure of central tendency. For data of this type, an alternative method for computing the correlation is necessary—a method which can obtain all of the necessary information about relationships solely from rank order.

Two such alternatives exist for describing the magnitude of relationship between two ordinal, rank-order variables. For purposes of illustration, however, we will present but one: the Spearman Rank-Order Correlation Coefficient (r_S). The formula for calculating this statistic is actually quite simple, and is expressed in Eq. 9.7.

$$r_S = 1 - \frac{6 \sum_{i=1}^{N} d_i^2}{N^3 - N} \tag{9.7}$$

where d_i is the difference between the ith ranked observation on variable X and its companion ranking on variable Y. As usual, N is the number of observations in the data set. Despite its completely different appearance, Eq. 9.7 is derived directly from Eq. 9.6, when it is assumed that the values of both X and Y are ranks. Due to its complexity, we will not present this derivation. For further information and discussion, see the thorough explanation by Siegal (1956, pp. 203–204).

The application of Eq. 9.7 can be illustrated by employing the data in Table 9.3. In this example, a sample of nine people were rank-ordered in terms of their ability on two separate nonverbal skills: sensitivity of nonverbal communication reception (SNR), and sensitivity of nonverbal communication transmission (SNT). In addition, the table displays each difference score between ranks (d_i), as well as each difference score squared (d_i^2). Applying Eq. 9.7,

$$r_S = 1 - \frac{6(49 + 36 + 25 + 25 + 4 + 1 + 16 + 36 + 0)}{(9 \times 9 \times 9) - 9}$$

$$= 1 - \frac{1152}{720}$$

$$= 1 - 1.6$$

$$= -.60$$

TABLE 9.3. Rank-Orders for Sensitivity of Nonverbal Reception (SNR) and Sensitivity of Nonverbal Transmission (SNT)

OBS	SNR	SNT	Diff	Diff^2
1	9	2	7	49
2	1	7	-6	36
3	8	3	5	25
4	6	1	5	25
5	3	5	-2	4
6	7	6	1	1
7	5	9	-4	16
8	2	8	-6	36
9	4	4	0	0

As a result of these calculations, one could reasonably conclude that the relationship between these variables in this sample is both inverse and moderately strong. This correlation would seem to suggest that those individuals who are good receivers of nonverbal cues tend to be relatively poor senders, and vice versa. At first, a puzzling finding, but perhaps not. Although these data are purely hypothetical, a similar conclusion concerning nonverbal sensitivity is supported by the research (and real data) of Lanzetta and Kleck (1970). They argue that such differences in nonverbal skills could be accounted for by differential patterns of socialization as children. In any case, these data illustrate clearly how a relationship between two ordinal variables would be calculated and described using rank-order correlation.

Much Ado About Nothing

In several places throughout this book, we have expressed our belief that distinctions between weak and strong measurement, as well as the type of statistics applicable to each, are often superfluous. Numbers are numbers, regardless of whether they represent names, ranks, or continua. Hence, while levels of measurement may well have implications for the theoretic interpretation of findings, they do not affect the statistical procedures required to produce such findings.

Despite what we consider a well-reasoned and cogent argument (naturally), the time has come to prove this point to yourself using the statistical skills you currently possess. Recall that the data in Table 9.3 represent the rank orders of individuals' sensitivity to nonverbal reception and transmission. Moreover, the calculation of Eq. 9.7 produced a correlation of $-.60$. Now apply Eq. 9.6 for computing the Pearson correlation to these data. If your calculations are correct, you will find that the $SP = -36$, and $SS_{SNR} = SS_{SNT} = 60$. Accordingly,

$$r = \frac{-36}{\sqrt{60 \times 60}} = \frac{-36}{60} = -.60$$

The results are exactly the same! We did not select a contrived example which luckily produced these results. If additional examples were available, you would find the Pearson r would closely approximate the Spearman r in every instance. They would not always be exactly the same, but the results would seldom be so different as to alter substantive interpretation.

This point has been made much more emphatically by Harris (1975, p. 18), and we will conclude this section with his comments.

> *The Pearson* r *was developed specifically for normally distributed (continuous) variables. A number of alternative measures of correlation have been developed for situations where one or both measures are dichotomous or rank-order variables, but with few exceptions . . . these alternative measures are either numerically identical to Pearson* r, *blindly applied to decidedly nonnormal ranks, or 0–1 measures . . . or are exercises in wishful thinking whose numerical value is equal to the value of Pearson* r *which "would have" been obtained had the normally distributed measures presumably underlying the imperfect data been available for analysis. . . . None of the descriptive aspects of Pearson* r *are altered by applying it to "imperfect" data . . . the present text therefore, will not use the more specialized name when Pearson* r*'s are computed on dichotomous or "merely" ordinal data.*

Amen!

The Concept of Shared Variance

Our discussion of relationships has emphasized the point that from an empirical or statistical point of view, a relationship is defined by its covariance: that amount (either in raw or standard units) that the two variables "vary together." We also described relationships in terms of concomitant variation: Changes in the values of X are accompanied by simultaneous changes in the values of Y. These descriptions lead directly to the final descriptive characteristic of empirical relationships, the concept of *shared variance*. Not only is shared variance extremely important in terms of describing and conceptualizing relationships, but it is the most important statistical concept when it comes to the empirical process of explanation.

To review, Pearson r has been presented as an index of standardized covariance. It describes the magnitude of a relationship on a scale ranging from $+1.0$ to -1.0. It is useful to remember, however, that the relationship being described by the correlation coefficient is bidirectional. It represents the extent to which X is related to Y, as well as the amount by which Y is related to X. Hence, while it certainly indexes the magnitude of relationship, it does *not* assess the proportion of variance X or Y share. Fortunately, this figure can be easily obtained by computing r^2. Unlike r, r^2 can range only between 0.0 and $+1.0$. Consequently, r^2 can be interpreted as the common variance between X and Y, or alternatively, as the proportion or percentage (out of 100%) of variance that X and Y share.

Increased understanding can be gained by returning to the concept of a perfect relationship. If X and Y are perfectly related, they would be measuring, for all practical purposes, exactly the same concept or construct. Moreover, such a relationship would be indexed by $r = +/-1.0$ and $r^2 = 1.0$, with the latter statistic indicating that X and Y share 100% of their variance. Conceptually, this makes sense. Any variable would obviously hold in common 100% of the variation with an exact replication of itself.

To be more realistic, assume a more moderate relationship between X and Y, say $r = +.50$. Accordingly, $r^2 = .25$, indicating that X and Y share 25% of their variance. Figure 9.5 portrays this relationship visually. For illustration, the variance of both X and Y is represented by two circles. If X and Y are standardized into z-scores (i.e., $\sigma_X^2 = \sigma_Y^2 = 1.0$), the circles will be of equal area. Although these variables are correlated ($r = .50$), the r^2 statistic indicates that each circle will share 25% of its area with the other.

Equally important, Figure 9.5 suggests that X and Y each possesses a considerable proportion of their variance which does not overlap, which they do not share. Since the total area of either circle is 1.0, the amount of uncommon or unshared variance is $1.0 - r^2 = .75$. Stated differently, 75% of the variance in X and Y is unrelated in any systematic way.

Earlier we suggested that shared variance was particularly useful in terms of scientific explanation. Moreover, at the outset of this chapter we said that the description and explanation of relationships was at the heart of every scientific endeavor. Statistically, such explanation is defined as *the ability to account for or explain variance*. It is taken for granted that individual observations will vary in their scores or values on some measure. The goal, therefore, is to explain *why* that variance occurred—i.e., to account for that variance by exhibiting the existence of concomitant (shared) variance with a second, explanatory variable.

Both r^2 and its opposite $1 - r^2$ are the statistical indicants of this explanatory ability. Quite literally, r^2 represents the amount of information provided by X and Y which is *redundant*, i.e., that information about one variable, Y, which is available because one has information about X. For example, obtaining an $r^2 = .25$ indicates that one's knowledge of variable X allows one to explain or account for 25% of the variance in Y (or vice versa). In a straightforward manner, this represents "knowledge." In contrast,

FIGURE 9.5. Shared Variance Between X and Y.

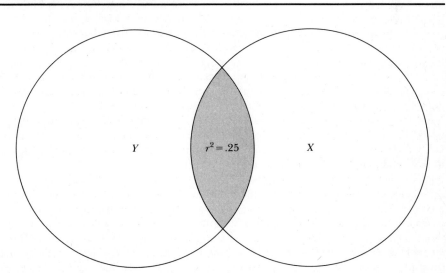

$1 - r^2 = .75$ represents what might best be conceptually labelled "ignorance." It is that proportion of Y that one's knowledge of X cannot explain. From the standpoint of theory, this is the most important component, for it represents (1) what is not known about Y, and hence (2) what future theoretic and empirical inquiry must attempt to discover.

These concepts can be reinforced by returning briefly to the hypothetical relationship between Loneliness and TV Hours. Assume, for example, that your interest is in explaining why people view TV as much or as little as they do. Earlier, you determined that the magnitude of relationship between Loneliness and TV Hours was $r = .8708$. Now, it can be calculated that $r^2 = .758$. What does this mean? The r^2 statistic suggests that slightly more than 75% of the variance in the amount of TV viewing can be explained by knowing how lonely a person is. Of the remaining 25%, certainly some is measurement error, while some may be due to additional explanatory variables which have not been considered. As a result, future investigations must attempt to reduce this ignorance by carefully considering other relevant variables, while also attempting to more precisely operationalize and measure the two already in hand.

Some Cautions About the Pearson r and Curvilinear Relationships

Throughout this chapter, we have stressed that the Pearson r is perhaps the most useful and interpretable statistic for assessing the magnitude of either direct or inverse relationships. These relationships, however, have been implicitly assumed to be linear in their form; i.e., they assume the general shape of a straight line. Several times we have briefly introduced the notion of curvilinear relationships (see, for example, Figure 9.4), but we have generally concentrated on understanding and assessing their linear counterparts.

It is important to realize that bivariate relationships need not be linear, and indeed many are not. Certainly, nothing in the discipline of statistics dictates linearity as the only measurable relationship between two variables. On the contrary, bivariate relationships may assume any number of shapes or forms other than a straight line: U-shape, inverted U-shape, J-shape, inverted J-shape, or a variety of other, more complex shapes which exhibit several peaks and valleys in their scatterplots. It is the purpose of statistics to describe and assess these nonlinear relationships as well, regardless of what shape they assume.

The purpose for introducing this cautionary note about the shape of relationships is to remind you that *the Pearson* r *assumes linearity.* It is capable of accurately describing only those relationships which conform to the shape of a straight line, e.g., Figures 9.1, 9.2, and 9.3. If the Pearson r were calculated for the curvilinear data in Figure 9.4, it would be very small, thus suggesting that there is no systematic covariation between Group Effectiveness and Self-esteem. Even a cursory glance at the scatterplot will indicate that such a conclusion would be unjustified. These two variables are highly related. Their relationship simply does not assume the shape of a straight line.

Two important points may be drawn from this discussion. First, we must reemphasize the importance of visually examining your data through the use of scatterplots. Summary indices such as the Pearson r are both important and necessary, but they cannot and frequently do not tell the whole story. They should not be used as substitutes for looking at data. Second, it is important to understand that when data do not correspond to the assumption of linearity, methods other than the Pearson r must be employed. A linear statistic (Pearson r) applied to curvilinear data cannot hope to provide accurate description and inference. The methods and statistics for assessing curvilinear relationships are somewhat more advanced than is appropriate for this introductory text. Accordingly, we will continue in subsequent chapters to concentrate on statistics designed for linear relationships. Excellent discussions of curvilinearity are presented in Cohen and Cohen (1975) and Kerlinger and Pedhazur (1973). These works should definitely be consulted when a nonlinear relationship between variables is suspected.

■ *Conclusion*

In this chapter, we have introduced several concepts and their statistical counterparts which are necessary to the understanding and description of bivariate relationships. Initially, we suggested that a good deal of preliminary insight could be gained by plotting the data on two-dimensional graphs and then simply looking for the patterns and trends which emerge. In addition, we introduced the conceptual attributes and statistical formula for the covariance—i.e., the amount that two variables "vary together." It was shown, however, that the covariance was not a particularly useful or interpretable statistic. As a result, we presented the Pearson r, the index of standardized covariation, as well as several alternatives for calculating it. Finally, we discussed the concept of shared variance, and argued that it was the most important statistical concept for the process of social scientific explanation.

Clearly, these various concepts and indices are extremely important if not indispensable to the study of human communication. Nevertheless, in their present capacity as descriptive statistics of a single sample of observations, they do not yet satisfy the primary criterion of science; namely, generalizability. In other words, the ability to describe a sample of observations is important and necessary, but not sufficient. The ability to generalize that information is the paramount goal of science. Such generalizability is accomplished by what we have called "inferential statistics." As shall be seen in subsequent chapters, the calculation of inferential statistics in no way differs from the descriptive indices just introduced. What must be added, however, are a number of assumptions and requirements about the sample of observations itself. Generally, that sample must be representative of the larger population from which it was drawn. Once these assumptions are satisfied, the task of generalizing can proceed with a relatively high degree of confidence.

10 *Chapter*

From Description
to Inference

If you were to take the book you are now reading, walk to the nearest window and throw it out, few people would have difficulty in predicting what would happen: The book would fall to the ground. (As its authors, we might also happily predict that book sales would rise due to the damage incurred.) We could predict with equal ease that *any* book thrown from *any* window by *any* person in *any* part of the world would suffer a similar fate. It is certainly not necessary to throw innumerable objects out of windows in order to confirm the law of gravity as a general and universal principle.

This example suggests that, based on a limited number of experiences, people are willing to generalize the effects of gravity to an infinite number of objects and situations that they have never personally observed. And so it is with any number of other physical principles: All fires are hot; all gasoline is combustible; a sharp blow will break glass; and so forth. People quite easily apply the process of generalization; from a limited sample of observations they make inferences about a much larger population which has never been observed.

The desire and ability to make similar kinds of generalizations is the cornerstone of all science, including communication research. Miller (1975, p. 232), in fact, has argued that *the* primary distinction between scientific and humanistic approaches to the study of human communication is generalization—i.e., "making factual generalizations about similar phenomena not encompassed by the observations that have been made." It matters little, therefore, which type of research methods are employed. Similarly, the scientific approach is not defined by the use of statistics or the computer. As we have indicated previously, any or all of these methods could be used in a purely descriptive (and thus, according to Miller, "humanistic") manner. What does define science, however, is whether the findings—the results of the statistics and methods—are generalizable to a larger, unobserved population.

Given this distinction, the purpose of this chapter is to outline the requirements, assumptions, and thinking processes involved in using statistics to make scientific generalizations. We will focus on two main points. First, we will discuss what attributes and characteristics the sample must possess in order to be representative of the larger population. Even at this preliminary stage of discussion it should be obvious that if the observations selected for study do not fairly and accurately depict the population from which they were sampled, any attempt to generalize will be flawed.

Second, we will describe the attributes that statistical findings (for example, Pearson r) must possess in order to permit inference to similar characteristics or relationships in the population. These attributes will be obtained by performing various statistical tests on the findings, then evaluating the outcomes of those tests. In this chapter, however, we will not present the methods for conducting specific statistical tests. These will be discussed in subsequent chapters. Our goal here is to sketch the logic and thinking which underlies all such tests of inference.

As you read this chapter, consider a final bit of qualification. The requirements and assumptions of scientific inference must be considered an ideal—the goal for which working scientists strive. They were derived by logicians, science philosophers, and mathematical statisticians in an effort to provide an ideal model for scientific generalization. These ideals often are not met in actual practice. The abstract world of the philosopher or mathematician is somewhat removed from the real world of the practicing researcher. Assumptions frequently are violated to a greater or lesser degree. Statistical inference, therefore, seldom conforms perfectly to the ideal model. Whether such violations prohibit inference entirely, however, cannot be answered in the abstract. Such questions must be evaluated on an individual, study-by-study basis. While we will provide some guidelines, they cannot be substituted for common sense and a thorough knowledge of the substantive area.

A Sample Versus the Population

A basic fact of scientific research is that, with few exceptions, an investigator cannot hope to use the entire population as the basis for observing the phenomenon of interest. Whether one is interested in atomic particles, the relationship between coffee and pancreatic cancer, or human beings communicating, it is neither practical nor possible to observe all of the instances of the phenomena which exist in the universe. Accordingly, a scientist must be content to select a representative sample of observations from that population or universe and employ tests of statistical inference to make generalizations to the population as a whole.

This basic fact of research raises an important question: What *is* a "representative" sample? Stated differently, in order for statistical tests of inference to be valid and thus one's generalizations to be accurate, what attributes or characteristics must the sample possess? The answer is at least partly dependent on the statistical test being performed. Each test has its own set of requirements. Nevertheless, several required characteristics of a sample are common to all tests of inference. In order for statistics to produce valid tests of inference, the investigator should possess an (1) *independent,* (2) *normally distributed,* (3) *sufficiently large,* and (4) *random* sample of observations. If these attributes characterize the sample, then a good deal of confidence can be placed in the subsequent statistical tests.

Below we will discuss each of these characteristics individually, presenting the rationale for each, as well as any negative effects which may result from incorrectly assuming them to be true. Such incorrect assumptions will be termed *violations.*

The Observations Are Independent.   The requirement of independent observations is designed to ensure that the score or measurement obtained from one observational unit (person, group, family, classroom, etc.) is unaffected by the scores of any other such unit. Perhaps the best way to illustrate this attribute is to describe a situation where it does not exist. Imagine that you are investigating the number of solutions to a problem which are generated by four-person groups engaged in "brainstorming." You assemble 10 such groups, tape-record their discussion, and have independent coders count the number of solutions proposed by each of the 40 discussants. Clearly, this is a relatively simple and uncomplicated procedure. Nevertheless, your ability to assume independent observations may be in serious jeopardy. Why?

An individual's ability to generate solutions probably is not unrelated to the solutions produced by the other members of the group. If person A suggests a particular solution, persons B, C, and D cannot suggest it, even though they may have "independently" derived the same solution. This problem becomes accentuated if several groups contain very dominant members who monopolize the discussion. Because they constantly hold the floor, other members are prohibited from discussing and producing solutions, not because these members possess any desire to be silent or nonproductive, but because their contributions to the group are dependent on the behavior of their fellow members.

It should be recognized that the problem outlined above is not unique to research on group communication. Researchers whose interests (to name just a few) might be communication patterns in the classroom, or communication behaviors and perceptions among family members (e.g., types of TV programs viewed) face similar concerns that an individual person's score is not independent. Fortunately, in such instances the problem is easily resolved. One simply designates the larger entity—the group, classroom, household, etc.—as the sampling unit rather than the individual members within that unit. As shall be seen shortly in our discussion of sample size, while this procedure has the disadvantage of reducing the number of observations, it does produce the independence of observations required.

The Effects of Violations. The effect of violating the requirement of independent observations is almost always a serious threat to the validity of statistical inference, perhaps the most serious of any of the requirements we will mention. Recall that in Chapter 9 we stated that one of the primary purposes of statistics was to explain or account for variation in the criterion variable, i.e., to partition variance into that which was systematically related to another explanatory variable and that which was totally random or unrelated. In fact, most tests of statistical inference are based on a comparison of how large the systematic variance is vis-à-vis the random variance.

Such tests become invalid whenever the observations are not independent, because the supposedly random component of the variance is no longer random. Instead, it is greatly affected by some unknown and unexpected systematic tendency, for example, the overly verbal discussant in a group, or the presence of an undisciplined and highly disruptive child in a grade school classroom. If such systematic sources of variance were known and expected, they could be included both statistically and theoretically as explanatory variables. Most often, however, systematic tendencies such as these result from oversight or procedural errors on the part of the investigator. As a result, they are unexpected and go undetected; they inappropriately influence the random component of variance in systematic ways; and as a result, they seriously undermine confidence in the validity of inferential tests and procedures.

The Observations Are Normally Distributed. In Chapter 9, we discussed the desirability and necessity of a normally distributed sample of observations from the point of view of description. A normal distribution of scores ensures that the mean will be an accurate index of the center of the data and that the indices of spread—the variance and the standard deviation—will not be affected by extreme scores or outliers. In short, the presence of a normal distribution increases the confidence with which an investigator can make descriptive statements about the sample of scores obtained.

A normal distribution is equally important to the process of inference, where the desire is to generalize certain attributes of the sample to the population as a whole. The normal distribution's importance goes beyond the obvious need to obtain accurate descriptive indices. The process of scientific generalization follows a rigorous inferential model developed by logicians and mathematicians. The normal distribution is an integral part of this model because its characteristics are well known and predictable. The role of the normal distribution in inference, however, is somewhat different from its straightforward use in description.

Assume that a researcher has calculated a statistical index of relationship (e.g., Pearson r) for two variables, X and Y. Further assume that Y is the variable of interest whose variance is to be explained, while X is the explanatory variable. If various tests of inference are to be used with an acceptable degree of confidence, assumptions about normality must be reasonably satisfied. One assumption that is *not* required by the process of inference is that the entire sample of Y scores be normally distributed. The same is true of the sample of X scores. No assumptions are made about the total distribution of either the X or Y variable. In this respect, inference clearly differs from description.

Assumptions about a normal distribution in the process of inference focus on subsamples or groupings of the Y scores. First, it is necessary to conceptualize the entire sample of Y scores as being divided into several groups. The group into which each Y score is placed is determined by the values of the X score with which it is associated. Thus, if the X variable consists of two scores (e.g., Male $= 1$, Female $= 2$), there would be one group of Y scores from the males and one from the females. Similarly, if the X variable consisted of seven scores derived from a semantic differential scale, seven distinct groupings of Y would be created. For an investigator to be confident that his or her statistical inference is accurate, *each* of these Y groupings must (1) be normally distributed, and (2) have the same variance.

In statistical jargon, these assumptions require the values of X to be "fixed effects" (see Cohen & Cohen, 1975). Each value of X—regardless of how many values there are—is assumed to be selected or operationalized by the researcher. When this assumption does not hold and the values of X are sampled from a larger population, the X variable is called a "random effect." Random effects require a completely different type of statistical treatment which we will not present in this book (see Winer, 1971). In subsequent chapters, therefore, the statistical treatment of every relationship will assume that (1) the explanatory variable X is characterized as a fixed effect, (2) the subsample of Y scores for each fixed value of X is normally distributed, and (3) the variance of each subsample of Y scores is equal.

The Effects of Violations.   As outlined here, the normal distribution is the ideal which underlies the logical process of inference. But real data do not always cooperate by conforming to this ideal. One or more of the subsamples of Y scores may not be normally distributed, and frequently the subsamples do not have equal variances. The question then arises: What effect does this have on statistical inference and scientific generalization? The answer, in the words of Lindquist (1953, p. 86), is "extremely gratifying." A number of empirical investigations have examined the effects of nonnormality on a variety of test statistics, and their conclusions are remarkably similar. The effect of moderate to even severe departures from normality is real and detectable, but in most cases is trivial for accurate statistical inference. In short, nonnormality often is not a difference that makes a difference.

This evidence does not imply that an investigator may blithely ignore the distribution of data while conducting statistical tests. The closer one's data conform to the ideal distribution, the more confidence one can place in the inferences which are made. Moderate departures from this ideal, however, are not cause for great alarm. If the investigator has a thorough knowledge of the descriptive aspects of the data (both graphic and numeric), he or she should be in a position to judge whether the assumption of normality is reasonably satisfied. In the final analysis, therefore, it is almost always a judgment call based on *informed* judgment.

The Sample Is Sufficiently Large.   The rationale behind the requirement that a sample be sufficiently large is, at the same time, both simple and complex. Simply stated, if an investigator wants his or her sample to represent the salient attributes of the population, then the sample must be large enough to model the population faithfully. This is really saying nothing more than that a large sample of observations will more accurately represent the population than a small sample. A sample of 1000 will provide a more accurate picture of TV viewing habits than will a sample of 10 to 15.

This commonsense realization can be recast a bit more formally. If a variable is normally distributed in the population, then the larger the sample the more closely it will approximate its "true" distribution. In statistics, this is frequently referred to as the *law of large numbers*. If a sufficiently large sample is obtained, not only will the population distribution be accurately represented, but the mean and standard deviation of the sample will be accurate estimates of those indices in the population.

Now for the more complex interpretation. Earlier we said that the sample must be "sufficiently large" to represent the "salient" attributes in the population. By salient attributes, we mean those relationships or differences in the population which are of theoretic interest to the investigator. The definition of "sufficiently large," therefore, depends directly on what relationships the researcher defines as salient. Some attributes or characteristics of the population are so pronounced and widespread that they can be detected with a relatively small sample. For example, if a researcher proposed the (admittedly trivial) hypothesis that adults with a college education have a larger vocabulary than junior high school students, a fairly small sample would be required to detect such a large and obvious difference. Attributes of this magnitude are referred to as *large effects*.

Suppose, in contrast, an investigator was interested in a relationship or difference that, although real, was small and unpronounced in the population; a *small effect*. Assume, for example, that a researcher proposes the hypothesis that females are more sensitive to nonverbal facial expressions than are males. Assume further that while this difference is real, it is quite small. Accordingly, the sample required to detect this difference would have to be considerably larger. In a small sample, the random variation would be so large as to overshadow any systematic tendency. As the sample becomes larger, however, this systematic trend would begin to emerge and eventually would reveal itself as large enough to be generalized to the population.

Fortunately, given this intricate relationship between the size of the effect and the size of the sample necessary to detect it, researchers need not rely on guesswork to estimate the exact number of observations required to be "sufficient." A number of formulas have been developed to calculate precisely the necessary number of observations. Cohen (1977) provides the most complete and thorough account of these procedures. He refers to this area of concern as "power planning"; i.e., the statistical tests must be sufficiently powerful to detect the relationship or difference of interest.

Later in this chapter, we will return to the topic of statistical power. For the present, the primary concept to be retained is that statistical power is not an inherent component of the test employed, but rather is a function of the relationship between effect size and sample size. If the sample is sufficiently large, the test will be sufficiently powerful.

The Effects of Violations. The effects of failing to obtain a sufficiently large sample are really quite simple. The investigator will not be able to generalize the relationship or difference of interest, even though it may actually exist in the population. As a result, the researcher's hypotheses will not be supported and theory construction will be inhibited. On the other hand, obtaining too many observations, while not affecting the validity of statistical inference, simply wastes time, energy, and money. The salient attributes can be detected with fewer observations. Therefore, the size of the sample is not a trivial, after-the-fact consideration. It is an integral part of the process of statistical inference and scientific generalization, and it should be accorded the thought, effort, and planning it deserves.

The Observations Are Randomly Sampled.

A random sample serves a fundamental and important role in the process of statistical inference: It helps to counter the effects of extraneous sources of variation. In any specified population, any number of factors or variables, although related to the variables of interest, are irrelevant to the theory under investigation. For example, a person's ability to recall the content of the evening news might be affected by the amount of sleep he or she had, or whether he or she had a hangover from the previous night's festivities. Similarly, an individual's interaction behavior in a dyadic situation might be altered or influenced by the fact that he or she recently had a serious argument with roommates, or just failed a midterm exam in chemistry.

Even though factors such as these possess the potential to affect the variables of interest, they are not systematic trends in the population. On the contrary, they are random, isolated factors which could not be predicted or anticipated in advance. As a result, they could not possibly be incorporated into theory. They are sources of variation which are extraneous to an investigator's theoretic interests. Accordingly, their effects must be minimized whenever possible.

This minimization is best and most easily accomplished by obtaining a sufficiently large, random sample. Certainly, any such random sample will contain a large number of extraneous factors. The worst possible thing that can happen, however, is for any of the extraneous factors to become systematic; to have a consistent, nonrandom effect on the scores or measurements which are obtained.

Fortunately, if a sample is sufficiently large and truly random, factors which are random in the population almost certainly will be equally so in the sample. Moreover, the effects of these random, extraneous factors will tend to negate or balance each other, with some exerting positive influence, while others have negative influence. As a result, systematic relationships or differences are allowed to emerge. The sample will be an accurate representation of the population, including all of the extraneous factors which the population contains.

Random Assignment as a Substitute for Random Sampling.   The concept of a random sample assumes that each and every person in the population of interest has an equal likelihood of being in the sample. Unless this population is very small and limited (e.g., sixth graders in one particular school district), this assumption is seldom satisfied. Pragmatic considerations such as money, time, geographical distance, etc., prohibit the researcher from obtaining a truly random sample.

Much more frequently, the researcher obtains access to several intact groups such as the students in the introductory communication course; the sixth graders in several, specified schools; or the doctors and nurses from three different hospitals. Clearly, none of these could be considered a random sample. Faced with this situation, the investigator can still attempt to minimize the effects of extraneous factors through the principle of *random assignment*. As the name suggests, random assignment requires that the available subjects or participants be assigned at random to the various conditions, treatments, or groups involved in the study. This procedure, like that of random sampling, ensures that extraneous sources of variation are dispersed randomly throughout conditions, thereby minimizing the probability that they will become systematic influences on the variables of interest.

The Effects of Violations.   The absence of either random sampling or random assignment creates the potential for serious sources of invalidity to enter the inferential process. Extraneous sources of variation can become systematic influences, and the confidence which can be placed in statistical tests of inference is dramatically decreased. In contrast, the substitution of random assignment whenever random sampling is impractical or impossible maintains the validity of statistical inference.

Random assignment, however, is not random sampling. Although random assignment allows the process of inference to be conducted with an acceptable degree of confidence, this confidence is not gained without a price. The price frequently is that the population to which the findings can be directly generalized is more limited in both scope and numbers. Many times, in fact, this limited population consists of college undergraduates, usually freshmen and sophomores. This realization has prompted one critic (McNemar, 1946, p. 33) to label all of social science as merely a "science of the behavior of sophomores."

The widespread use of college students as participants in communication research would not be a serious problem if either (1) an investigator's interest was in generalizing solely to college undergraduates, or alternatively (2) it could reasonably be argued that such students were a totally representative subset of the larger population, e.g., all American adults. For a particular study, however, neither of these assumptions may be valid. While many investigations are educationally oriented and thus have as their primary focus college students (see, for example, Hill & Courtright, 1981), these must be considered a small percentage of the total research in communication. In the much larger percentage of studies which do not focus on educational concerns, few investigators would be content to limit their generalizations to the student population from which they sampled.

On many variables, college students are not representative of society at large. A college campus is not a miniature copy of the United States. Students are younger, better educated, more intelligent, and more widely read than the average person. There are also data to suggest that the racial, ethnic, and religious composition of college students does not mirror that of the entire population. Add Rosenthal and Rosnow's (1969, p. 110) description of social science as "a science of just those sophomores who volunteer to participate in our research and who also keep their appointment with the investigator." Need we say more?

Before we discuss the implications of this lack of representativeness, a few words about survey research are in order. The sampling procedures typically associated with surveys allow for a much more representative sample of respondents. In fact, in a good many instances such samples are, indeed, random. But survey research methods are simply not viable approaches to all problems or questions in communication research. Moreover, survey samples are also composed only of those who agree to be surveyed, or who voluntarily complete and return their survey in the mail. Thus, to the extent that consent is an extraneous factor which affects a participant's responses, it is clearly a systematic effect in almost all social science research.

With this background information in mind, we will discuss the ramifications for communication research. What does all this mean for the process of scientific generalization? Have thousands of communication researchers wasted their time? Is communication research really a "science of the behavior of sophomores"?

The answer is not simple. Moreover, it depends in no small part on the substantive questions or hypotheses addressed in each study. In some areas of communication research the attributes which characterize college students would exert a systematic biasing effect. For example, college students might not provide a representative performance (i.e., representative of the population) on tasks such as idea generation and evaluation in small groups, the recall of communicated material, or the critical evaluation of persuasive evidence.

In contrast, there are certainly areas of communication behavior where the attributes typically associated with college students would have negligible effects. Why, for example, would one expect the greeting ritual or initial interaction behavior of college students to be different (at least in form) from that of the population? Is it not necessary for students to perform these behaviors in a functional manner with diverse types of people in numerous contexts and situations? Similarly, research by Motley, Camden, and Baars (1982) has investigated the cognitive processing in which people engage prior to uttering language. While it might be reasonable to argue that the content of the language of college students would be different, is it equally reasonable to argue that the basic psycholinguistic processes underlying that language are also different?

Ultimately, these are empirical questions to be answered conclusively only by well-designed and well-executed research. If this research were to indicate that such behaviors and cognitive processes were systematically influenced by education, race, amount of reading, etc., then previous findings in these areas must be seriously questioned. Such research, on the other hand, might indicate that these behaviors and processes vary much the same way in students as they do in the general population. If they do, then the confidence in the generalizability of such findings would be greatly increased.

In sum, we can neither condemn nor accept universally the sampling practices of communication researchers. But an attitude of "benign neglect" is inappropriate. As Rossiter (1976) maintains, students and practitioners of communication research must take a more active concern in sampling practices. Prior to conducting an investigation, researchers must devote thought and planning to the nature of the sample and its relationship to the level of scientific generalization desired. Perhaps more natural research settings, more unobtrusive measures (Webb et al, 1966), and/or a more representative sample of participants will provide partial remedies. In addition, more attention to detail must be paid to *describing* the sample in subsequent reports of research.

Finally, consumers of such research must be actively aware of sampling practices, especially as they relate to the process of generalization. While these suggestions will not totally alleviate problems, they can do much to reduce the controversy which surrounds them.

Statistical Indices: A Sample Versus the Population

We have gone to some length to describe and explain the requirements or assumptions a sample must fulfill to be considered an adequate representative of the population from which it was drawn. The rationale for this detailed discussion originates with the process of generalization: A representative sample facilitates valid generalization to the population. But the generalization of what? In the previous sections, we have been purposely vague on this issue, suggesting that our interest was in generalizing "findings," "attributes," or "characteristics." A bit more precision is now required.

As usual, we will begin with a conceptual discussion of the problem. Several times we have suggested that the discovery, description, and evaluation of relationships is the primary goal of the scientific enterprise. More globally, a scientist investigates theoretic propositions that two or more concepts or constructs are related in a specified manner in the population. To investigate these propositions (usually called hypotheses), however, researchers must operationally define all of the relevant concepts in an acceptable manner. Second, a representative sample of observations must be obtained. Third, measurements and/or scores must be obtained from the sample by employing the operations and methods previously defined. Whatever characteristics are of interest to the investigator must be contained in or implied by these measurements.

Finally come the statistics. Through various statistical procedures, salient information about the sample is synthesized and summarized into various numerical indices such as the mean, standard deviation, Pearson r, r^2, etc. These and other statistics to be presented in later chapters are the "findings" to which we have referred. They are indicative of the relationships the investigator sought to discover.

For the present, "findings" will be defined as any statistical index which is calculated from the sample data. Empirical researchers in communication, however, will seldom be content to statistically describe only the sample. Rather, they desire to generalize their findings to the population. Thus the question becomes: Are the statistical indices of relationship obtained from the sample also present in the population as a whole? Stated differently: Are the statistical parameters calculated from the sample good "estimates" of those in the population? For dealing with particular statistical indices and a specific substantive problem, these questions can be phrased much more precisely. Nevertheless, the logic is the same. If the population as a whole was measured and statistical procedures applied, would the same relationship be empirically discovered?

In order to answer these questions, two additional logical concepts which are the unique property of statistical inference must be introduced. The first is the *null hypothesis*, or the prediction that the two variables of interest are totally unrelated in the population. This particular concept is crucial. As shall be seen, all statistical inference is based on a direct test of this prediction. The second important concept is that of *statistical significance*. To label a particular finding as "significant" is to imply that it exists in the population. Statistical significance and the null hypothesis are closely related and are both central to generalizing social scientific findings. Both, therefore, deserve more detailed attention.

The Null Hypothesis.   A basic maxim of scientific inference and generalization is: Science can never prove a prediction, a hypothesis, or even a theory to be true. No, you did not incorrectly read the previous sentence. It is beyond the province of science and the process of scientific generalization to prove the truth value of relationships. The best that a researcher can hope to achieve is to show that the hypothesis of "no relationship" is false.

At this point, this new twist of logic probably seems quite illogical, but a bit of amplification should help. Recall that a fundamental assumption of inference is that an investigator will infrequently, if ever, obtain measurements from the entire population. Accordingly, he or she obtains a representative and sufficiently large sample from which the desired measurements are obtained. Finally, if all of the requirements and assumptions necessary for valid inference are adequately fulfilled, the investigator generalizes the statistical parameters (i.e., the findings) to the population.

Now the important question. Does the investigator ever know *for certain* that the findings obtained from the sample *really* exist in the population? Of course not! If this kind of certainty were possible, we would not need lengthy discussions of inference and generalization. We would simply talk about scientific "Truth." Such certainty would exist only if the investigator were able to measure the entire population, which is a rarity in all branches of science. As a result, all generalization is subject to the potential for error, and thus no relationship can ever be proven to be absolutely "true." Even the strongest findings possess a probability (albeit small) that they resulted from the vagaries of random chance.

Despite the logical impossibility of scientifically asserting what is true, all is not lost. One can show beyond a reasonable doubt that hypotheses and predictions are false; that is, one can provide evidence that a relationship called "no" relationship does *not* exist in the population. There is always the potential for error (and hence the phrase "reasonable doubt"), but that potential for error can be calculated precisely. Researchers therefore can agree on how small this potential for error must be before it can be considered "beyond a reasonable doubt."

If this emphasis on "reasonable doubt" brings to mind images of courtrooms and lawyers, the analogy is appropriate. As Erickson and Nosanchuck (1977, pp. 145–49) suggest, there is a good deal of similarity between the logic of scientific generalization and the logic which underlies our system of jurisprudence. For example, all criminal proceedings begin with the presumption of innocence. The defendant need not prove the truth value of his or her claim of innocence. Rather, the prosecutor must provide admissible evidence which shows these claims to be false beyond a reasonable doubt. If the defendant's claim cannot be reasonably falsified, he or she is deemed "not guilty." (Notice that the word *innocent* is not used, because innocence need not be proven.) If, in contrast, the evidence suggests that innocence is a reasonably false presumption, it can be legitimately inferred that the defendant is guilty.

This process is quite similar to the process of science. Researchers obviously would not waste the time and effort to gather data if they did not believe some relationship to exist. Hence, the scientist is analogous to the prosecutor who believes (before an expensive and time-consuming jury trial) that the defendant is guilty. The researcher must embark on the process of generalization by presuming just the opposite—i.e., that there is no relationship between these variables in the population. The findings obtained from the sample, however, constitute potential evidence to the contrary. If this evidence is sufficiently compelling, the researcher can assert that the assumption of no relationship in the population is false and should be rejected. Accordingly, the assumption that the relationship exists, even though not proven true (which is impossible), has received strong empirical corroboration.

Perhaps a more substantive example will clarify further this logic. Earlier, in Chapter 3, we presented a description of the Courtright and Courtright (1979) study designed to investigate the best method for teaching language-disordered children certain grammatical rules which they did not possess. These researchers' desire to investigate this question was motivated by the belief that the variance in the children's ability to learn these rules was systematically related to methods by which they were taught. As a result, they began the study with what is called a *research hypothesis:* Modeling and other modeling methods would more successfully produce learning than would the mimicry method.

At this point in any study, the researcher wants and expects to find a relationship. Despite the myth of scientific objectivity (see Fisher, 1978), researchers have egos (sometimes large ones) and certainly want their theoretic predictions to be confirmed. These desires and expectations aside, the process of generalization requires the investigator to assume that no relationship exists. This assumption of no relationship is termed the *null hypothesis.* Usually, the null hypothesis is phrased as the exact logical opposite of the research hypothesis; in the current example, modeling, other modeling, and mimicry methods of teaching grammatical rules will produce no differences in the children's rate or amount of learning.

The task of the investigator is to provide acceptable evidence that the null hypothesis is false. If the null hypothesis can be rejected, there is reason to accept the research hypothesis as "not false." In short, it has received empirical corroboration. If enough such corroboration is provided (as in the law of gravity), the research hypothesis comes to be generally accepted as true. But even the law of gravity is no more than very strongly accepted as "not false."

Statistical Significance.   Throughout the previous discussion, we have referred to acceptable evidence which falsifies the null hypothesis beyond a reasonable doubt. In the courtroom, of course, the rules of evidence are quite clear and specific, but the final determination of what qualifies as "reasonable doubt" rests on the subjective judgment of the judge and jurors. With statistics, however, the concept of "doubt" can be very precisely quantified. It is possible to accurately state the precise probability that the null hypothesis is not false and thus should not be accepted. In short, it is possible to know the exact likelihood that any decision to reject the null hypothesis is incorrect. Such likelihood is what is meant by quantifying doubt. Granted, the concept of "reasonable" can still be debated, but that argument can always be attached to a specific probability of error.

In statistics, the concept of *statistical significance* is the equivalent of reasonable doubt. Recall that statistical inference always possesses some potential for error. There is always some probability that in the population the null hypothesis of no relationship is actually true. Statistical significance, therefore, refers to the *maximum probability of committing an inferential error that a researcher is willing to accept.* Normally, this probability will be quite small. By tradition and years of consensus, most social scientists have come to accept the maximum probability of error as less than 5 times out of 100 ($p < .05$). Many times the computed probability will turn out to be much lower—e.g., $p < .01$; $p < .002$; or $p < .0001$. Nevertheless, there must be some agreed-upon maximum, and a probability of erroneous inference of .05 has served as this criterion for some time.

What does $p < .05$ mean? To answer this question adequately, it is necessary to understand the intimate relationship between the sample, the null hypothesis, and statistical significance. A researcher begins the process of inference with the assumption of the null hypothesis that no relationship exists in the population. From the sample, however, he or she obtains statistical findings which may constitute evidence to the contrary. Finally, through a process we will discuss later, the investigator determines the probability that, indeed, there is no such relationship in the population. Assume for the sake of discussion that this probability is $p < .05$. Precisely stated, this means that a sample which exhibited a relationship of this magnitude could have come from a population containing absolutely no relationship only 5 times out of 100 by chance. Accordingly, if an investigator uses this evidence to infer that such a relationship exists, he or she will be wrong less than 5% of the time.

The process of scientific generalization clearly recognizes that the sample is not the population. Moreover, it recognizes that no matter how carefully one draws a sample, random error and dumb luck play a role in one's findings. The more representative the sample (i.e., the closer it comes to fulfilling the various requirements and assumptions outlined earlier), the smaller this role will be. Nevertheless, all attempts at generalization will be clouded by some doubt. The best a researcher can do is to keep this to a minimum, e.g., $p < .05$.

Significance Versus Meaningfulness.   Before leaving the topic of statistical significance, we must make an important distinction. Statistical significance should not be considered synonymous with theoretic meaningfulness or salience. Significance is a prerequisite for claiming that a finding is meaningful or important to theory construction. The two concepts, however, are far from the same.

To review, "statistical significance" is a label attached to findings which are large enough in magnitude to reject beyond a reasonable doubt the hypothesis of no relationship. The researcher has confidence that such relationships exist in the population. It is important to realize that a finding which is statistically significant may, nonetheless, be quite small in its absolute magnitude. As Kirk (1972, p. 109) suggests:

> *A test of significance provides information concerning the probability of committing an error in rejecting the null hypothesis. The fact that a test statistic is declared significant tells an experimenter nothing regarding the magnitude of the ... [relationship] or the practical importance or usefulness of the results.*

Kirk is really saying nothing more than in the population there may be "real" relationships which are quite small, perhaps even trivial in their explanatory ability. Accordingly, a significant relationship may not be large enough to contribute meaningfully to the theory under examination.

Perhaps the most important component for distinguishing between significance and salience is, simply stated, sample size. The relationship between sample size and significance is straightforward; the larger the size of the sample, the smaller the finding can be and still be considered statistically significant. For example, in Chapter 9 it was hypothetically shown that the relationship between Loneliness and the number of hours of TV viewed per week was very large, $r = .8708$. Moreover, the sample size for this calculation was $N = 15$. Again withholding the details until later, one can determine that for a sample size of 15, any Pearson r larger than .51 would be considered significant ($p < .05$).

Keep in mind that this determination of significance was achieved with only 15 observations. What value of r would be required for significance if the sample size were 100? Clearly, this is not an unreasonably large sample. For $N = 100$, it can be shown that any r larger than .195 would be considered significant. Given a relationship of this magnitude, the null hypothesis could be rejected beyond a reasonable doubt. The probability of committing an error of inference would still remain at .05, even though the evidence for such an inference was considerably smaller in magnitude.

Despite the valid claim of statistical significance, a researcher could not claim that $r = .195$ was indicative of a large or strong relationship. On the contrary, two variables with a correlation of this size would be considered weakly related. In fact, by calculating r^2 it can be shown that they share less than 4% of their variance ($r^2 = .035$). Hence, while the claim of significance would be beyond dispute, an investigator would have to provide additional evidence and rationale to convince an audience of communication researchers that his or her findings were substantively meaningful. This, of course, is not an impossible task. Perhaps this small relationship is the key component in a partially constructed theory; perhaps it represents an important counterintuitive finding. There is more to meaningfulness than simply the size of the relationship. Nevertheless, whenever a relationship is significant, yet small, the burden is on the researcher to provide good reasons for applying the term *meaningful* to that relationship.

Erroneous Inference.   This discussion of the role of statistical inference in scientific generalization has emphasized that by fulfilling certain requirements and assumptions a researcher can be reasonably confident that his or her generalizations are valid. The discussion also has suggested that despite the safeguards and precautions the process requires, the possibility for erroneous inference is always present. The likelihood of such errors may be quite small ($p < .05$), but errors of inference can and do occur. Consequently, we will explain the nature of these errors and their ramifications a bit more fully.

A researcher can make two types of inferential errors. *Type I errors* refer to the fact that a researcher may erroneously reject the null hypothesis as false, when in the population it is actually true. This is the type of error we have discussed at some length in previous sections. In contrast, *Type II errors* occur when a researcher accepts the null hypothesis as true (i.e., he or she infers no relationship in the population) when in fact it should be rejected as false. Obviously, neither type of error is desirable, and researchers do their best to avoid both. This is not as easy as it sounds, however, because these two types of errors are inversely related. As a researcher takes precautions to decrease the probability of committing a Type I error, he or she concomitantly increases the likelihood that a Type II error will occur. The reverse is also true: If the probability of Type II errors is decreased, the likelihood of a Type I error increases. For reasons we shall sketch shortly, researchers have agreed that a Type II error possesses less negative ramifications for the process of scientific generalization than the Type I variety.

To illustrate this reasoning, consider again the example of the courtroom. Ask yourself why the presumption of innocence (i.e., the null hypothesis) prevails. Why is the burden of proof on the prosecutor (i.e., the researcher) to provide compelling evidence to the contrary? The answer lies in the value judgment that it is more acceptable to let a guilty person go free than it is to punish the individual who is innocent. Consequently, the process is oriented in favor of the defendant. He or she may "really" be guilty, but if the prosecutor fails to disprove the presumed innocence, even because of a technical error, the defendant will go free.

A similar type of value judgment underlies the process of scientific generalization. If a researcher is going to make an error of inference, it is better that he or she accept a null hypothesis which is really false, than to reject a null hypothesis which, in the population, is actually true. This decision is based on the realization that significant findings are frequently accepted as empirical fact. Often they form the basis for future research and theory. If such findings are actually erroneous and the null hypothesis characterizes the true state of affairs, an entire stream of research may be led astray.

Few researchers simply give up their ideas and quit when they initially fail to reject the null hypothesis. (Recall our earlier comment about egos.) This is especially true if sound theoretic support underlies the research hypothesis. Instead, an investigator will search for the reasons behind failure to reject the null hypothesis. Was there undue measurement error? Was the sample badly drawn? Was the questionnaire poorly constructed? Assuming that the null hypothesis was really false and should be rejected, a researcher will quite often remedy methodological and/or procedural errors, and thus eventually reject it. Unlike the courts, there is no such thing as "double jeopardy" when it comes to scientific research. If after additional research the null hypothesis still cannot be rejected as false, the researcher can legitimately reconceive his or her theory in appropriate ways.

In sum, a Type II error seldom produces additional erroneous inferences. Instead, the investigator must halt his or her stream of research and attempt to remedy any procedural flaws—sometimes successfully, sometimes not. In either case, the result is usually more accurate and more confident generalization. In contrast, Type I errors possess the very real potential to compound themselves, thus creating a succession of erroneous inferences. Eventually, the errors will be detected, but it may be too late to undo the damage.

Erroneous Inference and Statistical Power. The probability of committing a Type I error is exactly the same as the concept of statistical significance. It is the probability that the null hypothesis is true. The value judgments outlined above, therefore, have prompted researchers to place a heavy emphasis on statistical significance. In fact, in areas of scientific research where errors of inference might be harmful (e.g., experimentation with new pharmaceuticals), the maximum acceptable probability of error has been lowered drastically (e.g., $p < .00001$). Imagine the consequences, if 5 out of every 100 people who took a new medicine became ill and died. Although the consequences of inferential errors in communication research are hardly as drastic, researchers have still taken great pains to guard against Type I error.

Serious concern about Type II error, on the other hand, has been a relatively recent phenomenon, pioneered by the work of the psychologist, Jacob Cohen (1962; 1973; 1977). To say the least, calculating the probability of committing a Type II error is considerably more complex, requiring special formulas, tables, and so forth. Nevertheless, the logic of the procedure is fairly easy to comprehend. Once again, it is primarily a matter of sample size. Earlier, we suggested that as N becomes larger, the smaller a finding can be and still be considered significant. Because larger samples are presumably more representative of the population, they need less evidence to reject the null hypothesis beyond a reasonable doubt. As the sample size becomes larger, the statistical tests become more "powerful."

This so-called "power" refers to their ability to avoid making a Type II error. If a sample is sufficiently large, null hypotheses which should be rejected as false will be incorrectly accepted as true much less often. Those relationships which are actually present in the population will also tend to be present (and large enough to be significant) in the sample. As a result, a straightforward relationship can again be stated: The larger the size of the sample, the lower the probability of committing a Type II error.

This simple maxim, however, is not meant to suggest that huge samples are necessarily superior to smaller ones. As was mentioned during the discussion of large and small effects, at some point, gathering more observations produces diminished returns. This break-even point depends on a combination of (1) the magnitude of the relationship (i.e., the effect size) one considers meaningful, (2) the maximum risk of a Type I error one is willing to accept, as well as (3) the risk of a Type II error one considers tolerable. In some cases, this combination might suggest that a relatively small sample (for example, $N = 25$) will be sufficiently large to detect the relationships of interest. To gather more observations would simply be a waste of time and effort. At other times, when the relationships of interest are smaller or a Type I error might be harmful, a much larger sample would be required.

Table 10.1 illustrates several combinations of these three variables and thus allows for a more concrete discussion. Notice in Table 10.1 that four different sample sizes are presented—25, 50, 100, and 200. While it is clearly possible to gather a much larger or smaller sample, these four N's provide a reasonably inclusive range for illustrating these principles. In addition, this table contains three separate values of Pearson r: $r = .10$, .30, and .50. These correspond to what Cohen (1977) argues are small, medium, and large effect sizes for most social science research. Translated into our earlier terminology, these represent the size of Pearson r a researcher is willing to accept as meaningful. Finally, the several combinations of effect size and sample size are tabled separately for two levels of significance—$p < .05$ and $p < .01$.

The entries in the table are what Cohen terms "statistical power." They are the probability of rejecting a null hypothesis which is false in the population. In other words, they are the likelihood of *not* committing a Type II error. If you study these probabilities carefully, you will perceive a distinct pattern. First, as the sample size increases, the probability of finding a correlation to be significant increases also. In some cases (e.g., $r = .10$), these probabilities remain remarkably small, but they nevertheless increase. Similarly, as the size of r one considers meaningful is allowed to increase, the likelihood of finding that r significant (for any N) increases. Finally, notice that the various cell probabilities become larger as one allows the risk of committing a Type I error to increase from .01 to .05. As the risk of committing a Type I error increases, the probability of committing a Type II error decreases. This is the inverse relationship of which we spoke earlier.

Although the individual relationships among sample size, effect size, significance, and power are important, Table 10.1 gains its fullest meaning when all four variables are considered in combination. This realization can be extremely useful in planning research. If an investigator can determine or fix the value of any three of these components, the fourth can be readily determined from tables such as 10.1. For example, a researcher decides (before gathering data) that: (1) the maximum risk of a Type I error should be .05; (2) only Pearson rs of .30 or larger should be considered theoretically meaningful and hence significant; and (3) statistical power should be .80 or higher. From Table 10.1 it could be determined that slightly less than 100 observations are required to achieve these several conditions.

Table 10.1 is greatly abridged. Before attempting any analysis such as that described above, you should consult Cohen (1977) for a thorough explanation of the procedures, as well as the complete and unabridged set of tables. Perhaps the most

TABLE 10.1. Statistical Power Values for Different Values of r and Different Sample Sizes

	Significance $= p < .01$		
		r	
N	.10	.30	.50
25	.02	.13	.51
50	.03	.33	.89
100	.06	.69	.99+
200	.12	.96	.99+
	Significance $= p < .05$		
		r	
N	.10	.30	.50
25	.08	.31	.75
50	.11	.57	.97
100	.17	.86	.99+
200	.29	.99	.99+

The entries in the Table represent the probability of rejecting a false null hypothesis. As such, they are the probability of *not* committing a Type II error.

From Jacob Cohen, *Statistical Power Analysis for the Behavioral Sciences*, pp. 90–93. Copyright © 1977, by Academic Press, Inc.

important point, however, is that this consultation should occur *before* you obtain the sample and gather the data. It is of little help to find, after the fact, that one's sample size was too small to detect the relationships of interest as significant. In contrast, a researcher who carefully follows Cohen's advice before the fact will enhance the confidence with which his or her findings can be generalized.

■ *Conclusion*

This chapter has presented the requirements, assumptions, and thinking processes which are the foundation of scientific generalization. This concern is necessitated by the fact that seldom, if ever, do scientists have access to an entire population of observations. Instead, they must employ a sample of observations drawn from that population. The task, therefore, becomes one of generalizing the relationships discovered in the sample to the population as a whole.

For this generalization to be as valid and as error-free as possible, several requirements must be fulfilled. The sample of observations should be (1) independently sampled, (2) normally distributed, (3) sufficiently large, and (4) randomly drawn. Each of these requirements, of course, has the potential to be violated, and the effects of such violations were discussed. To the extent that these requirements can be shown or can be assumed to characterize the sample, however, valid generalization to the population is enhanced.

In the social sciences, this generalization is accomplished through a process called statistical inference. Statistical inference, much like courtroom proceedings, begins with the presumption of the null hypothesis—that is, the assumption that no relationship exists in the population. It is the task of the researcher to disprove this hypothesis by providing evidence obtained from the sample. If the evidence is sufficiently compelling, the null hypothesis can be rejected beyond a reasonable doubt. In statistics, doubt can be precisely quantified, and what constitutes reasonable doubt can be determined a priori. This predetermined value is referred to as statistical significance and by tradition has been set at $p < .05$. Any null hypothesis whose probability of being true is less than 5 out of 100 will be labeled as statistically significant and thus rejected as false.

The final sections of this chapter emphasized that despite the most stringent precautions, errors of inference can and do occur. Two types of error—Type I and Type II—were discussed and their ramifications on theory construction were presented. Researchers have typically regarded Type I error as the most harmful, thus explaining the traditional emphasis on statistical significance. The Type II error was also discussed and its relationship to the Type I variety was articulated. Finally, the notion of statistical power was introduced, and an example of how these concepts could be used in planning research was offered.

If the concepts and relationships discussed in this chapter could be synthesized into a single phrase, it would be: *Plan Ahead.* Hardly new advice. Although resisting the impulse to launch into a brief sermon on this topic, we cannot emphasize too strongly that many of the important components of communication research can and should be planned and decided upon before the research begins. Questions about significance, meaningfulness, statistical power, generalization, sampling, and so forth are actually more conceptual than statistical. They should be thoughtfully and responsibly addressed before one expends the considerable time and energy for any research project. Almost any practicing communication researcher will attest to the wisdom of this advice. They have proven it themselves, usually, the hard way.

Statistical Inference: Relationships and the Linear Model

The basic logic of statistical tests of inference has been alluded to and briefly discussed several times in previous chapters. This chapter will present that logic in detail. In addition, several specific tests of relationships will be presented and discussed. Our purpose for withholding these specifics until now is quite simple: We want you to *understand* how and why they are used, not just accept and memorize them because they are in this book. Far too many students have been exposed to statistics via this mechanical method, with the outcome frequently being technical proficiency in the relative absence of conceptual understanding.

An Overview of Statistical Tests

To review, the goal of social scientists is to account for and explain the variation in some specified human behavior. In this book, of course, our concerns focus primarily on communicative behavior. This variation can be numerically represented by several indices, e.g., variance, sum-of-squares, or standard deviation. In oversimplified terms, the first task of statistics is to inform a researcher how much of that variation is explained by one or more selected explanatory variables. This task is achieved by statistics such as r^2, which indicates the percentage or proportion of variance shared by two variables in the sample. Similarly, $1 - r^2$ indicates what percentage of variance cannot be explained. These and similar statistics designed to describe a sample of observations were presented in Chapter 9.

The second task of statistics is to aid the researcher in making inferences about and generalizations to the population. Chapter 10 presented the logical and empirical requirements for valid generalization. As was suggested, the job of the researcher is to provide compelling evidence to reject the null hypothesis beyond a reasonable doubt. This evidence is provided by statistical tests of inference. All such tests operate similarly. They synthesize the information contained in various statistical indices into a single number—a test statistic. If the test statistic is larger than a predetermined value (frequently referred to as the "critical value"), the relationship is considered significant, and the null hypothesis is rejected. If the test statistic does not surpass the critical value, the null hypothesis is not rejected and the relationship is deemed nonsignificant.

191

Performing such tests requires little more than taking previously calculated indices and plugging them into a formula. Hardly an intellectual challenge. However, to understand what such tests are attempting to accomplish, you must first comprehend (as always) the logic which underlies them. In previous chapters, we have shown that the variation of any criterion variable can be decomposed into two parts: (1) that which can be explained by (i.e., is shared with) other variables, and (2) that which cannot. The first component will be referred to as the *systematic variance*. It is that percentage of the variance which is systematically related to an explanatory variable or variables.

In contrast, the second component of variance—that which cannot be explained or is not shared—will be termed the *random variance*. This is the percentage of the variance which is unrelated in any systematic manner to the explanatory variable(s). Frequently, this component is labeled the *residual variation*, i.e., that which is left over after the systematic variance is removed. Perhaps more often this component is simply called *error*, a reference which will assume more meaning during the subsequent discussion of statistical prediction. Irrespective of its name, this component of variance represents scientific ignorance. It is what a researcher does not know or cannot explain about the criterion variable of interest.

These two components of variance form the basis for all statistical tests of inference. Different tests will employ different procedures to calculate them. Moreover, some calculational procedures are relatively complicated, while some are quite simple. In either case, the end result of these calculations is one index of systematic variance and one index of random variance. From this point, all tests proceed in much the same manner: They determine the size of the systematic variance relative to the random component. Stated differently, they calculate a test statistic based on the ratio of the systematic variance to the random variance. As Eq. 11.1. suggests:

$$\text{test statistic} = \frac{\sigma^2_{\text{Systematic}}}{\sigma^2_{\text{Random}}} \tag{11.1}$$

In short, the test statistic is a ratio of what is known to what is not; of knowledge compared to ignorance. Notice that as the size of the systematic variance increases relative to the random component, the test statistics become larger. Conversely, as the percentage of variance which can be explained becomes smaller and thus the random, unsystematic variance becomes larger, the test statistic decreases in size. This inverse relationship is absolutely inherent. When these two components are combined, they must total 100% of the variance. Consequently, for one component to become larger, the other must, by definition, decrease.

From the point of view of the researcher, large test statistics are desired. They indicate that what can be explained is considerably larger than what cannot. As test statistics become larger, they imply that the researcher can more confidently reject the null hypothesis as false, and accept the research hypothesis as "not false." As discussed in Chapter 10, however, the test statistic must be sufficiently large to reject the null hypothesis beyond a reasonable doubt. The question then becomes: How large is large enough?

At this point the concept of the critical value is required. For every test statistic, statisticians have calculated a distribution. This distribution is simply all of the possible values a test statistic might assume, as well as the frequency with which each value would be expected to occur by chance—i.e., under the assumption of complete randomness. Although most of these distributions are considerably different in form from the bell-shaped, normal distribution, they share an important commonality. It is possible to use the expected frequency of occurrence to determine the exact probability or likelihood that any value will occur by chance alone, i.e., the probability of obtaining a nonzero value of a test statistic from the sample, when the null hypothesis is true in the population.

Armed with this distribution, the researcher can determine the exact probability that the null hypothesis is false. In general, however, researchers do not want or need the entire distribution of probabilities. Rather, they are content to know those values of a test statistic which occur at particularly salient levels of probability—for example, $p < .05$, .025, .01, etc. The values associated with these probabilities are called "critical values." They are the values a test statistic must surpass for an investigator to claim statistical significance and thus reject the null hypothesis beyond a reasonable doubt. In this sense, they are indeed "critical" to the process of scientific generalization.

In this book, Appendices $B–E$ contain tables of critical values for several test statistics. Shortly, you will learn how to employ them, but for now rest assured that the procedure is simple and straightforward. In the meantime, let us put into perspective the previous discussion. Chapter 10 focused on the logic of generalization, emphasizing that for the null hypothesis to be rejected, the investigator must produce sufficient evidence from the sample data. Thus far, this chapter has specified what constitutes that evidence: test statistics which are sufficiently large to surpass the predetermined critical value. This is the relationship between statistical inference and scientific generalization. Tests of statistical inference provide the evidence from which investigators can make decisions about the accuracy or truth-value of their research hypotheses. In the final analysis, this is what inferential (as opposed to descriptive) statistics are all about. They are tools to aid the scientist in making valid generalizations.

Testing the Pearson r

The most basic statistical index of relationship is the Pearson correlation co-efficient, r. We have described it as an index of standardized covariance, and have suggested several desirable properties it possesses for describing the strength or magnitude of a relationship. The Pearson r is additionally useful, because r^2 is a direct indication of the percentage of variance that two variables share in common. Similarly, $1 - r^2$ represents the percentage of variance which is not shared. In terms of the previous section, r^2 is an index of systematic variation, while $1 - r^2$ provides an estimate of the random or residual variance.

As long as an investigator is content to describe only the sample at hand (which is seldom), generalization to the population is not an issue. In contrast, if the investigator desires to make inferences about the entire population of observations which have not been observed, the requirements and assumptions discussed in Chapter 10 must be invoked. The sample correlations are then thought of as "estimates" of those in the population. As such, they must be tested to determine if they constitute sufficient evidence to reject the null hypothesis.

To illustrate how such testing would proceed, some data are required. Table 11.1 presents the scores obtained from 49 children on two measures. These measures were adapted from a recent study by Courtright and Courtright (1983) on the relationship between the development of verbal and nonverbal competency in children. The first variable of interest is termed *Language Age* (LA). It represents the children's level of development in their use of language constructions. Measured in months, this score is the age level at which the child is producing language, which may be quite different from their actual, chronological age. The second variable is the number of correct responses each child produced on a test designed to measure their recognition of emotional meaning solely from the vocal cues of a speaker. This test was entitled Measurement of Vocalic Sensitivity (MOVS). Each child listened to a tape of different speakers producing a neutral phrase ("Bring that to me"), but adding vocal intonation to produce the emotions of happy, angry, loving, and sad. Each of the four emotions was presented three times, thus allowing for a maximum possible score of 12. Table 11.1 provides all of the univariate descriptive statistics, as well as various indices of relationship.

From this table it can be seen that the correlation between LA and MOVS is $r = .412$, with $r^2 = .170$. Obviously, these values are somewhat lower in magnitude than those of previous examples. These, however, are *real* data, not the invented variety we

TABLE 11.1. Data and Sample Statistics for Study of Verbal and Nonverbal Development in Children

OBS	MOVS	Language Age	OBS	MOVS	Language Age
1	4	39	26	8	24
2	9	31	27	6	32
3	8	45	28	3	24
4	4	40	29	5	37
5	7	41	30	6	32
6	5	65	31	7	32
7	8	55	32	5	32
8	7	86	33	7	18
9	8	67	34	6	39
10	4	64	35	4	32
11	8	68	36	6	39
12	8	44	37	4	34
13	7	81	38	7	39
14	5	50	39	5	32
15	7	70	40	5	29
16	8	82	41	3	41
17	9	88	42	7	39
18	7	68	43	6	34
19	6	88	44	7	45
20	5	54	45	7	44
21	7	72	46	6	40
22	9	105	47	5	45
23	6	56	48	8	37
24	7	80	49	6	56
25	3	26			

	Univariate Statistics		Bivariate Statistics	
	MOVS	**Language Age**		
$\sum Y_i$	305.00	2421.00	$SP =$	652.51
$\overline{X}$	6.22	49.41	$COV =$	13.59
SS	124.53	20093.80	$r =$	.412
σ^2	2.59	418.62	$r^2 =$	.170
SD	1.61	20.46	$1 - r^2 =$	.830

have used in some other examples. Despite this adventure in realism, the task remains the same: to test whether the null hypothesis can be rejected. In this instance, the null hypothesis is that the correlation coefficient in the population is actually zero. Several alternative approaches to testing are available.

The *F*-Ratio Approach

The first alternative to be presented is the most heuristic, because it corresponds closely to the concepts presented in Eq. 11.1. For reasons to be discussed later, it is also the least frequently used. Recall that Eq. 11.1 stated that all test statistics represent a ratio of the systematic variance to the random variance. When considering the Pearson r, the two components are quantified as r^2 and $1 - r^2$, respectively. Consequently, these two indices will be involved in any statistical test one might construct.

Eq. 11.2 presents the formula for a common and very important test statistic, the *F*-ratio.

$$F = \frac{r^2/p}{1 - r^2/N - p - 1} \qquad (11.2)$$

As previous logic would suggest, this equation makes prominent use of r^2 and $1 - r^2$. They are the sample's best estimates of systematic and random variation. In addition, Eq. 11.2 indicates that both indices should be divided by other numbers *before* their ratio is constructed. These "other numbers" are formally referred to as *degrees-of-freedom* (abbreviated simply as *df*). They aid in determining the appropriate distribution of the *F*-statistic to be consulted for the critical value. As these parameters change, so does the distribution of *F*.

For testing Pearson r, N always equals the number of observations in the sample, and the parameter p is always 1. (The logic of exactly how p is determined will be saved until the next section on predictive models.) As a result, Eq. 11.2 for the Pearson r can be somewhat simplified as:

$$F = \frac{r^2}{1 - r^2/N - 2} \qquad (11.3)$$

To conduct this test, first take the appropriate values from Table 11.1 and place them in Eq. 11.3. This results in the following:

$$F = \frac{.17}{.83/47}$$

$$= \frac{.17}{.0177}$$

$$= 9.60$$

with 1 and 47 *df*.

This test statistic indicates that in the sample the systematic variance is 9.6 times larger than the random variance. Obviously, this ratio is relatively large, but is it large enough? Is it sufficient to reject the null hypothesis? To answer this question, turn to Appendix C, which provides the critical values for several different significance levels. First, locate the column which represents the *df* for the numerator (in this case, 1). Next, find the row which represents the df for the denominator, $N - p - 1$. Since the row for 47 df is not explicitly tabled, some estimation between the lines is necessary. Finally, decide upon the level of significance desired, i.e., the maximum acceptable probability of committing a Type I error. For this illustration, begin with $p < .05$.

Using these three parameters, you can now determine that the critical value is somewhere between 4.17 and 4.06, about 4.12. The exact value is more or less superfluous, because the F-ratio of 9.60 will no doubt surpass it. In fact, a bit more inspection of this table will suggest that the obtained F-ratio (again, considering only 1 and 47 df) will surpass the critical values for several other significance levels ($p < .025, .01$, and $.005$; but *not* $p < .001$). Thus, the probability of committing a Type 1 error is somewhere between 1 and 5 times out of 1000. (The exact probability, as determined by computer, is $p < .0032$.) Clearly, the probability of the null hypothesis being true is minuscule. As a result, it can be rejected as false and the correlation declared significant. There is strong and compelling evidence for assuming that the relationship between these indices of verbal and nonverbal development is *not* zero in the population.

The *t*-Ratio Approach

The second alternative test statistic for testing Pearson r is the t-ratio, frequently referred to simply as the t-test or Student's t. The t-test is closely related to the F-ratio; in fact, the t-ratio is simply the square root of the F. The t-statistic is more frequently used to test the significance of correlations for the simple reason that it was designed specifically to examine bivariate relationships. The F-ratio, on the other hand, is capable of testing relationships involving more than two variables.

Given the relationship between F and t, the t-statistics can be derived as follows:

$$t = \sqrt{F},$$

Thus Eq. 11.3 suggests

$$t = \sqrt{\frac{r^2}{1 - r^2/N - 2}},$$

Therefore

$$t = \frac{r}{\sqrt{1 - r^2/N - 2}} \tag{11.4}$$

Although Eq. 11.4 can be derived directly from Eq. 11.3, there is an important difference. Because r rather than r^2 is used in the t-test, the statistic obtained from Eq. 11.4 can be directional. It can be either positive or negative, depending on whether the relationship being tested is direct or inverse. The F-ratio will always be positive, because the direction of the relationship is eliminated when the correlation is squared. Frequently, the direction of a relationship is not at issue. An investigator will be interested solely in its magnitude. On occasion, however, researchers will specify in advance the direction a relationship is expected to assume. If an F-ratio is used in those instances, the researcher must take into account the sign of the correlation coefficient, as well as the magnitude of the test statistic.

To illustrate the use of the t-test, the data and sample estimates from Table 11.1 will again be used.

$$t = \frac{.412}{\sqrt{1 - .17/47}}$$

$$= \frac{.412}{\sqrt{.0177}}$$

$$= \frac{.412}{.133} = 3.097,$$

or with rounding

$$= 3.10$$

To illustrate the relationship between F and t:

$$t = \sqrt{F}$$
$$= \sqrt{9.60}$$
$$= 3.098,$$

or with rounding

$$= 3.10$$

Ignoring the slight difference prior to rounding, these formulas produce exactly the same information.

Once again, the question arises: Is $t = 3.10$ large enough to reject the null hypothesis? For this particular relationship, the answer is already known, because the F-ratio has been tested and found significant. Nevertheless, it will be instructive to examine the t-test independently. Appendix B contains the critical values for the t distribution. For this statistic, however, no numerator degrees-of-freedom are needed. Because the t-test is capable of testing *only* bivariate relationships, this parameter will always be 1. As a consequence, only the row corresponding to $N - 2$ (e.g., 47) need be located, and the desired significance level (e.g., $p < .05$) be determined.

The specific critical value for 47 df is again not tabled, so some form of estimation is required. The exact critical value for this t-test is somewhere between 2.021 and 2.000. As with the F-ratio, great specificity is not required because $t = 3.10$ far surpasses even the most stringent estimate. Also corresponding to that previous experience, $t = 3.10$ surpasses the critical values for all significance levels except $p < .001$. As a result, the decision to reject the null hypothesis is the same. To be sure, the manner in which the evidence is presented (t instead of F) has been altered, but the information that evidence gives is exactly the same.

Testing Pearson r Directly

Having taken the rather tortuous route through two different test statistics, we must now admit that a much simpler and more direct method is available for determining the significance of a Pearson r. This third approach involves nothing more than comparing the value of r obtained from the sample to a table containing critical values of *r*. This table can be found in Appendix D. Notice there is no conversion of *r* to a test statistic required. One simply locates the row corresponding to $N - 2$, decides upon the appropriate significance level, and finds the critical value of *r* which must be surpassed.

For the previous example, therefore, *r* with 47 *df* must exceed an approximate critical value of .280 to be significant at $p < .05$. From the previous two tests, the fact that this happens comes as no surprise. Moreover, further examination indicates, as before, that $r = .412$ is significant somewhere between $p < .01$ and $p < .001$. Thus, for a third time the evidence for rejecting the null hypothesis is exactly the same.

Given the relative simplicity of this approach, you are no doubt wondering what justifies discussion of the *t*- and *F*-statistics. The answer, simply stated, is increased understanding. While the direct approach to testing *r* is admittedly simple and direct, it offers absolutely no insight into the logic of testing per se. For example, it is worthwhile to ask where the critical values of *r* in Appendix D came from? How were they determined? They were calculated by working backward from the critical values of the *F*- and *t*-statistics in the other tables. By using Eqs. 11.3 or 11.4, it is possible to calculate the precise value of *r* which is required to achieve the critical value for *F* or *t*.

In short, using Appendix D is simply a shortcut approach which avoids all the work of calculating test statistics. It also avoids all the thinking, which at this point in your understanding of statistics may not be especially desirable. The professional statisticians who calculated the critical values of *r* in Appendix D do not need to be reminded of the logic which underlies statistical inference. We assume, at least for the present, that you do. In practice, therefore, use Appendix D for the purpose for which it was intended: a convenient computational shortcut. In your thinking, however, continually recall that the formula for statistical inference (i.e., Eq. 11.4) is what makes this convenience possible.

In summary, we have presented three methods for testing the significance of a Pearson correlation coefficient. The *F*-ratio and the *t*-test approaches require the calculation of a test statistic, which is then compared to the critical value for the appropriate distribution—that is, the distribution with 1 and *N*-2 degrees-of-freedom. Two important aspects of these test statistics are worth recalling. The *F*-ratio corresponds most closely to the conceptual model of statistical inference. Nevertheless, because it requires additional computations, it is seldom used in practice. Second, the *t*-test is the square root of the *F*-ratio, and was designed specifically to test relationships involving only two variables. It has the capability of testing the directionality of a relationship, as well as its magnitude.

The third approach for testing Pearson *r* was simply called the direct approach. It involves nothing more than comparing the value of *r* obtained from the sample to a critical value of *r* for *N*-2 *df*. It requires no calculation of a test statistic and is both quick and convenient. As was suggested, however, the critical values of *r* were derived directly from the *F*- and *t*-statistics. Hence, despite the increase in convenience, the logic of statistical inference and scientific generalization remains unaltered.

These three methods make it possible to test the significance of any Pearson *r* one might obtain. As long as one knows the values of *r* and *N*, one can enter the appropriate table for *N*-2 *df* and determine the critical value of *F*, *t*, or *r*. In many instances, the precise critical value may not be tabled, which will require a bit of estimation (formally called "interpolation"). Usually, such estimation will suffice. If you require *precise* critical value, you can find an unabridged volume of statistical tables in the reference section in most libraries.

One final point before proceeding. Thus far, we have been concerned solely with the notion of testing and generalizing relationships. It has been sufficient to discover and test that two variables are related, i.e., that they share a significant proportion of their variance. In the course of constructing and testing meaningful theory, however, the fact that two variables are merely related is frequently not sufficient. The researcher must examine and specify *why* they are related. This requires a researcher to designate one variable as the concept or construct to be explained (the criterion variable), and the others as the variables to do that explaining (the explanatory variable(s)). Although this constitutes a slight shift in conceptualization, this analytic strategy is rooted firmly in the notion that two related variables share their variance. This shared variation, however, can also be thought of as "explained" variation—the knowledge of one variable allows the explanation of the variation in the other. This revised approach employs the knowledge of relationships in a much more powerful and predictive manner.

Statistical Models of Relationships

For students of human communication, the desire to model or depict a complex phenomenon in a simpler, more understandable fashion should not be new. Textbooks in communication routinely present two-dimensional, visual representations of the communication process. These pictorial models display only the basic, fundamental components of human communication, usually deleting or ignoring the details—the subtleties, complexities, or gaps in understanding. The goal, of course, is to make the model both accurate, yet relatively simple; frequently, these are mutually exclusive outcomes.

Statistical models operate in a remarkably similar fashion. Their goal is to depict accurately and faithfully the relationship between variables, yet keep this depiction as simple and parsimonious as possible. Frequently, these two goals cannot be achieved simultaneously, which underscores the realization that (1) many social phenomena are not simple, and (2) the theories which guide the construction of statistical models are not entirely accurate. Neither of these realizations have deterred researchers from attempting to construct models of relationships (see McPhee & Poole, 1982). As statistical models continue to add to the theoretic understanding of communication phenomena, this understanding should contribute to the construction or more accurate models. Whether such models will ever be simple is an empirical question.

Models as Explanatory

The purpose of statistical models is to depict a relationship. As suggested, the process of constructing such models requires a general reconceptualization of what relationships represent. In past discussions, relationships were defined as the degree to which two variables vary together, i.e., covariation. From this definition, the notion of shared variance was conceptually and empirically derived. None of these basic concepts will be altered; nor, for that matter, could they be altered. They are logical and mathematical fact.

What will be changed, however, is the information to be drawn from the empirical discovery that two variables are (or are not) related. Previously, evidence that two variables were significantly correlated was sufficient. This relationship was bidirectional:

X was related to Y, and Y was related to X. These variables simply shared variance to a greater or lesser degree.

Such bidirectional thinking will not suffice for the construction of a statistical model. Instead, one and only one variable must be designated as the variable of interest, the criterion variable, or the phenomenon which the investigator wishes to explain. The investigator must declare that it is the variance of a particular variable (usually symbolized as Y) that he or she wishes to explain or account for.

Needless to say, this is not a statistical task. Theory, previous research, or even an educated guess may compel a researcher to be interested in a particular communicative phenomenon. Whatever the reason, statistics has no role in this decision. Once it is made, the investigator will designate an additional variable(s) as the explanatory variable(s) (symbolized as variable X). Again, from established theory or previous research, the investigator has reason to believe that knowledge of the explanatory variable(s) will provide knowledge of *why* the criterion variable varies. In short, there is reason to believe that they are systematically related.

Notice that the discussion has quickly returned to the topic of relationships. The focus is still squarely on how much variation two variables share. Shared variance, however, begins to assume a different interpretative thrust: *shared variance is explained variance.* To the extent that the explanatory variable, X, shares variance with the criterion variable, Y, that proportion of the Y variance is explained. It is accounted for by the investigator's knowledge of X. As always, some proportion of the variance of Y will not be shared with X. Accordingly, this variance is unexplained. More research and/or more accurate theory is required.

Models as Predictive

Although we have thus far refrained from doing so, we can easily cast this discussion in the framework of prediction. Given the knowledge of an individual's X score, how accurately can the investigator predict that person's score on variable Y? To illustrate with a previous example, given the knowledge of how many hours of TV an individual watches per week, how accurately can one predict this person's score on the Loneliness index?

At first glance, such a question may seem totally unrelated to previous concerns about explaining variance. At the very least, the level of interest seems altered: Variance is explained at the level of the entire sample, while predictions are made for each individual within the sample. Despite this distinction, these concerns are closely allied. If a researcher can account for a relatively large proportion of the Y variation, then he or she can make relatively accurate predictions of individual Y scores based solely on the knowledge of a person's score on X. As shared variance decreases, the prediction of individual Y scores becomes proportionately imprecise.

A fuller understanding of this logic can be gained by returning to the concept of a perfect relationship. If two variables are perfectly related, then they share all of their variance. X accounts for 100% of Y. Similarly, in this situation to know an individual's X score is to know exactly the value of Y. X and Y will, of course, be the same and prediction will be perfect.

Even though perfect relationships do not occur in practice, this principle can be generalized. A high percentage of shared variance between X and Y implies a similarly high degree of accuracy in predicting individual Y scores. Low proportions of shared variance lead to relatively imprecise prediction. As you can see, the simple concept of a relationship begins to assume more interesting and potentially more insightful interpretations.

Constructing the Model

All statistical procedures carry out the construction of a statistical model in two phases. First, during the *estimation phase,* the data obtained from the sample are used to estimate the parameters of the model. The magnitude of the relationship, proportion of shared variance, predicted Y scores, and other statistics will be calculated from the data at hand. Second, in the *testing phase* the accuracy of the model is evaluated. Tests of statistical inference are performed to evaluate whether the model explains a significant proportion of the variation in Y. Stated differently, can the model as estimated from the sample be generalized to the population? As always, the null hypothesis will be that it cannot; that the explained variance in the population is zero. Each of these phases will be discussed separately.

Estimating the Model

A statistical model of a relationship can be conceptualized in two different ways. The most obvious is *mathematical:* The model will mathematically manipulate the X scores in some fashion to derive the predicted values of Y. More on that later. In a second and more heuristic conceptualization, such models can be thought of as primarily *visual.* Given a scatterplot of the values of X and Y, it is possible to overlay the model on this plot. In short, it is possible to see the model and how well it represents the relationship. It is important to realize that the ability to draw the model comes directly from the mathematical manipulations—the mathematics provide the numbers which can then be transferred to the scatterplot. Nevertheless, more insight and understanding can be gained if one works backward from the visual to the mathematical approach.

Models as Visual. Figure 11.1 (p. 202) presents a plot of the data from Table 11.1. The vertical axis represents the MOVS instrument, while the horizontal axis is scaled for Language Age. Given this plot, what is the goal? What does a statistical model ideally attempt to accomplish? The ultimate goal of a model is to produce a line which connects as many data points as possible—ideally, all such points. This would be easy if it were not for the second constraint of "simplicity." It would require little effort or thought to connect all the points with lines—much like a child's coloring book where the numbers are connected and a picture emerges. It is an elementary fact of geometry that any N points can be connected with N-1 lines. Clearly, no theoretic insight or understanding would be gained from such an exercise.

In recognition of this fact, all of the models discussed in this book will endeavor to connect as many points as possible with a *single straight line.* They will thus be termed *linear* models. Such models will attempt to construct what is often referred to as the "line-of-best-fit" through the cloud of data points, connecting as many as possible. This single line may slope upward or downward on the plot, depending on whether the relationship between X and Y is direct or inverse. Similarly, this slope (irrespective of direction) may be very steep or somewhat more gradual, depending on the magnitude of the relationship.

Finally, in all but the rarest of instances the linear model will *not* connect all of the

FIGURE 11.1. Plot of Relationship Between MOVS and Language Age, Including Line-of-Best Fit.

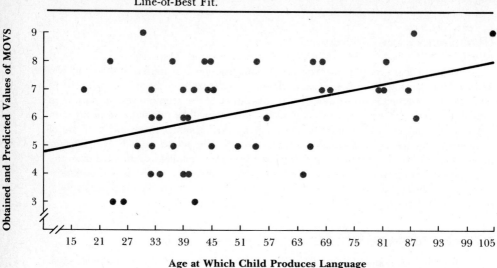

points. In fact, in many situations it will connect only a few. As a result, the model will always be inaccurate to some extent. Accordingly, the accuracy of the model is not judged by whether it connects all of the points, or even by how many points it connects. Rather, the "goodness-of-fit" of the model is evaluated by how close the line comes to each data point; i.e., by the spacial distance between each point and the line-of-best-fit.

The line-of-best-fit is already displayed in Figure 11.1. As expected, it does not connect all of the points on the plot. It comes close to some and misses others by far. This, of course, only reflects what statistical information is already possessed: $r = .412$. The relationship is moderate in its magnitude. Also, because the relationship is direct and the Pearson r positive, the linear model slopes gradually upward. Hence, this model seems to capture the salient attributes of the relationship which have been previously discussed.

A key question, however, still remains to be answered. What is the meaning of this straight line? Exactly what does it model? Recall that we earlier said that one outcome of constructing a linear model was to obtain a predicted value of Y (the criterion variable) for each value of X. Moreover, this predicted value would be accurate or inaccurate, depending on the magnitude of the relationship and thus r^2. The straight line in Figure 11.1 is a visual representation of these predicted values. For each value of X (Language Age), the corresponding point on the line represents the value of Y (MOVS) predicted by the model. The accuracy of the prediction, as suggested above, is judged by how close or how far away each observed data point is from the line—that is, the predicted data points. Moreover, it is now apparent why the goal of the model is to connect all of the points with a single straight line. If all of the points were on the line, prediction would be perfect.

Before turning to the mathematics which produce the linear model, a word or two about shared variance is in order. Earlier, we said that shared variance and accuracy of prediction are closely related. Some additional thinking about scatterplots and the information they contain should reinforce this point. In Chapter 9, we suggested that a good deal of information about a relationship could be obtained by examining such plots. Recall that strong relationships with large r's will manifest a clear and discernible pattern. The points will tend to be closely clustered in either an upward or downward trend. In contrast, weak relationships will exhibit a diffuse and scattered plotting of the data points, with no recognizable pattern being apparent.

These contrasting situations (for $r = .80$ and $r = .20$) are illustrated in Figures 11.2 and 11.3, respectively. Notice also that the line-of-best-fit is drawn in both figures. In Figure 11.2 where r and r^2 are relatively large, the points cluster tightly around the line. Recall that if the relationship were perfect, r^2 would equal 1.00 and all of the points would fall on the line. This relationship, of course, is not perfect. Nevertheless, its large correlation suggests that a good deal of the variance in Y is captured by the linear model through the points. Similarly, the distance of each point from its corresponding point on the line is relatively small. Hence, both the accuracy of the prediction and the variance accounted for are quite high.

A different situation is depicted in Figure 11.3 (p. 204). The data points do not cluster tightly around the line. Some are close, but many are not. Consequently, much of the variance of this criterion variable remains unexplained by the model. Moreover, the accuracy of predicting the individual values of Y is very low. The researcher's knowledge of X offers little insight or understanding into *why* Y varies.

Figures 11.2 and 11.3 illustrate the obvious: Models can be no better or no more accurate than the relationships they represent. They are merely visual depictions of the information contained in statistics such as r^2, $1 - r^2$, etc. Models can do no more than

FIGURE 11.2 Plot of Relationship for $r = .80$, Including Line-of-Best-Fit.

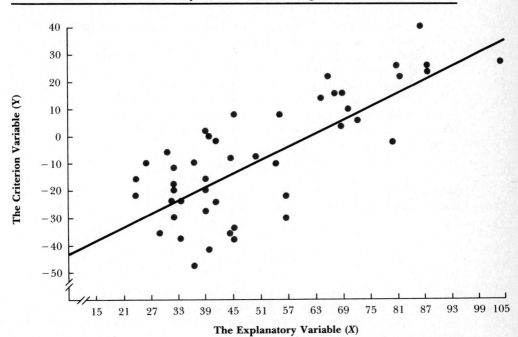

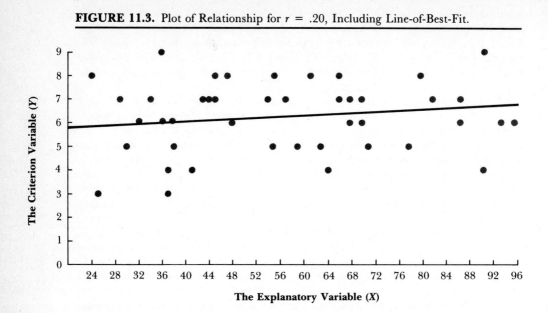

characterize the X variable selected by the investigator as explanatory. If the X variable is, indeed, explanatory, the model will fit the data quite closely. If not, then goodness-of-fit will be poor. In either case, both the statistics and the model are merely reflections of the substantive, theoretic understanding of the researcher.

Models as Statistical.   The goal of this section should be readily apparent. Given that the end result of a model is to produce the line-of-best-fit, one must understand how the numbers corresponding to that line—i.e., the predicted values of Y—are obtained. For the remainder of this discussion, the predicted values of Y will be symbolized as $\hat{Y}$ (pronounced as Y-hat). In terms of prediction, the goal of the model is to make the difference (the spacial distance on the plot) between the ith Y score (Y_i) and its corresponding predicted value ($\hat{Y}_i$) as small as possible; that is, to minimize the error of prediction. The smaller the difference, the better the prediction. This goal is symbolized in Eq. 11.5.

$$\text{Minimum Error} = (e_i) = (Y_i - \hat{Y}_i) \tag{11.5}$$

Moreover, this goal can be extended to all N observations in the sample, thus suggesting that the sum of the difference should be as small as possible.

$$\text{Minimum Total Error} = \sum_{i=1}^{N}(Y_i - \hat{Y}_i) \tag{11.6}$$

Eq. 11.6, however, is subject to the same problem encountered in Chapter 9 when we considered the calculation of spread. The signs of the various difference scores will cancel each other, thus producing a total error of zero. As before, the solution is one of squaring the difference scores prior to summing.

Thus error of prediction can be conceptualized and calculated as:

$$\text{Error} = \sum_{i=1}^{N}(Y_i - \hat{Y}_i)^2 \qquad (11.7)$$

In statistics, Eq. 11.7 is referred to as the formula for *least-squares error*. It is also referred to as sum-of-squares for error. The goal of the linear model is to produce Y predictions which *minimize* this quantity.

These comments have addressed the issue of prediction. But what about the closely allied concept of shared variance? As suggested, if error of prediction is minimized, the percentage of variance accounted for by X should be maximized. From this latter perspective, the goal of the model is to produce $\hat{Y}$ values which are maximally correlated with Y. In the bivariate case, this correlation will be exactly the same as the correlation between X and Y. Subsequently, when models with multiple explanatory variables $(X_1, X_2, X_3,$ etc.) are discussed, this will not necessarily be the case.

The quantity produced by Eq. 11.7, however, has another, equally important interpretation. It is the quantity represented by $1 - r^2$. This index, of course, represents the unexplained variance as a percentage. This percentage must be a percentage of some calculable quantity. For the linear model, this quantity is SS_Y, or the total variation of the criterion variable. In other words, 100% of the variance is equal to SS_Y. Consequently, the following relationships can be derived:

$$SS_{\text{Model}} = r^2 SS_Y \qquad (11.8)$$

$$SS_{\text{Error}} = (1 - r^2)SS_Y = \sum_{i=1}^{N}(Y_i - \hat{Y})^2 \qquad (11.9)$$

$$SS_Y = SS_{\text{Model}} + SS_{\text{Error}} \qquad (11.10)$$

where: SS_{Model} is the actual quantity of the variance accounted for by the linear model; and SS_{Error} is that actual quantity of the Y variation which is unexplained or unaccounted for.

In terms of understanding the allied concepts of predictive accuracy and explained variance, it is instructive to note that the quantities produced by Eqs. 11.7 and 11.9 will always be the same. Least-squares error, therefore, is equivalent to the model's inaccuracy or error of prediction. It is also exactly that percentage of the variance which cannot be explained by X. Once again, it can be seen that prediction and explanation, at least from the standpoint of the linear model, are virtually synonymous concepts. The goal of every statistical model is to produce accurate $\hat{Y}$ values. Whether these values are thought of as minimizing the error of prediction or maximizing the shared variance is not an either/or choice. They happen simultaneously.

Now, down to the business of presenting the actual model. The complete linear model can be symbolized as:

$$Y_i = a + BX_i + e_i \qquad (11.11)$$

where: Y_i is the obtained or measured score for the ith observation; a is the constant term which is added to each X score; and B is another constant term which is multiplied times each X score. Finally, e_i represents the error of prediction, and was defined previously in Eq. 11.5 as $(Y_i - \hat{Y}_i)$. By combining Eqs. 11.5 and 11.11, it can be shown that:

$$Y_i = a + BX_i + (Y_i - \hat{Y}_i)$$
$$Y_i - (Y_i - \hat{Y}_i) = a + BX_i$$

therefore

$$\hat{Y} = a + BX_i$$

As a result, the predicted value of Y_i (i.e., $\hat{Y}_i$) is calculated by (1) multiplying X_i times the coefficient B, and (2) adding another constant term, a. Obviously, whether the resulting predicted values of Y are accurate or inaccurate will depend totally on which values are selected for a and B. These values could be determined by trial and error, but a more efficient method is to employ the sample data to calculate them directly. In more complex models, these calculations involve either calculus or matrix algebra, and almost necessarily require the use of a computer. For the present bivariate model, however, these calculations are straightforward and simple. They involve the basic statistics already estimated.

It is first necessary to calculate B, which is often referred to as the "regression coefficient" or simply as the "beta weight." This coefficient is interpreted as *the number of units the Y variable changes for each single unit of change in X*. Formally, the regression coefficient, B, is defined as:

$$B = \frac{SP_{XY}}{SS_X} \tag{11.12}$$

For the bivariate case, therefore, B is simply the sum-of-products divided by the sum-of-squares for the explanatory variable, X. It is a ratio which compares the covariance *(SP)* to the variance or spread *(SS$_X$)* of the explanatory variable. It can be shown that if the relationship were perfect ($r = 1.0$), then $SP = SS_X$, and $B = 1.0$. Because in this case, X and Y would have exactly the same value, a unit of change in X would be accompanied by a single unit of change in Y. Most often, however, the SS_X will be either smaller or larger than the SP. The relationship will not be perfect, and B will not equal 1.0.

Using the data from Table 11.1, it can be seen that:

$$SP = 652.51$$
$$SS_X = 20,093.80$$

therefore,

$$B = \frac{652.51}{20,093.80}$$

$$= .0325$$

At first glance, the regression coefficient seems very small. From Table 11.1, however, it can be seen that Language Age is measured in a much different and much larger metric (months) than is MOVS. The rather small B, therefore, simply reflects and adjusts for this basic difference in measurement.

Table 11.1 also suggests that the means of MOVS and Language Age are considerably different. It is the function of the constant term, a, to adjust for this difference. Accordingly, a is defined as:

$$a = \bar{Y} - B\bar{X} \tag{11.13}$$

It is the difference between the mean of the criterion variable and the mean of the appropriately weighted explanatory variable, X. When applied to the current example,

$$\begin{aligned} a &= 6.22 - (.0325)49.41 \\ &= 6.22 - 1.60 \\ &= 4.62 \end{aligned}$$

The entire linear model for the present example, therefore, is:

$$\hat{Y}_i = 4.62 + (.0325)X_i$$

This equation will produce the most accurate prediction of the individual Y scores (i.e., "most accurate" given the magnitude of relationship between X and Y), in addition to producing the maximum correlation between Y and $\hat{Y}$.

Table 11.2 displays the original values of the MOVS instrument, as well as (1) the predicted or $\hat{Y}$ values for each score, and (2) the errors of prediction (or residuals) as calculated from Eq. 11.5. In the abstract, these lists of numbers defy interpretation. Consequently, some important statistics are also included. Using the data in the table, you should attempt to verify the accuracy of the values for yourself.

First, note the several univariate statistics. Notice that Y and $\hat{Y}$ have exactly the same mean. This equivalence is ensured by the constant term, a, in the linear model, $\hat{Y}_i = a + BX_i$. The sole purpose of this constant is to adjust the X scores so that the mean of the predicted values is exactly the same as the mean of the obtained values. Notice also that the mean of the errors, as discussed earlier, is 0.00. Each e_i value represents a deviation between two scores $(Y_i - \hat{Y}_i)$, which have exactly the same mean value. As a result, the sum of the deviations and thus their mean will always balance out to be zero.

Equally important are the sums-of-squares generated for these three variables. It can be seen that the SS for $\hat{Y}$ and the SS for Error can be added to obtain the SS for MOVS or SS_Y. This reflects an earlier assertion that the variance for any criterion variable can be decomposed into two separate pieces—that which can be explained and that which cannot. The SS for $\hat{Y}$ and Error are numerical equivalents of those two pieces. Because they can be added in this manner, they are considered "independent" or non-overlapping components of the Y-variation. They are not related in any way. Stated differently (and in a way you can prove to yourself), the correlation between the $\hat{Y}$ values and the residual or error values will always be $r = 0.00$.

The bivariate statistics in Table 11.2 (p. 208) provide equally useful information. For example, the correlation between Y and $\hat{Y}$ is .412, which is exactly the same as the value of Pearson r between Y and X (i.e., MOVS and Language Age). Accordingly, the values of r^2 and $1 - r^2$ will also be the same. This equivalence is hardly coincidental. On the contrary, it reinforces the fact that the relationship between X and Y is what underlies

TABLE 11.2. Listing of Original Values, Predicted Values, and Errors of Prediction for MOVS

OBS	MOVS	$\hat{Y}$	Errors (e_i)	OBS	MOVS	$\hat{Y}$	Errors (e_i)
1	4	5.88650	−1.8865	26	8	5.39941	2.6006
2	9	5.62672	3.3733	27	6	5.65919	0.3408
3	8	6.08134	1.9187	28	3	5.39941	−2.3994
4	4	5.91898	−1.9190	29	5	5.82156	−0.8216
5	7	5.95145	1.0485	30	6	5.65919	0.3408
6	5	6.73081	−1.7308	31	7	5.65919	1.3408
7	8	6.40607	1.5939	32	5	5.65919	−0.6592
8	7	7.41274	−0.4127	33	7	5.20457	1.7954
9	8	6.79575	1.2042	34	6	5.88650	0.1135
10	4	6.69833	−2.6983	35	4	5.65919	−1.6592
11	8	6.82823	1.1718	36	6	5.88650	0.1135
12	8	6.04887	1.9511	37	4	5.72414	−1.7241
13	7	7.25038	−0.2504	38	7	5.88650	1.1135
14	5	6.24371	−1.2437	39	5	5.65919	−0.6592
15	7	6.89317	0.1068	40	5	5.56177	−0.5618
16	8	7.28285	0.7172	41	3	5.95145	−2.9515
17	9	7.47769	1.5223	42	7	5.88650	1.1135
18	7	6.82823	0.1718	43	6	5.72414	0.2759
19	6	7.47769	−1.4777	44	7	6.08134	0.9187
20	5	6.37360	−1.3736	45	7	6.04887	0.9511
21	7	6.95812	0.0419	46	6	5.91898	0.0810
22	9	8.02973	0.9703	47	5	6.08134	−1.0813
23	6	6.43855	−0.4385	48	8	5.82156	2.1784
24	7	7.21790	−0.2179	49	6	6.43855	−0.4385
25	3	5.46435	−2.4644				

	Univariate Statistics		Bivariate Statistics	
	$\overline{Y}$	SS		
$\hat{Y}$	6.22	21.19	$r_{Y\hat{Y}} = .412$	
Errors	0.00	103.34	$r^2 = .170$	
MOVS	6.22	124.53	$1 - r^2 = .830$	

$$\frac{SS_{\hat{Y}}}{SS_{MOVS}} = \frac{21.19}{124.53} = .170 = r^2$$

$$\frac{SS_{Error}}{SS_{MOVS}} = \frac{103.34}{124.53} = .830 = 1 - r^2$$

the entire model; the model simply reflects this relationship. Neither the predictive nor explanatory power of the model can exceed the magnitude of the relationship which went into its construction.

Finally, the two ratios between *SS* presented in Table 11.2 suggest another important conceptual relationship. Throughout this book we have emphasized the concept of "percentage of variance," and have therefore stressed the r^2 statistic. We have frequently stated that r^2 must represent a percentage of some numerical quantity, namely, the SS for the criterion variable Y. Eqs. 11.8, 11.9, and 11.10 illustrated several of these conceptual relationships, while the ratios in Table 11.2 exemplify still others. Regardless of whether a model is presented in terms of SS or in terms of r^2, the explanatory and predictive information is exactly the same. Each researcher will select the method of presentation which he or she finds most meaningful. As a reader or consumer of research, therefore, you must be prepared to accept and understand each.

In summary, we have suggested that linear models can be conceptualized in two ways. As a visual model, they can be thought of as trying to overlay the line-of-best-fit on the scatterplot of data points. The goodness of this fit is how close this line comes to connecting the data points. When viewed mathematically, the linear model is represented by the equation $\hat{Y}_i = a + BX_i$, which produces the best possible predictions of each Y_i score (i.e., it minimizes error), as well as maximizing the correlation between Y and $\hat{Y}$. It is exactly these $\hat{Y}$ scores which are depicted in the visual model by the line-of-best-fit.

The linear model will provide the maximum amount of both prediction and explanation, subject only to the magnitude of the original X/Y relationship which produced the model. As with all statistical procedures, however, it is necessary to raise the question: Is it good enough? Is the predictive and explanatory power of the model beyond chance expectation, or does the null hypothesis more accurately characterize the population? To answer these questions, a testing phase is required.

Testing the Model

The logic which underlies tests of the adequacy of the linear model is exactly the same as the test of correlation discussed earlier. Their purpose is to provide the investigator with a tool of statistical inference, and thus aid in making scientific generalizations. Accordingly, one begins with the null hypothesis that in the population the explanatory and predictive power of the model is nonexistent; i.e., the model does not fit. Although phrased somewhat differently, this null hypothesis is the same as that for the correlation coefficient: the relationship in the population is zero.

As might be expected, the construction of the test statistic proceeds along the same lines as it did for Pearson r. Recalling Eq. 11.1, our concerns focus on the ratio of systematic variance to random variance. By altering the labels slightly to comform to the terminology of the linear model, Eq. 11.1 can be recast as:

$$\text{test statistic} = \frac{\sigma^2_{\text{Explained}}}{\sigma^2_{\text{Unexplained}}} \qquad (11.14)$$

While the labels have been changed, the test statistic remains unaltered. When a large proportion of the variance can be explained, the test statistic becomes larger. When a large proportion of variance is unexplained, the value of the test statistic decreases. As before, sufficiently large test statistics (i.e., those which surpass the appropriate critical value) are required before scientific generalization can take place.

Before presenting specific test statistics, we must discuss another important similarity. In tests of the Pearson r between X and Y, the primary index of systematic variation was r^2. Accordingly, the F-ratio for testing the magnitude of relationship between X and Y was given by Eq. 11.2

$$F = \frac{r^2/p}{1 - r^2/N - p - 1} \tag{11.2}$$

where, p is always 1 for bivariate relationships, and N is the number of observations in the sample. The discussion of obtained, predicted, and residual values presented in Table 11.2, however, raised an important equivalence: specifically, $r^2{}_{XY} = r^2{}_{Y\hat{Y}}$. This equality is inherent in what a linear model purports to model, namely, the relationship between an explanatory variable (X) and a criterion variable (Y).

For purposes of testing, this equality suggests that the F-ratio in Eq. 11.3 is the appropriate test statistic for *both* the simple correlation coefficient and the bivariate linear model. Only the interpretation of the test changes. When applied to Pearson r, the F-ratio tests whether X and Y *share* a significant proportion of their variance. In contrast, the F-ratio for the linear model indicates whether X *explains* or accounts for a significant proportion of the Y variation. Obviously, the sample estimate of r^2 is the same in both cases, as is the resulting F-ratio. Consequently, which of these interpretations one chooses is totally a matter of the theoretic question one is examining. The statistical procedures and tests supply the same information; only the researcher can convert that information into meaningful scientific generalizations.

Alternate Calculation of the F-Ratio

Thus far, test statistics have been presented solely in terms of percentage of the total variance, thus relying on the r^2 statistic. Table 11.2 and the subsequent discussion of the statistics it contains, however, provide an alternative method for calculating this ratio. Rather than employing r^2 and $1 - r^2$ as proportions of the variance, one can use the various sums-of-squares as direct numerical indicants of these components. Eqs. 11.8 and 11.9 indicate:

$$r^2(SS_Y) = SS_{\text{Model}} = SS_{\hat{Y}} \tag{11.8}$$

and

$$(1 - r^2)(SS_Y) = SS_{\text{Error}} \tag{11.9}$$

Together, these two pieces of the variance combine to equal $SS_Y = SS_{\text{Model}} + SS_{\text{Error}}$ which is equivalent to asserting that $r^2 + (1 - r_2) = 1.0$; or 100% of the variance.

From previous discussion and Eq. 11.3, it is clear that SS_{Model} is the best sample estimate of the explained variation. Similarly, Eq. 11.7 states that SS_{Error} is the best, least-squares estimate of the unexplained variance. If these components are inserted into the formula for the F-ratio (Eq. 11.2), the following is obtained:

$$F = \frac{SS_{\text{Model}}/p}{SS_{\text{Error}}/N - p - 1} \tag{11.15}$$

where, p and $N - p - 1$ represent the degrees-of-freedom. The parameter p is the number of explanatory or predictor variables in the model. Thus, for the bivariate linear model, p is always 1. When sums-of-squares are divided by their respective degrees-of-freedom, they are called *mean squares* (MS). Thus, Eq. 11.15 can be rewritten as:

$$F = \frac{MS_{Model}}{MS_{Error}} \tag{11.16}$$

To illustrate the calculation of this test statistic, the various sums-of-squares from Table 11.2 are inserted.

$$F = \frac{21.19/1}{103.34/47}$$

$$= \frac{21.19}{2.20}$$

$$= 9.63$$

with 1 and 47 *df*.

Recall that the F-ratio using r^2 was 9.60. Thus the two approaches to calculating this test statistic are equivalent within rounding error. Similarly, an examination of the F tables in Appendix C will produce exactly the same critical value for 1 and 47 *df*, and thus the same conclusion. The null hypothesis of no relationship must be rejected.

Which of these calculational procedures to use is a matter of personal choice. To calculate the Pearson r between any two variables, SS_Y is required. It requires little additional effort, therefore, to use Eqs. 11.8 and 11.9 to find the necessary sums-of-squares. While the choice itself is relatively trivial, understanding why the choice exists is not. In reports of research, investigators will frequently present tests based on sums-of-squares and mean squares, and then discuss their findings in terms of percentage of variance explained. Hence, understanding the equivalence between these two forms of expression is crucial.

■ *Conclusion*

In this chapter, two important concepts were presented. As an extension of our earlier discussion of statistical inference and scientific generalization, we discussed the basic logic for testing the significance of a relationship as indexed by Pearson r. In addition, two test statistics—the F-ratio and the t-test—were presented and calculated. The procedure for comparing the obtained value of the test statistic to the appropriate critical value was also discussed.

In the latter part of this chapter, we introduced the logic and procedures for constructing the linear model. Substantial emphasis was devoted to this model, because it forms the foundation for almost all statistical procedures. This is not to suggest that all relationships are linear in nature, or that researchers should not postulate and investigate curvilinear or nonlinear relationships among and between variables. On the contrary, statistical procedures designed to model and represent such curvilinearity are well developed and widely used. In most instances, such models are direct extensions or special cases of the linear model (see Kerlinger & Pedhazur, 1973). Hence, a thorough understanding of the basic linear model will provide the best preparation for comprehending and utilizing these more complex alternatives.

Finally, throughout this chapter there has been an implicit assumption that the explanatory variable, X, was measured on some form of a continuum. Without rehashing the tired litany on "levels of measurement," we simply mean that the X data did not consist of nominal, mutually exclusive categories, such as High/Low, Male/Female, Treatment 1/Treatment 2, etc.

Frankly, we perceive no reason to maintain this assumption. Chapter 12, therefore, dismisses it entirely and discusses relationships and models in which X is a nominal, classification variable. The criterion variable, however, will always be treated as continuous. What will be discovered is that both the logic and calculations of the linear model remain unchanged; only the interpretation of the information it provides is altered.

Statistical Inference: Differences and the Linear Model

The discussion of "levels of measurement" in Chapter 6 provides the basic premise from which to begin this discussion: Data need not be and frequently will not be ordinal, interval, or ratio (i.e., continuous) in form. It is a fact of empirical life in the social sciences that a researcher will sooner or later face the task of analyzing a set of variables, at least some of which are composed of nominal (i.e., categorical) data. Given this fact, the purpose of this chapter is twofold: (1) to show that the linear model can easily represent the relationship between a continuous Y variable and a dichotomous explanatory variable, X; and (2) to show the equivalence between the linear model of such relationships and the more "traditional" approach to this problem, the Analysis of Variance (ANOVA).

This chapter discusses those situations in which the explanatory variable X is a dichotomy containing only two discrete categories. This is obviously the simplest case of categorization, and as a result somewhat limited in its applicability to real-world data. Analyses containing multiple-category variables are somewhat more complex, requiring the model to contain more than one X variable to adequately represent all of the categories. Such models are direct extensions of the bivariate (one X, one Y) case, and are discussed in Chapter 13. For the present, the simple, two-category case will afford ample understanding, while avoiding unnecessary complexity.

The Origins of Categorical Data

A word or two about categorical variables is in order, especially about how they originate in research. The most obvious reason for obtaining categorical variables is that the concepts they represent are truly nominal classifications of various types of people. Variables such as gender (male/female), religion (Protestant, Catholic, Jew), political preference (Democrat, Republican, Independent), and so forth cannot be conceived of and measured at any other level. It might be possible in some instances to create additional categories (e.g., Moslem, Buddhist, Greek Orthodox, etc.), but these attempts at finer discrimination do not alter the basic categorical nature of the data.

A second reason for obtaining categorical data originates as a pragmatic response to difficulties in measurement. Even though some variables may be conceptualized as continuous, it is impossible or at least extremely difficult for a researcher to measure the underlying continuum. Thus, he or she is forced to classify the observations into broader categories. An excellent example of such a variable is personal income. Many people will simply not disclose their exact income in dollars. They feel that only they and the IRS have a right to know, and many exclude even the IRS. These same people, however, are much more likely to indicate a general range of income, e.g., $10,000–$20,000, $20,000–$30,000, etc. Similarly, many individuals will not provide their exact age (even on anonymous questionnaires), but will check a general category (20–25, 26–30, and so forth). In such instances, a researcher is not overjoyed to obtain data which are less precise than they could be, but has no other choice.

Perhaps the most prevalent situation in which categorical variables are obtained occurs when data result from a controlled experiment. By their very nature, experiments require that the participants be subdivided into categories, frequently referred to as groups, treatments, conditions, and the like. These subdivisions may have natural origins such as gender, or they may involve some experimental "manipulation" on the part of the investigator. In either case, the object is to obtain measurements on the criterion variable—in the jargon of experimentation, the "dependent" variable—and to compare or contrast the magnitude of these scores across the categories—the "independent variable." In the analysis of data from experiments, therefore, confrontations with categorical data are inevitable.

Finally and on a more negative note, categorical variables occasionally arise from inappropriate empirical procedure. Sometimes in the course of research an investigator will modify a continuous variable in order to make it categorical. For example, a researcher might take an inherently continuous variable such as the "number of minutes per week spent reading magazines and newspapers," and dichotomize it into two categories: heavy readers and light readers. The result, of course, is to discard information (more specifically, variance) which may be useful in detecting relationships with other variables. As Cohen and Cohen (1975, p. 299) suggest, "This has immediate negative consequences to the amount of variance such a crippled variable can account for and concomitantly to the power of the statistical test of its contribution."

Fortunately, as knowledge of the flexibility and generality of the linear model becomes more widespread, this inappropriate practice is becoming less prevalent. It reflects, without a doubt, poor research procedure as well as an equally poor grasp of the statistical logic being stressed in these pages. Such procedure should once and for all be abandoned.

The Linear Model with Categorical Explanatory Variables

The realization that a researcher must frequently include categorical variables into his or her analyses alters neither the basic conduct nor goal of such analyses. The purpose of statistics remains to aid the investigator in obtaining statistical inferences about relationships, thus allowing the formulation of valid scientific generalizations to a larger population. What has been altered is that one of the variables, X, describes a person's membership in a discrete category or group, rather than his or her position on a measurement continuum. This difference does entail some modification of how a relationship is substantively or theoretically interpreted, but *not* how it is statistically detected, described, or tested.

To illustrate these similarities and differences, Table 12.1 presents a two variable data set which again employs the Measurement of Vocalic Sensitivity (MOVS) instrument as the criterion measure (see Courtright & Courtright, 1983). As in Chapter 11, each of these 49 scores was obtained from a child between the ages of three and seven. In this example, however, the explanatory variable, Group, represents each child's membership in one of two mutually exclusive categories. Based on screenings and diagnoses by qualified speech clinicians, approximately half of these children ($n = 24$) were classified as "normal" in their language acquisition and development. The remaining children ($n = 25$) had been diagnosed as delayed or disordered in the acquisition and development of language. Accordingly, these children were receiving speech and language therapy at the time the data were gathered.

As always, the question of interest is the covariation between these two variables. Is there a relationship between a child's performance in acquiring language and his or her ability to recognize vocal cues of emotion? Stated statistically, do MOVS and Group share a significantly large proportion of their variance? Because Group is a dichotomy, however, the question addressed by the linear model can be phrased a bit differently: Does the knowledge of the Group into which the children have been classified account for or explain a significant proportion of the variance in their MOVS scores? This difference

TABLE 12.1. Listing of Data for MOVS Instrument and Categorical Variable, Group

Children Classified as Normal			Children Classified as Disordered		
OBS	MOVS	Group	OBS	MOVS	Group
1	4	1	25	3	0
2	9	1	26	8	0
3	8	1	27	6	0
4	4	1	28	3	0
5	7	1	39	5	0
6	5	1	30	6	0
7	8	1	31	7	0
8	7	1	32	5	0
9	8	1	33	7	0
10	4	1	34	6	0
11	8	1	35	4	0
12	8	1	36	6	0
13	7	1	37	4	0
14	5	1	38	7	0
15	7	1	49	5	0
16	8	1	40	5	0
17	9	1	41	3	0
18	7	1	42	7	0
19	6	1	43	6	0
20	5	1	44	7	0
21	7	1	45	7	0
22	9	1	46	6	0
23	6	1	47	5	0
24	7	1	48	8	0
			49	6	0

in phrasing the question reflects the realization that the explanatory variable is categorical. The purpose and approach of the linear model—both visually and mathematically—is exactly the same. In the subsequent discussion of the procedure called the Analysis of Variance, this same question will be modified further to ask: Is there a significant difference between the means of the two groups on the MOVS instrument? As remote and distinct as it may seem, this question is seeking exactly the same information as the question posed by the linear model. Despite its emphasis on the examination of differences, it is really a question of relationship in disguise.

Numerical Coding of Categorical Data

Before any of these questions can be addressed adequately, a more fundamental issue must be resolved. A review of the discussion of levels of measurement will reveal an inherent characteristic of nominal variables. They identify the category or class to which an observation belongs in a purely symbolic fashion. Such categories do not possess mathematical properties such as more than, less than, etc. For example, it is possible to label the two categories for a variable such as Gender with the symbols Men/Women, Males/Females, or simply M/F, and still convey the same information.

But alphabetic labels do not suffice for statistical analyses using the linear model. Statistical procedures are applied to numbers, not letters. Accordingly, one must label the discrete classes of a categorical variable with numerical rather than alphabetic symbols. This substitution creates what is referred to as a *dummy variable*. The designation "dummy" is applied because these numbers are not really numbers at all. They are merely surrogate symbols—symbols which possess numerical properties that make them amenable to statistical analysis. Whether the assignment of such numbers even constitutes "measurement" is a debate into which we will not enter; it does not really matter. Because they are numbers, albeit "dummy" numbers, they can be used in the calculation of various statistics—e.g., $\bar{X}$, SS, Pearson r, etc. As a result, they allow information about Group membership to be included as a legitimate explanatory variable in statistical analysis.

In Table 12.1, the Group labels "normal" and "disordered" have been replaced with the numerical symbols 1 and 0. The selection of these numbers was totally arbitrary. We could just as easily have selected $1/-1$ or $217/12$. Because they are substitute symbols, it makes no difference which numbers are chosen, as along as every member of a category receives the *same* number. Even though any two dummy numbers will produce exactly the same results when entered into the calculations for Pearson r or the linear model, certain pairs of numbers facilitate the calculation and interpretation of these results. The codes 1 and 0 are one of these pairs.

The choice of 1 and 0 as dummy codes is additionally advantageous because they possess a certain intuitive appeal as categorical symbols. Each observation coded as a 1 can be thought of as belonging to the category represented by a particular X variable. Each of these observations, therefore, can be conceptualized as possessing the quality or characteristic which defines that category, e.g., maleness, Protestantness, or in the present example, "normalness" in language development. The observations coded 0, on the other hand, are considered not to possess the defining quality or characteristic. Females do not possess the characteristic of maleness, Catholics do not exhibit Protestantness, and so on. As a consequence, they do not belong to the group or category coded 1. Instead, they receive a 0 to indicate they belong to some other, unidentified category.

Notice that despite this conceptual interpretation of dummy codes, it does not require more than one dummy variable to represent two categories. In Table 12.1, for example, the dummy variable Group identifies only those children who belong to the "normal" classification. The children diagnosed as disordered are not identified. Or are they? When there are only two groups or categories, those observations which do not belong to Group $= 1$ must, by process of elimination, belong to the second group. If a child has not been classified as normal, then he or she must be disordered. There are no other options.

This process of elimination makes it unnecessary to include a second dummy variable to explicitly identify the disordered children. Because these children have already been identified by the fact that they are not categorized as "normal," a second dummy variable would be redundant. Any information it would carry is already possessed by the first. As Chapter 13 will suggest, this principle of "process of elimination" can be extended to the coding of multiple (more than two) categories. If the observations are categorized into k groups (say 5), then it requires only $k - 1$ $(5 - 1 = 4)$ dummy variables to completely represent them. The last or kth group is always indirectly identified by a process of elimination, i.e., by the fact that its observations do not belong to any other group.

Describing the Relationship

We have said several times that the inclusion of a categorical variable does not alter the procedures for calculating the Pearson r or applying the linear model. This constancy can be illustrated on the data presented in Table 12.1. A variety of univariate and bivariate summary statistics for these data are displayed in Table 12.2. Using the formulas presented earlier, you should verify the accuracy of each of these values.

The univariate statistics for MOVS are the same as those calculated in Chapter 11. Perhaps the most important thing to keep in mind is that $SS = 124.53$ is the numerical equivalent of 100% of the variance. It is the quantity which the linear model will attempt to explain and account for. The mean and SS for Group, on the other hand, clearly reflect the 1/0 dummy coding used to quantify that variable. For example, the mean is simply the number of 1's (24) divided by N: $24/49 = .4897$.

This is not a meaningful, interpretable statistic; nor is it intended to be. The sole reason for quantifying this nominal variable is to examine its relationship to MOVS. The

TABLE 12.2. Univariate and Bivariate Statistics for MOVS and Group

	N	Mean	SS
MOVS	49	6.22	124.53
Group	49	.49	12.25

$$SP = 13.61$$
$$COV = .284$$
$$r = .348$$
$$r^2 = .121$$
$$1 - r^2 = .879$$

univariate statistics for Group, therefore, offer no insight by themselves. Their only value is as a vehicle for calculating Pearson r and applying the linear model. Throughout this process, one must never forget that the numbers assigned to categorical variables are "dummy" numbers. They are an arbitrary creation of the investigator, and thus no meaning should be attached to the values they produce.

In contrast, the bivariate statistics displayed in Table 12.2 are highly meaningful. They are indicants of the relationship between these two variables. The sum-of-products (SP) and covariance (COV) were calculated using Eqs. 9.1 and 9.2.

$$COV = \frac{\sum_{i=1}^{N} (X_i - \bar{X})(Y_i - \bar{Y})}{N - 1} \tag{9.1}$$

$$COV = \frac{SP_{XY}}{N - 1} \tag{9.2}$$

As discussed in Chapter 9, the covariance is the primary index of relationship, but is difficult to interpret and almost impossible to compare meaningfully to other relationships. Consequently, a standardized index of covariation, the Pearson r, is required. Eq. 9.6 allows the direct calculation of Pearson r, without performing the laborious task of transforming both MOVS and Group into z-scores.

$$r = \frac{SP_{XY}}{\sqrt{SS_X SS_Y}} \tag{9.6}$$

When the values obtained from the present example are inserted,

$$r = \frac{13.61}{\sqrt{12.25 \times 124.53}}$$

$$= \frac{13.61}{39.06}$$

$$= .348$$

Based on this value of Pearson r, the calculation of $r^2 = .121$ and $1 - r^2 = .879$ follow accordingly.

Therefore, *in this sample* we have discovered a relationship between the children's classification as normal or disordered and their ability to interpret vocal cues of emotion as operationalized by the MOVS instrument. Moreover, the fact that this relationship is direct rather than inverse also requires interpretation. This finding suggests that as "scores" on the classification variable, Group, become larger, there is a tendency for scores on the MOVS instrument to do likewise. In this problem, it was arbitrarily decided to give the normal children a numerically larger code (1) than the disordered group (0). These numbers, however, perform like *real* numbers in calculation. Consequently, this finding suggests that normal children tend to score higher on the MOVS instrument than their disordered counterparts.

Thus far, these findings must be confined solely to the sample at hand. In order to generalize them to the population, a test of statistical inference must be conducted. The null hypothesis is that the correlation coefficient in the population is zero. In Chapter 11, three approaches to testing the acceptability of this null hypothesis were outlined—the

F-ratio, the t-test, and the direct approach. To avoid redundancy, only the t-test will be calculated for these data.

Eq. 11.4 presented the formula for calculating the t-statistic.

$$t = \frac{r}{\sqrt{1 - r^2/N - 2}} \qquad (11.4)$$

where, $N - 2$ are the degrees-of-freedom needed to refer to the appropriate distribution in Appendix B. Recall that the t-test is both calculationally and conceptually treated as the square root of the F-ratio. Its primary advantage is that it allows the test statistic to be directional, i.e., to assume either a positive or negative value.

In the current problem,

$$t = \frac{.348}{\sqrt{1 - .121/47}}$$

$$= \frac{.348}{\sqrt{.0187}}$$

$$= \frac{.348}{.1367} = 2.5457,$$

or with rounding

$$= 2.55$$

In Appendix B, the critical value at $p < .05$ for a t-test with 47 degrees-of-freedom is approximately 2.01. The obtained test statistic of $t = 2.55$ surpasses this critical value. Thus, it can be concluded that in the population this relationship is not zero, assuming one is willing to take the risk of being wrong 5 percent of the time. Further examination of Appendix B, however, suggests that the risk of committing a Type I error (i.e., rejecting a true null hypothesis) is actually much lower. The obtained value of the test statistic surpasses the critical value for $p < .02$ (2.40), and comes quite close to the critical value for $p < .01$ (2.68). Determined by computer, the precise probability is $p < .0141$.

As a result of this test, we can conclude with relatively high confidence that MOVS and Group (as currently dummy-coded) are directly related in the population. Recall the manner in which Group was dummy-coded: normal = 1, disordered = 0. This suggests a significant tendency for normal children to score higher on the MOVS instrument. They are more accurate in interpreting vocal cues of emotion. It must be acknowledged, of course, that an $r^2 = .121$ leaves considerable explanation still to be accomplished. Nevertheless, at least one salient component of that explanation has been discovered.

Applying the Linear Model

The goal of the linear model, $\hat{Y} = a + BX$, is to discover the constants a and B which (1) minimize the difference between the obtained and predicted values of the criterion variable, while simultaneously (2) maximizing their correlation. The best estimate of these constants will come from the sample data. First, we must estimate the regression coefficient, B. Eq. 11.12 defined this constant as:

$$B = \frac{SP_{XY}}{SS_X} \tag{11.12}$$

The insertion of the appropriate values from Table 12.2 reveals,

$$B = \frac{13.61}{12.25} = 1.11$$

Similarly, Eq. 11.13 provides the formula for determining the intercept term, a.

$$a = \bar{Y} - B\bar{X} \tag{11.13}$$

In the present example,

$$
\begin{aligned}
a &= 6.22 - (1.11).49 \\
&= 6.22 - .54 \\
&= 5.68
\end{aligned}
$$

Thus, the entire linear model for the relationship between MOVS and Group is

$$\hat{Y}_i = 5.68 + (1.11)X_i$$

Some important features of the model are worth noting. Although we have not yet done so, we might calculate separately the means for the two groups on the MOVS instrument. These calculations will show that the group of normal children produced $\bar{Y}_n = 6.79$, while the disordered children exhibit a mean of $\bar{Y}_d = 5.68$. These results lead directly to two observations.

First, the intercept term, a, is the same as the mean of the "disordered group: 0." This equivalence, in fact, will hold for all linear models with 1 and 0 dummy coding.

$$a = \bar{Y}_0 \tag{12.1}$$

Second, the regression coefficient, B, is equal to the *difference* between these means:

$$
\begin{aligned}
B &= \bar{Y}_1 - \bar{Y}_0 \tag{12.2} \\
&= 6.79 - 5.68 \\
&= 1.11
\end{aligned}
$$

Thus, despite the fact that these constants were calculated from Eqs. 11.12 and 11.13 for the linear model, they automatically reflect the dichotomous nature of the dummy-coded, explanatory variable. While any pair of numbers will produce the correct Pearson r and r^2, only the codes 1 and 0 will produce the equalities expressed in Eqs. 12.1 and 12.2. This is one of the advantages inherent in using this set of dummy codes.

A second advantage becomes apparent when the X_i are inserted into the linear model. The variable Group possesses only two values. Moreover, these values have been arbitrarily designated as 1 and 0. Thus, only two predicted values will be produced. When $X_i = 1$ for the normal group,

$$\hat{Y}_i = 6.79 = 5.68 + 1.11\,(1)$$

For the disordered group coded $X_i = 0$,

$$\hat{Y}_i = 5.68 = 5.68 + 1.11\,(0)$$

In short, the two predicted values produced by the linear model turn out to be the means of the two groups calculated separately. Table 12.3 exhibits this result, displaying the obtained, predicted, and residual values for the current problem. In retrospect, this outcome should not be especially surprising. Within a given group, the value of the explanatory variable was the same for each member of the group. The model provided no additional information with which to discriminate among observations within the same group. Between groups, of course, that discrimination was possible because distinct dummy codes, 1 and 0, were assigned.

Equally understandable is the finding that the predicted value for each child is the mean of his or her group. The only information possessed about that child was the group to which he or she belonged. Consequently, the mean of that group would be the most logical, expected value for the $\hat{Y}_i$'s to assume. The mean truly becomes the "central

TABLE 12.3. Listing of Original Values, Predicted Values, and Errors of Prediction for MOVS

| | Group Classified as Normal | | | | Group Classified as Disordered | | |
OBS	MOVS	$\hat{Y}$	Error	OBS	MOVS	$\hat{Y}$	Error
1	4	6.79167	−2.7917	25	3	5.68000	−2.6800
2	9	6.79167	2.2083	26	8	5.68000	2.3200
3	8	6.79167	1.2083	27	6	5.68000	0.3200
4	4	6.79167	−2.7917	28	3	5.68000	−2.6800
5	7	6.79167	0.2083	29	5	5.68000	−0.6800
6	5	6.79167	−1.7917	30	6	5.68000	0.3200
7	8	6.79167	1.2083	31	7	5.68000	1.3200
8	7	6.79167	0.2083	32	5	5.68000	−0.6800
9	8	6.79167	1.2083	33	7	5.68000	1.3200
10	4	6.79167	−2.7917	34	6	5.68000	0.3200
11	8	6.79167	1.2083	35	4	5.68000	−1.6800
12	8	6.79167	1.2083	36	6	5.68000	0.3200
13	7	6.79167	0.2083	37	4	5.68000	−1.6800
14	5	6.79167	−1.7917	38	7	5.68000	1.3200
15	7	6.79167	0.2083	39	5	5.68000	−0.6800
16	8	6.79167	1.2083	40	5	5.68000	−0.6800
17	9	6.79167	2.2083	41	3	5.68000	−2.6800
18	7	6.79167	0.2083	42	7	5.68000	1.3200
19	6	6.79167	−0.7917	43	6	5.68000	0.3200
20	5	6.79167	−1.7917	44	7	5.68000	1.3200
21	7	6.79167	0.2083	45	7	5.68000	1.3200
22	9	6.79167	2.2083	46	6	5.68000	0.3200
23	6	6.79167	−0.7917	47	5	5.68000	−0.6800
24	7	6.79167	0.2083	48	8	5.68000	2.3200
				49	6	5.68000	0.3200

tendency" for the members of a particular group. Given no other information, it is the model's "best guess."

Testing the Linear Model

The test of this linear model follows exactly the procedures outlined in Chapter 11. It is necessary to construct an F-ratio, whose purpose as a test statistic is to compare the explained with the unexplained variation. For reasons to be discussed later, the various sums-of-squares will be used to construct the F-ratio for this problem, rather than their r^2 equivalents.

In Table 12.2, the quantity the model is attempting to explain is SS_{MOVS}, which was shown to be 124.53. The first step is to decompose this total sum-of-squares into its component parts, i.e., SS_{Model} or the explained variance, and SS_{Error}. Eqs. 11.8 and 11.9 accomplish this task.

$$
\begin{aligned}
SS_{Model} &= r^2 \, (SS_{MOVS}) & (11.8)\\
&= .121 \,(124.53)\\
&= 15.07\\
SS_{Error} &= 1 - r^2 \,(SS_{MOVS}) & (11.9)\\
&= .879 \,(124.53)\\
&= 109.46
\end{aligned}
$$

Because these are independent pieces of the variance,

$$SS_{MOVS} = SS_{Model} + SS_{Error}$$

and

$$124.53 = 15.07 + 109.46$$

As indicated by Eq. 11.15, the next step is to insert these two SS's into the formula for the F-ratio.

$$F = \frac{SS_{Model}/p}{SS_{Error}/N - p - 1} \tag{11.15}$$

which can be rewritten in terms of the respective mean squares (MS).

$$F = \frac{MS_{Model}}{MS_{Error}} \tag{11.16}$$

Thus for the present problem,

$$F = \frac{15.07/1}{109.46/47}$$

$$= \frac{15.07}{2.33}$$

$$= 6.47$$

with 1 and 47 df.

To show that this finding is equivalent to the earlier t-test of the Pearson r ($t = 2.55$), recall that

$$t = \sqrt{F},$$

thus

$$t = \sqrt{6.47}$$
$$= 2.54$$

which is exactly the same except for rounding error.

The next step in the testing process would be to compare the obtained F-ratio to the appropriate critical value in Appendix C. The outcome of this comparison, however, would be exactly the same as the t-test conducted earlier: the probability of rejecting the null hypothesis when it is actually true (i.e., a Type I error) is $p < .0141$. Consequently, we can conclude that this model is a significantly accurate representation of the relationship in the population.

To summarize, this discussion has focused on relationships in which one of the two variables is categorical rather than continuous. Such variables arise in research for a variety of reasons, and an investigator must be prepared to include them in his or her statistical procedures. Such inclusion is not problematic. Once the categorical labels have been replaced with dummy, numerical codes, the Pearson r can be calculated as the statistical index of relationship. Similarly, no alterations in the calculations are required in order to apply the linear model.

The conclusion to be drawn from this discussion is most important. It forms the bedrock for generalizing the bivariate model to more complex, multivariate contexts. Stated simply, the construction and interpretation of the linear model is unaffected by the type of information carried by X, the explanatory variable. The X variable may be categorical or continuous. More importantly, a model with multiple X variables may simultaneously contain both types of variables. No statistical restrictions apply to what type of information may be deemed "explanatory" and thus included in a model.

We will reemphasize this point in a subsequent chapter. In the meantime, however, we will focus on the most traditional and perhaps most frequently used statistical procedure: the Analysis of Variance. This procedure can be shown to be equivalent in all respects to the linear model which we have just presented.

The Analysis of Variance

The exact origins of the Analysis of Variance (ANOVA) are difficult to specify. Around the turn of this century, a number of influential mathematicians and statisticians in Great Britain were concerned with basic statistical issues. Many of these scholars were interested in substantive problems in genetics, applying correlation and linear model procedures to large samples of observations. In today's terminology, these would be called surveys or field studies. At the same time, however, several scholars addressed the issue of small-sample statistics, i.e., statistics to be used to analyze controlled experiments with a limited number of observations. The credit for first synthesizing these ideas into the ANOVA is awarded to Sir Ronald A. Fisher (1925), whose classic book, *Statistical Methods For Research Workers,* was published in 12 editions and seven languages. In fact, one of the primary tests of statistical inference was named the F-ratio in honor of Fisher's accomplishments.

This brief historical account paves the way for a more contemporary description of the use and influence of ANOVA. In all of its various forms, ANOVA has been the most widely used statistical procedure in contemporary social science, including communication research. To describe it as commonplace, widespread, or even ubiquitous is almost understatement. For many years, it was *the* statistical procedure used by nearly all researchers in the social sciences. There are two reasons for this popularity, both of which require a bit more history.

The ANOVA is especially suited for the statistical analysis of controlled experiments. In such experiments, a sample of subjects is subdivided into groups, each of which receives a different "treatment" or combination of treatments. Experiments have been the traditional mode of empirical inquiry in most branches of science, and communication research is no exception. Scholarly journals are replete with examples of controlled experiments. Almost all of these studies have employed ANOVA as the primary method for analyzing data. It is, therefore, a highly familiar commodity among researchers.

Second and perhaps more important, the ANOVA was designed to be computed or calculated by hand. Even in its most complex forms, the statistics necessary for ANOVA require little more than a pencil, paper, and some basic arithmetic to calculate. Needless to say, this attribute contributed greatly to the popularity of ANOVA, especially before the widespread availability of computers. More recently, the advent of computerized statistical analysis has dramatically reduced researchers' reliance on hand calculations. As might be expected, the sole reliance on experimentation and ANOVA has declined accordingly. Investigators, it seems, have "discovered" a host of additional statistical procedures and techniques. Such procedures were available in theory all the time, but not amenable to hand calculation.

Despite this decline, the Analysis of Variance is still a valid and viable approach to analyzing data, and experiments still constitute a scientifically accepted means for investigating human communicative behavior. The logic and design of experiments was presented in Chapter 2. The logic and calculations for ANOVA are to follow.

The Logic and Calculation of ANOVA

The ANOVA is a statistical procedure applied to a sample of observations which a researcher has divided into mutually exclusive and exhaustive groups or categories. These categories may represent a naturally occurring classification over which the experimenter has no control, e.g., gender, race, marital status, and so forth. Alternatively, the subjects in a sample may be randomly subdivided into groups, with no regard to preexisting attributes or characteristics. It is assumed that such individual differences are unrelated to the phenomenon under investigation. Or if they are related, randomization will prohibit any systematic effect or trend from emerging.

Instead, in this instance, differences between the groups of subjects are created or "manipulated" by the actions of the researcher. Each group is assumed to be the same at the outset (except for random differences), but they are exposed to a different combination of situational or communicative conditions which are theoretically salient. When the exposure to these conditions is complete, data from each subject in every group are gathered using the same instrument or procedure. These data are then submitted to ANOVA.

Regardless of whether the groups to which subjects are assigned result from natural classification or experimental manipulation, the logic of ANOVA is the same.

This reasoning is closely allied with the logic of experimental design. It begins with the scores which have been obtained from the subjects. Like all data, these scores are expected to exhibit variance. Under these circumstances, however, the researcher expects significant parts of this variance to be due to the conditions or classification he or she has created. In other words, much of this variance is assumed to be due to differences *between* the groups. This assumption is based on the design of the experiment. By the procedures used to classify or manipulate the groups of subjects, the researcher has attempted to instill differences between these groups which should cause their criterion scores to vary. But vary how? In what way?

If the researcher's procedures are successful, the means of the groups on the criterion or "dependent" measure should be substantially different. If they are, the mean for each group will vary around the overall or grand mean for all of the groups considered together. The grand mean may be thought of as the "mean of the group means," and is symbolized as $\bar{\bar{Y}}$ (pronounced Y double-bar). The larger the differences between the means of the groups, then (1) the more these means will vary around the grand mean, and hence (2) the larger will be the sum-of-squares between the groups (SS_{BG}). Because this source of variance reflects intentional differences in classification and/or experimental manipulation, the researcher expects the differences between the group means and thus the between-group variance to be large.

In contrast, the researcher expects subjects *within* the same group to exhibit relatively little variance among themselves. Subjects within the same group possess the same natural attributes or have been exposed to the same experimental conditions. As a result, their scores should be very similar, although certainly not the same. Scores from subjects within the same group *will* vary. Nevertheless, if the theory which guided the experiment is correct and the researcher made no procedural errors, this within-group variance should be due solely to random, individual differences among the subjects. No factor should systematically contribute to this variance. Accordingly, the within-group variance should be relatively small when compared to the variance attributable to between-group differences. It should be a minimal percentage of the overall variation.

To synthesize, these assumptions suggest that the total variation for the entire sample of observations—SS_{Total} or SS_Y—can be attributed to two distinct sources. Conceptually, these can be thought of as (1) variance due to some theoretically salient difference between distinct groups of subjects, and (2) variance due to differences among individual subjects within the same group. Rephrased statistically, the total variance, SS_{Total}, can be decomposed into two independent pieces: sum-of-squares between groups and sum-of-squares within groups. Symbolically,

$$SS_{\text{Total}} = SS_{BG} + SS_{WG} \qquad (12.3)$$

If the theoretic assumptions and empirical procedures of the investigator are correct, these two components of the overall variance should be much different in their relative magnitude. Because differences between groups of subjects have been intentionally created, SS_{BG} is expected to be relatively large. This component of the variance should reflect differences on all of the relevant variables which affect the criterion score. SS_{WG}, on the other hand, should reflect only random and theoretically trivial differences among individual subjects. This independent piece of the variance, therefore, should be relatively small.

As we have said several times, these expectations are based on the logic and design of the experimental investigation. They represent what "should" happen if the researcher's assumptions are accurate. This accuracy can never be simply taken for granted. It is an inherently empirical question. The purpose of ANOVA, therefore, is to statistically examine the feasibility of these assumptions, to perform a statistical test to determine whether the between-groups variance is indeed "substantially" larger than the variance within the groups.

Recall that the variation between groups is the result of differences between the means of these groups. Consequently, the empirical question of interest addressed by ANOVA can be phrased as: Is there a significant difference between the means of the groups? This question is purposely phrased to be global and something less than precise. It simply asks: Is there any difference, anywhere, among any of the means? It is the most general question that ANOVA can address. On occasion, the substantive theory under investigation will require more precision in phrasing this question. A given theory may suggest which group means are expected to differ, and/or what direction (more than or less than) these differences should be expected to exhibit. While such precision in specifying the research question will certainly alter what the investigator looks for, it does not change how he or she goes about looking.

As with all statistical procedures, legitimate interpretation and generalization can take place only after a test of statistical inference has been conducted. For ANOVA, the test statistic to be used will be the now familiar F-ratio. It will compare the between-groups variance (the variance systematically created by the researcher) to the within-groups variance (the supposedly random variance among subjects in the same group). Stated differently, it will compare the variance which the investigator can explain (primarily, because he or she intentionally created it) to the variance which the investigator cannot explain. If the obtained F-ratio is sufficiently large to surpass the appropriate critical value, the theoretic assumptions and experimental procedures of the investigator are assumed to be valid. The task of generalizing these findings to the larger population can then take place.

Before proceeding to an example, we note that in the preceding discussion of a test statistic, differences among means were not discussed or even mentioned. Earlier, however, we suggested that the primary question addressed by ANOVA was: Do the means differ? And so it is! The differences among the means of the groups are exactly what produces between-groups variation—the larger the differences, the larger the SS_{BG}. Do not be confused, therefore, by the terminology of the test statistic and the seemingly different terminology of the substantive question. All test statistics are based on a ratio of explained to unexplained variance. In ANOVA, the explained variance (SS_{BG}) results from the very differences between the groups which the substantive question seeks to address.

Applying the ANOVA: An Example

The discussion thus far has been a fairly abstract account of ANOVA and its applications. Perhaps a substantive example will serve to reinforce this logic, as well as to introduce the calculational formulas required by this procedure. Table 12.4 contains totally hypothetical data from an experimental study of effective brainstorming in small groups. Thirty-six four-person groups were randomly assigned to either (1) one of two experimental conditions or (2) a control condition. The two experimental conditions consisted of different methods of instructing groups in how to organize and conduct their brainstorming sessions. Groups in the control condition received no instructions and were allowed to brainstorm as they saw fit.

The criterion or dependent measure was the number of ideas generated by each group during a single, one-hour brainstorming session. In this study, the group rather

TABLE 12.4. Data from Experimental Study of Brainstorming in Small Groups Score = Number of Ideas Generated by Each Group

	Method = 1	Method = 2	Control
	55	35	28
	23	41	4
	39	36	32
	26	40	50
	54	39	23
	21	37	24
	39	49	24
	25	29	42
	23	33	8
	47	49	26
	35	39	21
	43	53	31
Group Total	430	480	313
N Per Group	12	12	12
$\bar{Y}$	35.83	40.00	26.08
SS For Group	1657.667	554.000	1746.917

Total N = 36
Total Score = 1223
Grand Mean = 33.972
SS_{Total} = 5182.972

than its individual members was used as the observational unit in order to avoid the problem of nonindependent observations discussed in Chapter 10. As suggested at that time, the disadvantage of this approach is that many more individual subjects are required: 144 subjects were needed to compose the 36 groups in this study. Any other approach, however, would almost certainly invalidate the assumption of independence of the data.

The data in Table 12.4 are arrayed so that the three conditions can be easily compared. Several features of these data are worth noting before a formal statistical test is discussed and calculated. First, the means of the three experimental conditions do differ. Groups in the control condition generated fewer ideas ($\bar{Y}_C$ = 26.08) than those in either of the two conditions where instructions were provided ($\bar{Y}_1$ = 35.83; $\bar{Y}_2$ = 40.00). In addition, groups which received the instructions in Method = 1 produced fewer ideas than their counterparts in Method = 2. One can conclude that the different approaches to brainstorming did create differences in the performances of these groups and thus between-groups variance. Whether these differences are significant and hence whether they can be generalized to the population remains to be seen.

A second noteworthy aspect of these data is that the scores within each of the three conditions do indeed vary. This within-groups variance is represented by the sum-of-squares for each condition. Shortly, we will present the method of calculating these quantities. For now, note that the scores within each group are far from being equal. They do vary—substantially. Can this variance be attributable to purely random differences among the groups, or were systematic, yet unknown and uncontrolled factors operating to produce this variance? This answer must also await the formal application of a statistical test of inference.

Before this test, the *F*-ratio, can be constructed, we will discuss its component parts and how they are calculated. Eq. 12.3 stated,

$$SS_{\text{Total}} = SS_{BG} + SS_{WG} \qquad (12.3)$$

Each of these three sums-of-squares requires a different computational formula to calculate its value, and thus each must be discussed separately.

Total Sum-of-Squares

The logic which underlies the concept of the "spread" of data was presented in Chapter 8. At that time, the basic formula for calculating sums-of-squares was presented by Eq. 8.2 as,

$$SS_Y = \sum_{i=1}^{N}(Y_i - \bar{Y})^2 \qquad (8.2)$$

This formula simply operationalized the concept of spread as "the sum of squared deviations from the mean." It is the most basic formula for calculating sum-of-squares, and all others can be viewed as offshoots or special cases of it.

Eq. 12.4 defines SS_{Total} as,

$$SS_{\text{Total}} = \sum_{j=1}^{k}\sum_{i=1}^{n_j}(Y_{ij} - \bar{\bar{Y}})^2 \qquad (12.4)$$

Despite its totally different appearance, Eq. 12.4 is essentially the same as Eq. 8.2. The additional symbols are required in an ANOVA problem because the *N* observations for the entire sample have been divided into *k* groups, each of which contains n_j observations. Thus, it is not only necessary to sum the squared deviation scores, but also to sum them across *k* separate groups. To ensure clarity, these new symbols will be defined and discussed.

First, the symbol Y_{ij} identifies the *i*th score or observation just as before. In this case, however, each score has been placed into one of the *k* groups. Hence, a double subscript is required to identify both the score *(i)* and the group *(j)*. The symbol $\bar{\bar{Y}}$ has been referred to previously as the mean of the total sample of scores: $\bar{\bar{Y}} = \sum_{i=1}^{N} Y_{ij}/N$. Finally, the two summation signs indicate that one must sum all of the *n* squared deviations across all *k* of the groups. Because,

$$N = \sum_{j=1}^{k} n_j$$
$$= n_1 + n_2 + \cdots + n_j + \cdots + n_k$$

this is the same as requiring the squared deviation scores to be summed across the entire sample.

The similarity between Eqs. 8.2 and 12.4 becomes even more apparent if, for the moment, one simply ignores the fact that the sample has been divided into groups; i.e., momentarily drop all references to j. As a consequence, one of the summation signs can be deleted, and Y_{ij} can be expressed simply as Y_i. Thus, $\bar{\bar{Y}}$ becomes defined as

$$\bar{\bar{Y}} = \frac{\sum_{i=1}^{N} Y_i}{N}$$

$$= \bar{Y}$$

In other words, when the necessity for symbolizing the groups is removed, Eq. 12.4 reverts to Eq. 8.2. As a result of this similarity, it is possible to reexpress Eq. 12.4 in a form more suitable to the actual calculation of SS_{Total}.

$$SS_{Total} = \sum_{j=1}^{k} \sum_{i=1}^{n_j} Y_{ij}^2 - \frac{\left(\sum_{j=1}^{k} \sum_{i=1}^{n_j} Y_{ij}\right)^2}{N} \tag{12.4a}$$

It is helpful to discuss the parts of this formula separately. Eq. 12.4a first directs one to $\sum_{j=1}^{k} \sum_{i=1}^{n_j} Y_{ij}^2$; in words, to square every score in every group, and then add all of those squared scores together. Again, except for the use of double subscripts and summation signs, the actual procedure is the same as that first presented in Eq. 8.3. The second half of Eq. 12.4 directs one to (1) add all of the socres together, (2) square that total, and (3) divide that squared total by N. Finally, this latter quantity is subtracted from the former.

These calculations can be illustrated using the data from Table 12.4

$$\sum_{j=1}^{k} \sum_{i=1}^{n_j} Y_{ij} = (55^2 + 23^2 + 39^2 + \cdots + 26^2 + 21^2 + 31^2)$$

$$= 46,731$$

$$\frac{\left(\sum_{j=1}^{k} \sum_{i=1}^{n_j} Y_{ij}\right)^2}{N} = \frac{(1223)^2}{36}$$

$$= \frac{1,495,729}{36}$$

$$= 41,548.03$$

$$SS_{Total} = 46,731 - 41,548.03$$

$$= 5182.97$$

This quantity, 5182.97, represents the sum-of squares for the entire sample. It is the equivalent of 100% of the variance so frequently mentioned in previous sections. It is the task of ANOVA to decompose this overall variation into its systematic (SS_{BG}) and random (SS_{WG}) components.

Between-Groups Sum-of-Squares

The variation between the means of the experimental conditions results from the systematic classification or manipulation of the investigator. As a consequence of having been intentionally created, it is also explainable—the investigator knows its source or origin. This between-group variation reflects the fact that the group means ($\bar{Y}_j$) deviate from the grand mean ($\bar{\bar{Y}}$). This deviation is transformed into sum-of-squares by Eq. 12.5.

$$SS_{BG} = \sum_{j=1}^{k} n_j (\bar{Y}_j - \bar{\bar{Y}})^2 \tag{12.5}$$

This formula directs the researcher to (1) subtract each of k means from the grand mean, (2) square those deviations, (3) multiply the obtained values by n_j, and (4) sum the values obtained from steps (1)–(3). Notice that Eq. 12.5 is very similar in form to Eq. 8.2. The primary difference is that SS_{BG} represents the variation among a set of k conditions, treatments, or classifications rather than among individual observations.

From the data in Table 12.4, the means for the three conditions can be calculated as $\bar{Y}_1 = 35.83$; $\bar{Y}_2 = 40.00$; and $\bar{Y}_C = 26.08$. The grand mean remains the same, $\bar{\bar{Y}} = 33.97$. When these values are inserted into Eq. 12.5,

$$SS_{BG} = \sum_{j=1}^{k} n_j (\bar{Y}_j - \bar{\bar{Y}})^2$$
$$= 12(35.83 - 33.97)^2 + 12(40 - 33.97)^2 + 12(26.08 - 33.97)^2$$
$$= 41.52 + 436.33 + 747.03$$
$$= 1224.88$$

As these calculations indicate, Eq. 12.5 is a relatively simple and straightforward formula to apply. Nevertheless, an alternative approach to calculating SS_{BG} is presented by the formula

$$SS_{BG} = \sum_{j=1}^{k} \frac{\left(\sum_{i=1}^{n_j} Y_{ij}^2 \right)}{n_j} - \frac{\left(\sum_{j=1}^{k} \sum_{i=1}^{n_j} Y_{ij} \right)^2}{N} \tag{12.5a}$$

Eq. 12.5a directs one to find the sum of the scores within each group separately, square each total, and divide each squared total by the number of scores in that group, n_j. Once this procedure has been completed for each of the k groups, the quantities are added together. The latter part of Eq. 12.5a again tells one to find the total of all N scores, square it, and divide by N. Notice that this will be the same quantity obtained from Eq. 12.4a.

When applied to the data in Table 12.4,

$$\sum_{j=1}^{k} \frac{\left(\sum_{i=1}^{n_j} Y_{ij}^2\right)}{n_j} = \left(\frac{430^2}{12}\right) + \left(\frac{480^2}{12}\right) + \left(\frac{313^2}{12}\right)$$

$$= \frac{184,900}{12} + \frac{230,400}{12} + \frac{97,969}{12}$$

$$= 15,408.333 + 19,200 + 8164.08$$

$$= 42,772.42$$

As before, $\left(\sum_{j=1}^{k} \sum_{i=1}^{n_j} Y_{ij}\right)/N = 41548.03$, and thus,

$$SS_{BG} = 42772.42 - 41548.03$$
$$= 1224.39$$

which, except for rounding error, is the same as the value calculated from Eq. 12.5.

This value, 1224.88, represents the systematic variation which the investigator can explain. When converted to a percentage, it can be seen that

$$r^2 = \frac{SS_{BG}}{SS_{\text{Total}}}$$

$$= \frac{1224.88}{5182.97}$$

$$= .2363$$

This also suggests that $1 - r^2 = .7637$. Given these percentages, Eq. 11.8 could be used to calculate the remaining component, SS_{WG}.

$$SS_{WG} = SS_{\text{Error}} = (1 - r^2)(SS_{\text{Total}}) \qquad (11.8)$$
$$= .7637(5182.97)$$
$$= 3958.09$$

Similarly, as suggested by Eq. 12.3,

$$SS_{\text{Total}} = SS_{BG} + SS_{WG} \qquad (12.3)$$

Thus,

$$SS_{WG} = SS_{\text{Total}} - SS_{BG}$$

In short, the remaining component could be obtained by simple subtraction.

$$SS_{WG} = 5182.97 - 1224.88$$
$$= 3958.09$$

Either of these methods calculates SS_{WG} by "default." They are based on the assumption that all of the previous calculations are totally correct—an assumption which should never be taken for granted. SS_{WG} should always be calculated directly using the formula in the following section. Because the subtraction and $1 - r^2$ approaches are incapable of detecting arithmetic error, they should only be employed as a check, after all of the sums-of-squares have been directly calculated.

Within-Groups Sum-of-Squares

As its name suggests, the SS_{WG} is a numerical indication of the overall variation within the k groups. The logic of the experimental design implies that this quantity should be due solely to random differences among individual subjects. SS_{WG}, therefore, is conceptually and calculationally straightforward. First, it is necessary to obtain a separate numerical index of the spread or variation for each experimental condition. Second, these separate estimates are summed to produce the overall within-groups variation. Eq. 12.6 symbolizes this logic.

$$SS_{WG} = \sum_{j=1}^{k} \left[\sum_{i=1}^{n_j} (Y_{ij} - \bar{Y}_j)^2 \right] \tag{12.6}$$

The brackets around part of Eq. 12.6 are technically not necessary. They do, however, heuristically depict the logic which is symbolically represented by the formula. The brackets indicate that all of the enclosed calculations be performed first; specifically, that a separate sum-of-squares be calculated for each condition or classification. Once this is completed, the second summation sign directs that those separate sums-of-squares be added to obtain the total SS_{WG}.

Once again it is possible to calculate SS_{WG} in a more efficient manner by employing an alternative formula.

$$SS_{WG} = \sum_{j=1}^{k} \left[\sum_{i=1}^{n_j} Y_{ij}^2 - \frac{\left(\sum_{i=1}^{n_j} Y_{ij} \right)^2}{n_j} \right] \tag{12.6a}$$

The portion of Eq. 12.6a which is within the brackets again directs us to calculate the SS for each group *separately*. The method of calculation, despite the different symbols, is simply a modification of that originally presented in Eq. 8.3. Each group is treated as a separate set of n_j scores. The summation sign outside of the brackets indicates that these separate SS's should be added together. In the current problem,

$$
\begin{aligned}
SS_{WG_1} &= (55^2 + 23^2 + \ldots + 35^2 + 43^2) - (430^2/12) \\
&= 17066 - 15408.333 \\
&= 1657.667 \\
SS_{WG_2} &= (35^2 + 41^2 + \ldots + 39^2 + 53^2) - (480^2/12) \\
&= 19754 - 19200 \\
&= 554 \\
SS_{WG_c} &= (28^2 + 4^2 + \ldots + 21^2 + 31^2) - (313^2/12) \\
&= 9911 - 8164.0833 \\
&= 1746.917
\end{aligned}
$$

The second summation sign can then be applied to obtain:

$$SS_{WG} = SS_{WG_1} + SS_{WG_2} + \ldots + SS_{WG_k}$$
$$= 1657.67 + 554 + 1746.92$$
$$= 3958.59$$

Either of the two "default" methods for obtaining SS_{WG} can now be applied as a check on these calculations. By the subtraction method it was found that $SS_{WG} = 3958.09$. It seems reasonable to conclude, therefore, that the value obtained by direct calculation is within rounding error of being exactly the same.

The three formulas for calculating the various sums-of-squares are summarized in Table 12.5. This table provides a convenient reference to be used when actually calculating an ANOVA problem. In the current example it was determined that $SS_{BG} = 1224.88$ and $SS_{WG} = 3958.09$. Now that the SS_{Total} has been divided into its component parts, a test of statistical inference can be performed to evaluate whether the difference due to the experimental conditions in the sample can be generalized to the population.

Tests of Significance in ANOVA

The null hypothesis for statistical tests in ANOVA is that the means of the experimental conditions or classification groups do not differ beyond chance expectation. In other words, the null hypothesis assumes that the between-groups variation is due to random chance and not to the intentional classification or manipulation of the researcher. If this is so, the variance which can be explained will be no larger than the

TABLE 12.5. Summary of ANOVA Formulas

	Conceptual Formulas	
Source of Variation	SS	df
Between-Groups	$\sum_{j=1}^{k} n_j(\bar{Y}_j - \bar{\bar{Y}})^2$	$k - 1$
Within-Groups	$\sum_{j=1}^{k} \sum_{i=1}^{n_j} (Y_{ij} - \bar{Y}_j)^2$	$N - k$
Total	$\sum_{j=1}^{k} \sum_{i=1}^{n_j} (Y_{ij} - \bar{\bar{Y}})^2$	$N - 1$

	Computing Formulas	
Source of Variation	SS	df
Between-Groups	$\sum_{j=1}^{k} \left(\sum_{i=1}^{n_j} Y_{ij}^2 / n_j \right) - \left(\sum_{j=1}^{k} \sum_{i=1}^{n_j} Y_{ij} \right)^2 / N$	$k - 1$
Within-Groups	$\sum_{j=1}^{k} \left[\sum_{i=1}^{n_j} Y_{ij}^2 - \left(\sum_{i=1}^{n_j} Y_{ij} \right)^2 / n_j \right]$	$N - k$
Total	$\sum_{j=1}^{k} \sum_{i=1}^{n_j} Y_{ij}^2 - \left(\sum_{j=1}^{k} \sum_{i=1}^{n_j} Y_{ij} \right)^2 / N$	$N - 1$

variance which cannot, resulting in a small test statistic. As always, the larger the test statistic, the more evidence the researcher has for rejecting the null hypothesis.

The test statistic used by ANOVA is the F-ratio. Previous discussion has described the F-ratio as

$$F = \frac{\sigma^2_{\text{Explained}}}{\sigma^2_{\text{Unexplained}}} \qquad (11.14)$$

When working with a sample of data, these two variances are estimated from the data. For ANOVA,

$$F = \frac{SS_{BG}/k - 1}{SS_{WG}/N - k} \qquad (12.7)$$

where: $k - 1$ and $N - k$ are the degrees-of-freedom, and k is the number of experimental conditions or classification groups created by the researcher. In the current problem, $k = 3$; therefore, $k - 1 = 2$. Similarly, this example had a sample size of $N = 36$; therefore, $N - k = 36 - 3 = 33$.

When the SS are divided by their respective df, the result is a mean square. This statistic is *the sample's best estimate of the variance in the population*. Thus,

$$F = \frac{MS_{BG}}{MS_{WG}} \qquad (12.8)$$

When the several values from the current problem are inserted,

$$F = \frac{1224.88/2}{3958.09/33}$$

$$= \frac{612.44}{119.94}$$

$$= 5.10$$

with 2 and 33 df.

When we consult the table of critical values in Appendix C, we find that the probability of the null hypothesis being true is somewhere between $p < .025$ and $p < .01$. (By computer, the exact value is $p < .0117$.) The null hypothesis can therefore be rejected with a relatively high degree of confidence that a Type I error will not be committed. It is reasonable to conclude that in the population there are real differences among these three approaches to organizing and conducting brainstorming sessions in small groups.

Some Post Hoc Considerations

The various statistics calculated thus far are contained in Table 12.6. This "Summary Table" is the traditional format for compactly and efficiently presenting ANOVA results. It combines all of the information obtained from the ANOVA into an easily readable, visual summary. The conclusion it suggests, of course, is the same as above. These three approaches to brainstorming produced significant differences in the number of ideas generated by the groups.

TABLE 12.6. ANOVA Summary Table

Source	df	Sum-of-Squares	Mean Square	F Value
Exp Conditions (Between-Groups)	2	1224.88	612.44	5.10 $p < 0.011$
Error (Within-Groups)	33	3958.09	119.94	
Total	35	5182.97		

A moment's reflection, however, will reveal this conclusion to be incomplete. It does not provide sufficient information to address adequately the theoretic issues at hand. Although the ANOVA has indicated that some differences exist somewhere among these three means, it has not specified where the difference or differences may be. Are the two experimental conditions significantly different from the control condition? Do the two experimental conditions significantly differ from each other? Answers to these questions are central to a complete understanding of these data and the inferences which can be drawn from them. In their absence, theory construction cannot proceed.

Accordingly, some additional, *post hoc tests* of statistical inference must be conducted. These tests are referred to as post hoc or "after-the-fact" because they can be legitimately conducted only after the general test of significance has shown that real differences exist. Typically, these follow-up tests are conducted on *comparisons* or *contrasts* between specific pairs of means, or among carefully selected sets of means.

To illustrate one possible example: In the hypothetical problem currently under consideration, it would be instructive to statistically compare $\bar{Y}_2$ and $\bar{Y}_C$, because these means exhibit the largest difference. In terms of calculation, such a comparison would employ the same, basic formulas outlined earlier. First, it is necessary to calculate a new grand mean—one that is not influenced by Method$_1$.

$$\bar{\bar{Y}} = \frac{\bar{Y}_2 + \bar{Y}_C}{2}$$
$$= \frac{(40.0 + 26.08)}{2}$$
$$= 33.04$$

This new value can be inserted in Eq. 12.4 to obtain a modified SS_{BG}. In these calculations, the mean for Method$_1$ is simply ignored. The application of this formula will show that the between-group sum-of-squares for this specific comparison is $SS_{BG} = 1162.60$. To complete the test of statistical inference, the SS_{WG} *from the entire sample* is employed. Thus,

$$F = \frac{1162.60/1}{3958.09/33}$$
$$= 9.69$$

with 1 and 33 *df*.

The degrees-of-freedom for SS_{BG} have been reduced to 1 because only two groups are being compared. Thus, $k - 1 = 2 - 1 = 1$. Appendix C indicates that the critical value for the F-ratio with 1 and 33 df at $p < .05$ is approximately 4.15. The obtained value of $F = 9.69$ surpasses this and several other critical values as well.

Protecting the Probability of Error.   From this evidence it would seem safe to conclude that this particular difference between means is significant. Or is it? Recall that the concept of statistical significance is the same as the probability of rejecting a null hypothesis which is actually true; that is, the likelihood of making a mistake. This probability of committing a Type I error is based on the assumption of randomness. How likely would it be for this value of the test statistic to occur solely by chance? Post hoc tests such as the one just conducted are not characterized by such randomness, however.

On the contrary, the means selected for this comparison were chosen (1) after the data had been statistically described and tested, and (2) precisely because this examination revealed that these two means exhibited the largest difference. The subsequent, post hoc test can hardly be evaluated under the assumption of randomness. The selection of these means for testing was a highly systematic and purposeful action. As a result, the true probability of a Type I error is unknown. One thing is certain, however. Use of the critical value in Appendix C to assess significance would ensure that this probability would be considerably larger than .05. Some type of adjustment or modification is clearly in order.

A number of writers have addressed the problem of post hoc significance testing from a variety of different approaches. Unfortunately, any attempt to detail these alternatives is beyond the scope of this book. Instead, the present discussion will focus on the logic upon which these various post hoc tests are based. Both Kirk (1968) and Winer (1971) present extensive and highly lucid accounts of these procedures. They are recommended for those who desire additional conceptual or calculational detail.

In its simplest terms, the logic of post hoc testing is this: A difference between or among means which have been selected for testing post hoc must be a larger difference to be declared significant than if it had been tested before inspecting the data. This principle recognizes that while a post hoc comparison of means is intended to be exploratory (some call it "data snooping"), it is based on information and inferences drawn from the initial, overall test of significance. The investigator will almost certainly select the largest and most promising differences (or in some cases, all possible differences) for after-the-fact, exploratory testing.

The consequence of these purposeful actions is that the original probability level (e.g., $p < .05$) is no longer accurate. The original probability of making an inaccurate inference (1 in 20) is now greatly compounded by the investigator's decision to test differences of *known* magnitude and direction. If some remedial action is not taken, the deck will be stacked in the investigator's favor.

Accordingly, the purpose of post hoc testing procedures is to "protect" the probability of a Type I error from being dramatically inflated—i.e., to provide the remedial action discussed above. This protection is achieved by raising or increasing the critical value of the F-ratio which a post hoc test must surpass. As before, the larger the critical value, the smaller the probability that a test statistic will surpass it. It follows, therefore, that a larger difference among or between means is required to produce such a test statistic. The result is that the investigator's systematic and purposeful selection of means for testing is offset or accounted for by this modified critical value. When appropriately applied, these post hoc tests ensure that the probability of incorrect inference remains at or about the level specified by the investigator.

ANOVA Is the Linear Model in Disguise

On several occasions, we have suggested a high degree of similarity between ANOVA and the linear model. Other than these infrequent innuendoes, however, the discussion of both procedures has progressed along traditional lines. ANOVA and the linear model have been treated as relatively separate, unrelated approaches to analyzing totally distinct types of empirical data. The terminology, the calculational formulas, and even the conceptual underpinnings of these two statistical procedures are seemingly so different and remote as to preclude any claim of similarity or equivalence.

As real as these differences may seem, they are purely symbolic and superficial. To be more specific, ANOVA and the linear model are equivalent in all respects. They ask the same questions of data and provide exactly the same answers to those questions. Simply stated, they are the same statistical procedure. Shortly, an example will illustrate this equivalence quite clearly. In the meantime, we will offer a brief explanation of why ANOVA and the linear model seem so different, when in fact they are the same.

In the introduction to ANOVA, we said that one of the positive attributes of this procedure was the relative ease by which it could be calculated by hand. Even the most complex ANOVA problems are direct extensions of the basic formulas presented above. Unfortunately, calculational ease does not characterize the linear model. As soon as an investigator wishes to include more than two or three explanatory variables in a linear model, the calculations become burdensome, to say the least. The calculations for a model with, for example, 10 explanatory variables would be overwhelming. This is not to suggest that they could not be done by hand, but rather that the time and effort involved are so great as to be prohibitive.

Computers have made such concerns irrelevant, of course. In no more than a few seconds, a computer can perform calculations that would require a human several hours or days to duplicate. Such computational power is a recent development, however. Prior to its advent, researchers had only paper, pencil, and if they were lucky, an adding machine to perform their analyses. Under these circumstances, their unwillingness to routinely perform the calculations involved in linear models is understandable. Instead, they were trained and socialized into an ANOVA framework, which included not only the by-hand formulas, but an entire way of thinking as well.

One result of this socialization—ANOVA thinking—was that little or no mention was made of the linear model. It came to be treated as a totally unrelated statistical procedure which possessed its own symbols, terminology, and so forth. At the same time, no one trained in ANOVA thinking bothered to ask where ANOVA formulas came from. What was their origin? Had this question been asked by social scientists, the answer would have been the linear model. *ANOVA is really the linear model in disguise.*

Recall that the use of categorical variables in the linear model gives rise to some interesting and unique outcomes. For example, the predicted values ($\hat{Y}_i$) became the means of the various groups, to name but one. The inclusion of categorical, explanatory variables, therefore, represents a special case of the more general linear model. From this special case, a number of "special" formulas can be derived; specifically, the ANOVA formulas described in Eqs. 12.4, 12.5, and 12.6. These formulas look much different and require totally different methods of calculation. Nevertheless, they produce the same statistical values as the linear model, but without the laborious calculations. As the example to follow will illustrate, they are direct descendants of the linear model.

An Example

To illustrate this equivalence, we will use the previous example of the relationship between the sensitivity to vocal cues of emotion (MOVS) and children's language abilities (normal versus disordered). The complete listing of these data was displayed in Table 12.1, with a variety of summary statistics presented in Table 12.2. This example was chosen because its linear model requires only one dummy-coded explanatory variable. It is, therefore, the simplest case in which the equivalence of ANOVA and the linear model can be demonstrated. Nevertheless, generalization to more complex models is direct.

To review, the previous discussion and computation of this problem revealed a significant relationship between MOVS and the categorical variable, Group. Because of the manner by which Group was dummy-coded (Normal $= 1$, Disordered $= 0$), the Pearson r ($r = .348$) suggested that normal children exhibited a significant tendency to score higher on the MOVS instrument than disordered children. When these data were used to calculate the linear model, it was found that $\hat{Y}_i = 5.68 + 1.11\ (X_i)$. In this problem, however, X_i could assume only two values, 1 or 0. Thus, only two predicted values were produced. These were found to be the means of the respective groups—$\hat{Y}_1 = \bar{Y}_n = 6.79$; $\hat{Y}_2 = \bar{Y}_d = 5.68$. For ease of reference, these findings as well as the results of the subsequent statistical tests are displayed in Table 12.7.

Shortly, these data will be rearranged slightly and reanalyzed using ANOVA and its special formulas. For the moment, however, it will be instructive to continue to consider them from a linear model perspective. The linear model which is numerically

TABLE 12.7. Summary of Linear Model Results for Illustrative Data

	N	Mean	SS
MOVS	49	6.22	124.53
Group	49	.49	12.25

$$SP = 13.61$$
$$COV = .284$$
$$r = .348*$$
$$r^2 = .121$$
$$1 - r^2 = .879$$
$$*(t = 2.55;\ df = 47;\ p < .0141)$$

$$Y = a + BX$$
$$= 5.68 + 1.11(X_i)$$
$$Y_1 = 5.68 + 1.111(1) = 6.79 = \bar{Y}_{\text{Normal}}$$
$$Y_2 = 5.68 + 1.111(0) = 5.68 = \bar{Y}_{\text{Disordered}}$$

$$SS_{\text{Model}} = 15.07$$
$$SS_{\text{Error}} = 109.46$$
$$F = 6.47;\ df = 1,\ 47;\ p < .0141$$

summarized in Table 12.7 is also visually depicted in Figure 12.1. The purpose of visually recreating the model is to overlay the line-of-best-fit on the scatterplot of points, thus allowing one to "see" and evaluate the model.

Recall from Chapter 11 that a good model—one which represents a strong relationship—will be one in which the line-of-best-fit comes relatively close to all of the data points (see Figure 11.2). In other words, the data points will cluster tightly around the line. A poor model, on the other hand, will show the data points to be far away from the line, scattered in a seemingly random fashion (see Figure 11.3). Because a poor model is based on a weak relationship, there is little or no systematic variation for it to depict.

One fact holds true for all models, regardless of the magnitude of the relationship portrayed. The lack of fit of the model is represented by the distance between each data point and the corresponding point on the line. The line-of-best-fit connects the predicted values of the criterion measure, the $\hat{Y}_i$ scores, while the individual data points stand for the obtained or measured values of Y. Accordingly, the spatial distance between the line and each point is error of prediction. It is the visual or spatial equivalent of $e_i = Y_i - \hat{Y}_i$. When all N of these distances are squared and summed, the result is equal to least-squares error:

$$\sum_{i=1}^{N} e_i^2 = \sum_{i=1}^{N} (Y_i - \hat{Y}_i)^2 = SS_{\text{Error}}$$

At first glance, these concepts and principles seem difficult to apply to the model in

FIGURE 12.1 Plot of Relationship Between MOVS and Group, Including Line-of-Best-Fit.

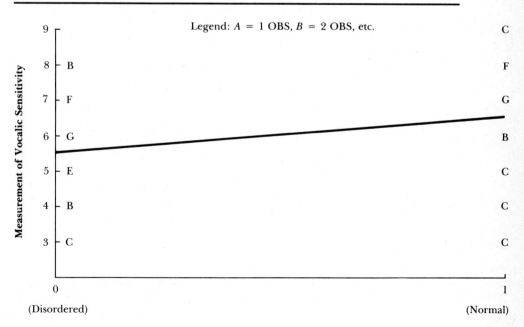

Figure 12.1. The positioning of the data points does not evoke images of a scatterplot. Instead, the points cluster into piles or groups at each end of the X-axis. This clustering, however, is exactly what has been mandated by the inclusion of a categorical explanatory variable. There is no continuum of measurement on the X-axis, but rather only discrete groups or categories of scores.

Despite these differences, the various components of this visual model are not altered. The line-of-best-fit still represents the predicted values, and the distance between each point and the line continues to be the error of prediction, e_i. As suggested above, this model is a special case of the general linear model. Consequently, even though all of the guiding principles of the linear model remain in force, they can be reconceptualized in some equally "special" ways. Earlier, it was demonstrated that this model has only two, dummy-coded values of the explanatory variable (1 and 0), and thus only two predicted values are produced. Moreover, as Table 12.7 indicates, these two values correspond to the means of the two groups—$\bar{Y}_n$ and $\bar{Y}_d$. The line-of-best-fit, therefore, connects only two points, specifically, the two means. As a consequence, the spatial distance between the line and each point which constitutes error (e_i) can be recast as the difference between each observed value and the mean of its respective group. Symbolically,

$$
\begin{aligned}
e_i &= (Y_i - \hat{Y}_i) \\
&= (Y_{ij} - \bar{Y}_j)
\end{aligned}
$$

where, the j has again been used as a subscript to designate to which of the k groups each individual observation (i) has been assigned. This equality can then be extended to obtain the overall, least-squares error of prediction.

$$
\begin{aligned}
SS_{\text{Error}} &= \sum_{i=1}^{N} e_i^2 \\
&= \sum_{i=1}^{N} (Y_i - \hat{Y}_i)^2 \\
&= \sum_{i=1}^{n_1} (Y_{i_1} - \bar{Y}_1)^2 + \sum_{i=1}^{n_2} (Y_{i_2} - \bar{Y}_2)^2 + \cdots + \\
&\quad \sum_{i=1}^{n_j} (Y_{ij} - \bar{Y}_j)^2 + \cdots + \sum_{i=1}^{n_k} (Y_{ik} - \bar{Y}_k)^2
\end{aligned}
$$

When this final, rather clumsy expression is collapsed across the several $(+)$ signs,

$$
SS_{\text{Error}} = \sum_{j=1}^{k} \sum_{i=1}^{n_j} (Y_{ij} - \bar{Y}_j)^2
$$

which, of course, is exactly the same as the symbolic expression for SS_{WG} as defined in Eq. 12.6. It is clear that this formula for calculating the within-groups variation was not just plucked out of thin air. On the contrary, it was derived directly from the basic formula for least-squares error which characterizes the linear model.

This conclusion can be reinforced by performing a similar demonstration on the SS_{Model}. Thus far, this component of the total variation has been calculated by Eq. 11.8, which employs r^2.

$$SS_{\text{Model}} = r^2(SS_Y) \qquad (11.8)$$

Nevertheless, it is possible to calculate this quantity directly, using only the predicted values from the linear model.

$$SS_{\text{Model}} = \sum_{i=1}^{N} (\hat{Y}_i - \bar{Y})^2 \qquad (12.9)$$

The use of $\bar{Y}$ in Eq. 12.9 reflects the fact that the use of the intercept term, a, in the linear model ($\hat{Y} = a + BX$) ensures that the means of the predicted and obtained values of the criterion variable will be exactly the same. Hence, while it might be technically more accurate to express this difference as $(\hat{Y}_i - \bar{\hat{Y}})$, Eq. 12.9 will produce exactly the same value for SS_{Model}.

Once again, the inclusion of a categorical variable gives rise to several "special" equalities. First, the mean of the entire sample, $\bar{Y}$, becomes the grand mean, or the mean of the group means. Thus, $\bar{Y} = \bar{\bar{Y}}$. Also, the predicted values become the means of the groups. Hence,

$$SS_{\text{Model}} = \sum_{i=1}^{N} (\hat{Y}_i - \bar{Y})^2$$

$$= \sum_{j=1}^{k} \sum_{i=1}^{n_j} (\hat{Y}_{ij} - \bar{\bar{Y}})^2$$

$$= \sum_{j=1}^{k} \sum_{i=1}^{n_j} (\bar{Y}_j - \bar{\bar{Y}})^2$$

Notice, however, that the quantity $(\bar{Y}_j - \bar{\bar{Y}})^2$ is a constant for all of the n_j scores in each group. As a result, the right-most summation sign, $\sum_{i=1}^{n_j}$, requires that the same number be added together n_j times. Since adding a constant n_j times is the same as multiplying that constant by n_j, this formula can be reexpressed as,

$$SS_{\text{Model}} = \sum_{j=1}^{k} \sum_{i=1}^{n_j} (\bar{Y}_j - \bar{\bar{Y}})^2$$

$$= \sum_{j=1}^{k} n_j (\bar{Y}_j - \bar{\bar{Y}})^2$$

which is the exact formula for SS_{BG} (Eq. 12.5).

In sum, we have demonstrated that the formulas for SS_{BG} and SS_{WG} are not as separate and unrelated to the linear model as traditional ANOVA thinking would suggest. In fact, just the opposite has been shown to be true. ANOVA formulas *are* the linear model formulas for those special cases when the explanatory variable is categorical. These two statistical procedures are more than related: They are identical.

This demonstration can be effectively concluded by actually reanalyzing the current problem using the ANOVA formulas. If it can be assumed that the previous equalities were not merely algebraic sleight of hand, then the results should be the same. Table 12.8 displays the data for the current problem in a more traditional ANOVA format. The first step is to calculate the SS_{Total}. According to Eq. 12.4,

TABLE 12.8 Reanalysis of MOVS Data Using ANOVA
Score = Measurement of Nonverbal Sensitivity (MOVS)

	Normal	Disordered
	4	3
	9	8
	8	6
	4	3
	7	5
	5	6
	8	7
	7	5
	8	7
	4	6
	8	4
	8	6
	7	4
	5	7
	7	5
	8	5
	9	3
	7	7
	6	6
	5	7
	7	7
	9	6
	6	5
	7	8
	•	6
Group Total	163	142
N Per Group	24	25
$\bar{Y}$	6.79	5.68
SS For Group	57.96	51.44

Total N = 49
Total Score = 305
Grand Mean = 6.22
SS Total = 124.53

$$SS_{Total} = \sum_{j=1}^{k} \sum_{i=1}^{n_j} (Y_{ij} - \bar{\bar{Y}})^2 \qquad (12.4)$$

When applied to the data in Table 12.8,

$$
\begin{aligned}
SS_{Total} &= (4 - 6.22)^2 + (9 - 6.22)^2 + \cdots + (6 - 6.22)^2 \\
&= 4.93 + 7.73 + \cdots + .049 \\
&= 124.53
\end{aligned}
$$

This is exactly the same quantity designated as 100% of the variance in the previous application of the linear model to these data (see Table 12.2).

In a similar fashion, Eq. 12.5 defines the between-groups variation as,

$$SS_{BG} = \sum_{j=1}^{k} n_j (\bar{Y}_j - \bar{\bar{Y}})^2 \qquad (12.5)$$

In the current problem,

$$
\begin{aligned}
SS_{BG} &= 24(6.79 - 6.22)^2 + 25(5.68 - 6.22)^2 \\
&= 7.79 + 7.29 \\
&= 15.08
\end{aligned}
$$

The value obtained from the linear model formula was 15.07. Thus, these two quantities are well within rounding error of being the same.

Finally, the formula for obtaining the within-groups variation is defined by Eq. 12.6 as,

$$SS_{WG} = \sum_{j=1}^{k} \left[\sum_{i=1}^{n_j} (Y_{ij} - \bar{Y}_j)^2 \right] \qquad (12.6)$$

The bracketed part of this equation is first applied separately to each group.

$$
\begin{aligned}
SS_{Normal} &= (4 - 6.79)^2 + (9 - 6.79)^2 + \cdots + (7 - 6.79)^2 \\
&= 7.78 + 4.88 + \cdots + 0.04 \\
&= 57.96
\end{aligned}
$$

$$
\begin{aligned}
SS_{Disord} &= (3 - 5.68)^2 + (8 - 5.68)^2 + \cdots + (6 - 5.68)^2 \\
&= 7.18 + 5.38 + \cdots + 0.10 \\
&= 51.44
\end{aligned}
$$

When the summation sign outside of the brackets is applied,

$$
\begin{aligned}
SS_{WG} &= SS_{Normal} + SS_{Disord} \\
&= 57.96 + 51.44 \\
&= 109.40
\end{aligned}
$$

The previous application of the linear model formula, $SS_{\text{Error}} = (1 - r^2)(SS_Y)$, resulted in the finding that $SS_{\text{Error}} = 109.46$. If the slight difference due to rounding error is ignored, it can be concluded that these values are identical.

Normally, at this point it would be desirable to conduct a test of statistical inference to determine if these two groups are significantly different in their sensitivity to vocal expressions of emotion. Previously, however, it was determined that MOVS and the dummy-coded variable, Group, were significantly *related*. It would, therefore, be somewhat superfluous to conduct this test again. Given that all aspects of ANOVA and the linear model are identical (except, of course, the terminology), the previous test of relationship is also the test of difference. You should check for yourself that the result would be: $F = 6.47$; $df = 1, 47$; $p < .0141$.

■ *Conclusion*

In this chapter, three important areas of concern were addressed. First, the use of categorical, explanatory variables in linear models was described and illustrated. Although such variables contain a much different type of explanatory information, it was shown that this information—specifically, group membership information—could be dummy-coded in a manner that substituted numerical symbols (e.g., 1 and 0) for alphabetic labels (e.g., male and female). It was further emphasized that the inclusion of these numerical codes as explanatory variables in no way altered the descriptive or inferential performance of the model. Through both discussion and example, we concluded that the linear model is capable of employing any type of empirical information in its attempt to explain and account for the variance of the criterion scores.

Second, this chapter presented a very traditional account of the statistical procedure known as the Analysis of Variance. The attributes which gave rise to the widespread use of ANOVA were described, and its primary conceptual underpinnings were detailed. In addition, the basic calculational formulas for ANOVA were derived and explained, and an extended example was computed. Finally, the logic of post hoc statistical inference was briefly discussed. It was suggested that by increasing the critical value necessary for significance, an investigator could engage in after-the-fact exploratory analysis, yet maintain the probability of making a Type I error at a predetermined and acceptable level (e.g., $p < .05$).

The final pages of this chapter were devoted to illustrating that ANOVA and the linear model, even though seemingly disparate and unrelated, are actually equivalent statistical procedures. When categorical explanatory variables are dummy-coded and included in the linear model, a number of "special" outcomes and results occur. It was shown that the basic ANOVA formulas simply take advantage of these special circumstances, thus allowing results to be calculated and tested by much simpler procedures—procedures which avoid the frequently laborious computations of the linear model. With the notable exception of terminology, it was concluded that ANOVA and the linear model are identical in all respects.

Perhaps a brief discussion of these differences in terminology is the most appropriate way to conclude this chapter. After reading this far, one could reasonably ask: Why this heavy emphasis on the equivalence of ANOVA and the linear model? Why all this fuss over a few differences in symbols and a little discrepancy in terminology? Is it really worth all the effort?

The answer to this last question, we believe, is an emphatic "Yes!" Moreover, it seems especially fitting that the rationale for this answer be taken directly from a well-known communication theory, the Whorfian hypothesis (Whorf, 1956). As described by Littlejohn (1978, p. 131), the Whorfian hypothesis asserts that "the structure of a culture's language determines the *behavior* and *habits of thinking* in that culture" (italics added). In other words, the perception and interpretation of the world around us—reality—is largely determined by the language we have for describing, labeling, and talking about that world. Each person's pattern of thinking as well as pattern of behavior is inextricably linked to the language that person possesses.

And so it is with statistics. Earlier in this chapter the concept of "ANOVA thinking" was introduced. Researchers who are trained and socialized in a traditional ANOVA framework come to be quite conversant with the symbols and terminology of that procedure. The language and formulas for between-group and within-group variance, post hoc testing, and so forth become second nature to them. After all, this is what socialization—in this case, being a good student—is all about.

At some point, however, ANOVA thinking tends to infiltrate the conceptualization of *substantive* questions and problems. Empirical inquiry becomes synonymous with experimental design; explanatory concepts become routinely operationalized as categorical, independent variables; and the search for continua of measurement is circumvented as subjects are classified into discrete and mutually exclusive groups or categories. As the Whorfian hypothesis would suggest, the language one possesses, i.e., ANOVA language, comes to shape one's pattern of thinking and thus one's behavior as a researcher.

Cannot the same be said of the linear model? Do not the concepts, terminology, and symbols of this procedure influence a researcher's substantive and empirical thinking in exactly the same way? Of course! There is a fundamental difference, however. The linear model is more aptly described as the *general linear model* (GLM), a reference we will use henceforth. It is the foundation for *all* parametric statistical procedures. ANOVA, on the other hand, is but a special case of the GLM. Stated differently, GLM thinking can easily incorporate or subsume all facets of ANOVA thinking, no matter how complex. The reverse is not true. Because ANOVA is a special case, it is limited to a relatively narrow range of empirical inquiry and statistical analysis.

The conclusion is that the GLM is a more flexible and thus ultimately a more utilitarian statistical procedure. It can be applied to a much wider range of statistical problems. Because ANOVA thinking has certainly not disappeared in communication research, familiarity with its terminology and formulas remains a necessity. Nevertheless, the frame of reference for that familiarity should be the GLM. If language does indeed structure one's thinking as the Whorfian hypothesis suggests, then the conceptual and statistical language of the GLM will provide the broadest and most flexible framework for the investigation of human communication behavior.

 *Chapter*

Extensions of the General Linear Model: An Overview

The previous discussions of the linear model and the various statistical procedures associated with it have focused on a single criterion variable and a single explanatory variable—Y and X, respectively. A comprehensive understanding of bivariate relationships was emphasized for two reasons. First, because they represent the simplest, most basic case of statistical analysis, their discussion could take place with a minimum of mathematical and computational detail. More emphasis could be placed on logic. Second, bivariate relationships and the linear model which depicts them can be generalized to a host of more sophisticated, *multivariate* procedures and techniques. The bivariate linear model, then, is really the most elementary instance of the general linear model (GLM).

The purpose of this chapter is to present these generalizations and extensions. This presentation, however, will indeed be an "overview." Each of the statistical procedures associated with the GLM has been the subject of many books and articles. We cannot hope to do justice to this massive amount of detailed information in the next few pages. Instead, this chapter is intended to be primarily heuristic: to provide preliminary insight into the logic and applications of the statistical procedures which constitute the GLM. Accordingly, many of the specifics of both calculation and interpretation will not be discussed. Similarly, a number of applications of the GLM (e.g., modeling curvilinear relationships) will not be included. Whenever appropriate, however, references to more detailed and complete accounts of these procedures will be included.

Table 13.1 both summarizes and previews the contents of this chapter. On the left, three forms of the GLM—labeled for easy references (a), (b), and (c)—are displayed. To the right are the names of various statistical procedures associated with these forms, depending on whether the explanatory variable, X, is continuous, categorical, or both. Shortly, each of the procedures will be described, and their relationship to the GLM will be explained. For the present, however, the alternate forms of the model deserve additional attention.

The models designated as (a), (b), and (c) in Table 13.1 are not intended to be accurate in a technical or statistical sense. They contain no symbols to denote an error term (for example, e_i), nor do they attempt to portray Y as a predicted value. Neither is

TABLE 13.1. Statistical Procedures Which Are Extensions of the General Linear Model

	Alternate Forms of GLM	X is Continuous	X is Categorical	X is Both
(a)	$Y = B_1X_1$	Pearson r Biv. Regr.	t-test	—
(b)	$Y = B_1X_1 + B_2X_2 + \ldots + B_pX_p$	Multiple regression	ANOVA (one-way, factorial)	ANCOVA
(c) $B_1Y_1 + B_2Y_2 + \ldots + B_qY_q =$	$B_1X_1 + B_2X_2 + \ldots + B_pX_p$	Canonical Correlation	MANOVA	MANCOVA

an intercept term, *a*, included in any model. Such technical precision is not their purpose. Rather, they are intended to depict heuristically the alternative ways in which relationships between and among variables may be modeled. As before, Y is treated as the criterion variable, or in some instances, the *set* of criterion variables. For this discussion, all variables symbolized as Y are assumed to be continuous. The X variable or variables represent the information available to explain or account for the variance of Y. This information may assume any quantitative or qualitative form—continuous, categorical, or both. Finally, the symbol B stands for the weights or coefficients by which a particular X or Y variable is multiplied.

By this time, model (a) should be quite familiar. It received extensive discussion in Chapters 11 and 12 as the model which underlies bivariate correlation and regression. In addition, Chapter 12 demonstrated that it is the model which underlies ANOVA when the X variable is coded categorically. It would seem, therefore, that further discussion of this model would be redundant. From time to time, concepts and formulas from these previous chapters will be used as a point of reference, but neither model (a) nor the statistical procedures associated with it will be directly addressed in this chapter.

Model (b), on the other hand, serves as the foundation for several procedures to be discussed subsequently. Like the bivariate model (a), it has a single criterion variable of interest. Model (b) extends model (a), however, by including several (i.e., p) explanatory variables in the equation. (Note that (a) is really a special case of (b) when $p = 1$.) In other words, model (b) attempts to combine the information contained in several X variables in an attempt to explain or account for the variation in a single Y. The basic principle which guides this attempt is still that of covariation or relationship. In this instance, however, the relationship is between a *set* of explanatory variables on one hand, and a single Y variable on the other.

Finally, model (c) depicts the situation in which an investigator desires to assess the relationships between two sets of variables. A combination of X variables is used to explain the variation of a combination of Y variables. Model (c), therefore, is a natural extension of model (b). In many senses, model (c) is *the* GLM, in that all other models can be derived as special cases of it. In the conduct of research, this model would apply whenever a researcher decided that the concept of interest could be most appropriately operationalized by several scores or measures. For example, a college entrance exam might be composed of separate scores on language usage, mathematics, general science, and so forth. An investigator could, of course, revert to model (b) and conduct separate analyses for each Y score. Such an approach, however, would not provide the "big picture," i.e., how the combined set of scores operated together to operationalize the concept.

From even this briefest of previews, it should be apparent that alternate forms of the GLM are different in many respects. They are applied to different research situations; they ask fundamentally different questions of the available data, and thus they provide the investigator with different answers and interpretations of the relationships among concepts. These differences become more numerous when it is recalled that the explanatory information may consist of any combination of categorical and continuous variables. Despite these differences, there are also some fundamental similarities among these models which cannot be ignored. These similarities are what unite all statistical procedures under the conceptual umbrella of the GLM.

Linear Combinations of Variables

One feature common to both models (b) and (c) is that they require two or more variables to be combined in an appropriate manner. Model (b) requires that only the X, explanatory variables be so combined, while model (c) necessitates that both the X and Y variables be treated as a combined set. More formally, what is required is a *weighted linear combination* of these variables. The term *weighted* refers to the fact that each variable is first multiplied by a weighting coefficient, symbolized by B_i. In general, the size of B_i depends on the importance of the ith variable to the overall relationship with the variable or variables on the other side of the equal sign. The reference to "linear combination" indicates that the variables are combined by addition, rather than some other method such as multiplication.

The computational method for obtaining the B_i as well as the criterion or criteria for determining the "importance" of a variable differ from procedure to procedure. Nevertheless, the result of a weighted linear combination is always the same: a single, combined score for each subject or observation. For simplicity, only the X scores in model (b) will be used to illustrate. From the logic outlined in Chapter 11,

$$\hat{Y} = a + B_1X_1 + B_2X_2 + \ldots + B_pX_p \tag{13.1}$$

In short, what results from the appropriate combination of these variables is a single predicted value, $\hat{Y}_i$. As shall be seen, the $\hat{Y}$ in Eq. 13.1 is the same in all respects as the predicted values obtained from the bivariate model (a). The only difference is that a larger number of X variables were combined to obtain it.

Assessing the Overall Relationship

A second common feature of these models is their concern with determining the overall relationship among variables. In the bivariate model (a), the relationship of interest (in fact, the only relationship) was the correlation between Y and X. Model (b), on the other hand, attempts to represent the relationship between Y and the set of explanatory X variables. This relationship is called the *multiple correlation,* and is symbolized as $R_{Y.12\ldots p}$. Finally, model (c) is designed to assess the relationship between two appropriately combined sets of variables. The term used to designate this relationship is the *canonical correlation,* and is most simply symbolized as R_C. Notice that the capital R is used to designate correlation whenever a set of variables is involved on either or both sides of the model.

Clearly, this discussion of sets of variables and relationships between weighted linear combinations has the potential to quickly become both complicated and confusing. This need not happen, however, if you will recall the earlier discussion about the *result* of a weighted linear combination. As Eq. 13.1 indicates, such a combination of variables produces a single predicted value for each observation. In other words, these *multiple* explanatory variables are combined (perhaps reduced is a better word) to produce a *single* $\hat{Y}$ score. Accordingly, the multiple correlation, $R_{Y.12 \ldots p}$, can more simply be conceptualized as $R_{Y\hat{Y}}$, the correlation between the obtained and predicted values of Y.

It also follows that model (c) can be conceptually reduced or simplified in a similar manner. The weighted linear combination of the X variables produces a single predicted value, $\hat{Y}_i$. At the same time, the appropriate combination of the Y variables produces its counterpart predicted value, $\hat{X}_i$. As a result, the canonical correlation, R_C, can be thought of as the correlation between these two predicted values, $R_{\hat{X}\hat{Y}}$.

In sum, the result of this conceptual simplification is that all multiple or multivariate relationships can be heuristically described as bivariate relationships (see Harris, 1975). All of these multivariate models eventually result in the equivalent of the familiar Pearson r. It must be stressed, however, that the purpose of this conceptual simplification is only to provide an elementary understanding of an otherwise sophisticated area of statistics. The actual application and computation of these multivariate models is somewhat different and considerably more complicated. Be that as it may, the primary concern of these computations is to determine how these multiple variables should be combined, i.e., calculating the appropriate B_i. Once these calculations are complete, the end result is always a single predicted value. Thus, the overall relationship can accurately be conceptualized as bivariate.

Contributions of the Individual Predictors

In addition to sharing a concern about the overall relationship, models (b) and (c) seek to determine the contribution of each individual variable to this relationship. Seldom will a researcher be content with only the knowledge that a weighted linear combination of variables is related to another variable or set of variables in a global, overall fashion. While the indices of multiple or canonical correlation are important, by themselves, they are not enough. It would seem reasonable to assume that the individual variables in a set—either the X or Y variables—were included in the model for some reason. The investigator must have believed from either theory or past research that these variables were relevant, that they were related in some meaningful way to other variables of interest. Accordingly, he or she will desire to assess individually each variable's contribution to the overall relationship.

This concept of a variable's individual contribution can be explained more completely by returning to the notion of shared variance. If $R_{Y.12 \ldots p}$ symbolizes the multiple correlation, then $R^2_{Y.12 \ldots p}$ stands for the variance shared in common between Y and the weighted linear combination of the X_i's. It should be possible, therefore, to distribute or decompose this overall variance among the p explanatory variables. And so it is, although this distribution is not always as simple and direct as one might assume.

FIGURE 13.1. Contributions of Individual Explanatory Variables When $r_{12} = .00$ (a) and $r_{12} = .50$ (b).

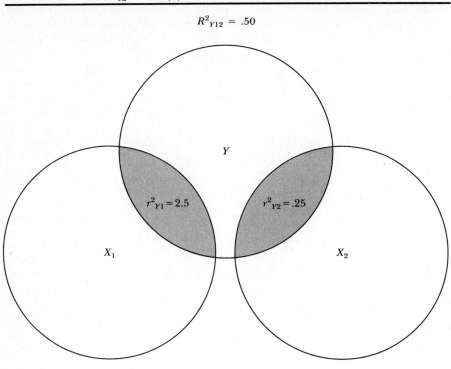

$R^2_{Y12} = .50$

(a)

In model (b), the simplest and most basic example of assessing individual contributions is the situation where all of the explanatory variables are related to Y, but absolutely unrelated ($r = 0.00$) among themselves. For the sake of simplicity, assume $p = 2$. Then,

$$R^2_{Y.12} = r^2_{Y1} + r^2_{Y2} \tag{13.2}$$

The overall variance accounted for by this entire model is simply the sum of the separate proportions of variance explained by the two variables individually. For example, if $r_{Y1} = .50$, $r_{Y2} = .50$, and $r_{12} = 0$, then $R^2_{Y.12} = (.50)^2 + (.50)^2 = .50$. This straightforward situation is illustrated graphically in Figure 13.1(a). Because there is no overlap between the circles representing X_1 and X_2, the amount of variance they account for separately can simply be added.

The situation depicted in Figure 13.1(a) is most characteristic of an ANOVA approach to the analysis of experimental designs. In experiments, the researcher controls the number of treatment or classification groups, the number of subjects assigned to each group, and (perhaps most importantly) the assignment of dummy codes to the several X_i variables. The researcher, therefore, can easily ensure that the experimental groups and

FIGURE 13.1. *(cont'd)*

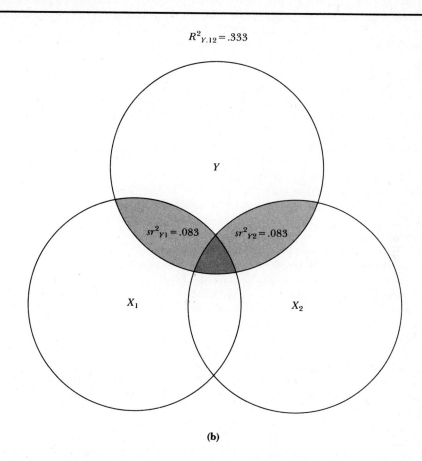

$$R^2_{Y.12} = .333$$

Y

$sr^2_{Y1} = .083$ $sr^2_{Y2} = .083$

X_1 X_2

(b)

the dummy codes which represent them are mutually uncorrelated. In fact, because of the straightforward, additive relationship between the multiple R^2 and the bivariate r^2's as expressed in Eq. 13.2, ANOVA is seldom concerned with the overall R^2. Since the parts simply add up to the whole, ANOVA focuses almost totally on the contribution of the parts—the individual variables.

Outside of controlled experiments, however, this rather simple, additive situation seldom occurs. More commonly, researchers select and measure explanatory variables precisely because they believe them to be correlated with the criterion, Y. As a consequence, these X variables will almost inevitably be correlated among themselves. They share variance not only with Y, but also with each other. The result is that Eq. 13.2 no longer obtains. In this situation, the explanatory information carried by X_1 is more or less *redundant* with the information contained by X_2. The more redundancy they exhibit, the less explanatory information X_2 provides over and above that already provided by X_1 (and vice versa). Similarly, as additional explanatory variables are included in the model, the amount of redundant information increases and the unique explanatory ability of each individual variable becomes smaller.

This more common situation is illustrated in Figure 13.1(b). In this example,

$r_{Y1} = 50$, $r_{Y2} = .50$, and $r_{12} = .50$. Thus X_1 and X_2 share 25% of their variance; $r^2_{12} = (.50)^2 = .25$. At least part of the variance they share with Y is also shared with each other, i.e., it is redundant. In Figure 13.1(b), this redundancy is represented by the intersection of the two circles representing X_1 and X_2. The shaded areas of this overlap is that proportion of the Y variance that the X variables account for jointly. In determining the overall relationship (i.e., R or R^2), this shaded area can be counted only once.

This redundant variation becomes problematic when it comes to assessing the explanatory contribution of the individual variables. Does this jointly explained proportion of the Y variation belong to X_1 or X_2? This is an important question for regardless of which variable is chosen, the other is automatically relegated to a less important explanatory role. Moreover, because there is no empirical or statistical criterion for deciding, the choice is totally arbitrary. Consequently, if such a decision is made, it should be guided solely by theory. The theory should unequivocally state that one variable is more salient than the other and thus should be given the redundant variation for its own. If more than one X variable is involved, then a complete ordering of the variables in terms of theoretic importance should be provided. Without such strong theoretic guidance, this arbitrary decision should not be made.

How, then, does one proceed? From a purely statistical point of view, the answer is simple. The redundantly explained variation belongs to neither variable. It is certainly considered a part of the overall explanation, R^2, but it is simply ignored in assessing the explanatory prowess of the individual variables. Instead, the contribution of each variable is evaluated by how much Y variation it explains *uniquely*. The relationship between X_i and Y is, accordingly, adjusted for this correlation between X_i and the other explanatory variables. This adjusted relationship is referred to as the *semipartial correlation*. With few exceptions, this semipartial correlation or its square will be smaller in magnitude than the unadjusted Pearson r or r^2. This decrease in magnitude simply reflects the fact that the former has had its redundant relationships removed. How much smaller it becomes, of course, will depend on the degree of correlation among the several X's.

These ideas can be illustrated further by returning to Figure 13.1. In Figure 13.1(a), X_1 and X_2 were uncorrelated and thus $R^2_{Y.12} = .50$. Without specifying formulas or calculations (see Cohen & Cohen, 1975, pp. 73–91), it can be demonstrated for Figure 13.1(b) that $R^2_{Y.12} = .333$. This reduction results from the fact that X_1 and X_2 are correlated and thus account for less variation overall. Similarly, in Figure (a) both X_1 and X_2 individually account for 25% of the Y variation. Because they are independent, their Pearson r's were simply squared. In Figure (b), by contrast, $r^2_{Y(1.2)} = .083$ and $r^2_{(2.1)} = .083$. Each variable *uniquely* accounts for 8.3% of the variance in Y, a considerable reduction to say the least. More than 16% of the Y variation is redundantly explained and thus is assigned to neither variable.

One obvious conclusion to be drawn from this discussion is that researchers should measure and employ explanatory variables (or in the case of model (c), both criterion and explanatory variables) which are uncorrelated among themselves. This is much easier said than done, however. The very act of measuring variables which are theoretically linked to Y will almost ensure that they will be statistically related to each other. No doubt, the ability to order the X variables in terms of their theoretic salience is most helpful, but such strong, unequivocal theory is seldom available. Hence, a researcher can do very little except make the necessary statistical adjustments. Although the semipartial r's will almost surely be smaller than the Pearson r's, this procedure guarantees that the final results will not be influenced by arbitrary and theoretically unsupported decisions of the investigator.

There are a number of additional similarities among these models, but their explanation would consist of exactly the type of computational and interpretational details which an overview must avoid. The three common features which have been outlined should suffice to show that these models are closely related. They are direct descendants of the GLM. Despite these similarities, the statistical procedures associated with these models serve fundamentally different purposes, which also require explanation. It is to these we now turn. As suggested by the format of Table 13.1, this discussion will be organized according to the type of X variable employed: continuous, categorical, or some combination of both.

Statistical Procedures When X Is Continuous

This section is devoted to the discussion of two procedures which are applied when the explanatory variables are continuous: multiple regression and canonical correlation. By continuous data, we mean any variable which contains more than nominally coded information—i.e., ordinal, interval, or ratio levels of measurement. As in previous discussions, it will be assumed that these variables (1) are independently sampled, (2) are normally distributed, and (3) contain a sufficient number of observations to be representative of the population (see Chapter 10).

Multiple Regression

The concepts of multiple regression are best introduced with an example. In a recent study, Hill and Courtright (1981, Abstract) "investigated the relationship between selected interpersonal variables and the perceived empathic ability of peer facilitators by students in a basic interpersonal communication course." The course was divided into (1) a traditional lecture component, and (2) an experiential component consisting of small groups led by trained undergraduate students called "facilitators." Previous research had indicated that the students' performance and success in these small group experiences were best predicted by how empathic or understanding they perceived their facilitators to be. Perceived empathy, however, may or may not be a reflection of actual empathic ability. Hence, this study attempted to discover what interpersonal characteristics—including actual empathy—were related to the perception of empathy.

Already in this brief description, we can see the elements of multiple regression emerge. Perceived empathy is the criterion variable (Y) of interest, and its relationship with other interpersonal attributes (implying more than one X) is being assessed. In the Hill and Courtright study, the attributes selected for study were actual empathy, trust, interpersonal attractiveness, and teaching effectiveness. These were used as the explanatory variables, whose weighted linear combination was used to produce the predicted ($\hat{Y}$) values of perceived empathy.

Table 13.2 (p. 254) displays the results of this statistical procedure. The R^2 statistic indicates that slightly more than 38% of the variance in the students' perception of their facilitators as empathic is accounted for by this combination of four variables.

Moreover, the *F*-ratio of 21.33 indicates that a multiple correlation of this magnitude could have occurred by chance only 1 in 10,000 times. Three additional pieces of information are located in the body of this table. First, the bivariate Pearson *r* for each variable is provided. This statistic, as always, describes the magnitude of relationship for each individual predictor variable with the criterion, while ignoring any interrelationships (i.e., redundancies) among the predictors. The critical value for Pearson *r* with $df = 141$ is .16, so all of these bivariate relationships are significant.

Second, Table 13.2 presents the weight by which each explanatory variable is multiplied to form the weighted linear combination. Because all of the variables were standardized to *z*-scores prior to the analysis, the size of these weights can be directly compared. Finally, the table indicates whether these weights are significantly larger than zero. In contrast to bivariate correlation, the weights take the interrelationships among the predictors into account. These redundancies operate to make all of these weights smaller than their corresponding Pearson *r*'s, and in two instances nonsignificant.

Although Hill and Courtright (1981) conducted additional analyses of these data, one of their primary conclusions can be drawn from the results presented in Table 13.2. The perception of empathy (i.e., being understood by the student facilitator) is largely determined by how interpersonally attractive and how effective as a teacher that facilitator is perceived. The facilitators' actual empathic ability and perceived trustworthiness, on the other hand, play a small and nonsignificant role in this perception. From this and other findings, Hill and Courtright were able to make a series of recommendations for the training of these student facilitators in the future.

This brief example provides a starting place from which to launch a more general discussion of multiple regression. As a procedure which is based on model (b), the goal of multiple regression is to relate a set of continuous explanatory variables to a single criterion variable, *Y*. The several (*p*) explanatory variables are subjected to a weighted linear combination which produces a single predicted value, $\hat{Y}_i$, for each observation. In the previous example, $p = 4$. According to Eq. 13.1,

$$\hat{Y} = a + B_1 X_1 + B_2 X_2 + \cdots + B_p X_p \qquad (13.1)$$

where all symbols are defined as before.

The statistical criterion for combining the X_i scores is to find values for the B_i which maximize the statistic, $R_{Y\hat{Y}}$, while simultaneously minimizing the value of

TABLE 13.2. Results of Multiple Regression Analysis with Perceived Empathy as Criterion

	Pearson		
$R^2 = .382$ ($F = 21.33$; $df = 4, 138$; $p < .0001$)			
Variable	*r*	Weight (B_i)	Significant
Actual Empathy	.22	.032	NO
Trust	.46	.058	NO
Attraction	.58	.349	YES
Teaching Effec.	.55	.271	YES

SOURCE: Adapted from Hill and Courtright (1981, pp. 222–23).

$$SS_{\text{Error}} = \sum_{i=1}^{N} e_i^2 = \sum_{i=1}^{N} (Y_i - \hat{Y}_i)^2 \qquad (13.3)$$

Eq. 13.3 will be recognized as the formula for least-squares error encountered earlier. In many ways, this formula is identical to that for the bivariate model (a). SS_{Error} represents that proportion of the overall variation (SS_Y) which cannot be accounted for or explained.

The use of p explanatory variables, however, does alter somewhat the concept of e_i—the error of prediction for an individual observation. Because model (a) was bivariate, its visual depiction could be presented in two dimensions, with the $\hat{Y}_i$ values being symbolized by the line-of-best-fit. Model (b), on the other hand, requires multiple dimensions in order to visually depict its multivariate nature. The predicted values, therefore, are represented as the "plane-of-best-fit" through the p-dimensionally arrayed data points.

Figure 13.2 illustrates this visual model for the case of $p = 2$. This is the most complex model that can be drawn on a two-dimensional page. Models with more dimensions are admittedly difficult to envision (most mathematicians cannot envision figures beyond four or five dimensions), but the principles are nonetheless directly generalizable. Visually, the concept of error is still represented by a spatial distance. In this instance, however, the distance is between each data point (o) and its corresponding point on the plane (·). As before, the smaller the combined distance (i.e., $\sum_{i=1}^{N} e_i^2$), the better the fit of the model.

The concept of error, however, in many senses represents the reverse side of an

FIGURE 13.2. The Visual Model for Multiple Regression When $p = 2$.

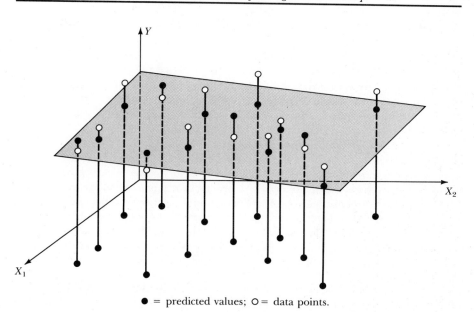

● = predicted values; ○ = data points.

investigator's true interest, namely, systematic relationship. This interest, of course, is indexed by the R^2 statistic, the amount of variance shared by Y and the weighted linear combination of the X variables. The null hypothesis is that R^2 in the population is zero. This hypothesis is tested by:

$$F = \frac{R^2_{Y.12\ldots p}/p}{1 - R^2_{Y.12\ldots p}/N - p - 1} \tag{13.4}$$

where p is the number of X_i variables in the model. This test statistic is compared to the appropriate critical value in Appendix C for degrees-of-freedom p and $N - p - 1$. Recall that in Table 13.2, $F = 21.33$. with 4 and 138 df. Because the obtained F-ratio surpassed the critical value of F for $p < .0001$, these investigators could confidently reject the null hypothesis of no relationship in the population.

Once the multiple correlation has been tested and found significant, an investigator may satisfy his or her interest in the contribution of the individual X_i variables in one of several ways. All of these approaches use $1 - R^2$ or its sum-of-squares equivalent as the error term for testing. First, a researcher might be interested in the question of whether each of the individual B_i is significantly different from zero. A weight of $B_i = 0$ would indicate that variable X contributed absolutely nothing to the explanation and prediction of Y.

This, of course, was the approach taken by Hill and Courtright (1981). Moreover, the finding that the null hypothesis of $B_i = 0$ could not be rejected for two of the four predictors allowed important (and in some senses, counterintuitive) conclusions to be drawn. It is interesting to note (proof not included) that the test of $B_i = 0$ is exactly the same as the test of the null hypothesis that the semipartial correlation (or its square) between Y and X_i is zero. This latter test examines whether the variance uniquely explained by X_i is significantly more than zero, i.e., no explanation. Either of these two tests, therefore, addresses the most basic question of the contribution of individual variables.

A very similar, but perhaps more heuristic approach to the same concept might be labeled the "incremental explanation" approach (see Cohen & Cohen, 1975). Suppose, for example, a researcher has constructed a model with one explanatory variable and found $r^2_{Y1} = .25$. Next, a second model is constructed (see Figure 13.1(b)) in which two X variables are included, and $R^2_{Y.12} = .333$. The question can then be raised: Did X_2 provide a significant increment in the explained variance? In other words, is $R^2_{Y.12} - r^2_{Y1} = .333 - .250 = .083$ a significant addition or increment to the explanatory power of the model? Did X_2 add something over and above X_1?

The reason for linking this example to Figure 13.1 is that the quantity under discussion is exactly the same as the semipartial correlation, $r^2_{Y(2.1)} = .083$. As stated, the semipartial correlation indexes the unique explanatory power of each variable. This concept of incremental explanation can be extended to 3, 4, or p variables, thus allowing the development of a more general concept. The unique contribution of the ith variable is the proportion of the variance it could explain or account for if it were entered into the model *last*, i.e., after all of the other X_i had been entered and had explained as much Y variance as they could. In this approach, redundantly shared variance would be of no value. Only unique contributions to the explanation of Y would increment the value of the R^2 statistic.

In sum, it should be obvious from even this brief discussion that multiple regression is a flexible procedure which allows the investigator to examine several different aspects of his or her data. When this fact is coupled with the recent development of sophisticated computer programs to perform the computations, it is no surprise that multiple regression has found widespread application. To cite but a few examples, multiple regression has been applied to the following topics: sexual socialization by the mass media (Baran, 1976); the effects of campaign commercials on voter defection (Joslyn, 1981); patterns of ethnic voting (Jeffries & Hur, 1979); relational communication (Courtright, Rogers, & Millar, 1980; Millar, Rogers-Millar, & Courtright, 1979); quality of group decision-making (Gouran, Brown, & Henry, 1978); and the role of TV, peer, and parent models in determining children's pro- and antisocial conflict behaviors (Roloff & Greenberg, 1980). Other examples abound! Multiple regression has become a staple in the researcher's repertoire of statistical tools.

Canonical Correlation

Prior to conducting a canonical correlation analysis, the researcher has measured a set of q outcome or criterion measures, and a set of p explanatory or predictor variables. Based on model (c), the statistical goal of the procedure is to identify the B_i's for both the X and Y sets which produce maximally correlated predicted values. These predicted values are referred to as *canonical variates*. The procedure calculates a $\hat{X}_i$ for the Y variables and a $\hat{Y}_i$ for the X variables whose bivariate correlation, $r_{\hat{x}\hat{y}}$, is as large as possible. The canonical correlation, R_C, is then subjected to a test of statistical inference to determine if it is significantly larger than zero.

A recent study by Courtright and Baran (1980) illustrates the application of this procedure. This study focused on the acquisition of sexual information by young people: How do young men and women obtain the information necessary to socialize them into appropriate and normative sexual behavior, attitudes, and values? To answer this question, the influences of family, peers, and the mass media were assessed by obtaining a number of variables representative of each.

As part of a series of analyses, the authors performed a canonical correlation analysis on the eight variables representing the influence of the media and the three variables which measured the social influence of peers and friends. These 11 variables had exhibited a large number of significant Pearson r's among and between themselves, thus making substantive interpretation impossible. The results of the canonical correlation analysis are presented in Table 13.3. The obtained R_C was .43, and a test of significance indicated that this relationship was significantly larger than zero: $\chi^2 = 90.44$; $df = 24$; $p < .0001$. (The χ^2 (pronounced ki-square) test statistic will be discussed in detail in Chapter 14.) A definition of the "loadings" will be provided shortly. For the present, these may be thought to represent how strongly a single variable is related to the entire combined set of which it is a member. The sign of the loading indicates the direction of that relationship.

Notice that Personal Sexual Activity possesses a very high positive loading on the social influence set, while almost all of the media variables possess negative loadings. This pattern of relationships allowed Courtright and Baran to draw a relatively straightforward conclusion: The more personal experience a person had with sexual activity, the less accurate and less influential media portrayals of such behavior were perceived to be. More salient to the present discussion, however, was that an unwieldly and uninterpretable set of bivariate r's were made manageable by the procedure. Only after canonical correlation procedures had been applied could meaningful interpretation proceed.

TABLE 13.3. Canonical Correlation and Canonical Loadings for Analysis of Social Influence Variables and Media Variables

$R_c = .43$ ($\chi^2 = 90.44$; $df = 24$; $p < .0001$)

Media Variables	Loadings
TV Sex is Real	$-.37$
Movie Sex is Real	$-.34$
Characters Have More Pleasure	$-.50$
Characters Perform Better	$-.34$
Too Much TV Sex	$-.50$
Hours Watching TV/Week	$-.73$
Number of Movies/Month	$+.30$
Social Influence Variables	
Personal Sexual Activity	$.98$
Friends' Sexual Activity	$.21$
Comparison of Friends-Self	$-.54$

SOURCE: Courtright and Baran (1980, p. 112).

With this example in mind, we will return to a discussion of canonical correlation per se. Because this procedure is truly multivariate, more than one linear relationship between the sets of variables can be identified. It is possible to calculate a second R_C, subject to the constraint that the second pair of predicted values be totally uncorrelated with the first. In fact, if there are q variables in the Y set and p variables in the X set, it is possible to identify a total of p or q (whichever is smaller) linear relationships between the two sets. Each of these R_C's is tested to determine its significance, although it is uncommon to find that more than the first few surpass the necessary critical value. For example, in the Courtright and Baran investigation, only one linear relationship was significant, even though three such relationships ($q = 8$, $p = 3$) were possible.

Because it is possible to discover more that one R_C, the concept of shared variation between the sets is not as simple as it was with model (b) and multiple regression. Accordingly, several analogous statistics have been developed for canonical correlation (see Levine, 1977). To date, the one most accepted by social science researchers is the "redundancy coefficient" developed by Stewart and Love (1968). This approach recognizes that simply squaring each R_C is not an acceptable method for assessing shared variation, and thus provides an alternative procedure. For example, the redundancy coefficient for the canonical correlation analysis in Table 13.3 was .083, indicating that approximately 8% of the variance in the perception of the media was explained by differences in social influences. For the conceptual and computational details of the redundancy coefficient, consult the original authors as well as Cohen and Cohen (1975), and Tucker and Chase (1976, 1980).

The multivariate nature of canonical correlation also requires the adoption of a different strategy for evaluating the contribution of the individual variables. Instead of examining the individual B's or the semipartial correlations for either or both sets, it is necessary to obtain and examine what are referred to as "canonical loadings" or "structure coefficients." These were outlined briefly during the discussion of Table 13.3.

A loading is the correlation between an individual variable in a weighted linear combination and the predicted value produced by that combination; that is, $r_{\hat{Y}X_i}$ for the set of explanatory variables, and $r_{\hat{X}Y_i}$ for the set of outcome measures. Since there is one canonical loading for each variable in the combination, this approach produces p loadings for the X variables and q loadings for the Y variables.

These loadings are recommended for use in assessing the importance of the individual variables for the simple reason that they are more "stable" than their corresponding B_i. That is, findings and interpretations obtained from loadings are more likely to hold up under replication. Subsequent investigations tend to support and reconfirm findings based on canonical loadings, while reconfirmation is not always possible when the B_i are used for interpretation. The reasons for this disparity are numerous and somewhat complicated, but the evidence supporting the use of canonical loadings is sound and compelling. Consequently, researchers who decide to use the B_i to evaluate the individual variables are generally required to provide a convincing rationale for their decision.

One final aspect of canonical correlation requires discussion. Simply stated, canonical correlation requires a relatively large number of subjects or observations. Weiss (1973), for example, recommends 20 observations per variable, while Tucker and Chase (1980) suggest a minimum of 200 observations with that number being increased as more variables are included in the model. Few other writers offer such specific suggestions, but all imply a similar conclusion: Canonical correlation should be applied only to large samples.

The reasoning behind this suggestion is that the calculation of the R_C is based solely on the bivariate correlations between and among the variables in the X and Y set. The number of observations, N, which produced these Pearson r's does not enter into these calculations, however. Thus the procedure for calculating R_C would be the same, regardless of whether the bivariate r's result from 15 or 1500 observations. From previous discussions, you will recall that Pearson r's based on small samples are likely to be unrepresentative of the population, containing large components of error due to random and extraneous factors. The procedure, however, has no way of taking the sample size into account. Unlike the F-ratio, t-test, or even the Pearson r itself, R_C is insensitive to N. Consequently, the burden falls on the investigator to ensure that the sample is sufficiently large and thus representative of the population under investigation.

Statistical Procedures When X Is Categorical

Categorical variables whose level of measurement is strictly nominal are included in the GLM whenever it is necessary to represent the membership of an observation or subject in a discrete group, category, or classification. The characteristics and possible origins of categorical variables were outlined in Chapter 12. Such variables have traditionally been associated with controlled experiments, and the typical approach to their analysis has been ANOVA. It was demonstrated, however, that ANOVA is really the GLM in disguise. It capitalizes on the unique characteristics inherent in the GLM when the X variables are categorical, thus allowing the calculations to be greatly reduced and simplified.

The previous discussion of ANOVA and the GLM focused exclusively on dichotomous classification and the bivariate model (a). In this section, the relationship will be extended and generalized to: (1) more complex forms of ANOVA, including a brief discussion of ANOVA with more than one independent variable; and (2) forms of ANOVA where multiple outcome or dependent measures are available—multivariate analysis of variance or MANOVA. Each of these procedures will be shown to be a special case of the GLM.

Analysis of Variance—ANOVA

The basic purpose of ANOVA is to decompose the overall variation in the criterion or dependent variable into two independent pieces: that which can be accounted for by the systematic classification or manipulation of the investigator, and that which cannot—i.e., random, uncontrolled error. As described by Eq. 12.3,

$$SS_{\text{Total}} = SS_{BG} + SS_{WG} \tag{12.3}$$

For dichotomous classifications, it was shown that this decomposition could be accomplished by either ANOVA procedures or by the simplest form of the GLM, model (a). By simply dummy-coding the group membership variable, the bivariate model produced the same results as ANOVA. More importantly, it was shown that ANOVA *is* the GLM for models where such dummy codes are included.

As these concepts are generalized to situations with k groups (where $k > 2$), the principles introduced in Chapter 12 remain intact. For example, the conceptual and calculational approach to within-group or error variation remains the same. It is still the sum of the within-group sums-of-squares, or symbolically,

$$SS_{WG} = \sum_{j=1}^{k} \sum_{i=1}^{n_j} (Y_{ij} - \bar{Y}_j)^2 \tag{12.6}$$

When generalized, the only difference is that more than two groups contribute to this estimate of random variation.

Similarly, the concept of between-groups variation for k groups is a direct extension of the dichotomous situation. As defined by Eq. 12.5,

$$SS_{BG} = \sum_{j=1}^{k} n_j (\bar{Y}_j - \bar{\bar{Y}})^2 \tag{12.5}$$

From the standpoint of ANOVA, this approach to estimating the systematic variance is the same regardless of how many discrete groups or classifications are involved. Because Eqs. 12.5 and 12.6 are based on the special characteristics of a dummy-coded GLM, they do not change.

What does change, however, is the form of the GLM itself. When $k > 2$, the relationship between the set of dummy-coded explanatory variables and the criterion variable must be represented by model (b). Each dummy variable is capable of symbolizing membership in one and only one group. Thus, if there are k groups, model (b) must contain $k - 1$ explanatory variables, $k - 1$ weighting coefficients or B_i, and an intercept term, a. The last or kth group is not directly symbolized, but rather is represented by the fact that its observations are not included in the other groups.

This extension to k groups does not alter the special characteristics of the model. The predicted values still turn out to be the means of the k groups. This is the primary attribute upon which ANOVA so successfully capitalizes to simplify the calculation of both between-groups and within-groups sums-of-squares. Despite this calculational equivalence, there is a conceptual difference. The estimate of the systematic or between-groups variation, SS_{BG}, is now composed of $k - 1$ sources of variation. Although the error term, SS_{WG}, is generally left as defined by Eq. 12.6, the SS_{BG} can be decomposed into $k - 1$ smaller pieces. Similar to the concept of semipartial correlation, each of these components can then be individually tested for significance.

In most ANOVA problems, the interest of the investigator is on these component parts, rather than on the more global relationship. While it is possible and on occasion desirable to obtain the R^2 statistic for the entire model, the overall index of shared variance is frequently not of primary interest. Instead, the investigator is concerned with how this overall shared variation is distributed among its $k - 1$ sources—i.e., the independent or explanatory variables and various comparisons among the groups they comprise. As a general rule, the more complex the ANOVA design, the less the investigator's interest in the variance explained by the model as a whole.

One-way ANOVA. The first and most obvious extension of dichotomous classification comes about by simply increasing the number of categories used to classify the observations or subjects. This approach is referred to as one-way ANOVA, because the additional categories continue to be subdivisions of a single variable or (in ANOVA parlance) factor. For the researcher, the advantage of including additional categories is increased discrimination, i.e., a more accurate labeling of the theoretically salient differences among the subjects. For example, it would be possible to dichotomize a variable like marital status into the categories "married" and "not married." More information might be gained, however, if the latter category were divided further into "single," "divorced," and "widowed." It is reasonable to assume that these labels represent considerably different experiences with matrimony, and thus might better explain the variance of some specified criterion variable.

An extended example of one-way ANOVA was presented in Chapter 12, although no attempt was made to link it to the GLM. Recall that the hypothetical example of an experimental study of brainstorming contained two manipulated conditions (Method$_1$ and Method$_2$) and a control group; that is, $k = 3$. A significant difference was discovered somewhere among the three groups, which in the present context is equivalent to finding a significant R^2. Further, it was shown that at least one after-the-fact comparison (Method$_2$ versus Control) was significant, even when it was compared to an appropriately modified critical value.

To make this problem amenable to analysis by model (b), $k - 1$ or 2 dummy-coded variables must be created. Although the actual calculations will not be presented (the results would be the same), it will be instructive to briefly examine these codes. Table 13.4 (p. 262) presents the 1/0 coding in abbreviated form. It suggests that all of the subjects in Method$_1$ receive a 1 for X_1 and a 0 for X_2, while exactly the reverse is true for the subjects in Method$_2$. The subjects in the Control groups never receive a 1, however. This indicates that they belong to neither of the experimental groups, and thus by the process of elimination must be control subjects.

To complete this analysis, these dummy codes would be inserted into model (b)

TABLE 13.4. Dummy Coding for One-way ANOVA with $k = 3$ (Each member of Group would receive same X_1 and X_2 Code)

Group	X_1	X_2
Method$_1$	1	0
Method$_2$	0	1
Control	0	0

and the calculations would be performed (ideally by computer). The results would indicate the size of the R^2 statistic and test it for significance. A significant R^2 would indicate that a difference somewhere among some means was large enough to create significant between-group variation. This is the most global test available, and almost certainly would be followed up by some more specific comparisons.

The nature of these comparisons is a direct result of the dummy codes. By changing the numbers used to symbolize membership in the test groups, a researcher can make a variety of comparisons among the three means. For example, in Chapter 12 it was shown that 1/0 codes have the desirable property of producing B's which are the *difference* between the group coded 1 and the last group which is always coded 0. An analysis using the codes in Table 13.4, therefore, would produce and test B's which represent comparisons between the two experimental conditions and the control group: $B_1 = (\bar{Y}_1 - \bar{Y}_C)$; and $B_2 = (\bar{Y}_2 - \bar{Y}_C)$. Other codes possess other properties, some desirable, some not. The specific choices involve a combination of the substantive question involved and the particular properties of a given set of dummy codes (see Cohen & Cohen, 1975; Kerlinger & Pedhazur, 1973).

In summary, one-way ANOVA where $k > 2$ is a direct extension of model (a) and dichotomous classification. In theory, the number of groups one may include is unlimited, but the pragmatics of sample size and statistical power cannot be ignored. Each group must possess a sufficient number of observations to estimate accurately the within-groups and between-groups components of variance. Regardless of the number of groups, however, one-way ANOVA can be analyzed by model (b) by simply including $k - 1$ dummy-coded explanatory variables. In addition, some forethought about the choice of dummy codes will allow the investigator to test simultaneously the global question of difference and specific comparisons of interest with only one run through the computer. No by-hand calculation need be involved, and considerable time and expense can be saved.

Factorial ANOVA. The discussion thus far has been focused on the situation where the subjects or observations have been classified into k groups on a single factor or dimension. Frequently, however, an investigator will wish to *cross-classify* the subjects on two or more factors. This amounts to assigning the subjects to a group (or experimentally manipulating the subjects within a group) based on two or more attributes or characteristics. Some writers refer to these cross-classification designs as two-way ANOVA, three-way ANOVA, etc., but we employ the label factorial ANOVA to refer to all designs which contain more than a single classification factor.

It is assumed that the additional classification factors will increase the proportion of the Y variance which can be explained. In many ways, this is equivalent to the investigator believing that the error variance is not completely random. Instead, it contains systematic sources of variation. If these nonrandom factors can be operationalized and included in the model as explanatory variables, the error variance will be decreased, while the systematic variance will be increased by that same amount. Whether such increments to the explained variance are significant is an empirical question to be answered only by the appropriate test of statistical inference.

This extension can be illustrated by returning to the previous hypothetical example of the experimental investigation of brainstorming. In addition to the hypothesis about differences between methods of organizing and conducting brainstorming sessions, a researcher might reasonably assume that differences in the cohesiveness of the groups would also affect their performance. Highly cohesive groups might exhibit increased motivation to produce more ideas, better ideas, and so forth. Accordingly, the researcher would experimentally manipulate the four-person groups on the cohesiveness dimension, as well as on the original dimension of methods for conducting brainstorming.

The results of this additional manipulation is that each group is cross-classified on two experimental factors. Figure 13.3 illustrates one of the several ways this cross-classification might be performed. This type of cross-classification would be described as a 3×2 factorial design, containing three categories of brainstorming method (control is now considered a method, i.e., no instructions), and two levels of cohesiveness—high and low. From a statistical standpoint, the designation 3×2 is meaningful, because it indicates that there are $k = 3 \times 2 = 6$ groups to be included in this analysis.

Figure 13.3 (p. 264) displays the symbols for the means of each of the six cross-classifications or "cells" of this design. It also displays the marginal means for the rows and columns. The marginal means represent only the effects of their particular classification, and ignore entirely any effects which might be introduced by cross-classifying their particular row or column. The marginal means, therefore, are those which would have been obtained if two separate one-way ANOVA's had been conducted on the brainstorming and cohesiveness factors. Shortly, it will be shown that if certain statistical requirements are met, this is exactly what happens. Factorial ANOVA becomes a set of one-way ANOVA's, with the distinct advantage that the error variance has been greatly reduced because additional, nonrandom factors have been extracted from it.

Despite this cross-classification, the analysis of this problem by model (b) of the GLM is a relatively direct extension. Because $k = 6$, it will be necessary to include $k - 1 = 5$ dummy-coded variables in the model. The origin of several of these is obvious. The three methods of brainstorming can be represented by two dummy variables. For simplicity, assume they are the same 1/0 codes presented earlier in Table 13.3. Cohesiveness, on the other hand, requires only one dummy variable; again, it can be a single 1/0 representation. Thus, three of the five dummy-codes X_i's are accounted for by simply combining one-way classifications.

The two remaining X_i's are needed to represent what is called *interaction*. Simply put, interaction is the distinction between factorial ANOVA and simply adding together a series of one-way classifications. In fact, interaction is frequently referred to as an estimate of "nonadditivity" (Winer, 1971, p. 318). It is best explained by returning to the current example. As described, the two dummy variables for brainstorming totally ignore the existence of a cohesiveness dimension. They are the same regardless of whether cohesiveness is included in the design. The same is true of the 1/0 coding for cohesiveness. It ignores the fact that the two levels of cohesiveness have been subdivided into three methods of brainstorming.

FIGURE 13.3. Illustration of 3 × 2 Cross-Classification ANOVA.

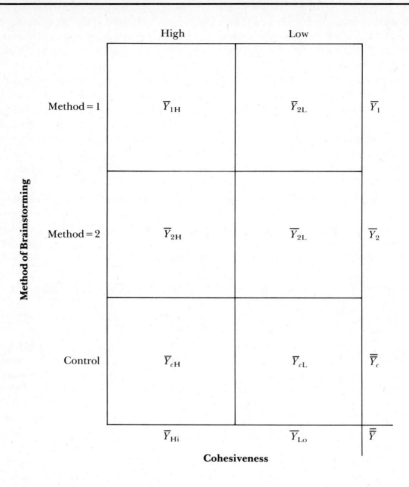

In other words, these variables are coded as if the effects of cross-classification do not exist, as if their effects can simply be added together. In many instances, however, the assumption of additivity is incorrect. For example, assume that Method₁ was a significantly better method of brainstorming than Method₂, if and only if the groups were highly cohesive. It might be that this method requires the motivation and esprit de corps that is characteristic of cohesive groups in order to be successful. In contrast, assume that Method₂ is significantly better than Method₁ for groups low in cohesiveness. Because it does not require the qualities which characterize high cohesiveness, Method₂ performs better in this condition. More succinctly stated, the difference between methods of brainstorming is completely dependent on which level of cohesiveness is being considered. As a result, the marginal means are no longer valid indicators of this difference. Because they are based on the assumption of additivity, tests of the marginal means should not be interpreted when a significant interaction is detected.

How, then, should such detection proceed? The statistical opposite of additivity is multiplication. Accordingly, the final two dummy variables are included to assess the presence of a multiplicative (i.e., nonadditive) relationship. To obtain the appropriate coding, the two dummy codes for brainstorming are simply multiplied times the single dummy variable for cohesiveness: thus, $X_4 = X_1X_3$; $X_5 = X_2X_3$. Table 13.5 displays the five dummy-coded explanatory variables which would then be inserted into model (b).

In the subsequent analysis, the pivotal test is of the two variables symbolizing the interaction. If X_4 and X_5 are found to be nonsignificant, the investigator can legitimately interpret the *main effects*. That is, the two one-way analyses can be treated as additive, and the marginal means can be directly interpreted. If these terms are significant, on the other hand, alternative analytic and interpretive strategies must be adopted. Although the details of these alternative approaches will not be discussed, they involve specific combinations of the cell means which do not assume additivity (see Cohen & Cohen, 1975; Winer, 1971).

Before concluding this section, we will note that the 3 × 2 design discussed above is still relatively simple. It contains only two factors and thus only a single interaction. Additional experimental or classification factors could easily be added, but because every factor can potentially interact with every other factor, the degree of complexity of the analysis increases rapidly. From a statistical point of view, however, the number of additional factors which may be included is limitless, subject only to the pragmatic constraints of (1) a sufficient number of subjects, and (2) the ability of the investigator to interpret the more complex findings which may result.

Multivariate Analysis of Variance—MANOVA

The natural extension or generalization of the ANOVA is to a multivariate analysis of variance or MANOVA. As a procedure associated with model (c), the purpose of MANOVA is to assess relationships between two sets of X and Y variables. In MANOVA, however, the explanatory information contained in the X set is in the form of categorization or classification into discrete groups. Thus, dummy-coding of some form is used to symbolize the X variables for inclusion into the GLM.

For all practical purposes, all of the information presented about dummy-coding explanatory variables in ANOVA is equally applicable to MANOVA. As Harris (1975,

TABLE 13.5. Dummy Coding for 3 × 2 Factorial ANOVA with $k = 6$ (Each member of Group would receive same X_1–X_5 Codes)

Group	X_1	X_2	X_3	X_1X_3 $\hat{X}_4$	X_2X_3 $\hat{X}_5$
HiCo-Method$_1$	1	0	1	1	0
LoCo-Method$_1$	1	0	0	0	0
HiCo-Method$_2$	0	1	1	0	1
LoCo-Method$_2$	0	1	0	0	0
HiCo-Control	0	0	1	0	0
LoCo-Control	0	0	0	0	0

p. 15) asserts, "a multivariate counterpart exists for every univariate analysis of variance design." In terms of models (b) and (c) in Table 13.1, the conceptualization and coding of the X_i variables on the right-hand side of the models are identical.

As models (b) and (c) further suggest, the primary difference between ANOVA and MANOVA is that the latter endeavors to include more than one outcome or criterion measure. Model (c) contains q Y variables, where $q > 1$. These several outcome measures must be weighted and linearly combined to produce a single predicted value. Statistically, the goal of MANOVA is to produce a weighted linear combination of the Y variables whose predicted values are maximally different among the various groups or classifications.

The application of MANOVA is clearly illustrated in a recent study by Daly, Richmond, and Leth (1979). These researchers were interested in the relationship between social communicative anxiety and perceptions of an individual's qualifications for and subsequent satisfaction with a job. Phrased as a question: Would individuals with high social communicative anxiety be perceived differently by potential employers than individuals with low anxiety? To examine this question, the researchers prepared two descriptions of a potential job applicant, one corresponding to high and one corresponding to low social communicative anxiety. Thus, high and low anxiety were treated as a single, dichotomous classification variable.

A variety of perceived characteristics of the two types of job applicants were rated on seven 9-point scales, which addressed such questions as willingness to interview the applicant, likelihood of recommending for a job, how successful in the future, how much training would be required, and so forth. Although each of these dimensions was analyzed by a simple bivariate ANOVA (see Chapter 12), the primary question was the relationship between communicative anxiety and the entire, combined *set* of perceptions which might result.

Table 13.6 contains a summary of the results for these several analyses. This table displays the sample sizes and the means for the seven outcome measures for both the high and low anxiety groups. The F-ratios and significance levels represent the results of the individual ANOVA's. Notice that all but one of the univariate ANOVA's resulted in significant differences between the high and low anxiety groups.

This table also displays the weights or the B_i's by which each criterion variable

TABLE 13.6. Results of Multivariate Analysis of Variance (MANOVA)

Variable	Low ($N = 21$)	High ($N = 20$)	$F(1137)$	P	Weight(B
Willingness to Interview	3.42	5.65	41.06	.0001	$-.07$
Recommended Salary	11,905.24	11,525.00	.03	ns	$-.25$
Necessity of Training	5.05	6.55	4.50	.04	$-.67$
Get Along with Co-workers	2.76	5.65	20.97	.0001	.03
Likely to Recommend	2.24	7.00	140.28	.0001	-1.49
Projected Success	2.52	6.30	78.47	.0001	$-.24$
Expected Satisfaction	6.09	12.75	46.66	.0001	.66
	$F = 24.68;\ df = 7,31;\ p < .0001$				

SOURCE: Daly, Richmond, and Leth (1979, p. 23). Published by permission of Transaction, Inc. from *Human Communication Research,* Vol. 6 Copyright © 1979 by the International Communication Association.

was multiplied to form the best weighted linear combination. Two pieces of information can be obtained from these weights. First, the relative size of the weights is indicative of the contribution each variable makes to the multivariate difference between the groups. Second, the sign of the weight indicates the direction of difference; in this case, a negative sign reflects less favorable perceptions of the high anxiety applications. This information suggests that three dimensions—Recommend, Training, and Satisfaction—were primarily responsible for the perceived difference between high and low anxiety applicants.

Finally, the authors report (p. 22) that the overall test statistic for the MANOVA was significant ($F = 24.68$; $df = 7,31$; $p < .001$). Hence, when this set of perceptions is taken as a whole, the high and low anxiety applicants are viewed much differently.

Although we have attempted to provide a brief introduction to and example of MANOVA, we have not addressed the most fundamental question: Why use it? If a researcher is faced with the task of analyzing q separate outcome measures, why not simply conduct q univariate ANOVA's? In the example displayed in Table 13.6, why not stop with the seven individual ANOVA's? After all, they would be simple both to calculate and to interpret. Basically, there are two reasons to avoid such a practice. The first involves an inherent characteristic of linear combinations, namely, intercorrelations among the combined variables. If the outcome measures are correlated, then so will be the individual ANOVA's and their univariate F-ratios. Univariate analysis and interpretation, however, will almost inevitably assume that the q Y variables are independent or uncorrelated. In Table 13.6, for example, six of the seven ANOVA's were significant, but only three variables (Recommend, Training, and Satisfaction) received relatively large weights. This difference can be traced directly to the fact that the seven outcome measures were intercorrelated. Hence, a smaller number of dimensions (in this case, three) contain the bulk of the information carried by the original seven. Whenever these interrelationships are not taken into account, the potential exists for spurious or erroneous inference to result.

The second reason for employing MANOVA instead of q ANOVA's concerns error-rate inflation. As suggested in Chapter 12, the probability of committing a Type I error for a set of tests is considerably larger than that for each individual test. In contrast, MANOVA is designed to ensure that tests on the weighted linear combinations maintain the Type I error rate preset by the investigator (e.g., $p < .05$). If a MANOVA test is significant, the investigator can be confident that the differences are not due to excessive and artificially inflated error rates. The probability of error is always present, but at least MANOVA maintains that probability at a specified and acceptable level.

Procedure When X is Both Continuous and Categorical

One of the justifications provided for so strongly emphasizing the GLM is its flexibility, its ability to incorporate a variety of statistical procedures under a general conceptual umbrella. The same basic model can contain either continuous explanatory variables as in multiple regression and canonical correlation, or categorical explanatory variables as in ANOVA and MANOVA. The purpose of this section is to suggest that the GLM can contain both in the same analytic procedure. The capability to include any type of explanatory information represents the ultimate flexibility of the GLM.

The discussion to follow will briefly overview two such procedures: analysis of covariance and multivariate analysis of covariance. Before proceeding, a brief aside. The procedures to be discussed have their origins rooted squarely in traditional ANOVA thinking. As a result, they are accurate, but relatively narrow approaches to the way data should be conceptualized and analyzed. Their incorporation under the umbrella of the GLM broadens their outlook considerably. Nevertheless, we will attempt to preserve the flavor of the original ANOVA thinking, while also indicating the advantages to be gained from the more flexible perspective of the GLM.

Analysis of Covariance—ANCOVA

The analysis of covariance (ANCOVA) is traditionally viewed as an alternative to the experimental control of explanatory variables. In the course of designing an experiment, a variable thought to be related to the outcome measure may not be amenable to classification or experimental manipulation. It may be impossible, for example, for a researcher to neatly classify his or her subjects into discrete groups based on some variable such as age, intelligence, amount of TV viewing, information processing abilities, and so forth. The requisite number of subjects may not be available or, alternatively, the available sample of subjects is simply not easily divisible into the necessary categories.

Despite the impossibility of appropriate classification, it is assumed by the researcher that such a variable affects the subjects' response on the outcome measure. Frequently, variables of this type are referred to as "nuisance" or "distractor" variables. Although they are related to the criterion measure, they are not considered theoretically salient, and are not included as part of the experiment. Rather, they are viewed as "getting in the way." Accordingly, the traditional purpose of ANCOVA is to substitute statistical control of this type of variable in the place of experimental control. In other words, because this "nuisance" factor could not be categorized or controlled experimentally, ANCOVA treats it as continuous and removes or partials out its effects prior to assessing the contribution and significance of the categorical, independent variables.

An example may help clarify. Assume that an investigator is interested in the effects of three different types of persuasive messages in convincing subjects to engage in proper dental hygiene. The differences in these messages are theoretically salient. In addition, the investigator believes that previous experience with dental problems (e.g., cavities, extractions, etc.) might influence this outcome. Subjects who possess a history of dental pathologies might, before the start of the study, possess different hygienic practices from subjects who do not. (Perhaps a few dozen hours in a dentist's chair are necessary to truly appreciate this example.)

Obviously, random assignment to experimental groups would eliminate any systematic effects of this variable. But the subjects within these groups would still vary considerably due to this factor, thus producing an unacceptably large error component—SS_{WG}. However, if this history could be validly operationalized and measured, ANCOVA could be applied to remove its influence. In essence, adjusting each subject's outcome score for their past history of dental pathology is statistically equivalent to "equalizing" the subjects on this dimension prior to the experiment. Any subsequent differences which are detected must therefore be due solely to the differential influence of the persuasive messages.

The statistical logic of ANCOVA is relatively simple. Assume the researcher starts with a continuous nuisance or "covariate" variable labeled A. He or she also possesses several categorical variables from either a one-way or factorial ANOVA design; for simplicity, label this *set* of variables B. Recall, the goal is to remove the effects of A prior to assessing the systematic variance explained by set B. Accordingly, ANCOVA would first assess the relationship between variable A and the outcome measure Y. For heuristic purposes, assume this is a simple bivariate regression model (a). This model would produce a r^2 which is the proportion of the Y variance which could be explained by A, and $1 - r^2$ which is the proportion of Y which could not. The former would then be discarded—it is extraneous or nuisance variation which the investigator wants to get rid of.

What remains, therefore, are the residuals (the e_i) and the residual variation $(1 - r^2)$ from this bivariate model. The ANCOVA is completed by using the categorical variables to perform a standard ANOVA on these residual values. The residual values are free from the effects of the covariate A, which have been discarded along with the proportion of the variance represented by r^2. Any differences which are discovered by the ANOVA, therefore, are due solely to the effects of classification or manipulation of the subjects.

Technically, this description of ANCOVA is incorrect, for it implies that the procedure consists of two separate analyses: a bivariate regression, followed by a separate ANOVA. In actual calculation, the continuous covariate and the categorical variables are included in the same model. What results, therefore, is quite similar to the "incremental explanation" approach discussed earlier. The categorical variables are entered into the model "last." Hence, the amount of Y variance these variables explain is over and beyond that already explained by the covariate variable A. It turns out, therefore, that ANCOVA is the same analysis as multiple regression, only both continuous and categorical variables have been included in the model.

As described thus far, traditional ANCOVA is a potentially useful procedure. Its ability to statistically control the effects of extraneous factors is a handy statistical tool. It is also evident, however, that its traditional and exclusive application to controlled experiments considerably narrows its range of applicability. When viewed from the perspective of the GLM, ANCOVA's range of application becomes much broader. This increased breadth begins with a fundamental shift in conceptualization. It is no longer necessary to view the covariate variables as carrying the effects of nuisance or distractor factors. Instead, they are more generally viewed as factors the investigator wishes to statistically control. Perhaps they create extraneous and unwanted variance in the outcome measure; or perhaps the investigator wants to control them in order to gain more precise insight into other relationships. Under this latter perspective, the covariates are not viewed as inconvenient nuisances to be summarily dismissed and forgotten. Instead, they may be theoretically salient factors in which the researcher is seriously interested. Their momentary control or statistical isolation, however, facilitates the statistical exploration of the data and may enhance the theoretic understanding of the substantive problem.

In addition to this conceptual shift, viewing ANCOVA from the perspective of the GLM offers several statistical advantages as well. First, the GLM allows several covariates to be included in the model. Thus, the effects of a set of several variables might be removed from the outcome measure prior to assessing the effects of a second set of so-called "explanatory" variables. Further, under the auspices of the GLM, the covariate set is *not* restricted to continuous variables. It may be composed of any combination of continuous and categorical variables. This fact greatly extends the type of information which can be taken into account prior to assessing the more theoretically salient relationships (see Courtright & Baran, 1980, for an example of multiple covariates).

Finally, the GLM provides the greatest generality to ANCOVA by not restricting the set B explanatory variables to categorizations or classifications. These variables may also be composed of any combination of categorical or continuous information. By generalizing the notion of semipartial correlation and uniquely explained variance, the process of adjustment can be extended to any type of data. The result, most importantly, is that ANCOVA is no longer restricted to purely experimental contexts. It is applicable to any set of data where the researcher believes certain factors should be "equalized" or held constant prior to assessing another set of relationships.

Multivariate Analysis of Covariance—MANCOVA

The discussion of the extension of ANOVA to MANOVA began with the basic premise that every univariate design has its multivariate counterpart. The same can surely be said of the generalization of ANCOVA to MANCOVA. The latter procedure is characteristic of model (c) in Table 13.1. The goal of this model remains to assess the relationship between two sets of variables—X and Y. In MANCOVA, however, these multivariate relationships are assessed only after the effects of a third set of variables— the covariate set—are removed or statistically controlled.

The similarity between models (b) and (c) again resides on the right-hand side of the equal sign. The previous characterizations of both the covariate and the explanatory variables remains unaltered. Each may be conceived of as a set of several variables, and each may contain any combination of continuous or categorical information. Model (c) thus continues the tradition of extreme flexibility. The major difference, of course, is that model (c) includes q Y variables in the analysis.

Heuristically, the MANCOVA analysis may be viewed as a multivariate generalization of the "incremental explanation" approach. It begins by conducting a canonical correlation between the set of outcome measures and the covariate set, A. A second canonical correlation is conducted between the Y set and the combination of the A and X sets. The difference in the variation explained by these two analyses is due solely to the incremental effects of the X set of explanatory variables. Because they were entered into the model "last," their ability to explain Y variation is independent of A—it is nonredundant or *unique*.

This incrementally explained variation is then subjected to a test of statistical inference. If it is found to be significant, substantive interpretation may begin. Unfortunately, the multivariate nature of the procedure makes interpretation of the contribution of the individual variables somewhat difficult. As with MANOVA, the weighted linear combination of the Y variables changes for every X variable. As Cohen and Cohen (1975, p. 438) point out, because the combination of Y variables changes, interpreting the individual X variables is like "shooting at a moving target." To their credit, these authors offer several alternative strategies by which investigators may improve their marksmanship. A discussion of these strategies, however, would go considerably beyond the bounds of an overview. Thus, we recommend highly these suggestions, but must forego their explication and amplification.

■ *Conclusion*

Perhaps the most appropriate way to conclude this chapter is to return to a predominant theme in this book: Empirical methods and statistical procedures are merely tools to aid the communication researcher in the development and examination of substantive theory. As methods of measurement and statistical analysis become more complex and sophisticated, this basic theme all too often gets lost in the shuffle—even by experienced researchers. The mechanical and uncritical application of these methods is too common: One simply constructs the appropriate model, partials a little variance here and there, and (poof) out pops knowledge.

It is impossible to imagine a more inaccurate conceptualization of the research process. No procedure—no matter how sophisticated it may be—is worth its weight in computer paper if it does not produce meaningful and interpretable results. We would suggest as a rule of thumb that the best empirical methods are the simplest methods which still meaningfully answer the theoretic questions of the investigator. Consider the results of a recent investigation which found, after a series of complex multivariate analyses, that television viewers perceived the prototypical female comedy character to be best represented by Lou Grant. We rest our case . . . .

14 Chapter

Cross-Classification Analysis of Nominal Variables

The adoption of the GLM as the basic and most general data-analytic model provides the researcher with the breadth and flexibility to handle a wide variety of empirical situations. One situation where the GLM is generally not recommended for use, however, is when *all* of the variables of interest are nominal or categorical in their level of measurement. Experience has shown that a GLM composed completely of categorical variables poses problems in terms of the accuracy of its estimation and testing, and thus eventually in the validity of its substantive interpretation.

As a result, statisticians have developed alternative methods and procedures for describing, testing, and interpreting relationships among such variables. It is not unreasonable to suggest, in fact, that the volume of literature devoted to this topic rivals that which has been written about the GLM. Some of the recommended approaches are basic and quite simple, while others are complex and sophisticated attempts to construct nominal data analogues of the GLM (see Bishop, Fienberg, & Holland, 1975).

This chapter will focus only on basic procedures used to statistically analyze nominal level data. As before, the discussion will begin at a conceptual level by presenting the *logic* which underlies these approaches. Subsequently, methods of calculation will be presented and illustrated by several examples.

Nominal-Level Relationships

The characteristics and origins of categorical variables have been discussed previously. Briefly, a variable of interest is operationalized by a set of mutually exclusive and exhaustive categories. Each observation is then classified into one and only one of the categories based on the attribute which that category identifies. In short, each observation is placed in a group with similar observations. The measurement process, then, is simply one of naming or labeling observations with numerical or alphabetical symbols. The primary characteristic of such nominal grouping is that the categories are incapable of being rank-ordered along some dimension. The concepts of more than and less than simply are not applicable.

Categorical variables, therefore, are characterized by the absence of what might be called "real" measurement. Despite this absence, the goal of the investigator remains exactly the same: to describe and assess relationships among and between these nominal variables. But the characteristics associated with nominal classification require a subtle reconceptualization of what it means for two categorical variables to be "related." The basic principles of relatedness do not change, but the manner in which they manifest themselves must take into account the inherent nature of the data.

The statistical principle which operationalized relationships between two continuous variables was that of covariation. Two variables were related if their values covaried, if the position of an observation on the continuum of measurement for variable X was affected by or related to that observation's position on the continuum for variable Y. This principle was explained in some detail in Chapter 9 and used as the basis for the development of the GLM. For categorical variables, however, there are no continua of measurement on which an observation or subject can be placed. Instead, there are simply memberships in discrete groups or categories. Thus, while the investigator still desires to know whether a person's "score" on one categorical variable influences or is influenced by that person's "score" on the other variable, the concepts associated with direct or inverse covariation will not provide the answer.

The answer, instead, must come from the categories themselves. The concept of relationship must be recast in terms of group membership. The researcher must ask: Is the category into which a person is classified on variable A influenced by (or does it influence) the category into which the same person is classified on variable B? For example, a researcher interested in politics and political communication might ask: Does an individual's race (black, white, chicano, etc.) influence the choice of the political party with which he or she would identify (Democrat, Republican, Independent)? Since neither variable is measured on a continuum, the concepts associated with covariation are of little use. The only available information exists in the frequencies and/or percentages of observations which are actually classified in the categories.

In such situations, the relationship between the categories of two nominal level variables is assessed through a process of *cross-classification*. Cross-classification was first encountered during the discussion of factorial ANOVA, where an experimenter may decide to simultaneously manipulate the subjects on two or more factors. The effects of such manipulations are then assessed by measuring the subjects on an outcome or criterion measure. The means of the outcome measure for each cell of the cross-classification matrix are then compared by the ANOVA procedure.

As shall be seen, there are several similarities between this type of ANOVA design and the cross-classification of nominal variables. The major conceptual difference is that the latter approach includes no outcome measure. There is no additional criterion measure on which the subjects are evaluated. Rather, the focus is on the cross-classification matrix itself, that is, on the relationship among the categorical groupings. The data of interest, therefore, become the number or frequency of observations which are cross-classified into each cell. How many blacks are Democrats, Republicans, or Independents? How many whites? And so forth. To the extent that these frequencies deviate from random expectations (as always, a question to be addressed formally by a test of statistical inference), it can be concluded that joint or concomitant membership in these categories is systematically related.

These basic ideas are illustrated further in Figure 14.1. This figure displays a 3×3 matrix in which N observations have been cross-classified on two categorical variables. This matrix is frequently referred to as a *contingency table* or *cross-tabulation table*. Figure 14.1 (p. 274) presents the symbolic notation usually employed in such matrices. The small n stands for the number of observations in a cell, and the subscripts identify the particular cell. Thus, n_{ij} indicates the number of observations which are jointly classified in the ith row and the jth column. The row and column marginal frequencies are indicated by the inclusion of a $(+)$ sign. The symbol n_{i+} represents the number of observations in the entire ith row, while n_{+j} symbolizes the same feature for the entire jth column.

In many instances, it is desirable to replace the actual frequencies with percentages or proportions. This is especially true with large samples of several thousand observations, where the raw frequencies become difficult to interpret meaningfully. This replacement, however, is easily accomplished by Eq. 14.1,

$$p_{ij} = \frac{n_{ij}}{N} \tag{14.1}$$

where p_{ij} is the percentage of all N observations which have been cross-classified into cell$_{ij}$. This percentage may also be interpreted as the *probability* of a single observation simultaneously possessing attribute$_i$ and attribute$_j$.

This symbolic notation is admittedly somewhat abstract, but will be used later to develop additional concepts. Figure 14.2 makes these ideas a bit more concrete by

FIGURE 14.1. Symbolic Notation Used in Cross-Classification Analysis.

	B_1	B_2	B_3	
A_1	n_{11}	n_{12}	n_{13}	n_{1+}
A_2	n_{21}	n_{22}	n_{23}	n_{2+}
A_3	n_{31}	n_{32}	n_{33}	n_{3+}
	n_{+1}	n_{+2}	n_{+3}	N

employing numbers instead of letters. This matrix displays the hypothetical cross-classification of $N = 100$ observations. Further, it has been constructed purposely to exhibit a complete absence of relationship or association between variables A and B. Notice that the row marginal frequencies show a perfect three-way division among the observations; an observation is equally likely to be in any of the three categories for variable A. In terms of variable B, 50 of the observations are classified into the third category ($n_{+3} = 50$), while the remaining observations are evenly split between categories 1 and 2 ($n_{+1} = n_{+2} = 25$). For future reference, it is worth noting that because $N = 100$, each of the cell and marginal frequencies can easily be converted to percentages: $p_{ij} = n_{ij}/100$.

Conceptualizing Statistical Independence

As suggested, this cross-classification table was constructed in such a way as to ensure total independence between variables A and B. A brief discussion of this situation should facilitate an understanding of the logic of nominal level relationships. In the

FIGURE 14.2. Hypothetical Cross-Classification Illustrating Statistical Independence.

	B_1	B_2	B_3	
A_1	9	8	17	34
A_2	8	9	16	33
A_3	8	8	17	33
	25	25	50	100

discussion of factorial ANOVA, we said that the presence or absence of an interaction was the key to determining how the several, combined one-way ANOVA's should be treated. If the interaction was tested and found nonsignificant, the effects of the several one-way ANOVA's in the design could simply be "added together." Accordingly, interpretations could focus on the marginal means. The individual cell means could safely be ignored, because the absence of an interaction indicated that they merely reflected the direction and magnitude of the differences exhibited by the marginal means.

Unlike ANOVA, of course, cross-classification analysis does not include an outcome measure. Instead, interest is focused solely on the frequency of observations which are classified into each category. Nevertheless, the logic of an interaction in ANOVA and a relationship or association in cross-classification analysis is remarkably similar. In both, the key concept is the presence or absence of symmetry between the cell entries (whether they be means or frequencies) and the marginal entries. Do the entries in the rows or columns of cells parallel those in the margin? An affirmative answer in ANOVA indicates an absence of interaction. In cross-classification analysis, such parallelism indicates that the variables of interest are *not* related.

Figure 14.2 provides a clear numerical example of the type of symmetry which characterizes independence between two categorical variables. Recall that the observations for variable A were equally divided among the three categories of this variable. Accordingly, an examination of any single column should reveal a similar three-way division. Because each column only contains a specified percentage of the $N = 100$ observations, the actual frequencies will be different. Their distribution or pattern of division, nevertheless, should be the same. And so it is. With only slight deviation, each column's distribution of observations is parallel or symmetrical to the marginal distribution.

For complete independence to hold, however, a similar parallel structure must be exhibited between the individual rows and the row marginals. In this case, category 3 has twice as many observations as categories 1 and 2. An inspection of the three rows reveals that this pattern holds throughout. Again slight deviations are apparent, but in general the distribution of observations in each row is symmetrical with how the observations are distributed in the margin.

The finding that two categorical variables are completely independent or unrelated, therefore, indicates that the variables can be examined *separately* as two one-way frequency distributions. All of the pertinent information about these variables is contained in their marginal distributions. No additional insight is gained by their combination or cross-classification. The same logic can be stated in reverse: The frequency of observations in an individual cell of the matrix is completely determined by the number of observations in the row and column for that cell. Since there is no information about any cell which is not already available from the marginal frequencies, the cross-classification into cells is superfluous. The two categorical variables can be examined separately without any concern for the fact that they might be related.

Conceptualizing Statistical Relationships

From the previous description it is clear that a relationship between two categorical variables is characterized by just the opposite state of affairs. There is no parallelism or symmetry between the distributions of individual rows and columns and their respective marginal distributions. As a result, the marginal frequencies do *not* determine the frequencies in the individual cells. Alternatively stated, there *is* information to be gained from the cell frequencies which is not available from the row and column marginals considered separately.

Described in yet another way, a relationship exists when the cell frequencies deviate from the number of observations which would be "expected" by a simple and independent combination of the categories of variable A and variable B. This is not to suggest that some slight deviation will not always occur. Errors due to sampling will inevitably cause random fluctuations to surface. For a significant relationship to exist, these deviations must be substantial. They must exceed the difference which would be attributed solely to chance.

The procedure used to test the significance of these deviations will be presented shortly. In the meantime, we will use another hypothetical example to illustrate the concept of a relationship between two categorical variables. Figure 14.3 displays a cross-classification matrix whose marginal frequencies are exactly the same as those in the previous example. The cell frequencies, however, are completely different. An examina-

FIGURE 14.3. Hypothetical Cross-Classification Illustrating Statistical Relationship.

	B_1	B_2	B_3	
A_1	13	5	16	34
A_2	7	6	20	33
A_3	5	14	14	33
	25	25	50	100

tion of any row or column will clearly indicate that the pattern of symmetry which characterizes complete independence simply does not exist.

A similar conclusion will be reached by an inspection of the individual cells. Recall that because $N = 100$, each of the frequencies can be viewed simply as a percentage of the total sample. Accordingly, it is possible to take any cell, say A_3B_2, and calculate how many observations should be present if the two categorical variables are independent. The marginal frequency for row A_3 indicates that 33% of the sample has been classified into the third category on variable A, while the marginal frequency for column B_2 suggests that 25% of the total N has been classified into the second category on that variable. Hence, when cross-classified, cell$_{32}$ should contain 33% of 25% of the total sample; that is, $.33 \times .25 = .0825$ or 8.25% of N. The actual frequency of this cell is $n_{32} = 14$ (i.e., 14%), thus indicating a deviation of almost 6% from that which is expected. A similar inspection of the other cells will reveal additional deviations. Clearly, something is happening within these cells which cannot be accounted for by the independent contributions of the marginal distributions. This "something" is a systematic relationship between variables A and B.

The Chi-Square (χ^2) Test of Relationship

The reason for emphasizing the contrast between statistical independence and statistical association between nominal level variables will soon become apparent. The primary test of statistical inference used in cross-classification analysis is the χ^2 (pronounced Kī-square) test. This test of significance is designed specifically to assess the degree to which a cross-classification matrix deviates from the assumptions of independence. The test statistic is frequently referred to as the *goodness-of-fit* χ^2. As the null hypothesis, it advances a model of a cross-classification matrix which corresponds exactly to statistical independence. It proposes that the row and column frequencies will parallel their respective marginal frequencies with complete symmetry. To conduct the test, the χ^2 then examines how "good" the fit is between the obtained data and this hypothetical cross-classification. If the deviation between the model advanced by the null hypothesis and the actual data is sufficient to surpass the critical value of the test statistic, the χ^2 is considered significant and the presence of a nominal level relationship is established.

The χ^2 test of statistical inference is defined by Eq. 14.2.

$$\chi^2 = \sum_{\text{all cells}} \frac{(O - E)^2}{E} \tag{14.2}$$

where O is the obtained or actual frequency of observations in each cell and E is the frequency which would be "expected" under the assumption of complete independence. The logic of this test is that it combines into a single index the deviation from independence of the entire cross-classification matrix. The minor deviation of one or two cells from their expected frequencies is not sufficient. Only the combination of deviations exhibited by each and every cell can validly determine whether the matrix as a whole is significantly different from the pattern of symmetry proposed by the null hypothesis.

The logic and calculation of the expected frequency, E, is a direct extension of the notion of probability. If the two variables under consideration are independent, the probability of a single observation falling into cell$_{ij}$ is the joint probability of simultaneously being classified in row$_i$ and column$_j$. As illustrated in the prior example, joint probabilities are determined by multiplying the marginal probabilities or percentages. Thus, $p_{ij} = p_{i+}p_{+j}$. For example, for cell A_3B_2 in Figure 14.2 it was shown that $E = .25 \times .33 = .0825$.

The χ^2 statistic, however, employs frequencies rather than probabilities or percentages in its calculation. Thus, the expected probability must be converted to an *expected frequency* by applying Eq. 14.3.

$$E = N(p_{ij}) = N(p_{i+}p_{+j}) \tag{14.3}$$

In situations where the investigator has not previously converted the various cell and marginal frequencies to percentages, Eq. 14.3 requires a considerable amount of additional calculation. It can be shown that the same value of E can be obtained directly from the available marginal frequencies by Eq. 14.4.

$$E = \frac{n_{i+}n_{+j}}{N} \tag{14.4}$$

Either Eq. 14.3 or 14.4 must be applied to every cell of the cross-classification matrix. For example, a 3×3 matrix would require that nine expected frequencies be calculated. Once an expected frequency for each cell is determined, it can be compared to the obtained frequency for that cell and the χ^2 statistic (Eq. 14.2) can be calculated.

The final step in this process of statistical inference is to compare the obtained value of the χ^2 to the appropriate critical value. Appendix E contains a representative listing of such critical values for several different levels of significance. As is the case with all test statistics, the critical value changes depending on the degrees-of-freedom *(df)* associated with the test. If, however, the test statistic surpasses the critical value, the null hypothesis can be rejected and the relationship can be generalized to the population.

The calculations required to determine the appropriate *df* are actually quite simple. As Eq. 14.5 indicates,

$$df = (r - 1)(c - 1) \tag{14.5}$$

where $r =$ the number of rows and $c =$ the number of columns of the cross-classification matrix. For example, a 3×3 matrix would have $df = (3 - 1)(3 - 1) = 4$. The obtained χ^2 would then be compared to the critical value for 4 *df*.

Conceptually, this suggests that only four of the nine cells in the matrix are actually free to vary. Recall that the frequency in the cells must sum across the rows and columns to equal their marginal frequencies. Moreover, the cross-classification analysis begins with these marginal frequencies in place—they are "given" by the separate one-way frequency distributions. Hence, once the frequencies for any $(r - 1)(c - 1)$ cells have been established, the number of observations in the remaining cells is fixed or determined. This is true no matter how large or how small the matrix may be. The frequencies in the remaining cells can assume one and only one value, i.e., they are *not* free to vary. In this instance, at least, the reference to degrees-of-freedom has an obvious and appropriate conceptual grounding.

Calculating the χ^2 Statistic: An Example

The calculation of the χ^2 statistic can be illustrated by applying Eq. 14.2 to the two cross-classification matrices displayed in Figures 14.1 and 14.2. These calculations are simplified because these matrices possess the same marginal frequencies and thus will produce the same expected frequencies for each cell. More importantly, calculating the χ^2 statistic for both matrices will again provide a clear comparison between the characteristics of statistical independence and statistical association.

To facilitate this comparison, Figure 14.4 displays a 3×3 matrix which contains only the expected frequencies for these two cross-classifications. These were obtained by applying Eq. 14.4 to the appropriate marginal frequencies for each cell. For example: $E_{11} = 34 \times 25/100 = 8.5$; $E_{12} = 34 \times 25/100 = 8.5$; $E_{13} = 34 \times 50/100 = 17$; and so forth. It will be recalled that these nine frequencies are those which would be "expected" under the condition of complete statistical independence. Thus, they exhibit the perfect symmetry or parallelism which is typical of that empirical state of affairs.

For the cross-classification matrix in Figure 14.2, the χ^2 is calculated by inserting the actual or obtained frequencies into Eq. 14.2.

$$\chi^2 = \sum_{\text{all cells}} \frac{(O - E)^2}{E} \tag{14.2}$$

FIGURE 14.4. Expected Frequencies for Previous Cross-Classifications.

	B_1	B_2	B_3	
A_1	8.5	8.5	17	34
A_2	8.25	8.25	16.5	33
A_3	8.25	8.25	16.5	33
	25	25	50	100

When these numbers are inserted:

$$\chi^2 = \frac{(9-8.5)^2}{8.5} + \frac{(8-8.5)^2}{8.5} + \frac{(17-17)^2}{17} +$$

$$\frac{(8-8.25)^2}{8.25} + \frac{(9-8.25)^2}{8.25} + \frac{(16-16.5)^2}{16.5} +$$

$$\frac{(8-8.25)^2}{8.25} + \frac{(8-8.25)^2}{8.25} + \frac{(17-16.5)^2}{16.5}$$

$$= .029 + .029 + 0 +$$
$$.008 + .068 + .015 +$$
$$.008 + .008 + .015$$
$$= .18 \text{ with } (3-1)(3-1) = 4 \text{ } df$$

This obtained value of $\chi^2 = .18$ is then compared to the critical value of this test statistic for the desired level of significance. Appendix E reveals that the critical value for $p < .05$ is 9.5. Clearly, the value obtained from this cross-classification is far from surpassing this critical value. The null hypothesis of statistical independence cannot be rejected.

Since this matrix was purposely constructed to display the complete absence of association, this nonsignificant test statistic is hardly surprising. It is worth noting, however, that even for this carefully constructed table the χ^2 is not 0.00. Random fluctuation in frequencies due to sampling error will always create some deviation, even if the variables are statistically independent. In this example, these small deviations were not nearly sufficient to produce a significant test statistic. Nevertheless, the logic of statistical inference is still operative and a Type I error is always a distinct (albeit remote) possibility.

In contrast, previous discussion has described the cross-classification matrix in Figure 14.3 as failing to exhibit the symmetry which is necessary for independence. To assess whether this absence of parallelism is sufficiently large, Eq. 14.2 is applied to these data in the same manner as before.

$$\chi^2 = \frac{(13-8.5)^2}{8.5} + \frac{(5-8.5)^2}{8.5} + \frac{(16-17)^2}{17} +$$

$$\frac{(7-8.25)^2}{8.25} + \frac{(6-8.25)^2}{8.25} + \frac{(20-16.5)^2}{16.5} +$$

$$\frac{(5-8.25)^2}{8.25} + \frac{(14-8.25)^2}{8.25} + \frac{(14-16.5)^2}{16.5}$$

$$= 2.38 + 1.44 + .059 +$$
$$.189 + .62 + .742 +$$
$$1.28 + 4.00 + .379$$
$$= 11.09 \text{ with } (3-1)(3-1) = 4 \text{ } df$$

When this obtained $\chi^2 = 11.09$ is compared to the critical value for $p < .05$ (critical value $= 9.5$), it surpasses this value. Further comparison indicates that it comes quite close to the critical value for $p < .025$ (critical value $= 11.1$). In fact, if the calculations had not been so severely rounded, the test statistic would have almost certainly surpassed this latter critical value. In either case, the obtained test statistic is large enough to reject the null hypothesis that these two categorical variables are unrelated or independent. The relationship between these two variables has been shown to be of sufficient magnitude to be generalized to the larger population.

Assumptions in the χ^2 Test

Although the χ^2 test of significance is extremely simple to conceptualize and calculate, its use entails certain assumptions about the data. These assumptions must be verified before substantive inferences can be accepted as valid. Unlike other test statistics, the assumptions associated with the χ^2 are minimally demanding and focus primarily on the appropriateness of the nominal level measurement itself. They are but three in number.

First, the categories making up the individual nominal level variables must be *mutually exclusive and exhaustive*. This is the same requirement which was first introduced in Chapter 4 as a requisite characteristic of coding schemes in observational analysis. Each person or observation must be classified into one and only one category, and the categories must "exhaust" all of the relevant classes of the variable.

This is such a simple and direct requirement that it seems hardly worth mentioning. Be that as it may, it has been violated in the past and no doubt will be again in the future; especially in the categorization of communication behavior where it is tempting to label a single behavior as simultaneously performing more than one communicative "function." As suggested, this assumption can be easily fulfilled by ensuring that one's measurement procedures conform to established practice.

The second assumption of the χ^2 statistic is that the observations are *independently sampled*. This is the same requirement which was introduced in Chapter 10 as requisite of all data, irrespective of the level of measurement or the type of statistic which is used. For categorical variables, this requires that the category to which one observation is assigned should in no way be affected by the classification of any other observation. For example, in classifying people in terms of their marital status, one would violate this assumption by classifying *both* members of a marital dyad as "married." Obviously, they are married, but to each other! An unwanted relationship is involved—both statistically and interpersonally—which will bias any subsequent attempt at statistical inference. As before, this type of problem can be avoided by simply planning ahead, by spending some time conceptualizing the research design and measurement procedures before the data are actually obtained.

The final assumption (perhaps "controversy" is a better term) concerns the expected frequencies for each cell: What is the *minimum* size of the expected frequencies for each cell? This question centers on the issue of accurate estimation. If the two marginal frequencies (or probabilities) are very small, the researcher cannot be confident that the subsequent "expectations" in the cross-classification analysis are accurate. Given that measurement or classification error is always present, even minimal changes in the small marginal frequencies would produce radical shifts in the expected frequencies in the cells.

We have no guaranteed remedy for this problem, but researchers have adopted a general rule of thumb. For larger matrices which contain more than a single degree-of-freedom, the minimum expected frequency in each cell for a valid χ^2 test is 5. For matrices with 1 *df* (i.e., 2 × 2 matrices), a minimum expected frequency in each cell of 10 is generally considered acceptable. For fuller confidence, larger expected frequencies are preferable.

When these minimum expected frequencies are not met, the researcher must proceed with extreme caution. The real potential exists that the χ^2 test of inference will be biased in unknown and unpredictable ways. Under these circumstances, an investigator would be unwise to use such a χ^2 as evidence to support substantive and theoretic generalizations.

The obvious solution is to gather additional observations. When this is not possible, the second possible remedy is to collapse categories, thus combining sparsely populated categories into larger, more general classifications. For instance, the categories "widowed," "divorced," and "single" might be collapsed into one category, "not married." This second alternative, while certainly possible, possesses a variety of pitfalls and should be employed *only* when a set of somewhat complicated assumptions about the data can be empirically justified (see Bishop, Fienberg, & Holland, 1975; Reynolds, 1977). When neither more observations can be obtained nor the assumptions for collapsing categories can be met, the sole recourse is to go back to the beginning and design a more rigorous investigation.

The Magnitude of Association in Cross-Classification Analysis

The χ^2 test statistic, much like the F-ratio and the t-test, is intended solely to determine whether a given relationship is significant, whether the association between two nominal variables is sufficiently large to surpass that which would be obtained by chance alone. The χ^2, however, is *not* designed to serve as an index of "meaningfulness." In other words, the size of the χ^2 statistic is generally not indicative of the magnitude of the relationship being tested. Some relatively weak relationships can generate large χ^2's (especially if N is large), while some relatively strong relationships can produce a small χ^2 (especially if N is small). It is apparent, therefore, that some additional measures of association are needed to provide this information.

When a researcher has employed a form of the GLM, such measures of association are almost inherent in its application: namely, the Pearson r, the multiple R, or their squares (r^2 and R^2). Moreover, these statistics have neat and tidy interpretations: A perfect relationship is indicated by $r = +/-1.00$, and no relationship is represented by $r = 0.00$. Any intermediate value of r or R, therefore, can be interpreted with respect to these upper and lower bounds. Numerous attempts have been made to capture these attributes in measures of association for nominal level variables, unfortunately, with a notable lack of success (see Reynolds, 1977). Some measures of association are accurate for 2×2 tables, but problematic for larger matrices; some are unduly affected by skewed marginal distributions, where one category is considerably more frequent than the others; and still other measures are applicable only to square matrices, where the number of rows and the columns are equal. Furthermore, many measures of association exhibit all three of these shortcomings.

Given these various problems, only four measures of association will be discussed below. Although several have various weaknesses, their wide use by social scientists in all disciplines warrants their discussion. Three of these four measures are based directly on the χ^2 statistic; these also happen to be the most problematic. The fourth approach to indexing nominal association is called "proportional reduction in error." Because it avoids many of the problems inherent in the other three (not to mention that it is a bit more complicated than the others), this approach will be discussed in some detail.

To facilitate this discussion, we have recreated the cross-classification matrix from Figure 14.3 in Figure 14.5. In this figure, however, these hypothetical data are accompanied by an equally hypothetical substantive problem. A number of communication researchers have been interested in the relationship between presidential debates and candidate preference (see Kraus, 1962, 1979). Accordingly, the variable on the rows represents the categorization of $N = 100$ respondents on the question: Who won the presidential debate between Carter and Reagan? The second variable, displayed on the columns, classifies these same respondents in terms of their candidate preference before the time of debate. Previous analysis of these data in Figure 14.4 has shown that these two variables are significantly related ($\chi^2 = 11.09$; $df = 4$; $p < .05$). The measures of

FIGURE 14.5. Hypothetical Cross-Classification Between Prior Candidate Preference and Perceptions of Debate Outcome.

Candidate Preference Prior to Debate

Perceptions of Who Won Debate	Carter	Reagan	Undecided	
Carter	13	5	16	34
Reagan	7	6	20	33
Draw	5	14	14	33
	25	25	50	100

association to be discussed below, therefore, attempt to assess the magnitude of that relationship.

The Phi (Φ) Coefficient

The χ^2 test statistic has been described as being sensitive to the size of the sample which is cross-classified. When N is large, even small departures from the expected frequencies (that is, small in terms of percent) can produce a large and highly significant χ^2 statistic. An obvious solution is to standardize the χ^2 by dividing it by N. The result is the phi-squared (Φ^2) coefficient defined by Eq. 14.6.

$$\Phi^2 = \frac{\chi^2}{N} \tag{14.6}$$

In the current example,
$$\Phi^2 = 11.09/100 = .1109$$

For the special case of the 2×2 matrix, Φ^2 is a most informative measure of association. Not only does it possess the desired upper and lower bounds (i.e., 1.00 and 0.00), but it provides exactly the same value as the Pearson r^2 which would be obtained if both variables were dummy-coded with 1/0 codes (see Hays, 1973). Accordingly, $\sqrt{\Phi^2} = r$. Both Φ and r share the drawback that they are highly sensitive to marginal distributions which are skewed. In such cases, a less sensitive measure may be preferable (see Reynolds, 1977). Given its other desirable properties, however, Φ is a useful measure for this special case of the 2×2 matrix.

In larger cross-classification (which will be denoted as $R \times C$) matrices, Φ is more problematic. It no longer possesses an upper limit, and interpretation is thus very difficult. For example, the computation of $\Phi = \sqrt{.1109} = .333$ reveals that some degree of relationship exists between candidate preferences and perceptions of debate performance—a conclusion which the significant χ^2 has already provided. Without an upper bound to which $\Phi = .333$ can be compared, it is impossible to decide whether the magnitude of this relationship is large or small. As a result, Φ or Φ^2 is not recommended as a measure of association for $R \times C$ cross-classifications which are larger than 2×2.

The Contingency Coefficient

The contingency coefficient *(C)* is an attempt to correct the deficiencies of Φ for larger, $R \times C$ matrices. It is defined as,

$$C = \sqrt{\frac{\Phi^2}{\Phi^2 + 1}} = \sqrt{\frac{\chi^2}{\chi^2 + N}} \tag{14.7}$$

For the present example,

$$C = \sqrt{\frac{.1109}{.1109 + 1}} = \sqrt{\frac{11.09}{11.09 + 100}} = .316$$

Thus, $C = .316$ is slightly less than $\Phi = .333$, but close enough to suggest a relationship of similar magnitude.

Once again, however, there is a serious problem of interpretation. Although C will always fall between the bounds of 1 and 0, it frequently cannot attain its upper limit of 1.0, even when the two variables are perfectly related. When the matrix is square and $R = C$, the maximum value of C can be determined and can be used to calculate an "adjusted" C (see Ott, Medenhall, & Larson, 1978). In tables where $R \neq C$, this adjustment is not possible and C, like Φ, becomes a difficult measure of association to interpret.

Cramer's V

The final measure of association was developed by Cramer (1946) and is labeled the V statistic. It is defined as:

$$V = \sqrt{\frac{\Phi^2}{S}} = \sqrt{\frac{\chi^2}{N \times S}} \tag{14.8}$$

where S is the smaller of $(R - 1)$ or $(C - 1)$. In the current problem, the matrix is square and $(R - 1) = (C - 1) = 2$. Thus,

$$V = \sqrt{\frac{.1109}{2}} = \sqrt{\frac{11.09}{100 \times 2}} = .235$$

Of these three measures of association, Cramer's V has the fewest deficiencies. It possesses an upper and lower bound of 1 and 0 respectively, and thus has a direct interpretation. Also, it can be readily calculated for nonsquare matrices, where $R \neq C$. Consequently, *if* a measure of association based on the χ^2 is chosen, Cramer's V is the statistic with the most positive and fewest negative attributes to recommend it.

Proportional Reduction in Error Measures

The various deficits just cited make the use of measures of association based on the χ^2 of limited value. In response, a completely different approach to assessing the magnitude of nominal level relationships has been advanced by what are called "proportional reduction in error" (PRE) measures. The logic of these measures conforms closely to the general scientific goal of increasing a researcher's ability to accurately explain and predict a person's "score" on a specified outcome measure.

For the GLM, it was shown that achieving this goal entails the search for explanatory variables which will significantly increase the amount or proportion of variance which can be explained, i.e., R^2. In cross-classification analysis, the general goal is the same, but its statistical implementation is somewhat different. Because no separate outcome measure exists, the researcher's purpose is to accurately classify each observation in terms of a particular categorical variable (say variable A). The concept of "reduction of error" enters the picture when a researcher asks: Will the knowledge of into which category each observation has been classified on variable B increase the accuracy of classification on variable A? And by how much? In short, the investigator is searching for additional "explanatory" variables which will reduce the error of classifying the observations on the categorical variable of interest. The fact that both the "explanatory" and "criterion" variables are nominal in their level of measurement alters the statistics involved, but not the conceptual goal which those statistics are designed to achieve.

An initial understanding of PRE measures can best be obtained by envisioning a sort of scientific guessing game. The ultimate goal is for the researcher to predict the category of each observation on variable A as accurately as possible. This process of prediction proceeds according to two simple "rules." The first rule operates under the assumption that variables A and B are statistically independent. It requires that the researcher predict the classification of each observation on variable A using no information from variable B, the explanatory variable. In short, the researcher observes the one-way frequency distribution of variable A and then "guesses" into which category each observation should be classified. Obviously, such guessing will produce a number of misclassifications. This frequency, in turn, is transformed into a percentage or probability of error, which is denoted as P_{e1}.

The second rule requires that these same observations be classified again, but this time the researcher utilizes the information about the category to which each observation is assigned on variable B. Again, misclassifications will occur, with the probability of error obtained from this procedure being labeled P_{e2}. To the extent that $P_{e1} > P_{e2}$, the second rule has produced fewer misclassifications than the first. Accordingly, the information about the observations which is provided by variable B has produced a *reduction in error*. To make this reduction "proportional," it is simply expressed as a percentage of the original probability of error, P_{e1}. Thus,

$$PRE = \frac{P_{e1} - P_{e2}}{P_{e1}} \tag{14.9}$$

Eq. 14.9 describes the logic which is inherent in all PRE measures: How much does the knowledge of the explanatory variable reduce the error of classifying observations on the criterion variable? The construction of Eq. 14.9 also ensures that the answer to this question will always fall between the values of 0 and 1.0. A value of PRE = 0 results when $P_{e1} = P_{e2}$, which indicates that variable B does nothing to enhance the accurate classification of observations on variable A. There are just as many misclassifications when B is used as when it is not. A value of PRE = 1, on the other hand, can only occur when $P_{e2} = 0$, that is, when the information obtained from variable B allows for the perfect classification (i.e., no errors) of variable A. Because of these conceptually meaningful upper and lower bounds, intermediate values of PRE measures can be interpreted as indicating the strength of explanation or prediction of variable B.

A less obvious, but nonetheless important attribute of Eq. 14.9 is that the PRE measure it defines is *asymmetric*. Unlike measures of association based on the χ^2 (Φ, C, and V), the value of a PRE measure will change depending on which variable is designated as the criterion. The ability of variable B to reduce the error of classification for variable A need not be and frequently will not be the same as A's ability to reduce the error classification for B. The attribute of asymmetry, therefore, requires the investigator to clearly specify which variable is the criterion and which is the predictor. So-called "symmetric" versions of some PRE measures have been developed, in which neither variable is designated as the criterion variable of interest. Without this specification, however, the logic of "reduction of error" loses its conceptual meaning and the interpretation of such symmetric measures becomes somewhat nebulous (see Ott et al., 1978, p. 360). As a consequence, PRE measures offer the greatest insight and utility in exactly the situations for which they were designed: when one categorical variable is used to predict or explain the distribution of observations of another.

Using the broad logic inherent in Eq. 14.9, statisticians have developed several different PRE measures. The primary distinction among these alternatives is the way in which the one-way frequency distribution of the criterion variable is used to guide the initial predictions (guesses) in the application of rule 1. Some PRE measures require that the entire distribution of variable A be employed to guide these initial predictions, while others use only the category with the largest frequency. These latter measures apply rule 1 by initially classifying all of the observations in one and only one category, i.e., the "modal" category.

The upshot of these differences in rule 1 is that these several PRE measures hold differing conceptions of what constitutes errors of classification. In short, the various PRE measures possess different ways to calculate P_{e1} and P_{e2}, thus producing a different numerical value for the proportion of error which has been reduced. As is the case with all statistics, the choice of a PRE measure is based on the empirical information the investigator wishes to obtain from the data. The discussion below will present and exemplify only the most basic PRE measure. For a complete discussion of the various alternatives, see Reynolds (1977).

Goodman and Kruskal's Lambda

Goodman and Kruskal (1954) developed a very basic PRE measure which they denoted as lambda (λ). It operates on a simple, yet highly logical conception of how rule 1 should be applied. It will be recalled from Chapter 8 that when no additional information about a person or observation is available, the best guess for that person's score on the criterion measure is the central tendency of that variable. For nominal level data of the type being considered here, the index of central tendency, of course, is the mode. Hence, for λ, rule 1 requires that all observations be assigned to the modal category of variable A. If A is assumed to occupy the rows, then the modal category can be symbolized as n_{m+}. (The subscript m symbolizes the "maximum" or modal row category.) Finally, to compute the errors of classification for rule 1 (E_1),

$$E_1 = N - n_{m+} \tag{14.10}$$

The second general rule for calculating λ requires that the information available from variable B be utilized before assigning the observations to an A category. This entails examining each column of variable B separately and assigning all of the observations in that column to the one and only one row with the maximum frequency. For each of the j columns, this row will be symbolized as n_{mj}, where mj indicates the maximum or modal row in the jth column. This procedure will, of course, also produce errors of classification (E_2), which are defined as,

$$E_2 = N - \sum_{j=1}^{c} n_{mj} \tag{14.11}$$

As suggested by Eq. 14.9, the applications of rules 1 and 2 allow λ to be calculated as:

$$\lambda_r = \frac{E_1 - E_2}{E_1}$$

where λ_r indicates that the criterion variable is arrayed on the *rows* of the cross-classification matrix. If the more complete expressions from Eqs. 14.10 and 14.11 are inserted,

$$\lambda_r = \frac{(N - n_{m+}) - \left(N - \sum_{j=1}^{c} n_{mj}\right)}{N - n_{m+}} \tag{14.12}$$

A bit of algebraic manipulation, however, will show that the two N's in the numerator of Eq. 14.12 cancel, thus producing

$$\lambda_r = \frac{\left(\sum_{j=1}^{c} n_{mj}\right) - n_{m+}}{N - n_{m+}} \tag{14.13}$$

Although at first glance the new notation makes Eq. 14.13 seem formidible, an example will show how simple its application actually is.

The data in Table 14.5 present the hypothetical association between perceptions of who won the 1980 presidential debate and candidate preference prior to the debate. Since λ, like all PRE measures, is asymmetrical, it is first necessary to specify which variable is the criterion of interest. In this example, it makes sense to assume that a person's prior candidate preference will influence his or her perceptions of the debate outcome. Thus, who won the debate will be treated as the criterion, necessitating the calculation of λ_r. Later, the asymmetry of this PRE measure will be illustrated by reversing these designations and calculating λ_c.

According to rule 1, the first step is to select the modal row frequency, n_{m+}. Although the three marginal row frequencies are almost equal, the first row contains 34 observations. Thus,

$$n_{m+} = 34$$

The second rule requires that each column of the candidate preference variable be examined separately, and the row with the largest frequency be identified. For column 1 (Carter), the first row is the largest, containing 13 observations. For column 2 (Reagan), the third row (14 observations) is selected, while for column 3 (Undecided), the second row contains the modal frequency of 20. When these frequencies are combined as required by rule 2,

$$\sum_{j=1}^{c} n_{mj} = 13 + 14 + 20$$

$$= 47$$

The final step is to insert these numbers into Eq. 14.13.

$$\lambda_r = \frac{47 - 34}{100 - 34}$$

$$= \frac{13}{66}$$

$$= .197$$

This result suggests that the knowledge of each person's candidate preference prior to the debate reduced the errors of classification on the criterion variable by approximately 20%. Given the meaningful bounds of 0 and 1.0 which are associated with PRE measures, a 20% reduction in error would be considered moderate at best. Nevertheless, prior candidate preference does possess information which is useful in explaining the respondents' perceptions of who won the debate. If this had been an actual study where substantive interpretation and discussion were required, this result would have provided valuable insight into this relationship.

Another, perhaps more interesting, point can be made by reversing the designation of criterion and explanatory variables and calculating λ again. The two rules are the same, but the rows and columns are simply interchanged in their application. Accordingly, λ_c is defined as:

$$\lambda_c = \frac{\left(\sum_{j=1}^{r} n_{im}\right) - n_{+m}}{N - n_{+m}} \tag{14.14}$$

Thus, rule 1 requires selection of the modal column. In this example,

$$n_{+m} = 50$$

Rule 2, on the other hand, requires that each row be examined separately and the modal column (n_{im}) be selected for each row. For these data: $n_{1m} = 16$; $n_{2m} = 20$; $n_{3m} = 14$. Thus,

$$\sum_{j=1}^{r} n_{im} = 16 + 20 + 14$$

$$= 50$$

When these values are inserted in Eq. 14.13,

$$\lambda_c = \frac{50 - 50}{50}$$

$$= 0$$

This result suggests that the knowledge of a person's perception of who won the debate offers absolutely no useful information when it comes to predicting prior candidate preference. Interesting, to say the least. From a substantive point of view, this finding indicates a much different type of relationship between these two variables, one that is clearly asymmetrical. Were these data to be formally interpreted, this result would certainly alter the nature of those theoretic conclusions.

This finding has equally interesting implications when viewed from a purely statistical frame of reference. Despite a significant χ^2 statistic, the second set of calculations revealed that $\lambda_c = 0$. Hence, even when the null hypothesis of statistical independence is clearly rejected, this PRE measure can obtain a value of zero. Some writers (e.g., Reynolds, 1977) consider this a shortcoming of λ, arguing that a measure of association should produce a value of zero *only* when the two variables are statistically independent.

Such arguments, however, seem to overlook the conceptual purpose for which PRE measures were developed. PRE indices are not measures of association in the traditional sense of "magnitude." Rather, they have been designed to assess association in the very specific and limited sense of the explanatory or predictive relevance of one categorical variable for another. If association in this sense does not exist—despite what other measures of association might indicate—then $\lambda = 0$ is not only legitimate, but desirable (see Bishop et al., 1975; Goodman & Kruskal, 1954). Ultimately, whether $\lambda = 0$ possesses great theoretic import or is merely a statistical aberration is *not* a statistical issue. The meaning of such a finding can be judged only in the context of past research and substantive theory.

In summary, the development of various PRE measures has offered researchers an alternative approach to the analysis and interpretation of relationships between nominal level variables. Not only do PRE measures avoid many of the shortcomings which characterize measures of association based on the χ^2, but they conform more closely to the general goal of scientific investigation—i.e., a reduction in error and thus a simultaneous reduction in scientific "ignorance." To illustrate how this goal is achieved, the λ measure was presented and its calculations were illustrated. λ, however, is but one of several PRE measures. While all pursue the same conceptual goal, each embodies different assumptions about the data and thus produces different results.

The choice of a PRE measure, therefore, should be guided solely by the theoretic concerns and empirical assumptions of the investigator. In many instances, however, this choice is best delayed until after the investigator has calculated and examined the complete array of measures of association which are available. As previously illustrated, different measures provided different insights and can often provide understanding which is not available from a single measure. As Reynolds (1977, p. 57) suggests:

> It usually pays to look at relationships from several points of view. . . . Unless one's theory explicitly assumes a particular definition [of association], which is almost never the case, he may overlook important aspects of the data by relying on a single index.

■ Conclusion

Perhaps the most fitting way to conclude this chapter is to reiterate its introduction. This chapter has only briefly surveyed the most basic logic and statistics associated with the analysis of nominal level variables. There are many more approaches and numerous additional statistics which have not been covered. It would not be an exaggeration to suggest that considerably more information about nominal variable analysis has been excluded than has been included.

One obvious reason for this relatively brief treatment is the nature of this book. As an introduction to research design and statistical analysis in communication, an in-depth discussion is neither expected nor desired. A second reason, however, can be traced to the field of communication itself. Simply stated, the analysis of nominal variables has not been and is not now a widely used approach to the empirical investigation of human communication phenomena. Exceptions exist, of course, especially in the areas of mass communication and political communication. Nevertheless, unlike investigators in social science disciplines such as sociology or political science, communication researchers have not made extensive use of nominal variables to operationalize their salient concepts and constructs.

Whether this tradition is good or bad is not the point—it just is. One thing is certain, however. If students of communication are not exposed to these relatively recent and sophisticated advances in nominal variable analysis, this tradition will not change. Change simply for the sake of change is not the primary concern. On the contrary, the primary concern is ignorance. A researcher who does not know that a certain analytic approach exists will be unable to capitalize upon it, even when that approach is the most appropriate or will provide the most theoretic insight.

Hence, despite the admittedly brief treatment in this book, we encourage readers to explore these more advanced procedures as fully as possible. Perhaps they will prove useful, perhaps not. In either case, to simply ignore them is to severely limit one's empirical perspective. At this point in the development of communication research as a social science, such artificial narrowness and limitation is highly undesirable.

Doing Communication Research: Some Practical Advice

The previous chapters have presented a number of aspects or components of the research process: research design, measurement procedures, data analysis, etc. Each of these is an important topic in its own right, but only their synthesis into a coherent, integrated whole makes communication research worthwhile.

Each of these topics is an abstraction. They can be pondered and discussed without linking them to an actual research context. You probably have never administered a set of semantic differential scales or actually conducted a content analysis. Perhaps you never will. Nevertheless, you have read about these and other methods in varying degrees of detail, and we hope that you have greater insight and understanding than you did before you began this book.

This chapter is much less abstract. It is about the practical, pragmatic, and to some even mundane aspects of actually *doing* communication research. Although the topics of design, measurement, and analysis receive the bulk of attention in most books (including this one), a number of details involved in actually designing, measuring, and analyzing require mention. This chapter does not contain profound words of wisdom or unique insights into complex methodological issues. Instead, it provides commonsense advice, some forceful prescriptions, and some very practical suggestions for organizing and communicating the results of research to others. These topics are not trivial. On the contrary, failure to execute competently each of these practical activities will endanger the success of the entire project.

Some Advice

Many people much of the time are neither interested in nor receptive to advice, no matter how perceptive and well intentioned that advice might be. They prefer instead to follow their own course and learn personally from mistakes and misjudgments. This school of "hard knocks" approach has a certain appeal, and we have obtained the basis for much of the advice that we are about to provide in that school. We will present three maxims. They represent the distillation of some of our experience with the research enterprise, both personal and vicarious. We encourage you to consider these maxims carefully, lest you learn them as we and many other researchers have done: the hard way.

Maxim 1: It Always Takes Longer Than You Think

Perhaps the most common mistake of inexperienced researchers is that they fail to estimate accurately how long a research project will take. Whether the study represents a class project, a master's thesis, or a doctoral dissertation, a common tendency is to underestimate (frequently, to *grossly* underestimate) the time required to carefully conduct social science research. The result is that some aspects of the research process—usually the data analysis and write-up—are rushed to completion under extreme time pressures. Or the research never reaches completion, and the data languish permanently on the shelf.

Make every effort to allow yourself time to complete the research project in an unhurried and meticulous fashion. Do not select deadlines that you cannot meet. If someone else (for example, your instructor) imposes deadlines on you, begin your work as soon as possible. When necessary, consult with other, more experienced researchers to determine their estimates of the time involved, and do not be surprised if their estimates are much longer than your own. Take their estimates seriously and plan accordingly.

More specifically: In something of a reversal of the traditional advice to "plan ahead," we suggest that you "plan backward." This will require you to construct a time line for your study. Begin by writing down the *last* step in the process, "report turned in to instructor," for example. Then think of the step that must immediately precede that one, "paper typed," for example. Estimate the time that will be required for typing the paper, and, working backward from the deadline, note the date at which you must begin typing the paper. Continue this process until you reach the beginning: e.g., "find research idea." Make your time frame conservative. Assume the worst. Respondents sometimes will not be at home. Helpers will become ill. Other projects will interfere.

This method of planning is sometimes called Performance Evaluation and Review Technique (PERT). A much more extensive description is available in Phillips (1966). You might find the technique useful for any complex project, not just social science research.

Maxim 2: Anticipate the Unanticipated

The social science research project is among the most fertile ground for the flowering of Murphy's Law: If something can go wrong, it will. Participants will fail to appear, recorders will malfunction (or the tape will break), the computer will go on sick leave, or (an actual experience of a colleague) thieves will steal your car, including its trunkful of data. These and many other events can turn a research project into a nightmare.

You cannot anticipate every possible malfunction, but with a bit of foresight you can be prepared for the most likely ones. Make extra copies of the measurement instruments. Bring extra tapes to the experimental sessions. Reserve an extra recording machine. Secure backup helpers and subjects who can be available at a moment's notice. Make an extra copy of your data sheets. Some scholars store their data in the refrigerator. The pages assimilate some strange odors, but they are relatively safe from fire.

The unanticipated occurrence is another reason to take Maxim 1 seriously. Realistically, a single afternoon may suffice to make copies of your measurement instrument—assuming that the copying machine is working, that you do not run out of paper, that the electricity does not black out, and that you do not encounter a line of seven people at the machine, each of whom intends to copy *War and Peace*.

Maxim 3: Do Not Trust Others to Do It If You Can Do It Yourself

A few years ago, one of us (Courtright) organized and conducted a complex study of group decision-making which required that discussion groups be videotaped. Each group was initially addressed by a helper, each of whom had been carefully selected for competence. These helpers were to instruct the participants and then turn on the video recorder before leaving the room. Only after the entire study was completed did Courtright discover that one of the helpers did not know how to operate a video recorder. An entire set of videotapes was blank, and the study was ruined. On the second attempt, Courtright personally controlled all of the video recording from a central control panel, thereby accepting this seemingly minor responsibility himself. This was a vivid, painful, and expensive lesson about the unnecessary delegation of responsibility.

This maxim implies a somewhat pessimistic view of others' goodwill and ability, and we do not hold a pessimistic view in general. Nevertheless, your study is your study. Friends and helpers do not have your investment of time, energy, and ego. The more helpers you have, the more likely it is that at least one of them will be incapable of performing the assigned tasks. Maintain for yourself as much responsibility as possible. Your relationships with friends, relatives, and colleagues will be less strained as a result.

Research Ethics and Standards

We presented the practical advice of the previous section as a set of suggestions which you may follow or ignore as you choose, reaping whatever fortune or misfortune that may ensue. In contrast, the subject matter of this section does not allow such discretion. Communication research is a social science whose primary focus is the behavior of human beings. Individuals who participate in social science research often voluntarily allow a researcher to observe and measure their behavior. They have *not* forfeited their basic human dignity.

When human beings are the subject of scientific inquiry, they are entitled to respect, courtesy, and consideration from the investigator. These are fundamental rights, not optional privileges that the investigator may grant or withhold. A researcher who thoughtlessly abuses, demeans, or exploits research subjects will quickly incur the wrath of the scientific community and possibly of the wider society.

What are the specific responsibilities of social science researchers? What particular behaviors or procedures constitute abuse or exploitation? Where does one draw the line between legitimate methods of inquiry and methods that endanger the integrity or self-concept of participants?

These are complex questions, almost impossible to answer except on a case-by-case, situational basis. We could easily, for example, criticize as unethical (in almost any situation) the use of severe electric shock or of hallucinatory drugs as predictor variables. Similarly, a researcher who knowingly induced destructive conflict into marriages probably would be open to serious criticism on ethical grounds.

But not all questions of proper ethical conduct are easily judged. Often, concerned, responsible, sincere individuals disagree about what procedures and methods are acceptable. Consequently, researchers must take extreme care.

Recognizing the complexity that frequently surrounds these decisions, several scholarly organizations such as the American Psychological Association and the American Sociological Association have written "codes of ethical conduct" for researchers to follow. These consist of general guidelines for appropriate behavior that the researcher must apply to a specific study. These codes are detailed, and differ among themselves somewhat depending on (1) the discipline, and (2) the type of research. We will not duplicate these codes here. Almost all university libraries have copies, and we encourage you to read them carefully before you begin any research project involving human subjects. In addition, many universities have committees whose purpose is to ensure in advance the rights and welfare of human subjects. You may be required to submit your plans for research to such a committee before you will be permitted to use human subjects in your research.

The rest of this section will outline in a general way the concerns of these several codes of conduct. This brief discussion is not an adequate substitute for the detailed presentation of these codes, nor does this overview release you from the responsibility to know and follow more detailed prescriptions. Our goal is to provide you with a global understanding of the topics that are of concern in research ethics.

As you read the rest of this section, you might pretend to be on the ethics review committee for the following proposals—each of which is of research that has actually been carried out, though before most universities had ethics review committees. In each case, would you approve the research as proposed? If so, how would you justify your decision? If not, would you insist on blanket disapproval, or would you suggest changes to the researcher that would make the proposal acceptable to you? What would those suggested changes be?

Case 1. Milgram (1974) proposes to discover the extent to which typical United States citizens will obey orders. In his research design, subjects will come to Milgram's Laboratory at Harvard University, having responded in answer to a newspaper advertisement. They will be paid a small amount, as promised, when they appear at the laboratory. Each subject will be introduced, upon arrival, to another "subject" (actually, Milgram's confederate), and the two will draw lots to determine which will be "teacher" and which will be "learner." (Actually, the drawing is rigged so that the subject will be the "teacher," the confederate the "learner.") The confederate will then go into another room where, allegedly but not actually, he will be hooked up to a mechanism through which he can receive electric shocks administered by the "teacher." The door to the other room will then be closed. The "teacher" will be instructed to administer what he or she perceives to be incrementally more severe electric shocks to the "learner" in response to the "learner's" wrong answers to questions. The dial on which the "shocks" are labeled ranges in its descriptions from "slight shock" to "danger: extreme shock." When the "teacher" reaches the "danger" point, he or she will hear groans and entreaties to stop from the "learner" in the other room. If a "teacher" refuses to increment the shocks beyond a certain point, the experimenter will express two mild prods (such as "the experiment requires that you continue"). If the "teacher" still refuses, he or she will be told the true nature of the experiment and released. All subjects will be told the true nature of the experiment at the end of their participation.

Case 2. Carmichael (1965) proposes to measure the effect of "frustration" and "ego-satisfaction" on the reception of persuasive messages. He will use as subjects intact classes in the required freshman speech and composition course. The experiment will be conducted near the end of the semester. Classes in the "frustrated" condition will be told by a bogus spokesperson for the department that the entire class has done extremely poor work through the course of the semester, that they must, within a short time, write an unexpected and complex research paper, and that they will be required to take another course in the department, though they had anticipated fulfilling the requirement by completing the course in which they are presently enrolled. Classes in the "ego-satisfied" condition will be told that they have done extremely well during the semester, that all will receive very high grades in the course, and that they will be excused from the final examination in the course. All classes will then listen to tape-recorded persuasive speeches and will fill out attitudinal criterion measures. When they have completed the criterion measures, all will be told the true nature of the study and that they should completely disregard the frustrating or ego-satisfying induction.

Case 3. Roberts (1972) proposes to use as subjects students about to graduate from a technical program in a community college. These subjects will be asked to role-play the applicant in a job interview. An observer will allegedly be taking notes during the interview. When the interview is over, the observer will critique the interview. (Actually, subjects will be randomly assigned to a condition in which they receive a positive critique or to a condition in which they receive a negative critique. The nature of the critique will be independent of the nature of the interview.) After the critique, subjects will complete various criterion measures, including a measure of their self-esteem. Finally, they will be told the true nature of the study and that they should disregard the critiques they received.

The Researcher Is Completely and Solely Responsible

No matter how detailed and specific a particular code of research ethics may be, it can always be reduced to one basic principle: As principal or primary investigator in a research project, you assume the full responsibility for the physical, emotional, and psychological welfare of your subjects. This is a *legal* responsibility. You must ensure that your participants are not coerced into participating. You must ensure that the procedures involved do not create unnecessary or intolerable anxiety or stress in your subjects. Your procedures must not cause long-term harm to your participants, such as negative changes in self-concept. Even revealing the true and specific purposes of a study, if that revelation does damage, may be unethical.

The primary investigator is also responsible for doing everything possible to ensure the ethical conduct of all employees, volunteer helpers, confederates, and co-investigators. These individuals, of course, are personally responsible for their own behavior. They are not free to behave irresponsibly simply because of their subordinate position. Nevertheless, someone must be ultimately responsible, and that someone is the principal investigator.

The Researcher Must Weigh the Costs and Benefits of the Research

Previous chapters frequently emphasized that a researcher must make decisions about procedures or methods based on their costs in terms of time, money, and energy. Such costs are borne by the researcher. In questions of ethics, a more important consideration is the cost to the participants. Will an excessive amount of time and energy be required? Will they be asked or otherwise induced to behave in ways that are contrary to their important beliefs or attitudes? Will they experience undue stress or anxiety as a result of their participation? Even if you cannot predict exact outcomes, you must take risks to the experimental subjects into account.

This is not to imply that costs to participants are always unacceptable. As a discipline, communication research recognizes that not all aspects of social behavior are pleasant. Real social situations do occasionally give rise to anxiety, embarrassment, anger, and conflict. These are clearly legitimate areas of study. But in studies where these kinds of forces operate, you must carefully weigh costs to participants against potential benefits of the study. When the benefits in terms of knowledge and understanding (not personal gain, such as earning a grade in a course) outweigh the risks to participants, the investigator can feel more confident about proceeding with the project.

On this value-laden decision, university committees frequently enter the picture. Researchers cannot be expected to perform the most objective and unbiased assessment of the costs and benefits of their work. Consequently, they often must submit their cases to a committee of uninvolved scholars (and sometimes others), several of whom may be selected from disciplines outside the social sciences. Such committees may offer suggestions or compromises, but eventually they must render a final judgment of ethical acceptability. Ask your instructor whether your university has such a committee to review proposed research involving the use of human subjects.

Participants Must Give "Informed Consent"

A general principle in all research involving human beings (including medical research) is that participants must give their *informed consent* to participate. Participants should be provided with all information that might reasonably be expected to influence their decision to take part in the study. They should be told what will happen to them, what will be expected of them, what kind of information they will be asked to provide, and what risks, if any, they will be incurring. Finally, they should be told that they are free to withdraw from participation at any time and for any reason.

The principle of informed consent does not require the researcher to provide subjects with more specific information about the study. For example, you need not (and probably should not) tell subjects the hypotheses or predictions of the study. Or how many treatments or conditions the study entails. Or what experimental cell subjects occupy. Or what statistical procedures will be used to analyze the data. Once the subjects' participation is complete, you may reveal these details in a session that is sometimes called a "debriefing."

The most difficult issue to be addressed under the topic of informed consent is *deception*. May an investigator deliberately deceive subjects to achieve the goals of a study?

It depends on many things. Basically, deception may sometimes be acceptable when (1) the benefits clearly outweigh the costs or risks, and (2) no other method of testing the hypothesis is possible. Deception should not be employed routinely. Neither can it be used as a substitute for creative design. The investigator must always try to find nondeceptive alternatives. When deception must be used, debriefing assumes added importance. Participants should not leave the study believing false or misleading statements made in the course of the study.

The Researcher Must Protect Participants From Unnecessary Anxiety or Stress

The key to understanding this particular responsibility is the word *unnecessary*. We said earlier that stress and anxiety are inherent consequences of various social situations, and researchers have both a right and an obligation to study the communication processes that occur in those situations. For example, the common communication event when a student presents a public speech to a classroom audience raises emotional reactions ranging from mild nervousness to extreme terror. The act of tape-recording the communication of some individuals raises their level of tension.

These facts do not preclude the study of public speakers and speaking or the use of tape recorders in research. These activities do not create *unnecessary* stress. A reasonable rule is this: Researchers should not evoke anxiety or stress in their subjects beyond that which is experienced in everyday civilized life. People give speeches and thus feel anxious in everyday life. People experience disagreement in everyday life. These experiences may not be especially enjoyable, but neither are they exceptional. Researchers who study such universal experiences probably will not be severely questioned on ethical grounds.

But keep in mind that the principle of "everyday life" is simply a useful rule. Not every situation that one might encounter in daily life is acceptable for a researcher. Life can be cruel, but the researcher cannot be so. People sometimes treat their fellow human beings in atrocious ways, but the researcher may not do so.

In everyday life, people have varying degrees of responsibility for the welfare of others. For researchers, however, that responsibility is total. Hence, if you are in doubt about the ethical acceptability of your procedures or methods, you should seek advice. Consult with other researchers, the appropriate university committee, or even with a pilot sample from the subject population. If you are still in doubt, discontinue the research or redesign it in a more acceptable manner. The right of your participants to be treated with human dignity is paramount.

Writing the Research Report

In this chapter devoted to the practical aspects of communication research, perhaps the *most* practical aspect is the need to communicate clearly and effectively the results of that research. Accordingly, this section describes the research report.

The research report is the written account of why the research was done (i.e., for what theoretic or applied reason), how it was done, what was discovered as a result, and, when appropriate, how theories must be adjusted as a consequence of the result. Usually, the anticipated audience is other researchers. Journalists, counselors, social workers, or others may be interested in the findings, but these audiences are usually secondary ones.

The organization of the research report has become relatively standardized as a result of tradition and consensus over a period of years. Although a certain degree of flexibility may accommodate innovative research approaches or unique findings, the conventional format ensures that the information necessary to understand and replicate the study is provided. The organization of a standard research report is:

1. Title of Study
2. Abstract of Study
3. Introduction to the Main Body of the Report
   a. General Statement of Problem
   b. Review of Relevant Literature
   c. Statement of Hypotheses or Research Questions

4. Method
   a. Description of Subjects
   b. Variables
      1. Predictor Variables
      2. Criterion Variables
   c. Procedure
   d. Statistical Method
5. Results
6. Discussion
7. References or Footnotes
8. Appendices (if any)

We will explain the purpose of each of these components of a research report, as well as what information they are expected to provide. However, we will not prescribe an exact method for providing that content—that is, how to do it. The exact content of a research report depends on (1) the subject matter and methodology of the study, and (2) the writing style of the researcher. Writing a research report, like any careful writing, is hard work. Only through experience and informed criticism will you develop the style and method that are comfortable and successful for you.

One general piece of advice is to make good use of available models in journals such as *Communication Monographs* and *Human Communication Research*. Pay special attention to those articles with topics or methods similar to yours. Notice their organization, style, placement and use of figures or tables, and the method of arguing from the general or theoretical to the specific, then back to the general or theoretical. How do the authors use their review of the literature to build the rationale for their study? How do they frame hypotheses or research questions? Report results? Pay close attention to their references. You can be reasonably confident that they are in the appropriate style for that particular journal. Only about 10 percent of the papers submitted to these journals are accepted for publication, so the ones published are likely to be acceptable models for your own studies.

Two general prescriptions about style that we have found useful for beginning researchers (though we have not always observed them ourselves, especially in Chapters 8–14, where the impersonal passive somehow seemed appropriate) are: (1) Avoid the passive voice. You can often do this by making an abstraction the active subject of a sentence. Instead of, "Three arguments can be made against this point of view" (a passive construction), try "Three arguments weaken confidence in this point of view." (2) Avoid the kind of sentence that begins with a nonreferential *It* followed by a form of the verb *to be*, or with a nonreferential *There* followed by a form of the verb *to be*. Instead of "It is difficult to reconcile theory A with theory B," or "There are inconsistencies between theory A and theory B," try "Aspects of theory A do not fit with aspects of theory B." Observing these negative injunctions will not necessarily make you a great writer, but they should force you to tighten the expression of your thought more than many social scientists do.

One other injunction about style. Most scholarly journals and organizations now require authors to use nonsexist style. Often, you can avoid the masculine first-person generic pronoun simply by changing its referent from singular to plural. This kind of change is usually more graceful than the somewhat inefficient expressions "he or she" and "his or her." So instead of "The experimenter told the subject that he or she . . . ," you might write "The experimenter told the subjects that they . . . ." The *Publication Manual of the American Psychological Association* (second edition) has an insertion,

"Guidelines for Nonsexist Language in APA Journals." We suggest that you read and follow these guidelines, which are very explicit.

Title and Abstract

The purpose of the title is obvious: to tell the reader what the study was about. Titles are frequently straightforward (for example, "Situational Determinants of Communication Anxiety"), though a bit of thought sometimes can produce a more attention-getting title ("Actions Speak Louder Than Words—Sometimes"). Even if you want an attention-getting title, you should never sacrifice descriptiveness to cleverness. Other scholars will be able to locate your paper as relevant to them only if your title contains the appropriate key words—or you supply those key words separately.

The abstract is a short description of the contents of the report, usually only 75–150 words long. Its purpose is to provide a synopsis of the study. It should succinctly describe the questions or hypotheses that you investigated, the methods you employed, and the findings that resulted.

Despite their brevity, the title and the abstract are crucially important. Many researchers use only these two pieces of information to decide whether to continue reading the report. Moreover, if another author references a research report, he or she will do so only with the title. And if a scholarly reference book (see Chapter 7) indexes or abstracts your research report, it will carry only your title, abstract, and possibly the key words. Based on this information alone, all other researchers must decide whether to invest additional time and energy to locate and read the study. Hence, the title and abstract must accurately represent the study.

Introduction

The introductory section of a research report consists of the first several pages of the manuscript, usually everything preceding the description of method. It normally has three distinct parts: (1) a general statement of the problem; (2) a review of relevant work previously done on this topic; and (3) a statement of the hypotheses and/or research questions addressed by the study.

Although the most obvious purpose of this section is to introduce the study, it must accomplish certain other goals along the way. It must explain to (and convince) the reader that the research described in this report is interesting and important. That is, it must provide a rationale for doing the study. It must isolate relevant knowledge available from previous research while also isolating gaps, inconsistencies, contradictions, or anomalies in that previous research. And it must indicate how the research being reported can be expected to fill in those gaps or resolve those inconsistencies, contradictions, or anomalies. These are important tasks. Once fulfilled, they provide the basic argument of the research report. Readers' reactions to the entire report will depend in large part on the quality of the introduction.

Statement of the Problem. The statement of the problem is the most general component of the introduction. It describes the topic of the study in global terms. Why is the topic interesting? Why is it significant to theories of human communication? What controversies surrounding the topic need resolution? Is the topic of special practical interest, for example to politicians, media executives, social workers, therapists? In this section, you are operating as a rhetorician, discovering "the available means" of persuading potential readers to take the study seriously.

Review of the Literature. Every research report must synthesize relevant previous research and/or theory on the topic. The length and completeness of this review will depend on the type of report. Theses and dissertations usually include comprehensive presentations of earlier work, but the review section of article-length manuscripts (whose total length is about twenty-five pages) is much shorter. In these shorter reviews, the previous work described is exemplary or representative rather than exhaustive, though references may be exhaustive.

A word of advice about *when* to work on your review of the literature. Almost certainly, you will actually write the review after you have completed your research. But do not wait until that time to read and critically synthesize the relevant literature. Unless you do your library search (see Chapter 7) early, you will risk missing insights that may be crucially important to you—and you may fail to discover that your entire study is redundant. Moreover, your review should be as encompassing as you can make it. The publications you discover—even if you do not use them in this particular report—will offer valuable insight into methods and data analysis, including pitfalls for you to avoid. What you learn in a broad review will help you in ways beyond this particular research report.

Hypotheses and/or Research Questions. The review of the literature should culminate in your presentation of the specific hypotheses or questions to be addressed by the study. Various formats for this presentation are acceptable. Some authors prefer to create a separate section labeled "Hypotheses," where they formally—sometimes mathematically—express their predictions. Others are not so formal. They work their predictions into the text, thus using them as the apparently natural outcome of their literature review. You will find models in published research that will help you decide on an approach.

Whatever approach you choose, remember that the organizational format is less important than the logical format. The hypotheses and/or research questions must *clearly and logically* emanate from the other two components of the introductory section. The reader should be able to understand with relatively little effort how and why you generated your specific hypotheses and/or research questions.

Finally, do not phrase your hypotheses in null form (for example, variable X and variable Y will not be related). Recall that inferential statistics all are designed to disprove the hypothesis of no relationship. Their failure to do so may result from the "truth" of the null hypothesis—or from sloppy procedures, unreliable and/or invalid measurement, or any other shortcomings of the study. Poor research methods almost always will fail to disprove the null hypothesis because they create random variance that is extremely unlikely to enter into systematic relationships. Hence, any attempt to "prove" the null hypothesis will be challenged by readers of the study. Only rarely does a researcher, through a systematic program of careful research, succeed in inducing the scientific community to accept as a generalization "no relationship" between two variables (as in recent research on videotape as a courtroom tool [Miller & Fontes, 1979]).

Method

Recall that one of the key concepts of the scientific method is replication, and a research report must present sufficient information and description to make replication possible. An acceptable method section, therefore, must provide information about four topics (five, if *predictor variables* and *criterion variables* each have their own section).

Subjects.   This subsection must answer a number of questions about the participants in the research and the likelihood that they are an adequate and representative sample of the population to which you hope to generalize. Collectively, who are they? College students? Unemployed workers? Fifth graders? How many participated? How did you sample them? If the study was an experiment, by what method did you assign them to cells in the design? If the study was a survey, what was the response rate? Did those who refused to participate have anything in common (besides their refusal)? How might the sample be described in terms of characteristics that might be relevant to the study such as age, sex, race, socioeconomic status? Did you use these characteristics to categorize the participants in any of your analyses?

Variables.   This subsection may in fact be divided in two, one on predictor variables and one on criterion variables, depending on the paradigm underlying the study. In this subsection, you must provide operationalizations of the variables used in the study so that another researcher can use the same variables by following your directions. You must describe any apparatus (machinery or equipment) in sufficient detail so that another person can build or acquire a similar system. For many studies in communication, this equipment consists of video or audio recorders. Generic descriptions usually suffice (for example, reel-to-reel, casette, color, two-camera, etc.). Specific brand names or specifications usually are unnecessary, unless the equipment enters into highly specialized purposes, such as very close analysis of film or videotape.

Researchers in communication are unlikely to use highly specialized apparatus such as learning mazes, machines to produce visual stimuli, conditioning devices, and the like. When they do, however, they must provide considerably more descriptive detail. Sketches or diagrams might be necessary. And, depending on the equipment, information about regularity of calibration or initial settings might be provided. The test of the description is another researcher's ability to replicate the study from it.

Far more common in communication research are materials such as survey questionnaires, paper-and-pencil tests and rating scales, scoring sheets, etc. You must thoroughly describe these in the research report. If you simply borrowed them from an earlier report, you need to give only a brief description and a complete citation of the earlier report.

When you construct the materials specifically for your study, you must present much more information, including the rationale for their construction, the methods used in their development, and the procedures employed for validation (for example, pretesting). Some researchers also present data on reliability of testing instruments in this subsection, though that may be reserved for the results section. If possible, you should present (in the form of a figure, perhaps) a copy of the entire instrument.

Procedures.   The purpose of this subsection is to describe, chronologically, the execution of the study. In what order did events occur? What instructions were given to participants? How long were they given to complete particular activities in the study? Where was the researcher during this time? After reading this section, your audience should have no doubt about what you did, when you did it, and how you did it. They should be able to imagine themselves as subjects in the study, and they should experience no gaps in those images.

Statistical Method.   Statistical method sometimes may be so obvious that it does not require its own subsection. Nevertheless, you as a beginning researcher probably should include it if only for the experience. The subsection names and provides citations for statistical techniques used to generate significance levels for the results of the study, including, often, main tests and follow-up tests. The possibilities are so numerous that we again will simply refer you to models in the published research.

Results

Previous sections of the research report have dealt with rationale and method. The purpose of the results section is to present outcomes. Of all the sections of the research report, the results section depends most on the specific study for its appropriate content and organization. Nevertheless, you may keep several general guidelines in mind.

First, what should you present? In an effort to understand and appreciate the information implicit in your data, you may have conducted a wide variety of statistical analyses. But you will not present all of these in the research report.

Focus sharply on the hypotheses or research questions that you presented at the end of the introductory section. Present only those findings bearing directly on those issues. But if your secondary or tangential "data snooping" activity produces an interesting finding (because it is counterintuitive or inconsistent with previous research), include it.

Do not interpret your findings in the results section. Simply present them. You will interpret them in the following, final section of the report. In the results section, you may appropriately say, "Variable X was directly correlated with variable Y at the .01 level of significance." You may not appropriately go on to say in the results section that "the predictions of the 'decremental hypothesis' as proposed by Jones and Smith (1982) are thereby confirmed." Save the theoretic explanation for later.

Tables and figures are most likely to appear in the results section. A well-chosen and carefully constructed visual representation does much to clarify results. A table of means and standard deviations or a well-conceived and skillfully drawn figure of the data can greatly facilitate understanding. But useful tables and figures may be difficult to construct. Be prepared to devote time and patience to the task, and anticipate making a number of revisions.

Again, use published research to give you models. This book provides a few of its own. Notice that no table or figure stands alone. Tables and figures are visual *aids,* and the text should be fully interpretable without them. For an excellent discussion of methods for visually displaying data, see Johnston and Pennypacker (1980).

The source of information for tables and figures, obviously, is the data analysis. If you followed our advice, then plotting and tabling the data were integral to that analysis. Focus on those graphs, plots, or tables that stimulated you to the greatest insight. They will need refining and revising before final presentation, but they are most likely to be meaningful to a reader.

A final bit of advice about the placement of figures and tables in the manuscript. In published research reports, tables and figures appear neatly where they "belong" in the report. The printer performs this task. In the typed manuscript, the author gives the printer directions for approximate placement by inserting in the manuscript,

---

PLACE FIGURE (OR TABLE) XX ABOUT HERE

The typist inserts all figures and tables (each on a separate page) at the end of the manuscript, after the references and appendices (if any).

Discussion

The discussion section is the culmination of the research report. It interprets the findings, usually in terms of theory but sometimes also in terms of practical application. Do the results confirm or disconfirm the predictions tested? Why or why not? Are the results consistent with the results of similar previous studies? What differences between your study and previous studies might explain inconsistent results? To what population can your results be generalized? Are alternative explanations—either theoretical or methodological—plausible for your results? Even if you consider them invalid, you should mention alternative explanations and refute them to the extent that you can do so.

The discussion section also should note any flaws in the study. No study is perfect, and minor shortcomings often become apparent to a researcher during or immediately following the execution of a study. You might discover a more appropriate testing instrument, or you might realize that another experimental condition would have been informative. You should discuss such insights so that future researchers in the area can benefit from your mistakes and your consciousness of those mistakes.

Finally, the discussion section often outlines an agenda for future research. If your study has fairly clear and testable implications for later studies, you should discuss those implications.

References

A reference gives credit (or blame) to others for their work. Provide citations for any direct quotations but also for more general ideas and approaches. Normally, these will be most heavily concentrated in the subsection of the introduction in which you review relevant literature. The appropriate citation of sources is ethically required, but, if you do it smoothly and control the argument, those citations will also impress the reader with your insight and argumentative skill.

Students sometimes overlook this second outcome, thinking that instructors will be impressed only with "independent" thinking. People, including instructors, are of course impressed by independent thinking. But they know that creativity is most likely to spring from comprehensive reading and critical analysis (see Chapter 7). Hence, your judicious use of references will enhance, not degrade, readers' perceptions of your competence.

Communication research recognizes two basic styles or formats for presenting references, and a number of variations on those formats. The citations and references in this book follow, with minor variations, the second edition of a manual published by the American Psychological Association (hence "APA style"). In the text, only authors' names and the date of publication appear. Complete references are located in an alphabetical (by last name of first author) listing in the "References" section at the end of the text. APA style also allows the use of explanatory or substantive footnotes to supplement ideas being advanced in the text.

The second basic method of citing and referencing sources follows a manual published by the Modern Language Association, hence "MLA style." This approach relies on footnotes rather than a final listing, and the footnotes are consecutively numbered throughout the manuscript. These footnotes may either cite another work or they may be explanatory supplements to the text. In published documents, the footnotes usually appear at the bottoms of pages, but in typed manuscripts you should place them in a separate section entitled "Notes" after the text. You should *double-space* footnotes and all other material in any manuscript for which you intend to seek publication. The editor will need the extra space for emendations or comments to the printer.

Your library should have both the APA manual and the MLA manual, but you will want to own them if you intend to do much writing in communication research. When you ask for them at your bookstore, be certain that you are acquiring the most recent edition.

Some instructors and journals will accept only one style, some the other. In journals, this preference is often expressed inside the front cover or among the other forematter. Decide which style to use before you begin preparing the research report. Revising a manuscript from one style to the other is laborious and often induces substantive and formal errors.

A Postscript: Reacting to Criticism

You probably are reading this postscript before you actually have written a research report. This is understandable, but also a bit unfortunate. Perhaps the best time to read and consider the advice we are about to give is after you have submitted your completed report to another person or persons for evaluation.

Usually, a report is not finished when you have written it. In life, unlike college, you do not end an activity when you have submitted it for evaluation. You will seek criticism, and you will get plenty of it. You will then use this criticism, if you are wise, to revise your project or even to redo it.

Your research report is almost certain to engender some negative response. How should you react? You have two options. You may take the criticism personally and become defensive as a result. Or you may take the criticism objectively (as it almost certainly was intended) and become a better researcher and writer as a result. As we mentioned earlier: The fact that national journals in communication research reject approximately nine of ten papers submitted might be evidence that most of us have substantial room for improvement.

Negative evaluations, of course, are disappointing. Nonetheless, you will be severely constraining your future if you allow that disappointment to inhibit your learning, especially in your early development as a scholar. To the extent possible, remove your ego from your research and writing. Use criticism constructively, to help you become a better social scientist, a better writer, and a better human being.

References

See also Appendix A for other references, indexed there by the names of variables.

Anderson, N. H. Scales and statistics: Parametric and nonparametric. *Psychological Bulletin,* 58 (1961), 305–316.

Ajzen, I., & Fishbein, M. *Understanding attitudes and predicting behavior.* Englewood Cliffs, N. J.: Prentice-Hall, 1980.

Auel, J. M. *The valley of horses.* New York: Crown, 1982.

Babbie, E. R. *Survey research methods.* Belmont, Cal.: Wadsworth, 1973.

Bailey, K. D. *Methods of social research.* New York: The Free Press, 1978.

Baran, S. J. How TV and film portrayals affect sexual satisfaction in college students. *Journalism Quarterly,* 43 (1976), 468–473.

Baran, S. J., & Courtright, J. A. Television portrayals of marriages as they affect married and divorced people's satisfaction in marriage. Presented at the International Communication Association Convention, Acapulco, Mexico, 1980.

Becker, S. L. The ordinal position effect. *Quarterly Journal of Speech,* 39 (1953), 217–219.

Becker, S. L. Rating scales. In Emmert and Brooks, 1970, 213–235.

Bem, D. Self-perception theory. In L. Berkowitz (ed.), *Advances in experimental social psychology.* New York: Academic Press, 1972.

Bem, D., & Allen, A. On predicting some of the people some of the time: The search for cross-situational consistencies in behavior. *Psychological Review,* 31 (1973), 506–520.

Bem, S. The measurement of psychological androgyny. *Journal of Consulting and Clinical Psychology,* 42 (1973), 155–162.

Berger, C. L. The covering law perspective as a theoretical basis for the study of human communication. *Communication Quarterly,* 25 (1977), 7–18.

Bernstein, B. (ed.). *Class, codes and control.* London: Routledge & Kegan Paul, 1971.

Bishop, Y. M., Fienberg, S. E., & Holland, P. W. *Discrete multivariate analysis: Theory and practice.* Cambridge, Mass.: MIT Press, 1975.

Bochner, A. P. On taking ourselves seriously: An analysis of some persistent problems and promising directions in interpersonal research. *Human Communication Research,* 4 (1978), 179–191.

Boring, E. G. *History, psychology, and science: Selected papers.* R. I. Watson and D. T. Campbell (eds.). New York: John Wiley & Sons, 1963.

Bowers, J. W. Language intensity, social introversion, and attitude change. *Speech Monographs,* 30 (1963), 345–352.

Bowers, J. W. The pre-scientific function of rhetorical criticism. In T. R. Nilsen (ed.), *Essays on rhetorical criticism.* New York: Random House, 1968.

Bowers, J. W. Content analysis. In Emmert and Brooks, 1970, 291–314.

Bowers, J. W. Beyond threats and promises. *Speech Monographs,* 41 (1974), ix–xi.

Bowers, J. W., & Ochs, D. J. *The rhetoric of agitation and control.* Reading, Mass.: Addison-Wesley, 1971.

Bradac, J. J., Bowers, J. W., & Courtright, J. A. Three language variables in communication research: Intensity, immediacy, and diversity. *Human Communication Research,* 5 (1979), 257–269.

Bradac, J. J., Bowers, J. W., & Courtright, J. A. Lexical variations in intensity, immediacy, and diversity: An axiomatic theory and causal model. In R. N. St. Clair and H. Giles (eds.), *The social and psychological contexts of language.* Hillsdale, N. J.: Erlbaum, 1980.

Bradac, J. J., Konsky, C. W., & Elliott, N. D. Verbal behavior of interviewees: The effects of several situational variables on productivity, disfluency, and lexical diversity. *Journal of Communication Disorders,* 9 (1976), 211–225.

Breed, W., & De Foe, J. R. The portrayal of the drinking process on prime-time television. *Journal of Communication,* 31 (Winter 1981), 58–67.

Broadhurst, A. R., & Darnell, D. K. Introduction to cybernetics and information theory. *Quarterly Journal of Speech,* 51 (1965), 442–453.

Browning, L. D. A grounded organizational communication theory derived from qualitative data. *Communication Monographs,* 45 (1978), 93–109.

Campbell, J. A. Darwin and the origin of species: The rhetorical ancestry of an idea. *Speech Monographs,* 37 (1970), 1–14.

Campbell, D. T., & Stanley, J. C. *Experimental and quasi-experimental designs for research.* Chicago: Rand McNally, 1963.

Cappella, J. N. Talk and silence sequences in informal communication II. *Human Communication Research,* 6 (1980), 130–145.

Carmichael, C. W. Attitude change as a function of the relevance of communications and their sources to frustrating experiences. Unpublished diss., University of Iowa, 1965.

Cegala, D. J., Savage, G. T., Brunner, C. B., & Conrad, A. B. An elaboration of the meaning of interaction involvement: Toward the development of a theoretical concept. *Communication Monographs,* 49 (1982), 229–248.

Cohen, J. A coefficient of agreement for nominal scales. *Educational and Psychological Measurement,* 20 (1960), 37–46.

Cohen, J. The statistical power of abnormal-social psychological research: A review. *Journal of Abnormal and Social Psychology,* 65 (1962), 145–153.

Cohen, J. Multiple regression as a general data-analytic system. *Psychological Bulletin,* 70 (1968), 426–443.

Cohen, J. Statistical power analysis and research results. *American Education Research Journal,* 10 (1973), 225–229.

Cohen, J. *Statistical power analysis for the behavioral sciences.* New York: Academic Press, 1977.

Cohen, J., & Cohen, P. *Applied multiple regression/correlation analyses for the behavioral sciences.* Hillsdale, N. J.: Lawrence Erlbaum Associates, 1975.

Conant, J. B. *Science and common sense.* New Haven: Yale University Press, 1951.

Courtright, J. A. Rhetoric of the gun: An analysis of the rhetorical modifications of the Black Panther Party. *Journal of Black Studies,* 4 (1974), 249–267.

Courtright, J. A. A laboratory investigation of groupthink. *Communication Monographs,* 45 (1978), 229–246.

Courtright, J. A. Using SPSS and SAS for Markov chain and lag sequential analysis: An alternative to custom programs. Presented at the International Communication Association Convention, Philadelphia, 1979.

Courtright, J. A., & Baran, S. J. Factors in the acquisition of sexual information by young people. *Journalism Quarterly,* 57 (1980), 107–114.

Courtright, J. A., & Courtright, I. C. Imitative modeling as a language intervention strategy: The effects of two mediating variables. *Journal of Speech and Hearing Research,* 22 (1979), 389–402.

Courtright, J. A., & Courtright, I. C. The perception of nonverbal vocal cues of emotional meaning by language disordered and normal children. *Journal of Speech and Hearing Research* (1983).

Courtright, J. A., Millar, F. E., & Rogers, L. E. Message control intensity as a predictor of transactional redundancy. In D. Nimmo (ed.), *Communication yearbook 4.* New Brunswick, N. J.: Transaction Books, 1980.

Courtright, J. A., Millar, F. E., & Rogers-Millar, L. E. Domineeringness and dominance: Replication and expansion, *Communication Monographs,* 46 (1979), 179–192.

Cramer, H. *Mathematical methods of statistics.* Princeton: Princeton University Press, 1946.

Cronbach, L. J. Coefficient alpha and the internal structure of tests. *Psychometrika,* 16 (1951), 297–334.

Cronbach, L. J., & Meehl, P. E. Construct validity in psychological tests. *Psychological Bulletin,* 52 (1955), 281–302.

Crow, B. K. Conversational pragmatics. Unpublished diss., University of Iowa, 1982.

Cushman, D. P. The rules perspective as a theoretical basis for the study of human communication. *Communication Quarterly,* 25 (1977), 30–45.

Czubaroff, J. Intellectual responsibility: A rhetorical problem. *Quarterly Journal of Speech,* 60 (1974), 155–164.

Daly, J. A., Richmond, V. P., and Leth, S., "Social Communicative Anxiety and the Personnel Selection Process: Testing the Similarity Effect in Selection Decisions," *Human Communication Research,* Volume 6, 1979, pp. 18–32.

Darnell, D. K. Semantic differentiation. In Emmert and Brooks, 1970.

Delia, J. G. Constructivism and the study of human communication. *Quarterly Journal of Speech,* 63 (1977), 66–83.

De Vries, P. *I hear America swinging.* Boston: Little, Brown and Company, 1976.

Ebel, R. L. Estimation of the reliability of rating. *Psychometrika,* 16 (1951), 407–424.

Edwards, A. L. *Techniques of attitude scale construction.* New York: Appleton-Century-Crofts, 1957.

Ellis, D. G. Relational control in two group systems. *Communication Monographs,* 3 (1979), 153–166.

Emmert, P. Attitude scales. In Emmert and Brooks, 1970, 197–211.

Emmert, P., & Brooks, W. D. (eds.). *Methods of research in communication.* Boston: Houghton Mifflin, 1970.

Erickson, B. H., & Nosanchuk, T. A. *Understanding data.* Toronto: McGraw-Hill Ryerson Limited, 1977.

Eysenck, H. J. The effects of psychotherapy. In H. J. Eysenck (ed.), *Handbook of abnormal psychology.* New York: Basic Books, 1961.

Feigl, H., & Brodbeck, M. *Readings in the philosophy of science.* New York: Appleton-Century-Crofts, 1953.

Festinger, H., Riecken, H., & Schachter, S. *When prophecy fails.* Minneapolis: University of Minnesota Press, 1956.

Fishbein, M., & Ajzen, I. *Belief, attitude, intention and behavior: An introduction to theory and research.* Reading, Mass.: Addison-Wesley, 1975.

Fisher, B. A. Information systems theory and research: An overview. In B. Ruben (ed.), *Communication yearbook 2.* New Brunswick, N. J.: Transaction Books, 1978. (a)

Fisher, B. A. *Perspectives on human communication.* New York: MacMillan, 1978. (b)

Fisher, R. A. *Statistical methods for research workers.* Edinburgh: Oliver and Boyd, 1925.

Folger, J. P., & Sillars, A. L. Relational coding and perceptions of dominance. Presented to the Speech Communication Association Convention, Washington, D. C., 1977.

Freedman, J. L., & Fraser, S. C. Compliance without pressure: The foot-in-the-door technique. *Journal of Personality and Social Psychology,* 4 (1966), 195–202.

French, J. R. P., Jr., & Raven, B. The bases of social power. In D. Cartright and A. Zander (eds.), *Group dynamics research and theory* (2nd ed.). Evanston, Ill.: Row, Peterson, 1960.

Gerbner, G., Gross, L., Jackson-Beeck, M., Jeffries-Fox, S., & Signorielli, N. Violence profile no. 9. *Journal of Communication,* 28 (Summer 1978), 176–207.

Gerbner, G., Holsti, O. R., Krippendorff, K., Paisley, W. J., & Stone, P. J. (eds). *The analysis of communication content: Developments in scientific theories and computer techniques.* New York: John Wiley & Sons, 1969.

Glaser, B. G., & Strauss, A. L. *The discovery of grounded theory: Strategies for qualitative research.* Chicago: Aldine, 1967.

Gillham, J., & Woelfel, J. The Galileo system of measurement: Preliminary evidence for precision, stability, and equivalence to traditional measures. *Human Communication Research,* 3 (1977), 222–234.

Goodman, L. A., & Kruskal, W. H. Measures of association for cross classifications. *Journal of the American Statistical Association,* 49 (1954), 732–764.

Gouran, D. S. Variables related to consensus in group discussions of questions of policy. *Speech Monographs,* 36 (1969), 345–352.

Gouran, D. S., & Baird, J. E. An analysis of distributional and sequential structure in problem-solving and informal group discussions. *Speech Monographs,* 39 (1972), 16–22.

Grünbaum, A. Causality and the science of human behavior. *American Scientist,* 40 (1952), 667. Reprinted in Feigl & Brodbeck, 1953.

Guetzkow, H. Unitizing and categorizing problems in coding qualitative data. *Journal of Clinical Psychology,* 6 (1950), 47–58.

Guildford, J. P. *Psychometric methods.* New York: McGraw-Hill, 1954.

Gurr, T. R. *Why men rebel.* Princeton, N. J.: Princeton University Press, 1970.

Guttman, L. A basis for scaling qualitative data. *American Sociological Review,* 9 (1944), 139–150.

Hansel, C. E. M. *ESP: A scientific evaluation.* New York: Charles Scribner's Sons, 1966.

Hart, R. P., Carlson, R. E., & Eadie, W. F. Attitudes toward communication and the assessment of rhetorical sensitivity. *Communication Monographs,* 47 (1980), 1–22.

Hatfield, J. D., & Weider-Hatfield, D. The comparative utility of three types of behavioral units for interaction analysis. *Communication Monographs,* 45 (1978), 44–50.

Hays, W. L. *Statistics for the social sciences* (2nd ed.). New York: Holt, Rinehart, and Winston, 1973.

Harris, R. J. *A primer of multivariate statistics.* New York: Academic Press, 1975.

Hawes, L. C. Alternative theoretical bases: Towards a presuppositional critique. *Quarterly Journal of Speech,* 65 (1979), 55–73.

Hewes, D. E., & Haight, L. The cross-situational consistency of communicative behaviors: A preliminary investigation. *Communication Research,* 5 (1979), 243–270.

Hewes, D. E. The sequential analysis of social interaction. *Quarterly Journal of Speech,* 65 (1979), 56–73.

Hill, S., & Courtright, J. A. Perceived empathy: Its relationship to selected interpersonal variables and students' interpersonal laboratory performance. *Western Journal of Speech Communication,* 45 (1981), 213–226.

Houck, C., & Bowers, J. W. Dialect and identification. *Language and Speech,* 12 (1969), 180–186.

Janis, I. L. *Victims of groupthink.* Boston: Houghton Mifflin, 1972.

Janis, I. L., & Field, E. B. Sex differences and personality factors related to persuasibility. In C. I. Hovland and I. L. Janis (eds.), *Personality and persuasibility.* New Haven: Yale University Press, 1959.

Jeffries, L. W., & Hur, K. K. Impact of ethnic issues on ethnic voters. In S. Kraus (ed.), *The great debates: Carter versus Ford, 1976.* Bloomington, Indiana: Indiana University Press, 1979.

Johnston, J. M., & Pennypacker, H. S. *Strategies and tactics of human behavioral research.* Hillsdale, N. J.: Erlbaum, 1980.

Joslyn, R. A. The impact of campaign spot advertising on voting defections. *Human Communication Research,* 7 (1981), 347–360.

Kelman, H. C. Processes of opinion change. *Public Opinion Quarterly,* 25 (1961), 57–78.

Kerlinger, F. N. *Foundations of behavioral research.* New York: Holt, Rinehart, and Winston, 1973.

Kerlinger, F. N., & Pedhazur, E. J. *Multiple regression in behavioral research.* New York: Holt, Rinehart, and Winston, 1973.

Kim, J. K. Explaining acculturation in a communication framework: An empirical test. *Communication Monographs,* 47, (1980), 155–179.

Kirk, R. E. *Experimental design: Procedures for the behavioral sciences.* Belmont, California: Brooks/ Cole, 1968.

Kirk, R. E. (ed.). *Statistical issues: A reader for the behavioral sciences.* Monterey, California: Brooks/ Cole, 1972.

Koestler, A. *The act of creation.* New York: Macmillan, 1964.

Kraus, S. (ed.). *The great debates: Background, perspective, effects.* Bloomington, Indiana: Indiana University Press, 1962.

Kraus, S. (ed.). *The great debates: Carter versus Ford, 1976.* Bloomington, Indiana: Indiana University Press, 1979.

Krippendorff, K. *Content analysis: An introduction to its methodology.* Beverly Hills, California: Sage, 1980.

Krivonos, P. D., & Knapp, M. L. Initiating communication: What do you say when you say hello? *Central States Speech Journal,* 26 (1975), 115–125.

Kuhn, T. S. *The structure of scientific revolutions* (2nd ed.). Chicago: University of Chicago Press, 1970.

Lanzetta, J. T., & Kleck, R. E. Encoding and decoding of nonverbal affect in humans. *Journal of Personality and Social Psychology,* 16 (1970), 12–19.

Leathers, D. The feedback rating instrument: A new means of evaluating discussion. *Central States Speech Journal,* 22 (1971), 32–42.

Leathers, D. Quality of group communication as a determinant of group product. *Communication Monographs,* 39 (1972), 166–173.

Levine, M. S. *Canonical analysis and factor comparison.* Beverly Hills, California: Sage, 1977.

Likert, R. A. A technique for the measurement of attitudes. *Archives of Psychology,* 1932, No. 140.

Lindquist, E. G. *Design and analysis of experiments in psychology and education.* Boston: Houghton Mifflin, 1953.

Liska, J. Situational and topical variations in credibility criteria. *Communication Monographs,* 45 (1978), 85–92.

Littlejohn, S. W. *Theories of human communication,* Second Edition. Belmont, California: Wadsworth, 1983.

Lord, F. M. On the statistical treatment of football numbers. *American Psychologist,* 8 (1953), 750–751.

Manheimer, S. An exploration of the relationship among unwillingness-to-communicate, self-concept, and the television viewing experience. Unpublished diss., University of Iowa, 1981.

Matlon, R. J. (Compiler). *Index to journals in communication studies through 1979.* Annandale, Virginia: Speech Communication Association, 1980.

McClelland, D. C., Atkinson, J. W., Clark, R. A., & Lowell, E. L. *The achievement motive.* New York: Appleton-Century-Crofts, 1953.

McCroskey, J. C. Oral communication apprehension: A summary of recent theory and research. *Human Communication Research,* 4 (1977), 78–96.

Merton, R. K. The Matthew effect in science. *Science,* 159 (January 5, 1968), 56–63. Cited in Zuckerman, 1977.

Meyer, K., Seidler, J., Curry, T., & Aveni, A. Women in July Fourth cartoons: A 100-year look. *Journal of Communication,* 30 (Winter 1980), 21–30.

Milgram, S. *Obedience to authority: An experimental view.* New York: Harper & Row, 1974.

Millar, R. E., Rogers-Millar, L. E., & Courtright, J. A. Relational control and dyadic understanding: An exploratory predictive regression model. In D. Nimmo (ed.), *Communication yearbook 3.* New Brunswick, N. J.: Transaction Books, 1979.

Miller, G. R. Humanistic and scientific approaches to speech communication inquiry: Rivalry, redundancy, or rapprochement. *Western Journal of Speech Communication,* 39 (1975), 230–239.

Miller, G. R. Editor's foreword. In G. R. Miller (ed.), *Explorations in interpersonal communication.* Beverly Hills, California: Sage, 1976.

Miller, G. R. The current status of theory and research in interpersonal communication. *Human Communication Research,* 4 (1978), 164–178.

Miller, G. R., & Berger, C. F. On keeping the faith in matters scientific. *Western Journal of Speech Communication,* 42 (1978), 44–57.

Miller, G. R., & Burgoon, M. Persuasion research: Review and commentary. In B. D. Ruben (ed.), *Communication yearbook 2.* New Brunswick, N. J.: Transaction Books, 1978.

Miller, G. R., & Fontes, M. E. *Videotape on trial: A view from the jury box.* Beverly Hills, Cal.: Sage, 1979.

Mongé, P. R. The systems perspective as a theoretical basis for the study of human communication. *Communication Quarterly,* 25 (1977), 19–29.

Montgomery, C. L., & Burgoon, M. An experimental study of the interactive effects of sex and androgyny in attitude change. *Communication Monographs,* 44 (1977), 130–135.

Morris, C. *Signs, language and behavior.* Englewood Cliffs, N. J.: Prentice-Hall, 1946.

Motley, M. T., Camden, C. T., & Baers, D. J. Toward verifying the assumptions of laboratory induced slips of the tongue: The output-error and editing issues. *Human Communication Research,* 8 (1981), 3–15.

Norton, R. W. Communicator style and teacher effectiveness. In B. Ruben (ed.), *Communication Yearbook 1.* New Brunswick, N. J.: Transaction Books, 1977.

Nunnally, J. C. *Psychometric theory* (2nd ed.). New York: McGraw-Hill, 1978.

Ogilvie, D. M., Stone, P. J., & Schneidman, E. S. Some characteristics of genuine vs. simulated suicide notes. In P. J. Stone, D. C. Dunphy, M. S. Smith, & D. M. Ogilvie, with associates, *The general inquirer: A computer approach to content analysis.* Cambridge, Mass.: M.I.T. Press, 1966.

O'Keefe, D. J. Logical empiricism and the study of human communication. *Speech Monographs,* 42 (1975), 169–183.

Olson, C. L. On choosing a test statistic in multivariate analysis of variance. *Psychological Bulletin,* 83 (1976), 579–586.

Osgood, C. E., Suci, G. J., & Tannenbaum, P. H. *The measurement of meaning.* Urbana, Illinois: University of Illinois Press, 1957.

Osgood, C. E., & Walker, E. G. Motivation and language behavior: A content analysis of suicide notes. *Journal of Abnormal and Social Psychology,* 59 (1959), 58–67.

Ott, L., Mendenhall, W., & Larson, R. F. *Statistics: A tool for the social sciences.* North Scituate, Mass.: Duxbury Press, 1978.

Parks, M. R. A test of the cross-situational consistency of communication apprehension. *Communication Monographs,* 47 (1980), 220–232.

Pearce, W. B. The coordinated management of meaning: A rules-based theory of interpersonal communication. In G. R. Miller (ed.), *Explorations in interpersonal communication.* Beverly Hills, California: Sage, 1976.

Perloff, R. M., Quarles, R. C., & Drutz, M. Social isolation, loneliness and television use among college students. Presented to Association for Education in Journalism, Boston, 1980.

Philipsen, G. Speaking "like a man" in Teamsterville: Culture patterns of role enactment in an urban neighborhood. *Quarterly Journal of Speech,* 61 (1975), 13–22.

Phillips, G. M. *Communication and the small group.* Indianapolis: Bobbs-Merrill, 1966.

Pingree, S., Hawkins, R. P., Butler, M., & Paisley, W. A scale for sexism in magazine advertising. *Journal of Communication,* 26 (Autumn 1976), 193–200.

Roberts, C. L. The effects of self-confrontation, role playing, and response feedback on the level of self-esteem. Unpublished diss., University of Iowa, 1972.

Rogers, L. E., Courtright, J. A., & Millar, F. E. Message control intensity: rationale and preliminary findings. *Communication Monographs,* 47 (1980), 201–219.

Rogers, L. E., & Farace, R. V. Analysis of relational communication in dyads: New measurement procedures. *Human Communication Research,* 1 (1975), 222–239.

Rogers-Millar, L. E., & Millar, F. E. Domineeringness and dominance: A transactional view. *Human Communication Research,* 5 (1979), 238–246.

Rosenthal, R., & Jacobson, L. *Pygmalion in the classroom.* New York: Holt, Rinehart, & Winston, 1968.

Rosenthal, R., & Rosnow, R. L. (eds.). *Artifact in behavioral research.* New York: Academic Press, 1969.

Rossiter, L. M. The validity of communication experiments using human subjects: A review. *Human Communication Research,* 2 (1976), 197–206.

Rowe, C. L. The connotative dimensions of selected display typefaces. *Information Design Journal,* 3 (1982), 30–37.

Sanders, R., & Martin, L. Grammatical rules and explanations of behavior. *Inquiry,* 18 (1975), 65–82.

Searle, J. *Speech acts.* Cambridge: Cambridge University Press, 1969.

Seibold, D. R. Communication research and the attitude-verbal report-overt behavior relationship: A critique and theoretic reformulation. *Human Communication Research,* 2 (1975), 3–32.

Skelly, G. U., & Lundstrom, W. J. Male sex roles in magazine advertising. *Journal of Communication,* 31 (Autumn 1981), 52–57.

Shimanoff, S. B. *Communication rules: Theory and research.* Beverly Hills, California: Sage, 1980.

Skinner, B. F. *Science and human behavior.* New York: Macmillan, 1953.

Siegel, S. *Nonparametric statistics for the behavioral sciences.* New York: McGraw-Hill, 1956.

Snider, J., & Osgood, C. (eds.). *Semantic differential technique: A sourcebook.* Chicago: Aldine, 1969.

Stark, R., Foster, B. D., Glock, C. Y., & Quinley, H. E. *Wayward shepherds: Prejudice and the protestant clergy.* New York: Harper & Row, 1971.

Stech, E. L., & Goldberg, A. A. Sampling discussion group interaction. *Speech Monographs,* 39 (1972), 312–314.

Stephenson, W. *The study of behavior.* Chicago: University of Chicago Press, 1953.

Stevens, J. Comment on Olson: Choosing a test statistic in multivariate analysis of variance. *Psychological Bulletin,* 86 (1979), 355–360.

Stevens, S. S. Mathematics, measurement, and psychophysics. In S. S. Stevens (ed.), *Handbook of experimental psychology.* New York: Wiley, 1951.

Stewart, D. K., & Love, W. A. A general canonical correlation index. *Psychological Bulletin,* 70 (1968), 160–163.

Tannenbaum, P. H. Entertainment as vicarious emotional experience. In P. H. Tannenbaum (ed.), *The entertainment functions of television.* Hillsdale, N. J.: Lawrence Erlbaum Associates, 1980.

Tedeschi, J. T., Schlenker, B. R., & Bonoma, T. V. *Conflict, power, and games.* Chicago: Aldine, 1973.

Thorndike, E. L., & Lorge, I. *The teacher's word book of 20,000 words.* New York: Teacher's College, Columbia University, 1927.

Thurstone, L. L. The measurement of attitudes. *Journal of Abnormal and Social Psychology,* 26 (1931), 249–269.

Thurstone, L. L., & Chave, E. J. *The measurement of attitude.* Chicago: University of Chicago Press, 1929.

Tompkins, P. K. *Communication as action.* Belmont, California: Wadsworth, 1982.

Tucker, R. K., & Chase, L. J. Canonical correlation in human communication research. *Human Communication Research,* 3 (1976), 86–96.

Tucker, R. K., & Chase, L. J. Canonical correlation. In P. R. Mongé and J. N. Cappella (eds.), *Multivariate techniques in human communication research.* New York: Academic Press, 1980.

Tukey, J. W. *Exploratory data analysis.* Reading, Mass.: Addison-Wesley, 1977.

Von Wright, G. H. *Explanation and understanding.* Ithaca, N. Y.: Cornell University Press, 1971.

Walker, H. M. Degrees of freedom. *Journal of Educational Psychology,* 31 (1940), 253–269.

Watzlawick, P., Beavin, J. H., & Jackson, D. *Pragmatics of human communication.* New York: W. W. Norton, 1967.

Watzlawick, P., Weakland, J., & Fisch, R. *Change: Principles of problem formation and problem resolution.* New York: W. W. Norton, 1974.

Webb, E. J., Campbell, D. T., Schwartz, R. D., & Sechrest, L. *Unobtrusive measures: Nonreactive research in the social sciences.* Chicago: Rand McNally, 1966.

Webb, E., & Roberts, K. H. Unconventional uses of content analysis in social science. In Gerbner, Holsti, Krippendorff, Paisley, & Stone, 1969.

Weiss, D. J. Canonical correlation analysis in counseling psychology research. *Journal of Counseling Psychology,* 19 (1972), 241–252.

Wheeless, L. R., & Grotz, J. The measurement of trust and its relationship to self-disclosure. *Human Communication Research,* 3 (1977), 250–257.

Whorf, B. *Language, thought, and reality.* New York: McGraw-Hill, 1971.

Williams, F. Language, attitude, and social change. In F. Williams (ed.), *Language and poverty.* Chicago: Markham, 1970.

Winer, B. J. *Statistical principles in experimental design.* New York: McGraw-Hill, 1971.

Woelfel, J. Foundations of cognitive theory: A multidimensional model of the message-attitude-behavior relationship. In D. P. Cushman and R. D. McPhee (eds.), *Message-attitude-behavior relationship: Theory, methodology, and application.* New York: Academic Press, 1980.

Woelfel, J., & Danes, J. E. Multidimensional scaling models for communication research. In P. R. Mongé and J. N. Capella (eds), *Multivariate techniques in human communication research.* New York: Academic Press, 1980.

Woelfel, J., Cody, M. J., Gillham, J., & Holmes, R. A. Basic premises of multidimensional attitude change theory: An experimental analysis. *Human Communication Research,* 6 (1980), 153–167.

Zipf, G. K. *The psychobiology of language: An introduction to dynamic philology.* Cambridge, Mass.: MIT Press, 1965. (Originally published, 1935.)

Zuckerman, H. *Scientific elite: Nobel laureates in the United States.* New York: The Free Press, 1977.

Appendix

What Are Some of the Variables Other Researchers Have Used?

This appendix consists of an index of variables, all relatively easy to use, that have been employed recently in communication research. Each entry lists the variable and, except for obvious variables such as age and sex, a reference to a journal or book where its operationalization may be found. All variables in the index were identified from a search of *Communication Monographs, Human Communication Research,* and *Journal of Communication* for the years 1979, 1980, and 1981.

We do not insert this index in order to encourage you to uncritically adopt (or adapt) conceptual variables that have been operationalized by others. You should pursue research problems that are interesting to you, and, if you discover that work on some of those interesting variables has already been done, you should investigate and evaluate that work before you use it as an intrinsic part of your own work. Not all of the recipes for making variables in this list will result in nutritional dishes.

But we do hope that this index will give you ideas—both general ideas about the kind of work others have attempted and specific ideas about the work you might do. If nothing else, we hope that it will lead you to experiment in small ways with some of these variables, and thereby to get an experiential idea of social science in communication.

We have used three abbreviations in this index. *Communication Monographs* is identified as *CM; Human Communication Research* is identified as *HCR;* and *Journal of Communication* is identified as *JC. Communication Monographs* was published under the title *Speech Monographs* through 1975, so in your library you probably will find *Speech Monographs* catalogued and shelved as the early volumes of *Communication Monographs.*

Recall that the entries in the References section were formatted in APA style. To illustrate an alternative, the citations in this appendix employ the MLA format. For periodical entries in this index, the number immediately following the title of the periodical is the volume number for that entry. Numbers at the end of entries refer to the page number(s) where the variable is described and discussed.

Ability to Function in an Organization (Perceived)
> J. A. Daly, V. P. Richmond, and S. Leth. "Social Communicative Anxiety and the Personnel Selection Process: Testing the Similarity Effect in Selection Decisions." *HCR*, 6 (1979), 20.

Academic Major

Academic Performance
>   S. G. Burton, J. M. Calonico, and D. R. McSeveney. "Effects of Preschool Television Watching on First-Grade Children." *JC*, 29 (Summer 1979), 166.

Acceptance (of Interactional Partner)
>   T. L. Thompson and D. R. Seibold. "Stigma Management in Normal-Stigmatized Interactions: Test of the Disclosure Hypothesis and a Model of Stigma Acceptance." *HCR*, 4 (1978), 236.

Access (Frequency of) Due to a Cue
>   C. J. Kasperson. "An Analysis of the Relationship Between Information Sources and Creativity in Scientists and Engineers." *HCR*, 4 (1978), 117.

Accuracy (of Communication)
>   J. E Grunig. "Accuracy of Communication from an External Public to Employees of a Formal Organization." *HCR*, 5 (1978), 45.

Acquaintance, Stages of
>   V. P. Richmond. "The Relationship Between Trait and State Communication Apprehension and Interpersonal Perceptions During Acquaintance Stages." *HCR*, 4 (1978), 340–341.

Acquaintance with Active Feminist Women
>   B. Bate. "Nonsexist Language in Transition." *JC*, 28 (Winter 1978), 143.

Advertisements (Perceived Influence of) on Consumer Decision
>   E. S. Schreiber and P. A. Boyd. "How the Elderly Perceive Television Commercials." *JC*, 30 (Winter 1980), 64.

Age

Aggression on Television (Content Analysis Scheme)
>   R. L. Welch, A. Huston-Stein, J. C. Wright, and R. Plehal. "Subtle Sex-Role Cues in Children's Commercials." *JC*, 29 (Summer 1979), 205.

Aggressiveness (Perceived)
>   J. R. Cantor. "Grammatical Variations in Persuasion: Effectiveness of Four Forms of Request in Door-to-Door Solicitations for Funds." *CM*, 46 (1979), 301.

Agreement Scale
>   P. H. Bradley. "The Folk-Linguistics of Women's Speech: An Empirical Examination." *CM*, 48 (1981), 80.

Alcohol Consumption on Television (Content Analysis Scheme)
>   W. Breed and J. R. Defoe. "The Portrayal of the Drinking Process on Prime-Time Television." *JC*, 31 (Winter, 1981), 58–67.

Alcohol Ingested (High vs. Low)
>   R. N. Bostrom and N. D. White. "Does Drinking Weaken Resistance?" *JC*, 29 (Summer 1979), 75.

"Allness" Terms
>   W. J. Jordan and W. G. Powers. "Verbal Behavior as a Function of Apprehension and Social Context." *HCR*, 4 (1978), 296.

Ambiguity, Intolerance of
>   J. Martin and F. Westie. "The Tolerant Personality." *American Sociological Review*, 24 (1959), 521–528.

Ambiguity, Tolerance of
>   S. Budner. "Intolerance of Ambiguity as a Personality Variable." *Journal of Personality*, 30 (1962), 29–50.

Androgyny
>   S. L. Bem. "The Measurement of Psychological Androgyny." *Journal of Consulting and Clinical Psychology*, 42 (1979), 55.

Anxiety of Message Source (Perceived)
>   See Ability to Function in an Organization, 24–25.

Anxiety (Perceived)
>   See Ability to Function in an Organization (Perceived), 20.

Assault Potential (of Potential Victims)
>   B. Grayson and M. I. Stein. "Attracting Assault: Victims' Nonverbal Cues." *JC*, 31 (Winter 1981), 70.

Attacking vs. Defensive Messages
>   W. J. McGuire. "Persistence of the Resistance to Persuasion Induced by Various Types of Prior Belief Defenses." *Journal of Abnormal and Social Psychology*, 64 (1962), 241–248.

Attentiveness Evaluation
>   R. W. Norton and L. S. Pettegrew. "Attentiveness as a Style of Communication: A Structural Analysis." *CM*, 46 (1979), 22.

Attentiveness Sensitivity
>   See Attentiveness Evaluation, 22.

Attentiveness Signals
>   See Attentiveness Evaluation, 21.

Attentiveness to Media
>   W. A. Lucas and W. C. Adams. "Talking, Television, and Voter Indecision." *JC*, 28 (Autumn 1978), 125.

Attitude
>   C. L. Montgomery and M. Burgoon. "The Effects of Androgyny and Message Expectations on Resistance to Persuasive Communication." *CM*, 47 (1980), 57.

Attitude Assessment
>   J. A. Daly, "Communication Apprehension and Behavior: Applying a Multiple Act Criteria." *HCR*, 4 (1978), 212.

Attitude Change
>   See Alcohol Ingested, 75–76.

Attitude Measures
>   M. D. Miller and M. Burgoon. "The Relationship Between Violations of Expectations and the Induction of Resistance to Persuasion." *HCR*, 5 (1979), 307.

Attitude Scale
>   D. Byrne. *The Attraction Paradigm.* New York: Academic Press, 1971.

Attraction
>   J. C. McCroskey and T. A. McCain. "The Measurement of Interpersonal Attraction." *Speech Monographs* (now *CM*), 41 (1974), 261–266.
>   See also Attitude Scale.

Attribute Scales (for Situations)
>   M. J. Cody and M. L. McLaughlin. "Perceptions of Compliance-Gaining Situations: A Dimensional Analysis." *CM,* 47 (1980), 137, 143.

Attributional Confidence Scale
>   G. W. Clatterbuck. "Attributional Confidence and Uncertainty in Initial Interaction." *HCR,* 5 (1979), 149.

Audience Sensitivity
>   A. Paivio, A. L. Baldwin, and S. M. Berger. "Measurement of Children's Sensitivity to Audiences." *Child Development,* 32 (1961), 721–730.

Avoidance (of Communication)
>   M. J. Beatty, R. G. Springhorn, and M. W. Kruger. "Towards the Development of Cognitively Experienced Speech Anxiety." *Central States Speech Journal,* 27 (1976), 181–186.

Behavioral Intention to Interact
>   D. J. O'Keefe and J. G. Delia. "Construct Differentiation and the Relationship of Attitudes and Behavioral Intentions." *CM,* 48 (1981), 152.

Belief Index
>   J. E. Danes, J. E. Hunter, and J. Woelfel. "Mass Communication and Belief Change: A Test of Three Mathematical Models." *HCR,* 4 (1978), 246.

Bem Sex Role Inventory (BSRI)
>   See Androgyny.

Body Movement Code (Category System)
>   See Assault Potential, 72.

Cartoons (Newspaper), Appearance of Women in
>   K. Meyer, J. Seidler, T. Curry, and A. Aven. "Women in July Fourth Cartoons: A 100-Year Look." *JC,* 30 (Winter 1980), 22.

Cartoons (Newspaper), Degree of Constraint on Depiction of Women in
>   See Cartoons (Newspaper), Appearance of Women in, 23.

Childhood Print Media Usage
>   E. C. Hirschman. "Social and Cognitive Influences on Information Exposure: A Path Analysis." *JC,* 31 (Winter 1981), 79–80.

Children's Television Programs, Formal Features of
>   A. C. Huston, J. C. Wright, E. Wartella, M. L. Rice, B. A. Watkins, T. Campbell, and R. Polts. "Communicating More than Content: Formal Features of Children's Television Programs." *JC,* 31 (Summer 1981), 39.

Choice of Issue to Be Argued For
>B. R. Schlenker and M. Riess. "Self-Presentations of Attitudes Following Commitment to Proattitudinal Behavior." *HCR,* 5 (1979), 329.

Church Attendance

Classroom Behavior of Children
>D. M. Zuckerman, D. G. Singer, and J. L. Singer. "Television Viewing, Children's Reading and Related Classroom Behavior." *JC,* 30 (Winter 1980), 170.

Cognitive Complexity
>W. H. Crockett. "Cognitive Complexity and Impression Formation," in *Progress in Experimental Personality Research,* ed. Brendan A. Maher. New York: Academic Press, 1965, II, 47–90.

Column Inches, Number of (in Issue of New York Times)
>A. Mazur. "Media Coverage and Public Opinion on Scientific Controversies." *JC,* 31 (Spring 1981), 112.

Commercials (Television), Formal Features of
>See Aggression on Television, 204–205.

Communication Anxiety
>W. Hensley and P. Batty. "The Measurement of Communication Anxiety Among Students in Public Speaking Courses." *Indiana Speech Journal* (November 1974), 7–10.

Communication Apprehension, Effect of Situation on
>M. R. Parks. "A Test of the Cross-Situational Consistency of Communication Apprehension." *CM,* 47 (1980), 227–228.

Communication Efficacy
>D. Stipek and K. Nelson. "Communication Efficacy of Middle and Lower SES Dyads." *HCR,* 6 (1980), 171.

Communication Strategies
>R. A. Clark. "The Impact of Self-Interest and Desire for Liking on the Selection of Communication Strategies." *CM,* 46 (1979), 260–264.

Communicative Behavior Questionnaire
>M. L. Knapp, D G. Ellis, and B. A. Williams. "Perceptions of Communication Behavior Associated with Relational Terms." *CM,* 47 (1980), 269–270.

Communicative Effectiveness (Perceived)
>D. R. Brandt. "On Linking Social Performance with Social Competence: Some Relations Between Communicator Style and Attributions of Interpersonal Attractiveness and Effectiveness." *HCR,* 5 (1979), 232.

Communicative Performance (in Persuasion)
>B. J. O'Keefe and J. G. Delia. "Construct Comprehensiveness and Cognitive Complexity as Predictors of the Number and Strategic Adaptation of Arguments and Appeals in a Persuasive Message." *CM,* 46 (1979), 237.

Communicator Style
>R. W. Norton. "Foundation of a Communicator Style Construct." *HCR,* 4 (1978), 103.

Communicator Style (Content Analysis Scheme)
> D. R. Brandt. "On Linking Social Preference with Social Competence: Some Relations Between Communicator Style and Attributions of Interpersonal Attractiveness and Effectiveness." *HCR*, 5 (1979), 227–228.

Communicator Style (Short Form)
> B. M. Montgomery and R. W. Norton. "Sex Differences and Similarities in Communicator Style." *CM*, 48 (1981), 128.

Compliance-Gaining Strategies
> M. W. Lustig and S. W. King. "The Effect of Communication Apprehension and Situation on Communication Strategy Choices." *HCR*, 7 (1980), 76–77.
> A. L. Sillars. "The Stranger and the Spouse as Target Persons for Compliance-Gaining Strategies: A Subjective Expected Utility Model." *HCR*, 6 (1980), 269.

Compliance-Gaining Strategies (Taxonomy for Content Analysis)
> R. L. Wiseman and W. Schenk-Hamlin. "A Multidimensional Scaling Validation of an Inductively-Derived Set of Compliance-Gaining Strategies." *CM*, 48 (1981), 257–258.

Compliance-Resisting Strategies
> M. L. McLaughlin, M. J. Cody, and C. S. Robey. "Situational Influences on the Selection of Strategies to Resist Compliance-Gaining Attempts." *HCR*, 7 (1980), 25–26.

Confidence in a Decision
> M. Burgoon, M. Cohen, M. D. Miller, and C. L. Montgomery. "An Empirical Test of a Model of Resistance to Persuasion." *HCR*, 5 (1978), 34.

Conflict Strategies (a Typology)
> A. L. Sillars. "Attributions and Communication in Roommate Conflict." *CM*, 47 (1980), 188.

"Constraint Recognition" in Organizations
> See Accuracy of Communication, 44.

Construct Comprehensiveness
> B. J. O'Keefe and J. G. Delia. "Construct Comprehensiveness and Cognitive Complexity." *Perceptual and Motor Skills*, 46 (1978), 548–550.

Consumer Spending on Mass Media
> M. E. McCombs and C. H. Eyal. "Spending on Mass Media." *JC*, 30 (Winter 1980), 154–155.

Contexts for Discussions about Sex
> J. S. Sanders and W. L. Robinson. "Talking and Not Talking About Sex: Male and Female Vocabularies." *JC*, 29 (Spring 1979), 25.

Conversation Styles on Soap Operas (Content Analysis Scheme)
> M. G. Fine. "Soap Opera Conversations: The Talk That Binds." *JC*, 31 (Summer 1981), 100.

Conversation Topics
> See Attentiveness to Media, 126.

Conversational Content (Coding Scheme)
   J. G. Delia, R. A. Clark, and D. E. Switzer. "The Content of Informal Conversations as a Function of Interactants' Interpersonal Cognitive Complexity." *CM*, 46 (1979), 278.

Counterarguments, Number of
   See Alcohol Ingested.

Corporate Political Advertising Typology (Content Analysis Scheme)
   R. G. Meadow. "The Political Dimensions of Nonproduct Advertising." *JC*, 31 (Summer 1981), 76–80.

Credibility
   J. Liska. "Situational and Topic Variation in Credibility Criteria." *CM*, 45 (1978), f.n. 8, 86.
   J. L. Whitehead. "Factors of Source Credibility." *Quarterly Journal of Speech*, 54 (1968), 59–63.

Credibility of the Media (Perceived)
   See Advertisements (Perceived Influence of) on Consumer Decision, 64.

Crime in the Mass Media, Coverage of (Content Analysis Scheme)
   D. A. Graber. "Is Crime News Coverage Excessive?" *JC*, 29 (Summer 1979), 82–83.

Cultivation Effect Instrument for Soap Operas
   N. L. Buerkel-Rothfuss with S. Mayes. "Soap Opera Viewing: The Cultivation Effect." *JC*, 31 (Summer 1981), 110.

Cultural Indicators "Mean World" Index
   S. Pingree and R. Hawkins. "U. S. Programs on Australian Television: The Cultivation Effect." *JC*, 31 (Winter 1981), 100.

Debates (Presidential), Exposure to
   G. F. Bishop, R. W. Oldendick, and A. J. Tuchfarber. "Debate Watching and the Acquisition of Political Knowledge." *JC*, 28 (Autumn 1978), 101.
   S. Kraus (ed.). *The Great Debates: Carter Versus Ford, 1976*. Bloomington, Indiana: Indiana University Press, 1979.

Decision Proposal System (Content Analysis Scheme)
   B. A. Fisher. "Decision Emergence: Phases in Group Decision-Making." *Speech Monographs* (now *CM*), 37 (1970), 55.

Defensive vs. Attacking Messages
   See Attacking vs. Defensive Messages, 241–248.

Degree of Closeness to Women's Movement
   See Acquaintance with Active Feminist Women, 142.

Dependency on Channels of Communication for Political Information
   G. J. O'Keefe and J. Liv. "First-Time Voters: Do Media Matter?" *JC*, 30 (Autumn 1980), 125.

Depictions of Elderly on Television (Perceptions of)
   F. Korzenny and K. Neuendorf. "Television Viewing and Self-Concept of the Elderly." *JC*, 30 (Winter 1980), 75.

Desirability of Verbal Response
J. B. Stull. "Rewards for Openness." *JC*, 28 (Winter 1978), 126.

Desired Liking
See Communication Strategies, 259.

Dialect Attitude Scale
A. Mulac. "Assessment and Application of the Revised Speech Dialect Attitudinal Scale." *CM*, 43 (1976), 238–245.

Dialectical Similarity (Perceived)
W. J. Schenck-Hamlin. "The Effects of Dialectical Similarity, Stereotyping, and Message Agreement on Interpersonal Perception." *HCR*, 5 (1978), 18.

Diffuse Support for the Political System
A. S. Tan. "Political Participation, Diffuse Support, and Perceptions of Political Efficacy as Predictors of Mass Media Use." *CM*, 48 (1981), 141.

Disclosure Tendencies
J. J. Bradac, L. A. Hosman, and C. H. Tardy. "Reciprocal Disclosure and Language Intensity: Attributional Consequences." *CM*, 45 (1978), 9.

Discrepancy of Attitude
M. J. Smith. "Discrepancy and the Importance of Attitudinal Freedom." *HCR*, 4 (1978), 310–311.

Discussant Contribution to Group
D. S. Gouran and J. E. Baird, Jr. "An Analysis of Distributional and Sequential Structure in Problem-Solving and Informal Group Discussions." *Speech Monographs* (now *CM*), 39 (1972), 16–23.

Discussion Quality
D. S. Gouran, C. Brown, and D. R. Henry. "Behavioral Correlates of Perceptions of Quality in Decision-Making Discussions." *CM*, 45 (1978), 51–63.
See Groupthink Indicators.

Dogmatism
M. Rokeach. *The Open and Closed Mind*. New York: Basic Books, 1960.

Dogmatism (Short Form)
V. C. Trohldahl and F. Powell. "A Short-Form Dogmatism Scale for Use in Field Studies." *Social Forces*, 44 (1964), 211.

Dominance
J. A. Courtright, F. E. Millar, and L. E. Rogers-Millar. "Domineeringness and Dominance: Replicaion and Expansion." *CM*, 46 (1979), 181–186.
P. H. Bradley. "Sex, Competence, and Opinion Deviation: An Expectation States Approach." *CM*, 47 (1980), 105.

Dominance in Depiction (of Women in Newspaper Cartoons) (Content Analysis Scheme)
See Cartoons (Newspaper), Appearance of Women in, 22.

Domineeringness
See Dominance.

Donations (to a Charity), Amount of
See Aggressiveness (Perceived), 301.

Donations (to a Charity), Number of
See Aggressiveness (Perceived), 301.

Drug Advertising (Exposure to) Index
C. R. Atkin. "Effects of Drug Commercials on Young Viewers." *JC*, 28 (Autumn 1978), 72–73.

Drug Approval
See Drug Advertising (Exposure to) Index, 75.

Drug Orientation
See Drug Advertising (Exposure to) Index, 74.

Drug Use on Television (Content Analysis Scheme)
C. F. Fernandez-Collado and B. S. Greenberg with F. Korzenny and C. K. Atkin. "Sexual Intimacy and Drug Use in TV Series." *JC*, 28 (Summer 1978), 32.

Dyadic Adjustment Scale
G. Spanier. "Measuring Dyadic Adjustment: New Scales for Measuring the Quality of Marriage and Similar Dyads." *Journal of Marriage and the Family*, 38 (1976), 15–27.

Editorial Quality (Perceived)
L. Bogart. "Editorial Ideals, Editorial Illusions." *JC*, 29 (Spring 1979), 13.

Education

Elderly Characters on Television, Attribute Ratings
D. Shinar, A. Tomer, and A. Biber. "Images of Old Age in Television Drama." *JC*, 30 (Winter 1980), 52.

Elderly (Perceived Depiction of) in Television Commercials
See Advertisements (Perceived Influence of) on Consumer Decision, 64.

Empathy
A. Mehrabian and N. Epstein. "A Measure of Emotional Empathy." *Journal of Personality*, 40 (1972), 525–543.

Encoding Consistency
F. L. Johnson. "Communicative Purpose in Children's Referential Language." *CM*, 47 (1980), 49–50.

Encoding Style
See Encoding Consistency, 50.

Equal Rights Amendment, Magazine Advocacy of
J. Farley. "Women's Magazines and the Equal Rights Amendment: Friend or Foe?" JC, 28 (Winter 1978), 190.

Equal Rights Amendment, Magazine Coverage of
See Equal Rights Amendment, Magazine Advocacy of, 189.

Ethnic Groups in Mass Media, Perceived Depiction of
> L. W. Jeffres and K. K. Hur. "White Ethnics and Their Media Image." *JC*, 29 (Winter 1979), 117.

Ethnic Homogeneity of Neighborhood
> See Ethnic Groups (Perceived Depiction of) in Mass Media, 118.

Ethnic Identification (Strength)

Ethnic Mass Media, Use of
> See Ethnic News Coverage (Perceived Quality of), 118.

Ethnic Network
> J. K. Kim. "Explaining Acculturation in a Communication Framework: An Empirical Test." *CM*, 47 (1980), 169.

Ethnic News Coverage (Perceived Quality of)
> See Ethnic Groups (Perceived Depiction of) in Mass Media, 118.

Ethnic Origin

Exhibitionism Scale
> See Audience Sensitivity.

External Involvement with Organization
> See Accuracy of Communication, 45.

Extroversion/Extraversion
> H. Eysenck. "A Short Questionnaire for the Measurement of Two Dimensions of Personality." *Journal of Applied Psychology*, 42 (1958), 14–17.
>
> A. Jensen. "The Maudsley Personality Inventory." *Acta Psychologica*, 14 (1958), 314–325.

Extroversion (Perceived)
> See Ability to Function in an Organization (Perceived), 21.

Eye Gaze
> D. J. Cegala, A. F. Alexander, and S. Sokuritz. "An Investigation of Eye Gaze and Its Relation to Selected Verbal Behavior." *HCR*, 5 (1979), 102.
> G. Robbins, S. Devoe, and M. Wiener. "Social Patterns of Turn-Taking: Nonverbal Regulators." *JC*, 28 (Summer 1978), 40.

Eye Movement
> J. E. Hocking and D. G. Leathers. "Nonverbal Indicators of Deception: A New Theoretical Perspective." *CM*, 47 (1980), 127.

Facial Features (Negroid vs. Caucasian)
> R. A. Kerin. "Black Model Appearance and Product Evaluations." *JC*, 29 (Winter 1979), 124.

Facial Movements
> See Eye Movement.

Family Communication Questionnaire
>S. H. Chaffee, J. M. McLeod, and D. B. Wackman. "Family Communication Patterns and Adolescent Political Participation," in *Socialization to Politics,* ed. J. J. Dennis. New York: J. Wiley, 1973.

Family Communication Patterns (Consumer Socialization Version)
>G. P. Moschis and R. L. Moore. "Family Communication and Consumer Socialization," in *Advances in Consumer Research,* ed. W. L. Wilkie. Ann Arbor, Michigan: Association for Consumer Research, VI, 1979.

Family Income

Family Size

Father's Interest in Politics
>See Dependency on Channels of Communication for Political Information, 125.

Fear of Crime (Self-Report)
>W. B. Jaehnig, D. H. Weaver, and F. Kico. "Reporting Crime and Fearing Crime in Three Communities." *JC,* 31 (Winter 1981), 92.

Feedback (in Organizations), Amount of
>C. A. O'Reilly, III, and J. C. Anderson. "Trust and the Communication of Performance Appraisal Information: The Effect of Feedback on Performance and Job Satisfaction." *HCR,* 4 (1980), 293.

Feedback (in Organizations), Developmental Nature of
>See Feedback (in Organizations), Amount of, 293.

Feedback (in Organizations), Perceived Accuracy of
>See Feedback (in Organizations), Amount of, 293.

FIRO-B (Fundamental Interpersonal Relations Orientations-Behavior)
>W. Schutz. *FIRO: A Three-Dimensional Theory of Interpersonal Behavior.* New York: Rinehart, 1957.

Food Consumption on Television (Content Analysis Scheme)
>L. Kaufman. "Prime-time Nutrition." *JC,* 30 (Summer 1980), 38–40.

Foreign News Coverage (Content Analysis Scheme)
>D. H. Weaver and G. Cleveland Wilhoit. "Foreign News Coverage in Two U.S. Wire Services." *JC,* 31 (Spring 1981), 58–61.

Forms of Request
>See Aggressiveness (Perceived), 297–300.

Frequency of Appearance of Women in Newspaper Cartoons
>See Cartoons (Newspaper), Appearance of Women in, 22.

Frequency of Channel Access
>See Access (Frequency of) Due to a Cue, 116.

Frequency of Discussions
>See Dominance (second reference), 187.

Frequency of Discussions About Political Candidates
See Attentiveness to Media, 127.

Frequency of Grammatical Variants per Turn
M. G. Fine, C. Anderson, and G. Eckles. "Black English on Black Situation Comedies." *JC*, 29 (Summer 1979), 23–27.

Gender of Pronoun in Sentence Completions
W. Martyng. "What Does 'He' Mean? Use of Generic Masculine." *JC*, 28 (Winter 1978), 133.

Gender-Related Terms and Phrases, Attitudes Toward
See Acquaintance with Active Feminist Women, 142.

Gender-Typed Situation
See Gender of Pronoun in Sentence Completions, 134.

Generic Terms, Use of
S. E. Purnell. "Politically Speaking, Do Women Exist?" *JC*, 28 (Winter 1978), 151–152.

Gestures (Illustrators, Adaptors, Hand to Face Gestures, Leg Movements, Foot Movements,
Overall Body Nervousness)
See Eye Movement, 126.

Goals of the Women's Movement
See Acquaintance with Active Feminist Women, 143.

Government Policies, Attitudes Toward
R. M. Entman and D. L. Paletz. "Media and the Conservative Myth." *JC*, 30 (Autumn 1980), 156–158.

Grandparent's Birthplace

Group Behavior (Dimension)
R. F. Bales. *Personality and Interpersonal Behavior*. New York: Holt, Rinehart, and Winston, 1970.

Group Behavior (Perception of)
See Discussion Quality, 53.

Group Effectiveness (Open-Ended Questionnaire)
N. L. Harper and C. R. Askling. "Group Communication and Quality of Task Solution in a Media Production Organization." *CM*, 47 (1980), 81.

Group Discussion (Perceived Quality of)
See Discussion Quality, 53.

Group Member Task Orientation
W. E. Jurma. "Effects of Leader Structuring Style and Task-Orientation Characteristics of Group Members." *CM*, 46 (1979), 286–287.

Group Procedural Order Questionnaire (GPOQ)
L. L. Putnam. "Preference for Procedural Order in Task-Oriented Small Groups." *CM*, 46 (1979), 199–200.

Group Satisfaction Scale
> F. M. Jablin. "Cultivating Imagination: Factors that Enhance and Inhibit Creativity in Brainstorming Groups." *HCR,* 7 (1981), 250.

Groupthink Indicators
> J. A. Courtright. "A Laboratory Investigation of Groupthink." *CM,* 45 (1978), 233.

Gun Control Legislation, Attitudes Toward
> D. F. Caetano. "The Domestic Arms Race." *JC,* 29 (Spring 1979), 41.

Gun Ownership
> See Gun Control Legislation, Attitudes Toward, 41.

Hair Style (Afro vs. Wavy)
> See Facial Features, 124.

Headline Accuracy
> F. T. Marquez. "How Accurate are the Headlines?" *JC,* 30 (Summer 1980), 30–35.

Health-Related Conditions (on Soap Operas) (Content Analysis Scheme)
> M. B. Cassata, T. D. Skill, and S. O. Boadu. "In Sickness and in Health." *JC,* 29 (Autumn 1979), 75.

Homophily
> P. A. Anderson and W. R. Todd de Mancillas. "Scales for the Measurement of Homophily with Public Figures." *Southern Speech Communication Journal,* 43 (1978), 169–179.

Hostility (Content Analysis Category)
> See Dominance (second reference), 105.

Idea Generation, Frequency of
> F. M. Jablin and L. Sussman. "An Exploration of Communication and Productivity in Real Brainstorming Groups." *HCR,* 4 (1978), 332–333.

Identification with Television Characters
> B. Reeves and G. E. Lometti. "The Dimensional Structure of Children's Perceptions of Television Characters: A Replicaton." *HCR,* 5 (1979), 251.

Inactivity (in Communication)
> See Attentiveness Evaluation, 20.

Individual Innovativeness
> H. T. Hurt, K. Joseph, and C. D. Cook. "Scales for the Measurement of Innovativeness." *HCR,* 4 (1977), 58–65.

Informativeness of Source
> L. M. Hanser and P. M. Muchinsky. "Performance Feedback Information and Organizational Communication: Evidence of Conceptual Convergence." *HCR,* 7 (1980), 70.

Intention (Behavioral) to Interact
> See Behavioral Intention to Interact, 152.

Intensity of Message
> See Disclosure Tendencies, 6–9.

Interaction Process Analysis (IPA)
>R. F. Bales. *Interaction Process Analysis.* New York: Addison-Wesley, 1950.

Interest in Product
>J. Bryant and P. W. Comisky. "The Effect of Positioning a Message Within Differentially Cognitively Involving Portions of a Television Segment on Recall of the Message." *HCR,* 5 (1978), 72.

Internal Involvement with Organization
>See Accuracy of Communication, 44.

Interpersonal Attraction
>See Attraction (first reference).

Interpersonal Communication Satisfaction Inventory
>M. L. Hecht. "The Conceptualization and Measurement of Interpersonal Communication Satisfaction." *HCR,* 4 (1978), 259.

Interpersonal Competency
>J. L. Holland and L. L. Baird. "An Interpersonal Competency Scale." *Educational and Psychological Measurement,* 28 (1968), 503–510.

Interpersonal Conflict
>See Conflict Strategies.

Interpersonal Judgment Scale
>D. Byrne. *The Attraction Paradigm.* New York: Academic Press, 1971.
>See Attitude Scale.

Interpersonal Situations (Short Term vs. Long Term)
>See Compliance-Gaining Strategies (second reference), 78.

Interpersonal Trust Scale
>J. B. Rotter. "A New Scale for the Measurement of Interpersonal Trust." *Journal of Personality,* 35 (1967), 651–665.

Intimacy of Message
>See Disclosure Tendencies, 6–9.

Issue Importance (Content Analysis Scheme)
>L. L. Swanson and D. L. Swanson. "The Agenda-Setting Function of the First Ford-Carter Debate." *CM,* 45 (1978), 349.

Issue, Importance of
>See Choice of Issue to Be Argued for, 328.

Job Description Index
>P. Smith, L. Kendall, and C. Hulin. *The Measurement of Satisfaction in Work and Retirement.* Chicago: Rand–McNally, 1969.

Job Satisfaction
>See Feedback, Amount of, 292.

Language Attitudes
>
> N. De La Zerda and R. Hopper. "Employment Interviewers' Reactions to Mexican-American Speech." *CM,* 46 (1979), 131.

Leader Structuring Style
>
> See Group Member Task Orientation, 285.
> See Groupthink Indicators.

Least Preferred Co-Worker Scale
>
> F. Fiedler. *A Theory of Leadership Effectiveness.* New York: McGraw-Hill, 1967.

Leisure Activities (Classification Scheme)
>
> G. F. McEvoy and C. S. Vincent. "Who Reads and Why?" *JC,* 30 (Winter 1980), 138.
> J. P. Murray and S. Kippax. "Children's Social Behavior in Three Towns with Differing Television Experience." *JC,* 28 (Winter 1978), 26.

Length of Interaction (in Minutes)

Length of Message
>
> W. G. Powers, W. J. Jordan, and R. L. Street. "Language Indices in the Measurement of Cognitive Complexity: Is Complexity Loquacity?" *HCR,* 6 (1979), 71.

Length of Statement
>
> P. H. Bradley. "Power, Status, and Upward Communication in Small Decision-Making Groups." *CM,* 45 (1978), 36–37.

Life Satisfaction Index
>
> See Cultivation Effect Instrument for Soap Operas, 111.

Likelihood of Verbal Response
>
> See Desirability of Verbal Response, 126.

Liking
>
> See Attitude Scale.
> See Length of Statement, 37.

Listener Adaptation (Coding Scheme)
>
> T. L. Thompson. "The Development of Communication Skills in Physically Handicapped Children." *HCR,* 7 (1981), 317.

Listening Comprehension
>
> J. I. Brown and G. R. Carlsen. *Brown-Carlsen Listening Comprehension Test.* New York: Harcourt, Brace, and World, 1955.

"Literate" Viewing of Television by Children
>
> A. A. Cohen and G. Salomon. "Children's Literate Television Viewing: Surprises and Possible Explanations." *JC,* 29 (Summer 1979), 157.

Locus of Control
>
> J. Rotter. "Generalized Expectations for Internal vs. External Control of Reinforcement." *Psychological Monographs,* 80 (1966), no. 1 (whole no. 609).

Machiavellianism
> R. Christie, unpublished scale, included in *Measures of Social Psychological Attitudes,* ed. J. R. Robinson and P. R. Shaver. Ann Arbor, Michigan: Survey Research Center, Institute for Social Research, 1973.

Magazine Type
> See Equal Rights Amendment, Magazine Advocacy of, 188.

Manifest Anxiety Inventory
> J. A. Taylor. "A Personality Scale of Manifest Anxiety." *Journal of Abnormal and Social Psychology,* 48 (1953), 285–290.

Marital Satisfaction
> See Dominance (first reference), p. 187, f.n. 9.

Marital Status

Marital Status of Television Characters
> G. Gerbner, L. Gross, M. Jackson-Beeck, S. Jeffries-Fox, and N. Signorielli. "Cultural Indicators: Violence Profile No. 9." *JC,* 28 (Summer 1978), 192.

"Mean World" Index
> R. P. Hawkins and S. Pingree. "Uniform Messages and Habitual Viewing: Unnecessary Assumptions in Social Reality Effects." *HCR,* 7 (1981), 294.

Media Involvement
> See Interest in Product, 69.

Media Use
> R. L. Moore and G. P. Moschis. "The Role of Family Communication in Consumer Learning." *JC,* 31 (Autumn 1981), 46.
> P. M. Poindexter. "Non-News Viewers." *JC,* 30 (Autumn 1980), 60.
> See also Diffuse Support for the Political System, 140–141.

Media Usage
> See Childhood Print Media Usage, 81.

Membership in Social Groups
> See Childhood Print Media Usage, 80–81.

Membership Organizations
> See Leisure Activities (first reference), 138.

Message Agreement (Perceived)
> See Dialectical Similarity (Perceived)

Message Coherence
> See Dialectical Similarity (Perceived), 19.

Message Control Intensity
> L. E. Rogers, J. A. Courtright, and F. E. Millar. "Message Control Intensity: Rationale and Preliminary Findings." *CM,* 47 (1980), 201–219.

Message Expectancy
>M. Burgoon, M. Cohen, M. D. Miller, and L. L. Montgomery. "An Empirical Test of a Model of Resistance to Persuasion." *HCR*, 5 (1978), 34.

Mode of Expression (Written or Spoken)

Moderate Intensity Messages
>See Attitude Measures, 307.

Monomorphic Opinion Leadership Test
>V. P. Richmond. "The Relationship Between Opinion Leadership and Information Acquisition." *HCR*, 4 (1977), 38–43.

Mood Scale
>B. S. Greenberg and P. H. Tannenbaum. "Communicator Performance Under Cognitive Stress." *Journalism Quarterly*, 39 (1962), 169–178.

Most Important Political Issue (Interpersonal Channel)
>W. Williams, Jr. and W. D. Semlak. "Structural Effects of TV Coverage on Political Agendas." *JC*, 28 (Autumn 1978), 115.

Mother's Viewing of Television (Time)
>E. A. Medrich. "Constant Television: A Background to Daily Life." *JC*, 29 (Summer 1979), 175.

Motivation (Perceived)
>See Alcohol Ingested, 76–78.

Movies (Theatrical) for Television, Attractiveness of
>B. R. Litman. "The Economics of the Television Market for Theatrical Movies." *JC*, 29 (Autumn 1979), 31.

Nationality of Television Characters (U. S. and Other)
>See Ethnic Groups in Mass Media, Perceived Depiction of.
>See Marital Status of Television Characters, 191.

Naturalness of Speaker
>W. G. Woodall and J. P. Folger. "Encoding Specificity and Nonverbal Cue Context: An Expansion of Episodic Memory Research." *CM*, 48 (1981), 46.

Negotiation Interact System (Coding Scheme)
>W. A. Donohue. "Analyzing Negotiation Tactics: Development of a Negotiation Interact System." *HCR*, 7 (1981), 278–280.

Network News Stories (on an Issue), Number of
>See Column Inches, Number of (in Issue of New York Times), 112.

Network News (Early Evening) Viewing
>See Attentiveness to Media, 125.

Network Showing Commercial
>J. Marecek, J. A. Piliarin, E. Fitzsimmons, E. C. Krogh, E. Leader, and B. Trudell. "Women as TV Experts: The Voice of Authority?" *JC*, 28 (Winter 1978), 161.

Newspaper Attributes (Perceived Importance to Editorial Quality)
See Editorial Quality, 14.

News Norm Scale
See Media Use (second reference), 63.

News Story Content (Content Analysis Scheme)
J. Charles, L. Shore, and R. Todd. "The *New York Times* Coverage of Equatorial and Lower Africa." *JC,* 29 (Spring 1979), 152.

News Story Types
M. R. Levy. "Disdaining the News." *JC,* 31 (Summer 1981), 25–26.

Neuroticism
See Extroversion/Extraversion (second reference).

Nonverbal Behaviors Associated with Deception
H. D. O'Hair, M. J. Cody, and M. L. McLaughlin. "Prepared Lies, Spontaneous Lies, Machiavellianism, and Nonverbal Communication." *HCR,* 7 (1981), 332.

Nonverbal Behaviors not Under Conscious Control
J. M. Wiemann. "Effects of Laboratory Videotaping Procedures on Selected Communication Behaviors." *HCR,* 7 (1981), 305.

Noun-Verb/Adjective-Adverb Ratio
W. J. Jordan and W. G. Powers. "Verbal Behavior as a Function of Apprehension and Social Context." *HCR,* 4 (1978), 296.

Novelty Experiencing Scale
P. Pearson. "Relationships Between Global and Specified Measures of Novelty Seeking." *Journal of Consulting and Clinical Psychology,* 34 (1970), 199–204.

Number of Statements (Directed Toward Confederate)
See Length of Statement, 37.

Occupation of Short Story Characters
C. Lazer and S. Dier. "The Labor Force in Fiction." *JC,* 28 (Winter 1978), 175.

Occupational Role of Characters in Commercial
See Network Showing Commercial, 161.

Occupational Status
R. W. Hodge, P. M. Siegel, and P. H. Ross. "Occupational Prestige in the United States, 1925–1963." *American Journal of Sociology,* 70 (1964), 290–292.

Openness of Verbal Response
See Desirability of Verbal Response, 126.

Opinion Leadership
J. C. McCroskey and V. P. Richmond. "The Effects of Communication Apprehension on the Perception of Peers." *Western Speech Communication,* 40 (1976), 14–21.

Opportunity to Interact
> D. E. Hewes and D. Evans. "Three Theories of Egocentric Speech: A Contrastive Analysis."
> *CM*, 45 (1978), 24–25.

Organizational Communication Variables
> See Informativeness of Source, 69–70.

Paralinguistic Features
> See Eye Movement, 127.

Parent's Education

Parent's Occupation

Past Participation in Elections
> See Attentiveness to Media, 123.

Pauses in Conversation
> See Eye Gaze (second reference), 40.

Performance Styles (in Interpersonal Relations)
> K. Ring and K. Wallston. "A Test to Measure Performance Styles in Interpersonal Rela-
> tions." *Psychological Reports,* 22 (1968), 147–154.

Personal Association with an Attitude
> See Choice of Issue to Be Argued for, 328.

Personal Report of Communication Apprehension (PRCA)
> J. C. McCroskey. "Validity of the PRCA as an Index of Oral Communication Apprehen-
> sion." *CM*, 45 (1978), 192–203.
> D. T. Porter. "An Empirical Appraisal of the PRCA for Measuring Oral Communication
> Apprehension." *HCR,* 8 (1981), 62.
> See Communication Apprehension, Effect of Situation on.

Personal Report of Communication Apprehension (PRCA)—Organizational Form
> M. D. Scott, J. C. McCroskey, and M. E. Sheahan. "Measuring Communication Apprehen-
> sion." *JC,* 28 (Winter 1978), 107.

Personal Report of Communication Apprehension (PRCA)—Short Form, 10 Items.
> See Personal Report of Communication Apprehension (PRCA).

Personal Report of Confidence as a Speaker
> H. Gilkinson. "Social Fears as Reported by Students in College Speech Classes." *Speech
> Monographs* (now *CM*), 9 (1942), 141–160.

Personal Report of Public Speaking Anxiety (PRPSA)
> J. C. McCroskey. "Measures of Communication-Bound Anxiety." *Speech Monographs* (now
> *CM*), 37 (1970), 269–277.

Personal vs. Social Context
> See Noun-Verb/Adjective-Adverb Ratio, 296–297.

Personnel Selection Questions
> See Anxiety of Source, 21–22.

Persuasion Situation
> See Attribute Scales (for Situations), 136.

Persuasive Messages
> See Compliance-Gaining Strategies (Taxonomy for Content Analysis), 257–258.

Persuasive Strategies
> See Compliance-Gaining Strategies (second reference), 269.

Persuasive Strategy, Highest Level (Coding Scheme)
> See Communicative Performance, 248–249.

Phrase Repetitions
> See "Allness" Terms.

Place of Residence (East, West, Midwest, South)

Pleasantness
> See Aggressiveness (Perceived), 301.

Political Affiliation

Political Campaign, Involvement with
> See Debates (Presidential), Exposure to (first reference), 102 (f.n. 3).

Political Cognitions
> W. D. Kimsey and L. E. Atwood. "A Path Model of Political Cognitions and Attitudes, Communication, and Voting Behavior in a Congressional Election." *CM,* 46 (1979), 225.

Political Efficacy
> See Dependency on Channels of Communication for Political Information, 125.
> See Diffuse Support for the Political System, 141.

Political Interest
> R. A. Joslyn. "The Impact of Campaign Spot Advertising on Voting Defection." *HCR,* 7 (1981), 352 (and f.n. 6).
> See also Dependency on Channels of Communication for Political Information, 125.

Political Issues (Content Analysis Scheme)
> See Most Important Political Issue, 115.

Political Knowledge
> See Attentiveness to Media, 123.

Political Momentum (Content Analysis Categories)
> R. A. Meyers, T. L. Newhouse, and D. E. Garrett. "Political Momentum: Television News Treatment." *CM,* 45 (1978), 384.

Political Orientation of Author (Content Analysis Scheme)
> G. L. Rous and D. E. Lee. "Freedom and Equality: Two Values of Political Orientation." *JC,* 28 (Winter 1978), 46–47.

Political Participation
> See Diffuse Support for the Political System, 141.

Reading History
> See Leisure Activities (first reference), 139.

Reasonableness (Content Analysis Category)
> See Dominance (second reference), 105.

Reasons for Reading
> See Leisure Activities (first reference), 139.

Recall
> See Naturalness of Speaker, 46.

Recognition Failure
> See Naturalness of Speaker, 46.

Recognition Rate
> See Naturalness of Speaker, 46.

Recognition Scores for Political Candidates
> See Prominence Ratings of Political Candidates, 303.

Referential Clarity
> See Encoding Consistency, 49.

Referential Communication
> S. Glucksberg, R. M. Krauss, and R. Weisberg. "Referential Communication in Nursery School Children: Method and Some Preliminary Findings." *Journal of Experimental Child Psychology,* 3 (1966), 333.

Relational Communication Coding Scheme
> L. E. Rogers and R. V. Farace. "Analysis of Relational Communication in Dyads: New Measurements and Procedures." *HCR,* 1 (1975), 222–239.
> See also Message Control Intensity.

Relational Dimensions Instrument (Representative Statements)
> M. A. Fitzpatrick and P. Best. "Dyadic Adjustment in Relational Types: Consensus, Cohesion, Affectional Expression, and Satisfaction in Enduring Relationships." *CM,* 46 (1979), 171.

Relational Scenarios
> L. A. Baxter. "Self-Disclosure as a Relationship Disengagement Strategy: An Exploratory Investigation." *HCR,* 5 (1979), 218.

Religious Affiliation

Religious Magazine Articles, Rhetorical Features of
> R. P. Hart, K. J. Turner, and R. E. Krupp. "A Rhetorical Profile of Religious News: *Time,* 1947–1976." *JC,* 31 (Summer 1981), 61.

Responsiveness
> A. Mehrabian. *Nonverbal Communication.* Chicago: Aldine Atherton, 1972.
> A. Mehrabian and S. Ksionzky. "Some Determinants of Social Interaction." *Sociometry,* 35 (1972), 588–609.

Retention of Information (Relative to Commercial Content)
    See Interest in Product, 72.

Rhetorical Sensitivity (RHETSEN)
    R. P. Hart, R. E. Carlson, and W. E. Eadie. "Attitudes toward Communication and the Assessment of Rhetorical Sensitivity." *CM,* 47 (1980), 6–7.

Role Construct Questionnaire
    W. H. Crockett. "Cognitive Complexity and Impression Formation," in *Progress in Experimental Personality Research, II,* ed. B. A. Maher. New York: Academic Press, 1965.

Role Construct Repertory Grid
    See Construct Comprehensiveness.

Role of Television Character—Major or Minor
    G. Gerbner, L. Gross, N. Signorelli, and M. Morgan. "Aging with Television: Images on Television Drama and Conceptions of Social Reality." *JC,* 30 (Winter 1980), 38.

Role Portrayed (by Women in Newspaper Cartoons) (Content Analysis Scheme)
    See Cartoons (Newspaper), Appearance of Women in, 22–23.

Role Relationships
    See Conversation Styles, 101.

Sales Tactics
    See product Choice, 93.

Saliency of Presidential Debate
    See Debates (Presidential) (first reference), Exposure to, 101.

Satisfaction with Group Process
    See Group Member Task Orientation, 290–291.

Self-Concept
    See Depictions of Elderly on Television (Perception of), 76.
    See also Cultivation Effect Instrument for Soap Operas, 111.

Self-Disclosure
    S. M. Jourard and R. Friedman. "Experimenter-Subject Distance and Self-Disclosure." *Journal of Personality and Social Psychology,* 8 (1971), 278–282.
    L. R. Wheeless. "A Follow-Up Study of the Relationships Among Trust, Disclosure, and Interpersonal Solidarity." *HCR,* 4 (1978), 148–149.

Self-Disclosure Avoidance
    L. B. Rosenfeld. "Self-Disclosure Avoidance: Why I Am Afraid to Tell You Who I Am." *CM,* 46 (1979), 68.

Self Disclosure—Revised Instrument
    See Self-Disclosure Avoidance, 67.

Self-Esteem
    M. Rosenberg. *Society and the Adolescent Self-Image.* Princeton, N. J.: Princeton University Press, 1965.

C. R. Berger. "Sex Differences Related to Self-Esteem Factor Structure." *Journal of Consulting and Clinical Psychology,* 32 (1968), 442–446.

Self-Esteem Scale for Blacks
   A. S. Tan and G. Tan. "Television Use and Self-Esteem of Blacks." *JC,* 29 (Winter 1979), 132.

Self-Esteem Scale for Whites
   See Self-Esteem Scale for Blacks, 133.

Self-Interest
   See Communication Strategies, 259.

Self-Monitoring
   M. Snyder. "Self-Monitoring of Expressive Behavior." *Journal of Personality and Social Psychology,* 30 (1974), 526–537.

Self-Perceived Role Enactment Competence (SPREC)
   E. M. Bodacker, T. G. Plax, R. N. Piland, and A. N. Weiner. "Role Enactment as a Socially Relevant Explanation of Self-Persuasion." *HCR,* 5 (1979), 206.

Sentence Construction (Language Behavior)
   See Eye Gaze (first reference), 103.

Setting of Television Commercials
   W. J. O'Donnell and K. J. O'Donnell. "Update: Sex-Role Messages in TV Commercials." *JC,* 28 (Winter 1978), 156–158.

Sex, Contexts for Discussion about
   See Contexts for Discussions About Sex, 25.

Sex of Adults in Commercial
   See Network Showing Commercial, 161.

Sex of Author By-Lines
   See Equal Rights Amendment, Magazine Advocacy of, 188.

Sex of Commercial Product Representative
   See Setting of Television Commercials, 156–158.

Sex of Experimenter

Sex of Intended Audience of Television Commercials
   See Aggression on Television, 204.

Sex of Magazine Staff Members
   See Equal Rights Amendment, Magazine Advocacy of, 188.

Sex of Message Source

Sex of On-Screen Character Delivering Expert Message in Commercial
   See Network Showing Commercial, 161.

Sex of Short Story Characters
   See Occupation of Short Story Characters, 175.

Sex of Subject

Sex of Voice in Voice Over
See Network Showing Commercial, 161.

Sex Role Expectation
See Attitude, 61.

Sex Role Inventory
See Androgyny.

Sexism in Advertisements (Content Analysis Scheme)
S. Pingree, R. P. Hawkins, M. Butler, and W. Paisley. "A Scale for Sexism." *JC*, 26 (Autumn 1976), 193–201.
G. V. Skelly and W. J. Lundstrom. "Male Sex Roles in Magazine Advertising." *JC*, 31 (Autumn 1981), 53.

Sexual Attractiveness
See Aggressiveness (Perceived), 301.

Sexual Behavior (Intimate) on Television (Content Analysis Scheme)
See Drug Use on Television, 32.

Sexual Behavior on Television (Content Analysis Scheme)
T. Silverman, J. N. Sprafkin, and E. A. Rubinstein. "Physical Contact and Sexual Behavior on Prime-Time TV." *JC*, 29 (Winter 1979), 34–36.
D. T. Lowry, G. Love, and M. Kirby. "Sex on the Soap Operas: Patterns of Intimacy." *JC*, 31 (Summer 1981), 92–94.
J. N. Sprafkin and L. T. Silverman. "Update: Physically Intimate and Sexual Behavior on Prime-Time Television, 1978–79." *JC*, 31 (Winter 1981), 36–38.
B. S. Greenberg, R. Abelman, and K. Neuendor. "Sex on the Soap Operas: Afternoon Delight." *JC*, 31 (Summer 1981), 84–85.

Sexual Terminology, Preferred
See Contexts for Discussions About Sex, 23–26.

Skin Pigmentation (Dark, Medium, Light)
See Facial Features, 124.

Similarity to Source
See Ability to Function in an Organization (Perceived), 21.

Situation Scenarios
See Compliance-Resisting Strategies, 22–23.

Soap Operas, Cultivation Effect Instrument for
See Cultivation Effect Instrument for Soap Operas, 110.

Soap Operas, Exposure to
See Cultivation Effect Instrument for Soap Operas, 110.

Sociability
H. G. Gough. *Manual for the California Psychological Inventory*. Palo Alto: Consulting Psychologist Press, 1957.
See also Academic Performance, 166.

Social Age
> See Role of Television Character—Major or Minor, 38.

Social Anxiety
> D. T. Lukken, A. Tellegen, and C. Katzenmeyer. "Manual for the Activity Preference Questionnaire (APQ)." *Reports from the Research Laboratory of the Department of Psychiatry, University of Minnesota, Report #PR-73-4,* October, 1973.

Social Anxiety and Distress Scale
> D. Watson and R. Friend. "Measurement of Social-Evaluative Anxiety." *Journal of Consulting and Clinical Psychology,* 33 (1969), 448–457.

Social Attractiveness (Perceived)
> See Communicator Style (Content Analysis Scheme), 232.

Social Desirability
> D. Crowne and D. Marlowe. *The Approval Motive.* New York: John Wiley, 1964.

Perceived Social Power
> W. A. Donahue. "An Empirical Framework for Examining Negotiation Processes and Outcomes." *CM,* 45 (1978), 253.

Social Reality (Perception of)
> G. Gerbner, L. Gross, N. Signorelli, M. Morgan, and M. Jackson-Beeck. "The Demonstration of Power: Violence Profile No. 10." *JC,* 29 (Summer 1979), 185–190.

Social Relaxation
> See Responsiveness.

Social Speech Functions (for Children)
> A. R. Ritti. "Social Functions of Children's Speech." *JC,* 28 (Winter 1978), 36–37.

Socioeconomic Status
> D. D. Duncan. "A Socioeconomic Index of All Occupations," in *Occupations and Social Status,* ed. A. J. Reiss, Jr. New York: The Free Press, 1961.

Solidarity
> See Self-Disclosure (second reference).

Source Character Appeal
> J. C. McCroskey. "Scales for the Measurement of Ethos." *Speech Monographs* (now *CM*), 33 (1966), 65–72.

Source Competence
> See Source Character Appeal, 65–72.

Source Credibility
> See Attitude Measures, 307.

Spatial Displacement in Pedestrians
> F. N. Willis, Jr., J. A. Gier, and D. E. Smith. "Stepping Aside: Correlations of Displacement in Pedestrians." *JC,* 29 (Autumn 1979), 34–36.

Speaker Internality
> See Disclosure Tendencies, 9.

Speech Anxiety, Behavioral Assessment of (BASA)
> A. Mulac and A. Sherman. "Behavioral Assessment of Speech Anxiety." *Quarterly Journal of Speech,* 60 (1974), 134–143.

Speech Behavior
> See Eye Gaze (first reference), 103.

Speech Dialect Attitude Survey
> A. Mulac. "Assessment and Application of the Revised Speech Dialect Attitudinal Scale." *CM,* 43 (1976), 238–245.

State-Trait Anxiety Inventory
> C. D. Spielberger, R. L. Gorsuch, and R. E. Lushene. *The State-Trait Anxiety Inventory: Preliminary Test Manual for Form X.* Tallahassee, Florida: Florida State University, 1968.

Status Differential (Perceived)
> See Idea Generation, Frequency of, 333.

Style of Talk (Confirming vs. Disconfirming) (Content Analysis Scheme)
> L. Dangott, B. C. Thornton, and P. Page. "Communication and Pain." *JC,* 28 (Winter 1978), 32–33.

Subjective Concern for Being Informed
> See Attentiveness to Media, 128.

Subjective Information Index
> See Belief Index, 246–247.

Superior-Subordinate Communication Openness (SSCO)
> F. M. Jablin. "Message-Response and 'Openness' in Superior-Subordinate Communication," in *Communication Yearbook II,* ed. B. D. Ruben. New Brunswick, N. J.: Transaction Books, 1978, 293–309.

Superior-Subordinate Status Differential
> F. M. Jablin and L. Sussman. "An Exploration of Communication and Productivity in Brainstorming Groups." *HCR,* 4 (1978), 329–337.

Superior's Upward Influence
> S. B. Bacharach and M. Aiken. "Structural and Process Constraints on Influence in Organizations: A Level-Specific Analysis." *Administrative Science Quarterly,* 21 (1976), 623–642.

Supervisory Leadership Scale
> J. Taylor and D. G. Bowers. *The Survey of Organizations: A Machine-Scored Standardized Questionnaire Instrument.* Ann Arbor, Mich.: Institute for Social Research, 1972.

Syllables per Word
> See "Allness" Terms, 296.

Task Difficulty
> See Opportunity to Interact, 24–25.

Task Attractiveness (Perceived)
> See Communicator Style (Content Analysis Scheme), 232.

Television Viewing, Functions of
See Depictions of Elderly on Television (Perceptions of), 72–74.

Television Viewing Rates (Attention to TV)
C. R. Corder-Bolz and S. O'Bryant. "Teacher vs. Program." *JC,* 28 (Winter 1978), 99.

Tension
See Acceptance (of Interactional Partner), 236.

Tension (About Communicating)
See Avoidance (of Communication).

Textbook Evaluation Questionnaire
J. Bryant, D. Brown, A. R. Silberberg, and S. M. Elliott. "Effects of Humorous Illustrations in College Textbooks." *HCR,* 8 (1981), 50.

Theme in Group Interaction (Content Analysis Scheme)
E. A. Mabry. "An Instrument for Assessing Content Themes in Group Interaction." *Speech Monographs* (now *CM*), 42 (1975), 291–297.

Threat
See Discrepancy of Attitude, 311.

Time Slot of Commercial
See Network Showing Commercial, 161.

Threat of Messages (Perceived)
See Message Expectancy, 34.

Threat (Perceived)
See Attitude Measures, 307.

Time Slot of Television Show (Daytime vs. Prime Time)
See Role of Television Character—Major or Minor, 38.

Time Spent on Activities Other than Television Viewing
See Academic Performance, 167.

Time Spent in Nonschool Activities
See Mother's Viewing of Television (Time), 172.

Time Spent with Media
See Leisure Activities (first reference), 137.

Tonal Inflection
See Eye Gaze (second reference), 40.

Topics of Conversation (in Soap Operas) (Content Analysis Scheme)
See Conversation Styles (on Soap Operas) (Content Analysis Scheme), 100.

Topic Situations
See Credibility (first reference), 87.

Touching Behavior
> C. M. Rinck, F. N. Willis, Jr., and L. M. Dean. "Interpersonal Touch Among Residents of Homes for the Elderly." *JC,* 30 (Spring 1980), 45–46.

Trust in Superior
> See Feedback, Amount of, 292.

Trust Scale, Individualized
> L. R. Wheeless and J. Grotz. "The Measurement of Trust and Its Relationship to Self-Disclosure." *HCR,* 3 (1977), 250–257.

Truthfulness of Source (Perceived)
> D. R. Brandt, G. R. Miller, and J. E. Hocking. "The Truth Deceptor Attribution: Effects of Familiarity on the Ability of Observers to Detect Deception." *HCR,* 6 (1980), 103.

Turn-Taking
> See Eye Gaze (first reference), 103.

Type of Residence (Rural, Metropolitan . . .)

Types of Utterances (Coding Scheme)
> R. Y. Hirokawa. "A Comparative Analysis of Communication Within Effective and Ineffective Decision-Making Groups." *CM,* 47 (1980), 316.

Type/Token Ratio
> See "Allness" Terms, 296.

Uncertainty
> See Acceptance (of Interactional Partner), 235–236.

Understanding
> See Naturalness of Speaker, 46.

Unwillingness to Communicate
> J. Burgoon. "The Unwillingness to Communicate Scale: Development and Validation." *CM,* 43 (1976), 60–69.

Usefulness of a Source
> See Access (Frequency of) Due to a Cue, 117.

Uses of Television (for Adolescents)
> See Television, Attachment to, 112–113.

Values
> M. Rokeach. *Beliefs, Attitudes, and Values.* San Francisco: Jossey-Bass, 1968.

Verbal Aggression
> D. L. Mosher, R. L. Mortimer, and M. Grebel. "Verbal Behavior in Delinquent Boys." *Journal of Abnormal Psychology,* 73 (1968), 454–460.

Verbal Categories for Assessing Interview Interaction
> L. C. Hawes. "The Effects of Interviewer Style on Patterns of Dyadic Communication." *Speech Monographs* (now *CM*), 39 (1972), 114–123.

Verbal Complexity
    See Length of Message, 71.

Verbal Fluency
    C. L. Hall. "Cognitive Complexity-Simplicity as a Determinant of Communication Effectiveness." *CM,* 47 (1980), 307.

Victimization
    See Gun Control Legislation, Attitudes Toward.

Violence in Society, Cultural Indicators of
    See Cultural Indicators "Mean World" Index, 99.

Violence in Society (Perceived)
    See "Mean World" Index, 293.

Violence Index for Television
    See Marital Status of TV Characters, 180–181.

Violence on Television (Content Analysis Scheme)
    See Social Reality (Perception of), 182–192.

Violence on Television
    G. Gerbner, L. Gross, N. Signorelli, M. Morgan, and M. Jackson-Beeck. "Violence Profile No. 10: Trends in Network Television Drama and Viewer Conceptions of Social Reality, 1967–78." Annenberg School of Communications, University of Pennsylvania, 1979.

Visual Treatment of New Stories (Content Analysis Scheme)
    See Most Important Political Issue, 116.

Vote Decision
    See Attentiveness to Media, 121.

Voter Intention
    D. A. Andersen and R. J. Kibler. "Candidate Valence as a Predictor of Vote Preference." *HCR,* 5 (1978), 8.

Voting, Concern About
    See Dependency on Channels of Communication for Political Information, 125.

Voting Efficacy
    See Dependency on Channels of Communication for Political Information, 125.

Willingness to Discuss
    See Relational Scenarios, 218.

B Appendix

Critical Values for the *t*-Statistic

Directions: Find the degrees-of-freedom *(df)* in the far left-hand column. These are always equal to $N - 2$. Next, read across to the appropriate row to find the desired level of significance (e.g., $p < .05$). The number in the table represents the critical value the obtained *t*-test must surpass in order to be considered significant.

df	Level of significance for nondirectional (two-tailed) tests					
	.20	.10	.05	.02	.01	.001
1	1.000	6.314	12.706	31.821	63.657	636.619
2	.816	2.920	4.303	6.965	9.925	31.598
3	.765	2.353	3.182	4.541	5.841	12.941
4	.741	2.132	2.776	3.747	4.604	8.610
5	.727	2.015	2.571	3.365	4.032	6.859
6	.718	1.943	2.447	3.143	3.707	5.959
7	.711	1.895	2.365	2.998	3.499	5.405
8	.706	1.860	2.306	2.896	3.355	5.041
9	.703	1.833	2.262	2.821	3.250	4.781
10	.700	1.812	2.228	2.764	3.169	4.587
11	.697	1.796	2.201	2.718	3.106	4.437
12	.695	1.782	2.179	2.681	3.055	4.318
13	.694	1.771	2.160	2.650	3.012	4.221
14	.692	1.761	2.145	2.624	2.977	4.140
15	.691	1.753	2.131	2.602	2.947	4.073
16	.690	1.746	2.120	2.583	2.921	4.015
17	.689	1.740	2.110	2.567	2.898	3.965
18	.688	1.734	2.101	2.552	2.878	3.922
19	.688	1.729	2.093	2.539	2.861	3.883
20	.687	1.725	2.086	2.528	2.845	3.850
21	.686	1.721	2.080	2.518	2.831	3.819
22	.686	1.717	2.074	2.508	2.819	3.792
23	.685	1.714	2.069	2.500	2.807	3.767
24	.685	1.711	2.064	2.492	2.797	3.745
25	.684	1.708	2.060	2.485	2.787	3.725
26	.684	1.706	2.056	2.479	2.779	3.707
27	.684	1.703	2.052	2.473	2.771	3.690
28	.683	1.701	2.048	2.467	2.763	3.674
29	.683	1.699	2.045	2.462	2.756	3.659
30	.683	1.697	2.042	2.457	2.750	3.646
40	.681	1.684	2.021	2.423	2.704	3.551
60	.679	1.671	2.000	2.390	2.660	3.460
120	.677	1.658	1.980	2.358	2.617	3.373
∞	.674	1.645	1.960	2.326	2.576	3.291

SOURCE: Appendix B is taken from Table III of Fisher & Yates: *Statistical Tables for Biological, Agricultural and Medical Research*, published by Longman Group Ltd., London (previously published by Oliver and Boyd, Edinburgh). Reprinted by permission of the authors and publishers. This abridgement is reproduced from John G. Peatman, *Introduction to Applied Statistics*. New York: Harper & Row, Publishers, 1963.

Appendix C

Critical Values for the *F*-Statistic

Directions: First find the degrees-of-freedom *(df)* for the denominator mean square (i.e., MS_{Error}). These are located in the far left-hand column (df_2). Second, locate the *df* for the numerator mean square, which are located on the top row (df_1). For each combination of *df*, there are seven critical values listed. These represent the percent or probability of committing a Type I error (e.g., 5% = $p < .05$). The number in the table which corresponds to the desired probability is the critical value the obtained *F*-statistic must surpass to be considered significant.

df_2 \ df_1		1	2	3	4	5	6	8	12	24	∞
1	0.1%	405284	500000	540379	562500	576405	585937	598144	610667	623497	636619
	0.5%	16211	20000	21615	22500	23056	23437	23925	24426	24940	25465
	1 %	4052	4999	5403	5625	5764	5859	5981	6106	6234	6366
	2.5%	647.79	799.50	864.16	899.58	921.85	937.11	956.66	976.71	997.25	1018.30
	5 %	161.45	199.50	215.71	224.58	230.16	233.99	238.88	243.91	249.05	254.32
	10 %	39.86	49.50	53.59	55.83	57.24	58.20	59.44	60.70	62.00	63.33
	20 %	9.47	12.00	13.06	13.73	14.01	14.26	14.59	14.90	15.24	15.58
2	0.1	998.5	999.0	999.2	999.2	999.3	999.3	999.4	999.4	999.5	999.5
	0.5	198.50	199.00	199.17	199.25	199.30	199.33	199.37	199.42	199.46	199.51
	1	98.49	99.00	99.17	99.25	99.30	99.33	99.36	99.42	99.46	99.50
	2.5	38.51	39.00	39.17	39.25	39.30	39.33	39.37	39.42	39.46	39.50
	5	18.51	19.00	19.16	19.25	19.30	19.33	19.37	19.41	19.45	19.50
	10	8.53	9.00	9.16	9.24	9.29	9.33	9.37	9.41	9.45	9.49
	20	3.56	4.00	4.16	4.24	4.28	4.32	4.36	4.40	4.44	4.48
3	0.1	167.5	148.5	141.1	137.1	134.6	132.8	130.6	128.3	125.9	123.5
	0.5	55.55	49.80	47.47	46.20	45.39	44.84	44.13	43.39	42.62	41.83
	1	34.12	30.81	29.46	28.71	28.24	27.91	27.49	27.05	26.60	26.12
	2.5	17.44	16.04	15.44	15.10	14.89	14.74	14.54	14.34	14.12	13.90
	5	10.13	9.55	9.28	9.12	9.01	8.94	8.84	8.74	8.64	8.53
	10	5.54	5.46	5.39	5.34	5.31	5.28	5.25	5.22	5.18	5.13
	20	2.68	2.89	2.94	2.96	2.97	2.97	2.98	2.98	2.98	2.98
4	0.1	74.14	61.25	56.18	53.44	51.71	50.53	49.00	47.41	45.77	44.05
	0.5	31.33	26.28	24.26	23.16	22.46	21.98	21.35	20.71	20.03	19.33
	1	21.20	18.00	16.69	15.98	15.52	15.21	14.80	14.37	13.93	13.46
	2.5	12.22	10.65	9.98	9.60	9.36	9.20	8.98	8.75	8.51	8.26
	5	7.71	6.94	6.59	6.39	6.26	6.16	6.04	5.91	5.77	5.63
	10	4.54	4.32	4.19	4.11	4.05	4.01	3.95	3.90	3.83	3.76
	20	2.35	2.47	2.48	2.48	2.48	2.47	2.47	2.46	2.44	2.43
5	0.1	47.04	36.61	33.20	31.09	29.75	28.84	27.64	26.42	25.14	23.78
	0.5	22.79	18.31	16.53	15.56	14.94	14.51	13.96	13.38	12.78	12.14
	1	16.26	13.27	12.06	11.39	10.97	10.67	10.29	9.89	9.47	9.02
	2.5	10.01	8.43	7.76	7.39	7.15	6.98	6.76	6.52	6.28	6.02
	5	6.61	5.79	5.41	5.19	5.05	4.95	4.82	4.68	4.53	4.36
	10	4.06	3.78	3.62	3.52	3.45	3.40	3.34	3.27	3.19	3.10
	20	2.18	2.26	2.25	2.24	2.23	2.22	2.20	2.18	2.16	2.13
6	0.1%	35.51	27.00	23.70	21.90	20.81	20.03	19.03	17.99	16.89	15.75
	0.5%	18.64	14.54	12.92	12.03	11.46	11.07	10.57	10.03	9.47	8.88
	1 %	13.74	10.92	9.78	9.15	8.75	8.47	8.10	7.72	7.31	6.88
	2.5%	8.81	7.26	6.60	6.23	5.99	5.82	5.60	5.37	5.12	4.85
	5 %	5.99	5.14	4.76	4.53	4.39	4.28	4.15	4.00	3.84	3.67
	10 %	3.78	3.46	3.29	3.18	3.11	3.05	2.98	2.90	2.82	2.72
	20 %	2.07	2.13	2.11	2.09	2.08	2.06	2.04	2.02	1.99	1.95
7	0.1	29.22	21.69	18.77	17.19	16.21	15.52	14.63	13.71	12.73	11.69
	0.5	16.24	12.40	10.88	10.05	9.52	9.16	8.68	8.18	7.65	7.08
	1	12.25	9.55	8.45	7.85	7.46	7.19	6.84	6.47	6.07	5.65
	2.5	8.07	6.54	5.89	5.52	5.29	5.12	4.90	4.67	4.42	4.14
	5	5.59	4.74	4.35	4.12	3.97	3.87	3.73	3.57	3.41	3.23
	10	3.59	3.26	3.07	2.96	2.88	2.83	2.75	2.67	2.58	2.47
	20	2.00	2.04	2.02	1.99	1.97	1.96	1.93	1.91	1.87	1.83

SOURCE: Appendix C is taken from Table V of Fisher & Yates: *Statistical Tables for Biological, Agricultural and Medical Research*, published by Longman Group Ltd., London (previously published by Oliver and Boyd, Edinburgh). Reprinted by permission of the authors and publishers.

df_1 df_2		1	2	3	4	5	6	8	12	24	∞
8	0.1	25.42	18.49	15.83	14.39	13.49	12.86	12.04	11.19	10.30	9.34
	0.5	14.69	11.04	9.60	8.81	8.30	7.95	7.50	7.01	6.50	5.95
	1	11.26	8.65	7.59	7.01	6.63	6.37	6.03	5.67	5.28	4.86
	2.5	7.57	6.06	5.42	5.05	4.82	4.65	4.43	4.20	3.95	3.67
	5	5.32	4.46	4.07	3.84	3.69	3.58	3.44	3.28	3.12	2.93
	10	3.46	3.11	2.92	2.81	2.73	2.67	2.59	2.50	2.40	2.29
	20	1.95	1.98	1.95	1.92	1.90	1.88	1.86	1.83	1.79	1.74
9	0.1	22.86	16.39	13.90	12.56	11.71	11.13	10.37	9.57	8.72	7.81
	0.5	13.61	10.11	8.72	7.96	7.47	7.13	6.69	6.23	5.73	5.19
	1	10.56	8.02	6.99	6.42	6.06	5.80	5.47	5.11	4.73	4.31
	2.5	7.21	5.71	5.08	4.72	4.48	4.32	4.10	3.87	3.61	3.33
	5	5.12	4.26	3.86	3.63	3.48	3.37	3.23	3.07	2.90	2.71
	10	3.36	3.01	2.81	2.69	2.61	2.55	2.47	2.38	2.28	2.16
	20	1.91	1.94	1.90	1.87	1.85	1.83	1.80	1.76	1.72	1.67
10	0.1	21.04	14.91	12.55	11.28	10.48	9.92	9.20	8.45	7.64	6.76
	0.5	12.83	9.43	8.08	7.34	6.87	6.54	6.12	5.66	5.17	4.64
	1	10.04	7.56	6.55	5.99	5.64	5.39	5.06	4.71	4.33	3.91
	2.5	6.94	5.46	4.83	4.47	4.24	4.07	3.85	3.62	3.37	3.08
	5	4.96	4.10	3.71	3.48	3.33	3.22	3.07	2.91	2.74	2.54
	10	3.28	2.92	2.73	2.61	2.52	2.46	2.38	2.28	2.18	2.06
	20	1.88	1.90	1.86	1.83	1.80	1.78	1.75	1.72	1.67	1.62
11	0.1	19.69	13.81	11.56	10.35	9.58	9.05	8.35	7.63	6.85	6.00
	0.5	12.23	8.91	7.60	6.88	6.42	6.10	5.68	5.24	4.76	4.23
	1	9.65	7.20	6.22	5.67	5.32	5.07	4.74	4.40	4.02	3.60
	2.5	6.72	5.26	4.63	4.28	4.04	3.88	3.66	3.43	3.17	2.88
	5	4.84	3.98	3.59	3.36	3.20	3.09	2.95	2.79	2.61	2.40
	10	3.23	2.86	2.66	2.54	2.45	2.39	2.30	2.21	2.10	1.97
	20	1.86	1.87	1.83	1.80	1.77	1.75	1.72	1.68	1.63	1.57
12	0.1	18.64	12.97	10.80	9.63	8.89	8.38	7.71	7.00	6.25	5.42
	0.5	11.75	8.51	7.23	6.52	6.07	5.76	5.35	4.91	4.43	3.90
	1	9.33	6.93	5.95	5.41	5.06	4.82	4.50	4.16	3.78	3.36
	2.5	6.55	5.10	4.47	4.12	3.89	3.73	3.51	3.28	3.02	2.72
	5	4.75	3.88	3.49	3.26	3.11	3.00	2.85	2.69	2.50	2.30
	10	3.18	2.81	2.61	2.48	2.39	2.33	2.24	2.15	2.04	1.90
	20	1.84	1.85	1.80	1.77	1.74	1.72	1.69	1.65	1.60	1.54
13	0.1	17.81	12.31	10.21	9.07	8.35	7.86	7.21	6.52	5.78	4.97
	0.5	11.37	8.19	6.93	6.23	5.79	5.48	5.08	4.64	4.17	3.65
	1	9.07	6.70	5.74	5.20	4.86	4.62	4.30	3.96	3.59	3.16
	2.5	6.41	4.97	4.35	4.00	3.77	3.60	3.39	3.15	2.89	2.60
	5	4.67	3.80	3.41	3.18	3.02	2.92	2.77	2.60	2.42	2.21
	10	3.14	2.76	2.56	2.43	2.35	2.28	2.20	2.10	1.98	1.85
	20	1.82	1.83	1.78	1.75	1.72	1.69	1.66	1.62	1.57	1.51
14	0.1	17.14	11.78	9.73	8.62	7.92	7.43	6.80	6.13	5.41	4.60
	0.5	11.06	7.92	6.68	6.00	5.56	5.26	4.86	4.43	3.96	3.44
	1	8.86	6.51	5.56	5.03	4.69	4.46	4.14	3.80	3.43	3.00
	2.5	6.30	4.86	4.24	3.89	3.66	3.50	3.29	3.05	2.79	2.49
	5	4.60	3.74	3.34	3.11	2.96	2.85	2.70	2.53	2.35	2.13
	10	3.10	2.73	2.52	2.39	2.31	2.24	2.15	2.05	1.94	1.80
	20	1.81	1.81	1.76	1.73	1.70	1.67	1.64	1.60	1.55	1.48
15	0.1	16.59	11.34	9.34	8.25	7.57	7.09	6.47	5.81	5.10	4.31
	0.5	10.80	7.70	6.48	5.80	5.37	5.07	4.67	4.25	3.79	3.26
	1	8.68	6.36	5.42	4.89	4.56	4.32	4.00	3.67	3.29	2.87
	2.5	6.20	4.77	4.15	3.80	3.58	3.41	3.20	2.96	2.70	2.40
	5	4.54	3.68	3.29	3.06	2.90	2.79	2.64	2.48	2.29	2.07
	10	3.07	2.70	2.49	2.36	2.27	2.21	2.12	2.02	1.90	1.76
	20	1.80	1.79	1.75	1.71	1.68	1.66	1.62	1.58	1.53	1.46
16	0.1%	16.12	10.97	9.00	7.94	7.27	6.81	6.19	5.55	4.85	4.06
	0.5%	10.58	7.51	6.30	5.64	5.21	4.91	4.52	4.10	3.64	3.11
	1 %	8.53	6.23	5.29	4.77	4.44	4.20	3.89	3.55	3.18	2.75
	2.5 %	6.12	4.69	4.08	3.73	3.50	3.34	3.12	2.89	2.63	2.32
	5 %	4.49	3.63	3.24	3.01	2.85	2.74	2.59	2.42	2.24	2.01
	10 %	3.05	2.67	2.46	2.33	2.24	2.18	2.09	1.99	1.87	1.72
	20 %	1.79	1.78	1.74	1.70	1.67	1.64	1.61	1.56	1.51	1.43
17	0.1	15.72	10.66	8.73	7.68	7.02	6.56	5.96	5.32	4.63	3.85
	0.5	10.38	7.35	6.16	5.50	5.07	4.78	4.39	3.97	3.51	2.98
	1	8.40	6.11	5.18	4.67	4.34	4.10	3.79	3.45	3.08	2.65
	2.5	6.04	4.62	4.01	3.66	3.44	3.28	3.06	2.82	2.56	2.25
	5	4.45	3.59	3.20	2.96	2.81	2.70	2.55	2.38	2.19	1.96
	10	3.03	2.64	2.44	2.31	2.22	2.15	2.06	1.96	1.84	1.69
	20	1.78	1.77	1.72	1.68	1.65	1.63	1.59	1.55	1.49	1.42

df_2		df_1 1	2	3	4	5	6	8	12	24	∞
18	0.1	15.38	10.39	8.49	7.46	6.81	6.35	5.76	5.13	4.45	3.67
	0.5	10.22	7.21	6.03	5.37	4.96	4.66	4.28	3.86	3.40	2.87
	1	8.28	6.01	5.09	4.58	4.25	4.01	3.71	3.37	3.00	2.57
	2.5	5.98	4.56	3.95	3.61	3.38	3.22	3.01	2.77	2.50	2.19
	5	4.41	3.55	3.16	2.93	2.77	2.66	2.51	2.34	2.15	1.92
	10	3.01	2.62	2.42	2.29	2.20	2.13	2.04	1.93	1.81	1.66
	20	1.77	1.76	1.71	1.67	1.64	1.62	1.58	1.53	1.48	1.40
19	0.1	15.08	10.16	8.28	7.26	6.61	6.18	5.59	4.97	4.29	3.52
	0.5	10.07	7.09	5.92	5.27	4.85	4.56	4.18	3.76	3.31	2.78
	1	8.18	5.93	5.01	4.50	4.17	3.94	3.63	3.30	2.92	2.49
	2.5	5.92	4.51	3.90	3.56	3.33	3.17	2.96	2.72	2.45	2.13
	5	4.38	3.52	3.13	2.90	2.74	2.63	2.48	2.31	2.11	1.88
	10	2.99	2.61	2.40	2.27	2.18	2.11	2.02	1.91	1.79	1.63
	20	1.76	1.75	1.70	1.66	1.63	1.61	1.57	1.52	1.46	1.39
20	0.1	14.82	9.95	8.10	7.10	6.46	6.02	5.44	4.82	4.15	3.38
	0.5	9.94	6.99	5.82	5.17	4.76	4.47	4.09	3.68	3.22	2.69
	1	8.10	5.85	4.94	4.43	4.10	3.87	3.56	3.23	2.86	2.42
	2.5	5.87	4.46	3.86	3.51	3.29	3.13	2.91	2.68	2.41	2.09
	5	4.35	3.49	3.10	2.87	2.71	2.60	2.45	2.28	2.08	1.84
	10	2.97	2.59	2.38	2.25	2.16	2.09	2.00	1.89	1.77	1.61
	20	1.76	1.75	1.70	1.65	1.62	1.60	1.56	1.51	1.45	1.37
21	0.1	14.59	9.77	7.94	6.95	6.32	5.88	5.31	4.70	4.03	3.26
	0.5	9.83	6.89	5.73	5.09	4.68	4.39	4.01	3.60	3.15	2.61
	1	8.02	5.78	4.87	4.37	4.04	3.81	3.51	3.17	2.80	2.36
	2.5	5.83	4.42	3.82	3.48	3.25	3.09	2.87	2.64	2.37	2.04
	5	4.32	3.47	3.07	2.84	2.68	2.57	2.42	2.25	2.05	1.81
	10	2.96	2.57	2.36	2.23	2.14	2.08	1.98	1.88	1.75	1.59
	20	1.75	1.74	1.69	1.65	1.61	1.59	1.55	1.50	1.44	1.36
22	0.1	14.38	9.61	7.80	6.81	6.19	5.76	5.19	4.58	3.92	3.15
	0.5	9.73	6.81	5.65	5.02	4.61	4.32	3.94	3.54	3.08	2.55
	1	7.94	5.72	4.82	4.31	3.99	3.76	3.45	3.12	2.75	2.31
	2.5	5.79	4.38	3.78	3.44	3.22	3.05	2.84	2.60	2.33	2.00
	5	4.30	3.44	3.05	2.82	2.66	2.55	2.40	2.23	2.03	1.78
	10	2.95	2.56	2.35	2.22	2.13	2.06	1.97	1.86	1.73	1.57
	20	1.75	1.73	1.68	1.64	1.61	1.58	1.54	1.49	1.43	1.35
23	0.1	14.19	9.47	7.67	6.69	6.08	5.65	5.09	4.48	3.82	3.05
	0.5	9.63	6.73	5.58	4.95	4.54	4.26	3.88	3.47	3.02	2.48
	1	7.88	5.66	4.76	4.26	3.94	3.71	3.41	3.07	2.70	2.26
	2.5	5.75	4.35	3.75	3.41	3.18	3.02	2.81	2.57	2.30	1.97
	5	4.28	3.42	3.03	2.80	2.64	2.53	2.38	2.20	2.00	1.76
	10	2.94	2.55	2.34	2.21	2.11	2.05	1.95	1.84	1.72	1.55
	20	1.74	1.73	1.68	1.63	1.60	1.57	1.53	1.49	1.42	1.34
24	0.1	14.03	9.34	7.55	6.59	5.98	5.55	4.99	4.39	3.74	2.97
	0.5	9.55	6.66	5.52	4.89	4.49	4.20	3.83	3.42	2.97	2.43
	1	7.82	5.61	4.72	4.22	3.90	3.67	3.36	3.03	2.66	2.21
	2.5	5.72	4.32	3.72	3.38	3.15	2.99	2.78	2.54	2.27	1.94
	5	4.26	3.40	3.01	2.78	2.62	2.51	2.36	2.18	1.98	1.73
	10	2.93	2.54	2.33	2.19	2.10	2.04	1.94	1.83	1.70	1.53
	20	1.74	1.72	1.67	1.63	1.59	1.57	1.53	1.48	1.42	1.33
25	0.1	13.88	9.22	7.45	6.49	5.88	5.46	4.91	4.31	3.66	2.89
	0.5	9.48	6.60	5.46	4.84	4.43	4.15	3.78	3.37	2.92	2.38
	1	7.77	5.57	4.68	4.18	3.86	3.63	3.32	2.99	2.62	2.17
	2.5	5.69	4.29	3.69	3.35	3.13	2.97	2.75	2.51	2.24	1.91
	5	4.24	3.38	2.99	2.76	2.60	2.49	2.34	2.16	1.96	1.71
	10	2.92	2.53	2.32	2.18	2.09	2.02	1.93	1.82	1.69	1.52
	20	1.73	1.72	1.66	1.62	1.59	1.56	1.52	1.47	1.41	1.32
26	0.1%	13.74	9.12	7.36	6.41	5.80	5.38	4.83	4.24	3.59	2.82
	0.5%	9.41	6.54	5.41	4.79	4.38	4.10	3.73	3.33	2.87	2.33
	1 %	7.72	5.53	4.64	4.14	3.82	3.59	3.29	2.96	2.58	2.13
	2.5%	5.66	4.27	3.67	3.33	3.10	2.94	2.73	2.49	2.22	1.88
	5 %	4.22	3.37	2.98	2.74	2.59	2.47	2.32	2.15	1.95	1.69
	10 %	2.91	2.52	2.31	2.17	2.08	2.01	1.92	1.81	1.68	1.50
	20 %	1.73	1.71	1.66	1.62	1.58	1.56	1.52	1.47	1.40	1.31
27	0.1	13.61	9.02	7.27	6.33	5.73	5.31	4.76	4.17	3.52	2.75
	0.5	9.34	6.49	5.36	4.74	4.34	4.06	3.69	3.28	2.83	2.29
	1	7.68	5.49	4.60	4.11	3.78	3.56	3.26	2.93	2.55	2.10
	2.5	5.63	4.24	3.65	3.31	3.08	2.92	2.71	2.47	2.19	1.85
	5	4.21	3.35	2.96	2.73	2.57	2.46	2.30	2.13	1.93	1.67
	10	2.90	2.51	2.30	2.17	2.07	2.00	1.91	1.80	1.67	1.49
	20	1.73	1.71	1.66	1.61	1.58	1.55	1.51	1.46	1.40	1.30

df_2	df_1	1	2	3	4	5	6	8	12	24	∞
28	0.1	13.50	8.93	7.19	6.25	5.66	5.24	4.69	4.11	3.46	2.70
	0.5	9.28	6.44	5.32	4.70	4.30	4.02	3.65	3.25	2.79	2.25
	1	7.64	5.45	4.57	4.07	3.75	3.53	3.23	2.90	2.52	2.06
	2.5	5.61	4.22	3.63	3.29	3.06	2.90	2.69	2.45	2.17	1.83
	5	4.20	3.34	2.95	2.71	2.56	2.44	2.29	2.12	1.91	1.65
	10	2.89	2.50	2.29	2.16	2.06	2.00	1.90	1.79	1.66	1.48
	20	1.72	1.71	1.65	1.61	1.57	1.55	1.51	1.46	1.39	1.30
29	0.1	13.39	8.85	7.12	6.19	5.59	5.18	4.64	4.05	3.41	2.64
	0.5	9.23	6.40	5.28	4.66	4.26	3.98	3.61	3.21	2.76	2.21
	1	7.60	5.42	4.54	4.04	3.73	3.50	3.20	2.87	2.49	2.03
	2.5	5.59	4.20	3.61	3.27	3.04	2.88	2.67	2.43	2.15	1.81
	5	4.18	3.33	2.93	2.70	2.54	2.43	2.28	2.10	1.90	1.64
	10	2.89	2.50	2.28	2.15	2.06	1.99	1.89	1.78	1.65	1.47
	20	1.72	1.70	1.65	1.60	1.57	1.54	1.50	1.45	1.39	1.29
30	0.1	13.29	8.77	7.05	6.12	5.53	5.12	4.58	4.00	3.36	2.59
	0.5	9.18	6.35	5.24	4.62	4.23	3.95	3.58	3.18	2.73	2.18
	1	7.56	5.39	4.51	4.02	3.70	3.47	3.17	2.84	2.47	2.01
	2.5	5.57	4.18	3.59	3.25	3.03	2.87	2.65	2.41	2.14	1.79
	5	4.17	3.32	2.92	2.69	2.53	2.42	2.27	2.09	1.89	1.62
	10	2.88	2.49	2.28	2.14	2.05	1.98	1.88	1.77	1.64	1.46
	20	1.72	1.70	1.64	1.60	1.57	1.54	1.50	1.45	1.38	1.28
40	0.1	12.61	8.25	6.60	5.70	5.13	4.73	4.21	3.64	3.01	2.23
	0.5	8.83	6.07	4.98	4.37	3.99	3.71	3.35	2.95	2.50	1.93
	1	7.31	5.18	4.31	3.83	3.51	3.29	2.99	2.66	2.29	1.80
	2.5	5.42	4.05	3.46	3.13	2.90	2.74	2.53	2.29	2.01	1.64
	5	4.08	3.23	2.84	2.61	2.45	2.34	2.18	2.00	1.79	1.51
	10	2.84	2.44	2.23	2.09	2.00	1.93	1.83	1.71	1.57	1.38
	20	1.70	1.68	1.62	1.57	1.54	1.51	1.47	1.41	1.34	1.24
60	0.1	11.97	7.76	6.17	5.31	4.76	4.37	3.87	3.31	2.69	1.90
	0.5	8.49	5.80	4.73	4.14	3.76	3.49	3.13	2.74	2.29	1.69
	1	7.08	4.98	4.13	3.65	3.34	3.12	2.82	2.50	2.12	1.60
	2.5	5.29	3.93	3.34	3.01	2.79	2.63	2.41	2.17	1.88	1.48
	5	4.00	3.15	2.76	2.52	2.37	2.25	2.10	1.92	1.70	1.39
	10	2.79	2.39	2.18	2.04	1.95	1.87	1.77	1.66	1.51	1.29
	20	1.68	1.65	1.59	1.55	1.51	1.48	1.44	1.38	1.31	1.18
120	0.1	11.38	7.31	5.79	4.95	4.42	4.04	3.55	3.02	2.40	1.56
	0.5	8.18	5.54	4.50	3.92	3.55	3.28	2.93	2.54	2.09	1.43
	1	6.85	4.79	3.95	3.48	3.17	2.96	2.66	2.34	1.95	1.38
	2.5	5.15	3.80	3.23	2.89	2.67	2.52	2.30	2.05	1.76	1.31
	5	3.92	3.07	2.68	2.45	2.29	2.17	2.02	1.83	1.61	1.25
	10	2.75	2.35	2.13	1.99	1.90	1.82	1.72	1.60	1.45	1.19
	20	1.66	1.63	1.57	1.52	1.48	1.45	1.41	1.35	1.27	1.12
∞	0.1	10.83	6.91	5.42	4.62	4.10	3.74	3.27	2.74	2.13	1.00
	0.5	7.88	5.30	4.28	3.72	3.35	3.09	2.74	2.36	1.90	1.00
	1	6.64	4.60	3.78	3.32	3.02	2.80	2.51	2.18	1.79	1.00
	2.5	5.02	3.69	3.12	2.79	2.57	2.41	2.19	1.94	1.64	1.00
	5	3.84	2.99	2.60	2.37	2.21	2.09	1.94	1.75	1.52	1.00
	10	2.71	2.30	2.08	1.94	1.85	1.77	1.67	1.55	1.38	1.00
	20	1.64	1.61	1.55	1.50	1.46	1.43	1.38	1.32	1.23	1.00

Appendix

Critical Values for the Pearson r

Directions: Find the degrees-of-freedom *(df)* in the far left-hand column. These are always equal to $N - 2$. Next, read across to the appropriate row to find the desired level of significance (e.g., $p < .05$). The number in the table represents the critical value the Pearson r must surpass in order to be considered significant.

df $N - 2$	.10	.05	.02	.01	.001
1	.98769	.99692	.999507	.999877	.9999988
2	.90000	.95000	.98000	.990000	.99900
3	.8054	.8783	.93433	.95873	.99116
4	.7293	.8114	.8822	.91720	.97406
5	.6694	.7545	.8329	.8745	.95074
6	.6215	.7067	.7887	.8343	.92493
7	.5822	.6664	.7498	.7977	.8982
8	.5494	.6319	.7155	.7646	.8721
9	.5214	.6021	.6851	.7348	.8471
10	.4973	.5760	.6581	.7079	.8233
11	.4762	.5529	.6339	.6835	.8010
12	.4575	.5324	.6120	.6614	.7800
13	.4409	.5139	.5923	.6411	.7603
14	.4259	.4973	.5742	.6226	.7420
15	.4124	.4821	.5577	.6055	.7246
16	.4000	.4683	.5425	.5897	.7084
17	.3887	.4555	.5285	.5751	.6932
18	.3783	.4438	.5155	.5614	.6787
19	.3687	.4329	.5034	.5487	.6652
20	.3598	.4227	.4921	.5368	.6524
25	.3233	.3809	.4451	.4869	.5974
30	.2960	.3494	.4093	.4487	.5541
35	.2746	.3246	.3810	.4182	.5189
40	.2573	.3044	.3578	.3932	.4896
45	.2428	.2875	.3384	.3721	.4648
50	.2306	.2732	.3218	.3541	.4433
60	.2108	.2500	.2948	.3248	.4078
70	.1954	.2319	.2737	.3017	.3799
80	.1829	.2172	.2565	.2830	.3568
90	.1726	.2050	.2422	.2673	.3375
100	.1638	.1946	.2301	.2540	.3211

SOURCE: Appendix D is taken from Table VII of Fisher & Yates: *Statistical Tables for Biological, Agricultural and Medical Research,* published by Longman Group Ltd., London (previously published by Oliver and Boyd, Edinburgh). Reprinted by permission of the authors and publishers.

Appendix

Critical Values for the Chi-Square Statistic

Directions: First find the degrees-of-freedom *(df)* in the far left-hand column. These are equal to the number of columns in the cross-classification matrix minus one multiplied times the number of rows in the matrix minus one; $df = (R - 1)(C - 1)$. The subscripted probabilities in the top row indicate the likelihood of existence of a real relationship. Hence, the probability of committing a Type I error is obtained by subtracting the subscripted probability from 1.00; e.g., $1.00 - .95 = .05$. The numbers in the table represent the critical value the obtained χ^2 must surpass in order to be considered significant.

df	$\chi^2_{.75}$	$\chi^2_{.90}$	$\chi^2_{.95}$	$\chi^2_{.975}$	$\chi^2_{.99}$	$\chi^2_{.995}$	$\chi^2_{.999}$
1	1.3	2.7	3.8	5.0	6.6	7.9	10.8
2	2.8	4.6	6.0	7.4	9.2	10.6	13.8
3	4.1	6.3	7.8	9.4	11.3	12.8	16.3
4	5.4	7.8	9.5	11.1	13.3	14.9	18.5
5	6.6	9.2	11.1	12.8	15.1	16.7	20.5
6	7.8	10.6	12.6	14.4	16.8	18.5	22.5
7	9.0	12.0	14.1	16.0	18.5	20.3	24.3
8	10.2	13.4	15.5	17.5	20.1	22.0	26.1
9	11.4	14.7	16.9	19.0	21.7	23.6	27.9
10	12.5	16.0	18.3	20.5	23.2	25.2	29.6
11	13.7	17.3	19.7	21.9	24.7	26.8	31.3
12	14.8	18.5	21.0	23.3	26.2	28.3	32.9
13	16.0	19.8	22.4	24.7	27.7	29.8	34.5
14	17.1	21.1	23.7	26.1	29.1	31.3	36.1
15	18.2	22.3	25.0	27.5	30.6	32.8	37.7
16	19.4	23.5	26.3	28.8	32.0	34.3	39.3
17	20.5	24.8	27.6	30.2	33.4	35.7	40.8
18	21.6	26.0	28.9	31.5	34.8	37.2	42.3
19	22.7	27.2	30.1	32.9	36.2	38.6	43.8
20	23.8	28.4	31.4	34.2	37.6	40.0	45.3
21	24.9	29.6	32.7	35.5	38.9	41.4	46.8
22	26.0	30.8	33.9	36.8	40.3	42.8	48.3
23	27.1	32.0	35.2	38.1	41.6	44.2	49.7
24	28.2	33.2	36.4	39.4	43.0	45.6	51.2
25	29.3	34.4	37.7	40.6	44.3	46.9	52.6
26	30.4	35.6	38.9	41.9	45.6	48.3	54.0
27	31.5	36.7	40.1	43.2	47.0	49.6	55.5
28	32.6	37.9	41.3	44.5	48.3	51.0	56.9
29	33.7	39.1	42.6	45.7	49.6	52.3	58.3
30	34.8	40.3	43.8	47.0	50.9	53.3	59.7

SOURCE: Adapted from Table 8 of E. S. Pearson and H. O. Hartley, *Biometrika Tables for Statisticians*, Vol. 1, Third Edition, 1966. Used by permission of the Biometrika Trustees. This abridgement is adapted from John G. Peatman, *Introduction to Applied Statistics*, New York: Harper & Row, Publishers, 1963.

Table of Random Numbers

5	27	115	453	1681	6007	913	1414	272	8905
978	5727	5559	1811	836	8715	4761	135	7959	6544
7628	6876	2602	3730	8958	176	436	1033	2278	4371
5722	4993	8461	5823	8794	358	2996	4757	1576	6648
5700	4366	4903	118	6584	8440	1385	2353	1654	8744
7576	6760	2378	3429	9176	4193	2572	7699	3045	8979
6467	7993	9753	6577	1689	939	429	4130	914	8315
1665	5155	5946	9286	2201	9629	7968	1148	5174	713
7710	9840	9655	9364	9291	1475	5228	8090	1489	6131
3379	5097	172	5161	9421	75	5657	3273	8721	2873
8745	6613	972	6319	9166	8126	6261	4426	211	1431
6686	7241	3270	4450	7272	3584	6055	4070	9927	2930
8239	3058	4200	7677	8265	494	8585	7057	5082	6977
6122	3941	8550	5832	8044	5776	2264	1600	9221	925
2560	7032	9153	1634	7426	9848	2255	4900	9104	521
1195	2475	4099	2319	7022	1261	4369	4862	9851	5348
3430	2450	3831	937	1139	8404	174	5411	895	6671
1971	1792	3013	1945	4558	9840	8020	9560	5179	5039
3623	6385	5700	6733	9100	4002	2109	6640	858	5383
4577	9018	2918	6344	1801	3714	6073	3011	3409	3358
9461	6550	4149	5943	8318	6415	3632	4056	1643	3360
5371	1981	3551	3468	8863	1965	2021	4444	8475	855
8854	5426	2870	8391	4513	1558	8733	8377	1662	4584
2543	4001	1119	702	4144	8545	3973	6936	5859	2729
3639	7276	906	9953	1568	9827	4854	679	391	6234
3883	7197	8230	4610	3589	38	7931	7243	2078	7278
4968	4305	1121	7976	7771	4839	9094	1012	4227	6252
9471	556	8097	3581	8610	9435	9113	9768	6592	1636
489	8209	4848	5206	7611	8806	4339	6782	1640	8800
8037	9022	1800	9606	1437	2168	73	924	4888	1012
2077	3357	1450	8485	7861	801	4061	7154	6372	3849
5748	9846	7346	5457	6631	675	4368	131	1480	7696
2856	7878	1561	8461	6719	4168	4538	9711	7428	7170
6165	2459	9271	3495	7528	3713	4521	3713	1584	6089
2279	8876	2741	6569	4739	9316	3248	5643	4624	6956
117	8100	7547	2379	6351	6699	3036	7923	217	9990
7992	8040	6313	5521	6308	8161	2189	9687	8421	3340
4255	5469	4520	7904	6742	9313	5198	7375	7462	8403
3254	3899	4109	9568	428	6451	4859	1090	2811	7053
7019	8640	8667	4246	7471	6613	2436	5098	8664	6105
8650	6959	3900	772	9532	242	5670	1839	4	3470
787	3494	3879	1828	6063	9922	4967	497	8286	5238
6854	3988	2240	7545	5109	2752	528	8401	5652	8301
8936	8913	3052	8094	1096	3727	2498	1446	6195	4157
9184	7690	3486	1708	8873	7865	7336	3235	3380	1167
6582	8995	4727	7412	1924	4840	1722	6771	5123	9802
2704	8013	3738	310	8218	6522	5169	2312	7355	3322
3738	2526	1518	6372	4573	86	9358	5377	8037	9827
6634	1359	8450	8465	4740	2255	867	4911	1660	5764
9643	5980	9092	729	2551	8742	9490	8268	4194	756

Index